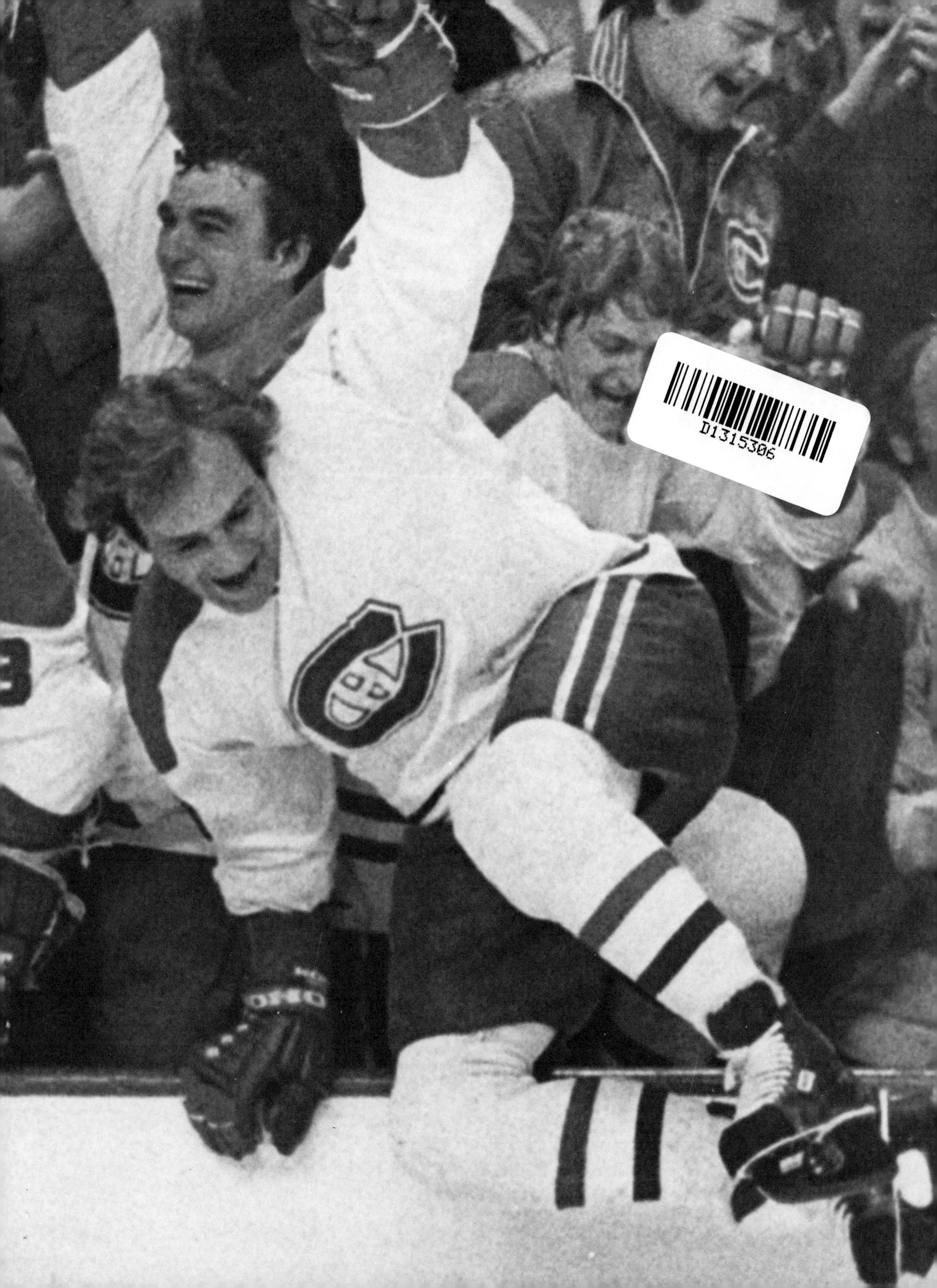

THE MONTREAL CANADIENS

A HOCKEY DYNASTY

THE MONTREAL CANADIENS

A HOCKEY DYNASTY

CLAUDE MOUTON

Van Nostrand Reinhold Ltd., Toronto
New York, Cincinnati, London, Melbourne

Published in Canada by Van Nostrand Reinhold Ltd., Toronto. Published simultaneously in the United States of America by Van Nostrand Reinhold Company, New York.

Publié aussi en français sur le titre, *Les Canadiens de Montréal: Une Dynastie du Hockey,* par Van Nostrand Reinhold Ltd., Toronto.
Édition française, ISBN 0-442-29636-3

Library of Congress Catalogue Number 80-52729

EDITORIAL CONSULTANTS: Camil DesRoches and John Roberts
EDITOR: James T. Wills
DESIGN: Artplus Ltd./Brant Cowie
FRONT JACKET PHOTOGRAPH: Press Internationale
BACK JACKET PHOTOGRAPH: Willie Dagenais Photographie
ENDPAPER PHOTOGRAPH: Jean-Guy Paradis
TYPESETTING: Compeer Typographic Services Limited
Printed and bound in Canada by The Bryant Press Ltd., Toronto
81 82 83 84 85 86 7 6 5 4 3 2

CANADIAN CATALOGUING IN PUBLICATION DATA

Mouton Claude, 1931-
The Montreal Canadiens: A Hockey Dynasty
Issued also in French under title:
Les Canadiens de Montréal: Une Dynastie du Hockey
Includes index
ISBN 0-442-29634-7

1. Montreal Canadiens (Hockey club),
1. Title.
GV848.M6M68 796.96′26 C80-094628-6

Halte-là, halte-là, Les Canadiens sont là. . . .

To:
Monique, Pierre and Michel for being so patient during all these years with the sport nut that I am.

A hockey match for the Canadian championship, Montreal, 1905 (The Montreal Victorias vs Montreal A.A.A.).

THE AUTHOR

Claude Mouton

Claude Mouton is Public Relations and Publicity Director for the Montreal Canadiens Hockey Club, a position he has held since 1973. For almost twenty years he has been a well known personality in Montreal sports circles. His career has included nine years as public address announcer at the Montreal Forum, the role of ball-park announcer for the first five years of the Montreal Expos Baseball Club, eleven years as a sportscaster for radio station CKAC, and three years as Sports Director for the Télé Média Radio Network. At various times he has also been boxing matchmaker for the Montreal Forum, President of the *Club de la Médaille d'Or,* Chief Organizer of the International Bantam Hockey Tournament in Montreal, and founder and organizer of the bicycle race, *Tour Cycliste de la Nouvelle-France.* In 1979 he added a further enterprise to his already busy life, a retail sporting goods store in which his wife and two sons are his partners.

THE CONTRIBUTORS

Bill LeGrand

Bill LeGrand was born in 1947 in Anse-au-Beau-Fils on Quebec's Gaspé Peninsula. His ancestors were French Protestants from Jersey in the Channel Islands, but his immediate family was English speaking. Mr. LeGrand grew up in the Gaspé listening to his father and friends reminiscing about the Montreal Maroons during the days when there was a friendly rivalry between supporters of Montreal's English and French hockey teams.

Surrounded as he was by memories of those old Montreal Maroons, he became deeply interested in the history of the team, an interest that has become a hobby in recent years. As a result, he has been collecting photographs and information about the Maroons and interviewing surviving players with the intention of writing a book about the team and about what he calls "hockey's golden years" from 1893 to 1947.

Bill LeGrand has been a teacher for the past eleven years and currently lives with his wife in London, Ontario.

Herbert Warren Wind

Forty-five years ago, at Yale University, Herbert Warren Wind began his distinguished career as a sports writer. He is perhaps best known today as North America's most brilliant golf writer; Bobby Jones has called his *The Story of American Golf* "truly monumental." Mr. Wind is an equally gifted analyst of all types of sport, attested to by his *The Gilded Age of Sport* which contains a sampling of his best magazine work from 1945 to 1960. A native of Brockton, Massachusetts, Herbert Wind has been a student of hockey since his teenage days. He has also been an enthusiastic admirer of the Montreal Canadiens (to whom he has dedicated several in-depth magazine articles) and in particular of Maurice Richard (to whom he dedicated his "Fire on Ice" in a 1954 issue of *Sports Illustrated*). "Les Canadiens Sont Là" appears in this book with the kind permission of Mr. Wind and the *New Yorker* magazine, where it first appeared on March 19, 1979.

Camil DesRoches

The career of Camil DesRoches reads like a history of the Montreal Canadiens. The youngest of nineteen children, he grew up in Montreal and after finishing school began as a sports writer on the staff of a small weekly newspaper called *Le Petit Journal*. By 1938, he was working on a daily paper, *Le Canada*, and at this point he became associated with the team. While still holding his job at *Le Canada*, he was hired by T. P. Gorman to translate all the team's English press releases into French. When Gorman left the team as General Manager in 1946 and Frank Selke took over, DesRoches was hired full-time as a public relations man. He has continued in the Canadiens' front office ever since. Today he is the Forum's Director of Special Events. Camil DesRoches' knowledge of hockey is immense, and he is the recognized authority of the history of the Canadiens.

Acknowledgments

"Les Canadiens Sont Là", by Herbert Warren Wind, first appeared as an article in *The New Yorker* magazine March 19, 1979. Reprinted by permission © 1979 The New Yorker Magazine Inc.

Every care has been taken to credit correctly the source of photographs where they appear. The author and publisher would welcome information that will enable them to rectify any errors or omissions in future printings.

"Those Old Montreal Maroons" appears for the first time in this book with the kind permission of the author, Bill LeGrand.

"Nine Glorious Epochs", "The Blue, White and Red", and "The Forum" have been written especially for this book by Camil DesRoches and are used with the author's kind permission.

Aurèle Joliat
HOCKEY HALL OF FAME, TORONTO

TABLE OF CONTENTS

PREFACE

The *Club de Hockey Canadien* is a national institution in Canada and well known to millions of hockey fans throughout the world. Strangely, so far as I know, there has never been an illustrated book that fully documents its triumphant history, although judging by all the questions I have been asked during my past twenty years in sport I am certain there are a great many people who would value one. With *The Montreal Canadiens: A Hockey Dynasty* I hope to succeed, at least partially, in satisfying these people and, indeed, all hockey fans everywhere.

This first edition of the book is the product of five years of work. Even so, it is certainly not perfect and I would be very happy to hear from interested readers who have new information or material that could be used to produce future editions and other books of the same type. In the meantime, I wish to thank all those who have generously helped me already, especially Alain Chantelois, Camil DesRoches, François Dupuis, Suzanne Lafranchise and Roger Leblond.

The Montreal Canadiens: A Hockey Dynasty is intended to be an album in which you will find a record of the great traditions of hockey's greatest team, its leading players of the past and present, and the momentous events that have made it so illustrious in the world of sport. I hope it will give pleasure and, if called upon to do so, supply many of those difficult-to-find bits of information that are always useful in settling a friendly wager.

CLAUDE MOUTON

May 16, 1976—Steve Shutt and Yvan Cournoyer with the Stanley Cup after defeating the Philadelphia Flyers at the Spectrum.

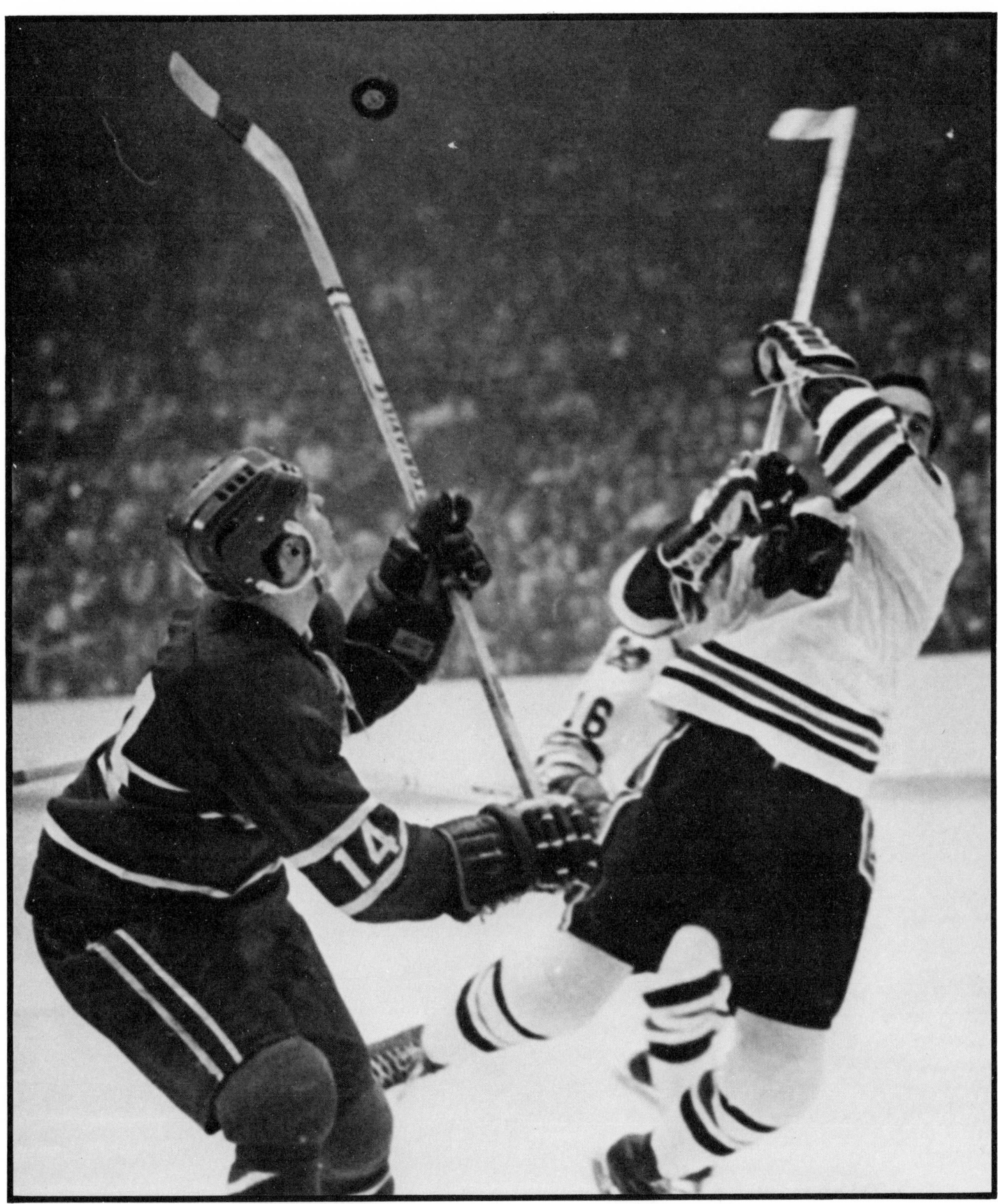

Réjean Houle and Doug Jarrett of the Chicago Black Hawks during the Stanley Cup playoffs, May 18, 1971.

1

THOSE OLD MONTREAL MAROONS!

BILL LEGRAND

Few memories of my youth are as clear as nostalgic recollections about the Montreal Maroons, an NHL club that captured the imagination of thousands of English-speaking Quebecers. Although I was born nine years after the team folded, the Maroons remain a part of my boyhood as vividly real as homemade ice cream and oven-fresh Gaspesian fish cakes.

My dad and almost all of his friends were avid fans of this spunky little team. Even though each and every one of them became impassioned supporters of the Montreal Canadiens after 1939, they still recalled the exploits of Maroon players. "Those old Montreal Maroons," my father would say, packing his pipe with Old Chum, "they was some hockey club. Why I remember going on the excursion train from Gaspé to Montreal, just to see Seibert and good old Hooley Smith play the Canadiens. One time there, Battleship Leduc and Hooley jabbed at each other for fifteen minutes. What noise in the Forum! All around me, Maroon and Canadien fans were copying the fellas on the ice. Hell, I even lost my hat when some guys fell over me. Boys, they were two good teams!"

This recollection, therefore, is an act of love. To the Maroons of the past I tip my hat. May this extraordinary team never be forgotten. They deserve a special place in the history of the NHL.

Jimmy Strachan, a Montreal businessman, decided to put this infant franchise on the ice in 1924. Canadiens' boss, Leo Dandurand sold half of the Canadiens' territorial rights to Strachan's Canadian Arena Company for a paltry $15,000. Actually, Dandurand's overt act of generosity was not as altruistic as it appeared on paper. "I figured that having an English team to compete with the French Canadiens would make for a great rivalry and I was proven right." Right, indeed! From the very beginning, the Maroon-Canadien drawing card caused a boom in Forum attendance.

Stories abound about the Maroons, especially those that are concerned with the bustling "Three S Line" of Nels Stewart, Babe Seibert and Hooley Smith, a unit that Stan Fischler describes as having "a collective butcher's touch." Eddie Shore, a Bruin of brutal renown, once experienced an unfriendly altercation with the "S" boys; after the match, the unfortunate Eddie had a broken nose, slashed face and several prominent teeth that had been extracted.

Hooley Smith was not known for his sportsmanlike conduct as an enthusiastic enforcer for the small Maroons. In a game at the Forum, Leo Dandurand once connected with a right to Smith's stomach, while Newsy Lalonde tried valiantly to behead the Maroons' captain. Mike Rodden, a veteran referee, found himself jammed among all three combatants.

In the period of their existence, the hefty Maroons were unmistakeably successful. They won their first of two Stanley Cups in 1926 by defeating the Pittsburgh Pirates, Ottawa Senators and Victoria Cougars for the coveted prize. Nineteen twenty-seven marked the beginning of Canadien-Maroon rivalry in the playoffs, when the Flying Frenchmen edged them out by one goal in a two game series. Once again in 1928 the plucky Maroons met their crosstown rivals, this time eliminating the Habs by a whisker. In the finals of that year, the Rangers and Maroons were engaged in a neck and neck series that the American team eventually won by three games to two. The enraged Maroons' fans heaved chairs and other debris on the Forum ice and proceeded to chase the referee.

Nineteen thirty ushered in an extraordinary Maroon renaissance that was only equalled by a handful of clubs in later years. Ending

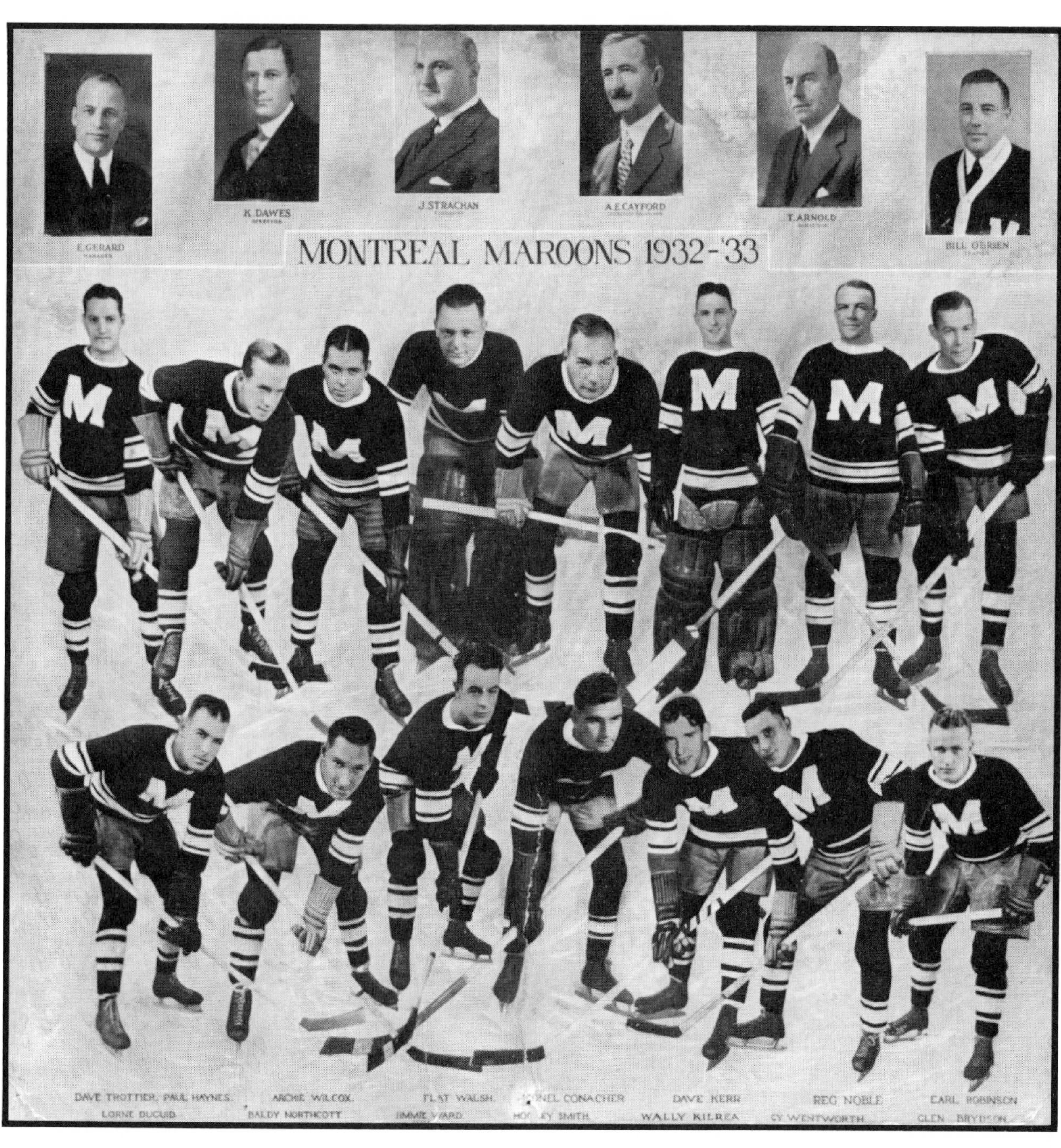
E. GERARD
K. DAWES
J. STRACHAN
A. E. CAYFORD
T. ARNOLD
BILL O'BRIEN
MONTREAL MAROONS 1932-'33
DAVE TROTTIER, PAUL HAYNES
LORNE DUGUID
ARCHIE WILCOX
BALDY NORTHCOTT
FLAT WALSH
JIMMIE WARD
NEL CONACHER
HO EY SMITH
DAVE KERR
WALLY KILREA
REG NOBLE
CY WENTWORTH
EARL ROBINSON
GLEN BRYDSON

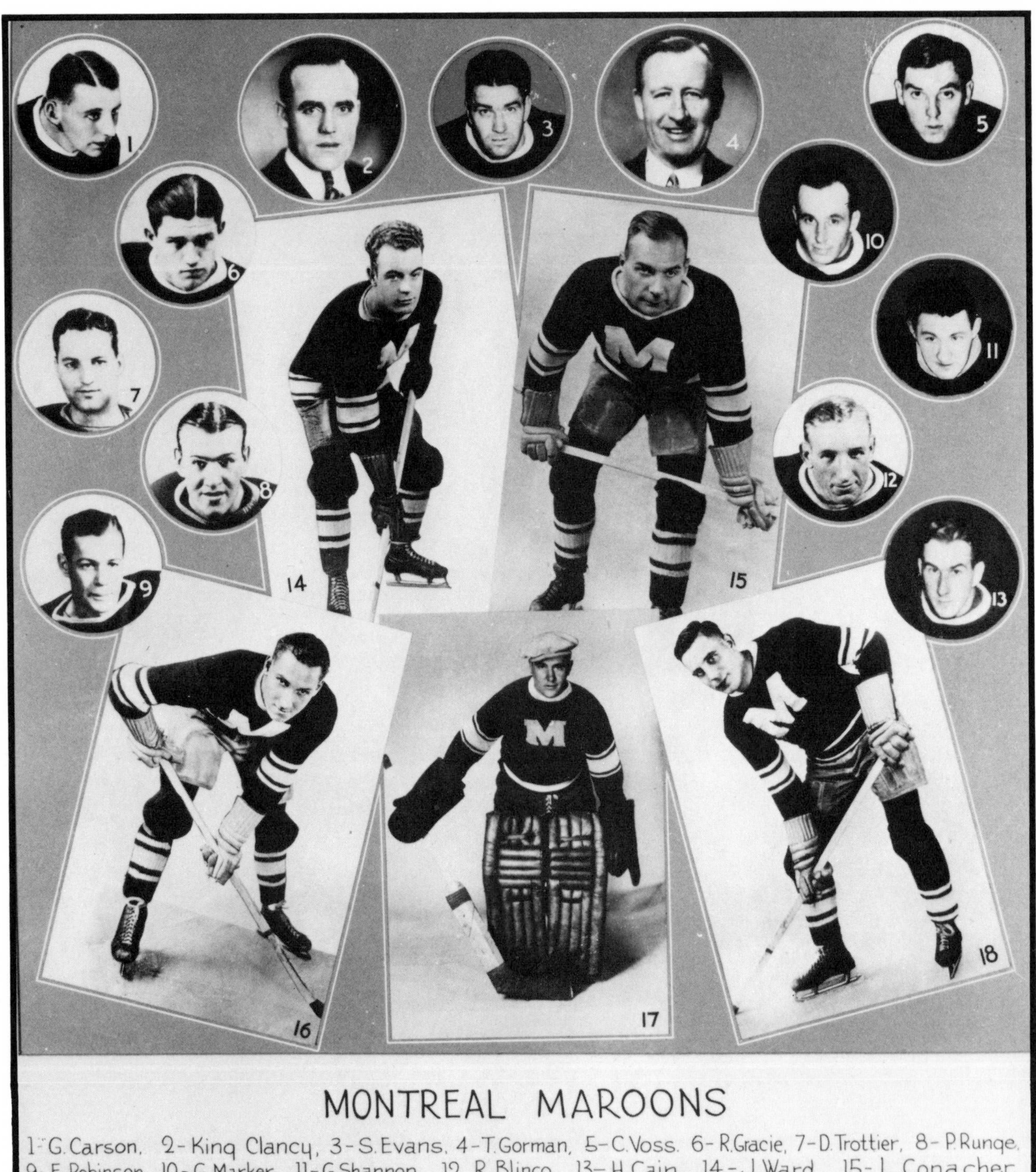

MONTREAL MAROONS

1- G. Carson, 2- King Clancy, 3- S. Evans, 4- T. Gorman, 5- C. Voss, 6- R. Gracie, 7- D. Trottier, 8- P. Runge, 9- E. Robinson, 10- G. Marker, 11- G. Shannon, 12. R. Blinco 13- H. Cain, 14- J. Ward, 15- L. Conacher, 16- L. Northcott, 17- W. Beveridge, 18- M. Wentworth.

HOCKEY HALL OF FAME, TORONTO

in fifth place in the Canadian Division the previous year, the unpredictable Maroons stormed to first place and the Canadian Championship. The bellicose Bostonians then subdued the Maroons three games to one. This year saw the resurgence of the Mighty Habitants, as they captured their first of two consecutive Stanley Cups in the 1930s.

In 1932, the Toronto Maple Leafs met the Maroons in a two game series. Few pundits would give the pesky Montrealers much chance of upsetting Conn Smythe's dream team with its famed "Kid Line" of Charlie Conacher, Joe Primeau and Harvey Jackson. The mighty Leafs were stunned after two games, as the fighting Maroons refused to accept defeat. Tied in goals, the two clubs played in overtime for eighteen minutes, until Bob Gracie rapped the puck by the Maroons' Flat Walsh. Toronto carried on their offensive style until they captured the Stanley Cup. Dick Irvin admitted afterwards that the Maroons had scared the arrogant Torontonians.

During the playoffs in 1933 and 1934, the once potent Maroon offense tended to sag. They lost out to the Detroit Red Wings and Chicago Black Hawks in each respective playoff session. As difficult as it is to understand in 1980, the Canadiens were on the verge of financial collapse at this time. There was talk that the Flying Frenchmen might be moved to Cleveland. Fortunately for hockey, the Canadiens survived to become the most successful franchise in the history of professional sports.

When the Finals arrived in 1935, the little Maroons found themselves faced with an onerous task. To capture a second Cup they had to overwhelm the highly-touted Maple Leafs. Most experts gave the Leafs heavy odds, for the Montrealers looked puny and vulnerable against superior Toronto scoring. Surprisingly enough, the Maroons failed to read the newspaper clippings about Leaf superiority; they vanquished the invincible Toronto club in three consecutive games. One of the memorable players on this Cup-winning team was a youthful Toe Blake. He would later star on the "Punch Line" for the revitalized Canadien champions of 1944 and 1946. This native of Victoria Mine, Ontario, would also become the most brilliant coach in history between 1955 and 1968.

In 1936, the Montreal Maroons won the elusive Championship in the Canadian Division. During the opening playoff round, they played the longest game in NHL history. The aggressive Detroit Red Wings were their opponent on that fateful night, and both teams endured six hours of exciting hockey to decide a 1-0 victory for the Red Wings. During the intermissions of this crucial game, the announcer for the Maroons, Chuck Harwood, was obliged to carry on a non-stop conversation with his radio audience without the benefit of commercials or music. The CFCF radio crew had all gone home.

Both the Canadiens and Maroons suffered financially during 1937 and 1938. As well as a drop in Forum attendance, both Montreal teams experienced a severe decline in morale. The untimely death of Howie Morenz, the legendary Canadien hero, seemed to signal an ominous note for all Montreal fans. The Maroons, sensing that their hopes for survival were ebbing away, played erratic hockey. In 1938, they failed to make the playoffs—a fate that would soon overtake the once-proud Canadiens. In short, the Depression and bad luck had weakened the Maroons.

It was decided in 1938 to end the illustrious history of the once-great Maroons. Although Montreal was a bilingual city, more than seventy per cent of its people were French Canadians. It was only fair that the Maroons should fold so that the Canadiens might live.

The Leafs score against the Montreal Maroons.
HOCKEY HALL OF FAME, TORONTO

They withdrew quietly before the start of the 1939 season.

Happier days awaited the citizens of Montreal as Maroons like Herb Cain, Stew Evans and Cy Wentworth joined the Canadiens. Quite soon Dick Irvin's "Punch Line" of Maurice Richard, Toe Blake and Elmer Lach would excite and arouse the passions of even the most sceptical Montreal fan. Henceforth a mighty chorus of bilingual cheers would pour over the magnificent Habs. The sounds of "Les Canadiens sont là" and "Go Habs Go" would breathe new life into the world's greatest hockey town.

Brian McFarlane in his authoritative work, *Stanley Cup Fever*, wrote a fitting eulogy to this unique, Montreal team: "Nothing like the rivalry between the Maroons and the Canadiens, with its built-in fan enthusiasm and box office success, has been known since their day. The departure of this colourful club was a loss to the game."

Yes, today the Montreal Maroons are almost a forgotten team; nonetheless, when elderly English-speaking Quebecers gather at the Forum to watch their Canadien heroes win yet another Stanley Cup, a rekindling of memories still occurs: "Remember when the Maroons beat Morenz, Lalonde and Joliat?" I can still remember my own father's face light up as he started to tell another story: "Why those old Montreal Maroons. . . ."

HOCKEY HALL OF FAME, TORONTO

Earl Robinson.
HOCKEY HALL OF FAME, TORONTO

P. Runge, M. Wentworth and D. Trottier of the Maroons.
HOCKEY HALL OF FAME, TORONTO

HISTORICAL NOTES

1. The extraordinary Clint Benedict was the first NHL goalie to record four shutouts in nine playoff games. This feat was achieved in 1928 against the Ottawa Senators, the Montreal Canadiens and the New York Rangers. No other NHL goalie has ever done better. In 1935, he had his finest hour, stopping a superior Maple Leaf team and helping the Maroons to win the Stanley Cup.
2. The Montreal Maroons and Detroit Red Wings participated in the longest overtime playoff game in NHL history. For 116 minutes and 30 seconds, the two teams went scoreless. When Detroit's Mud Bruneteau scored at 2:25 a.m., the entire match had lasted 176 minutes and 30 seconds. This happened on March 24-25, 1936.
3. When the Maroons won the Stanley Cup in 1935, they were the first NHL team to go through seven consecutive matches without a loss.
4. Nels Stewart of the Maroons holds the NHL record for scoring the fastest two goals. In a game against the Boston Bruins on January 3, 1931, Stewart blasted pucks into the Bruins' net at 8:24 and 8:28 during a 5-3 victory.
5. In 1926, Nels Stewart scored 34 goals and eight assists in 36 regular season games to become one of the greatest all-time scoring champions in history.

RECORD OF THE MONTREAL MAROONS 1924-1938

YEAR	POSITION	W	L	T	PTS	ACHIEVEMENT
1925	5th (NHL)	—	—	—	—	Out of Playoffs
1926	2nd (NHL)	—	—	—	—	*Won Stanley Cup*
1927	2nd (CDN DIV)	28	14	2	58	Eliminated in Playoffs
1928	2nd (CDN DIV)	24	14	6	54	Lost Finals
1929	5th (CDN DIV)	15	20	9	39	Out of Playoffs
1930	1st (CDN DIV)	23	16	5	51	Eliminated in 1st Playoff Round
1931	3rd (CDN DIV)	20	18	6	46	Eliminated in 1st Playoff Round
1932	3rd (CDN DIV)	19	22	7	45	Eliminated in 2nd Playoff Round
1933	2nd (CDN DIV)	22	20	6	50	Eliminated in 2nd Playoff Round
1934	3rd (CDN DIV)	19	18	11	49	Eliminated in 1st Playoff Round
1935	2nd (CDN DIV)	24	19	5	53	*Won Stanley Cup*
1936	1st (CDN DIV)	22	16	10	54	Lost 1st Round
1937	2nd (CDN DIV)	22	17	9	53	Lost 2nd Round
1938	4th (CDN DIV)	12	30	6	30	Out of Playoffs
1938	—	—	—	—	—	Suspended Operations (August 25)

6. Tommy Gorman, who coached and managed the Maroons to the Stanley Cup Championship in 1935, was the most successful hockey man of his era, an early version of Sam Pollock. He managed the following Cup-winning teams: Ottawa Senators (1919-1921, 1923), Chicago (1934), Maroons (1935) and Canadiens (1944, 1946).

The Maroons versus Leafs in 1932.
HOCKEY HALL OF FAME, TORONTO

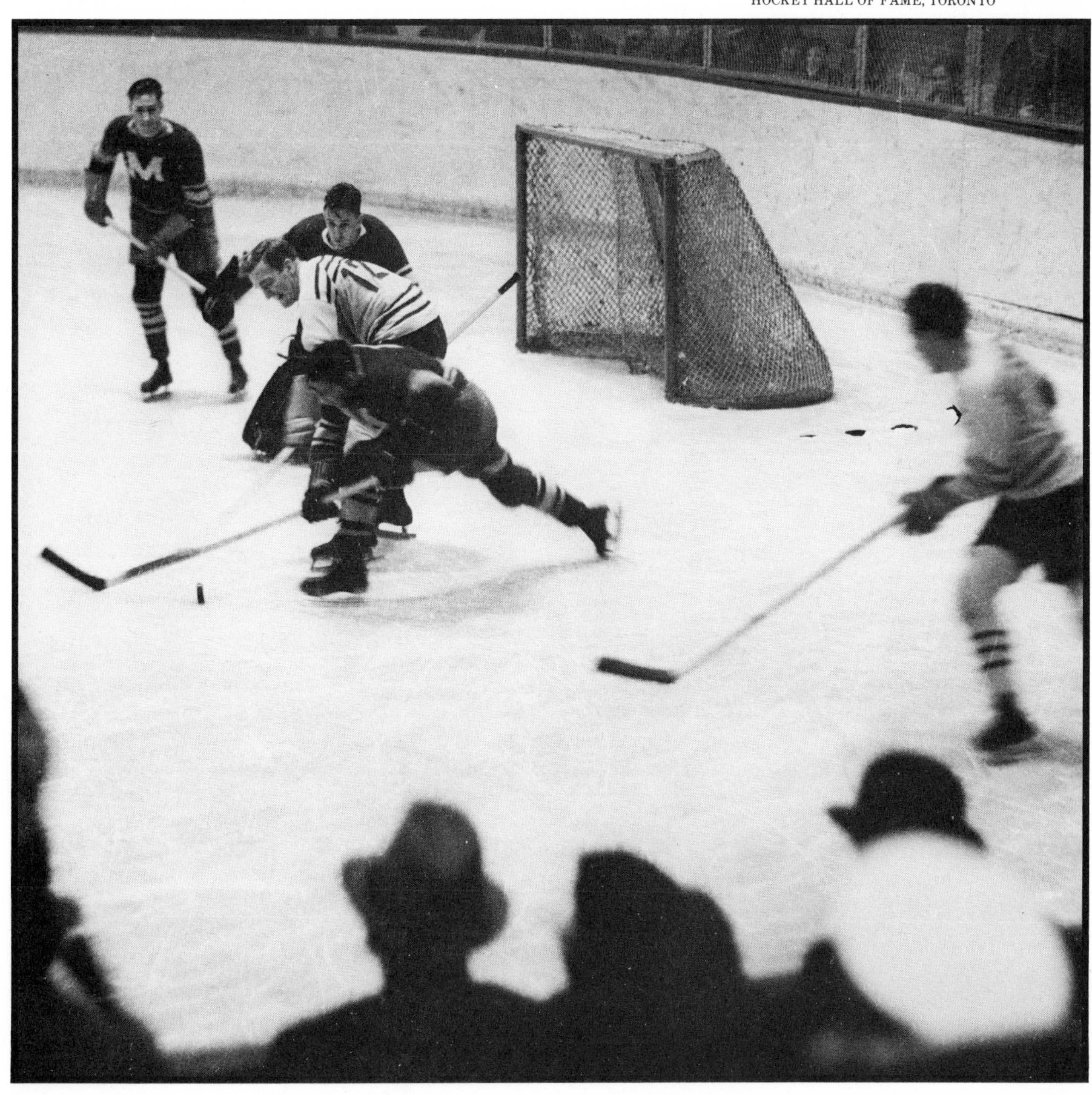

LES CANADIENS SONT LÀ

HERBERT WARREN WIND

Over the last half century, it has been accepted in professional hockey circles that most fans, as a rule, have two favorite teams—their home team and the Montreal Canadiens. There are several interrelated reasons for the Canadiens' vast and sustained popularity. To begin with, none of the other old, preëxpansion members of the National Hockey League, the top league in North America, has enjoyed as few losing seasons and as many glitteringly successful ones. At the end of the regular NHL schedule, for example, in the playoffs for the Stanley Cup, which is emblematic of the league championship (and, until the recent rise of splendid teams in Russia, Czechoslovakia, and Sweden, was assumed to be emblematic of world supremacy as well), the Canadiens have carried off the Cup twenty times. This is seven more times than the team with the next-best record, the Toronto Maple Leafs, earlier called the St. Pats and, before that, the Arenas. The appeal of the Canadiens has been based not only on their being a winning team but on the way they have gone about winning. Ever since the team came into existence, in 1909, it has been known for its *vitesse*—the players

A department store window display in Montreal of the 1931 team that won Canadiens' fourth Stanley Cup.
J. CATTARINICH FAMILY

skated like the wind. As often as not, the goals they scored, set up by subtle team maneuver or by dashing individual thrust, have had a sensational quality to them. Above and beyond this, the Canadiens have possessed a vital team spirit. While the group has always been made up of players of various ancestries, it has been composed primarily of young men of French descent drawn from the French-speaking province of Quebec. As one watched them in action, one felt that their flamboyant style reflected not only their Gallic temperament but a deep-rooted consciousness that, as the idols of French Canada, they had a responsibility to represent that minority region with heart and distinction.

THE FLYING FRENCHMEN

At the present time, when many Québécois support the separatist movement, which is committed to taking the province out of the Dominion of Canada and setting it up as a separate state, the differences between French and English Canada are of a grave and unhappy character. Of course, back in 1924, when the NHL first began to add teams representing American cities, this problem did

Henri Richard dekes Leafs' Ed Chadwick.
HOCKEY HALL OF FAME, TORONTO

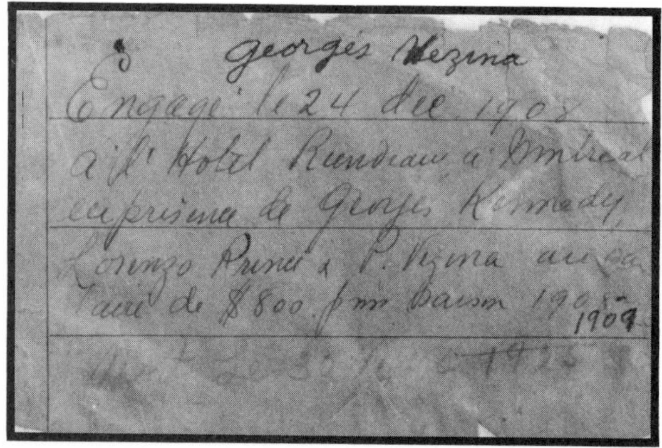

Georges Vezina
Engagé le 24 dec 1908
de $800 par saison 1908
1909

Georges Vezina's 1908-09 contract, calling for $800 yearly.
MONTREAL FORUM

not exist, and the new-to-hockey fans in this country, who saw nothing remarkable about the Maple Leafs—whose players, with few exceptions, came from English-speaking Canada (as did most of the players on the American teams)—were entranced by the very foreignness of the Canadiens, the "Flying Frenchmen." There was no doubt about it: the Canadiens had a romantic aura. They certainly looked the part, in their bright-red uniforms trimmed with blue and white—the famous *bleu, blanc, et rouge.* In the center of the jersey was a large "C," and, set inside the "C," a smaller "H." Many Americans deduced that the "H" stood for Habitants, for in the newspapers the Canadiens were often alluded to by that name, and called the Habs for short. This was not the case, though. The letters were the key initials of the official name of the organization, Le Club de Hockey Canadien. In any event, the Flying Frenchmen stirred the imagination as few teams in sport did. American fans who journeyed to Montreal to watch them on their home ice, the rink called the Forum, were charmed to find that at one end there was a so-called Millionaires Section, made up of workingmen who paid fifty cents for standing room, wore woollen toques in the Canadiens' colors, and cheered the team on by chanting *"Les Canadiens Sont Là!,"* an old French song adopted at the beginning of the century by Les Montagnards, a popular French-Canadian snowshoeing club, and later, when these clubs began to disappear and hockey began to boom in Montreal, adopted (with the substitution of *"Canadiens"* for *"Montagnards"*) by the Forum regulars.

THE STRATFORD STREAK

The Canadiens have been particularly fortunate in having a succession of bona-fide superstars to spearhead the team. The first of these, Howarth (Howie) Morenz, happened to be of German-Swiss, rather than French, lineage. He was born in 1902 in Mitchell, Ontario, and played Junior hockey for the team in the nearby town of Stratford. A young man of medium size—five feet nine, a hundred and sixty-five pounds—Morenz was far and away the finest skater and stickhandler in the Junior ranks in Ontario. He had one other invaluable trait: he loved to play hockey. Near the close of his career as a Junior, he was approached by many professional teams. He turned them all down until Leo Dandurand, the manager and coach of the Canadiens, made him an offer that far surpassed his wildest expectations: eight hundred and fifty dollars in cash and a contract for twenty-five hundred dollars a season. Dubbed the Stratford Streak during that heyday of all-out alliteration, Morenz in his rookie year, 1923-24, became a member of the Canadiens' first line, centering for Billy Boucher and Aurèle Joliat. Over a stretch of ten years, he averaged more than twenty goals a season at a time when a season consisted first of only twenty-four games and, later, of forty-eight. (The teams in the NHL today play eighty.) As a schoolboy, I was lucky enough to see Morenz in action several times. He was marvellous to watch. He combined well with his wingmen, but the rink-length rush was his specialty, and whenever he swung around his own net with the puck and started down the ice he brought the arena to life. His fantastic speed carried him quickly past the checking forwards, and he was flying when he neared the opposing team's blue line, where the two hefty defensemen were poised to step into him with a stiff body check. Sometimes they succeeded in doing this. More often they didn't. Morenz had a last-second shift that frequently fooled even veteran defensemen into thinking he would be cutting to the right when he was cutting to the left, or vice versa. This enabled him to slide around the defensemen and come roaring in with only the goalie to beat. He had a good, hard, rising shot. On these solo rushes, Morenz used a fairly wide repertoire of moves. For example, sometimes when he approached the two defensemen he had the audacity to feint to the outside and then to try to split the defense—to burst between the two men. One of his most dazzling feats came during a Stanley Cup game when his intention was to do exactly that. At the last moment, sensing that the defensemen expected him to attempt this and were all set for it, he poked the puck between them, swerved sharply out to the right, collected the puck behind them, and swooped in on the goalie and scored. He looked back and saw the two defensemen—they had collided—stretched out on the ice. Morenz's bravura performances changed the Canadiens from a team that the fans in and around Montreal thought highly of into something much more— their oriflamme, and the passion of their lives. Old-time hockey people also credit him with turning on the new American spectators in Boston, New York, Detroit, and Chicago to the beauty of the game, thus insuring the stability of those franchises and the future of the National Hockey League.

ROCKET RICHARD

In the 1943-44 season, a half-dozen years after Morenz had played his last game for the Canadiens, the team's next major star, Maurice (Rocket) Richard, arrived. The eldest son of Onésime Richard, a machinist—a much younger son, Henri, also became a star with the Canadiens—Maurice was a hometown boy from the parish of Bordeaux, which is situated close to the Rivière des Prairies, at the northern edge of the city. (Montreal and many of its suburbs occupy an island, about thirty miles long, at the confluence of the St. Lawrence River, to the south, and the Ottawa River, to the north. The street that serves as a sort of dividing line in Montreal is known as either Boulevard St. Laurent or St. Lawrence Boulevard, depending on whether one is of French or English descent. (The sprawling French section of the city lies to the east of the boulevard, while downtown Montreal and the principal English neighborhoods are to the west of it.) Richard's emergence as a star came, in a way, as a surprise. In 1940, when he was nineteen and in his first year with the Canadiens' farm team in the Senior Quebec Hockey League, he broke his left ankle. The next year, he broke his left wrist. Though he had missed most of these two seasons, he earned a spot with the Canadiens in the autumn of 1942. He started off very well, but in the sixteenth game he broke his right ankle when he was checked into the boards, and was out for the rest of *that* season. The general feeling was that Richard was obviously too brittle to make it in a slam-bang game like top-level hockey, but he came back the following season to score thirty-two goals for the Canadiens, playing right wing (though he was a left-hand shot) on a forward line that had Elmer Lach at center and Hector (Toe) Blake at left wing, and that went on to become one of the most

Maurice Richard, who announced his retirement five months later, surrounded by the press, including Jim Coleman (center) and Bruce Walker (right) during the 1960 playoffs. HOCKEY HALL OF FAME, TORONTO

productive lines in history. The next year, the 1944-45 season, Richard scored fifty goals in a fifty-game schedule—a pace that no NHL player had ever before approached. His NHL career lasted eighteen years in all, and when he retired, in the summer of 1960, he had accumulated a record total of five hundred and forty-four goals in regular-season competition and another eighty-two goals in Stanley Cup competition. Year after year, his performances in the playoffs, when the pressure is enormous, were almost unbelievable: he scored the winning goal in eighteen games (six of them in sudden-death overtime play), and he scored three or more goals in seven games (including five goals in one game and four goals in two others). A husky, broad-shouldered fellow who played with a flaming aggressiveness, Richard had such strength and determination that he frequently managed to score goals when opposing players were holding him, hooking him, or were draped all over him. Nobody else ever got shots off as fast as he did. The instant before a spectator told himself, "He'll shoot now," he had already fired the puck. It was often said that Richard, a terribly intense man, lived to score goals, and indeed he probably did.

Richard had a strong-featured face, set off by black hair brushed smoothly back. It was his gleaming dark eyes that one always noticed, for they projected the full force of his fierce pride, his short-fused temper, and the deep, elemental emotions that surged through him. He was without a doubt one of the most magnetic athletes of this century—you couldn't take your eyes off him when he was on the ice, even if he was doing nothing of

Jacques Plante leaps for the puck with Eddie Shack and Dick Duff of the Leafs at the doorstep.
HOCKEY HALL OF FAME, TORONTO

consequence at the moment. Montreal and all of Quebec adored him. After his extraordinary gift for putting the puck in the net had become evident, a large number of the Canadiens' fans began to keep notebooks in which they listed each goal he scored, along with a description of how he had done it. These Richard experts were unanimously agreed that his most dramatic goal was the one against the Boston Bruins in the seventh and deciding game of the Stanley Cup semifinals in 1952. In the second period, after his head had hit the ice following a collision, six stitches were taken above his left eye. He sat silently on the bench in the third period, still dazed, but with the score tied 1-1 late in

The shot that won the Stanley Cup in 1971. Henri Richard follows through to beat Black Hawks goalie Tony Esposito to put the Canadiens ahead, 3–2.

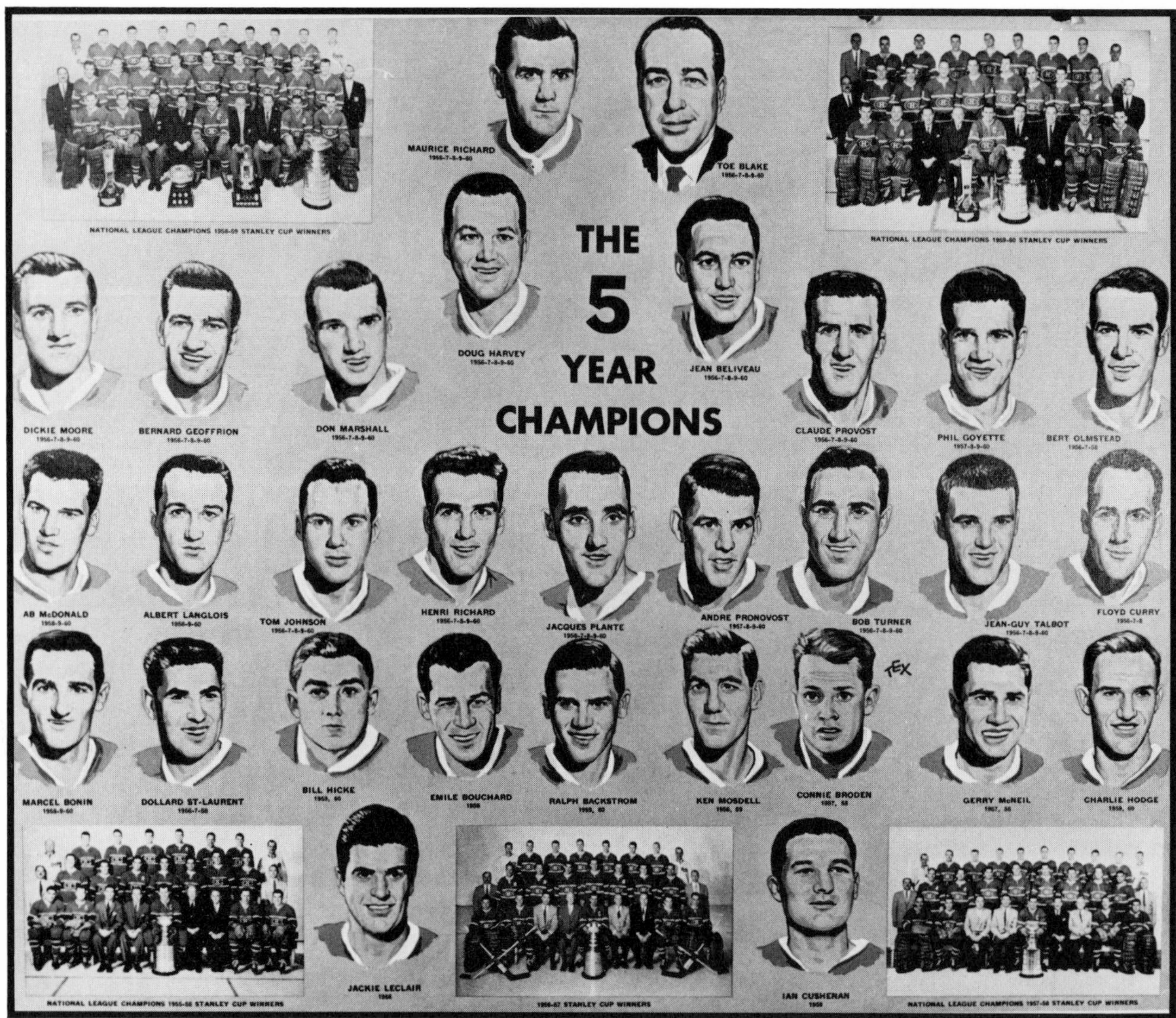

WILLIE DAGENAIS

the period he indicated that he was ready to take his regular turn with the line. Operating almost entirely on courage and instinct, Richard, his eyes glazed, got control of the puck deep in the Canadiens' zone. He twisted his way up the ice and warded off a check by a Bruin defenseman, Bob Armstrong, but he was ridden into the corner to the right of the goal by the other defenseman, Bill Quackenbush. Then, with a tremendous effort, he broke free of Quackenbush and, skating laterally across the ice, closed in on the Bruins' goalie, Jim Henry, and lifted the puck past him for the goal that won the game. A four-minute ovation shook the Forum. I can think of only two postwar athletes who matched Richard in their total dedication to the game they played—Ben Hogan, the golfer, and Bob Cousy, the leader of the Boston Celtics basketball team during their championship era in the nineteen-fifties and sixties. What these three men didn't give they simply didn't have to give.

Jean Béliveau, un immortel du hockey.
Jean Beliveau, a Canadien immortal.

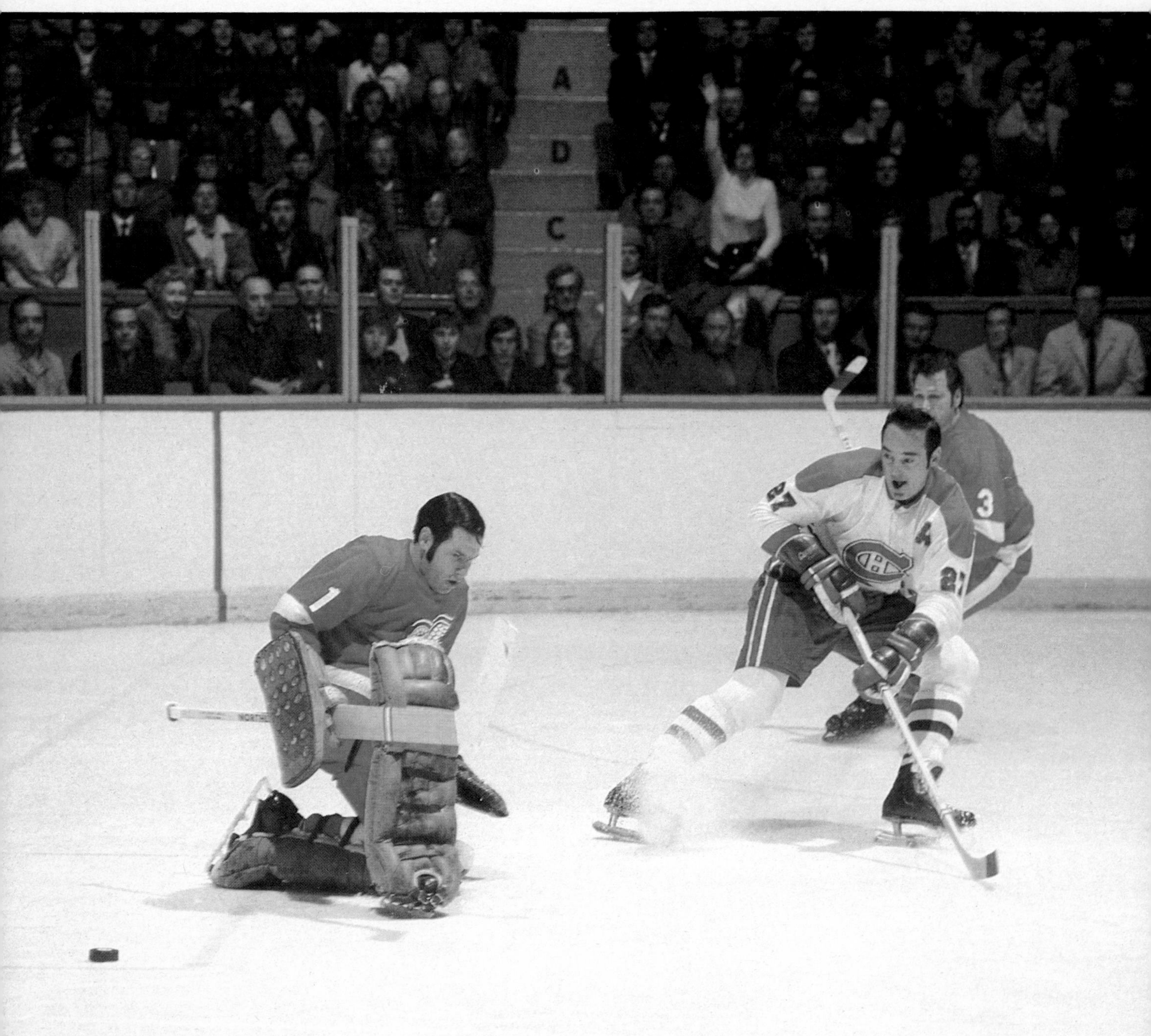
A
D
C
1
27
3

John Ferguson, un des joueurs les plus durs au hockey.
John Ferguson, one of the toughest men to play the game.

Roger Doucet chante l'hymne national.
Roger Doucet sings the National Anthem.
WILLIE DAGENAIS

Frank Mahovlich lance bien à côté du filet des Red Wings.
Frank Mahovlich shoots wide of the Red Wing net.
WILLIE DAGENAIS

Guy Lafleur compte lors d'un mêlée contre les Islanders.

Guy Lafleur scores through a traffic jam against the Islanders.

Bob Gainey à l'esseau du filet des Rangers.
Bob Gainey charges the Ranger net.

Le banc des joueurs de Montréal pendant l'hymne national.

The Montreal bench during the National Anthem.

WILLIE DAGENAIS

Scotty Bowman.
WILLIE DAGENAIS

Ken Dryden se prépare à recevoir un lancer.

Ken Dryden braces for a shot.
WILLIE DAGENAIS

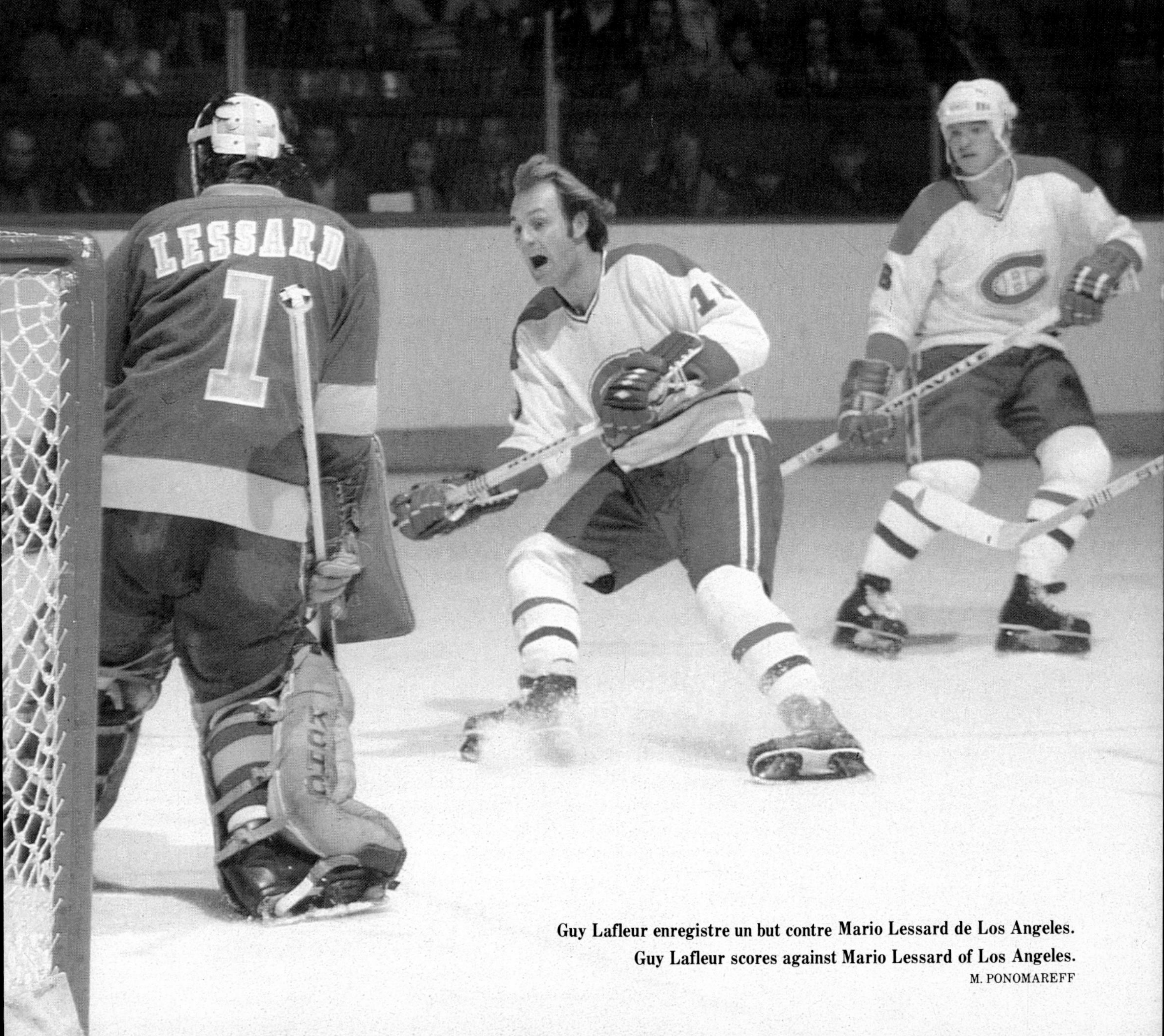

Guy Lafleur enregistre un but contre Mario Lessard de Los Angeles.
Guy Lafleur scores against Mario Lessard of Los Angeles.
M. PONOMAREFF

Steve Shutt et Larry Robinson félicitent Peter Mahovlich à la suite d'un autre but.

Steve Shutt and Larry Robinson congratulate Peter Mahovlich after another goal.

WILLIE DAGENAIS

Yvon Lambert en action.

Yvon Lambert in action.

WILLIE DAGENAIS

Guy Lafleur faisant échec arrière contre les Islanders.

Guy Lafleur backchecking against the Islanders.

M. PONOMAREFF

Lors d'une joute contre Boston, Guy Lafleur se dirige vers les buts mais la rondelle refuse d'y pénétrer; Pierre Mondou attend un retour.

Guy Lafleur heads for the net but the puck stays out in a game against Boston, as Pierre Mondou looks for a rebound.
M. PONOMAREFF

Murray Wilson lance contre St. Louis.

Murray Wilson shooting against St. Louis.

WILLIE DAGENAIS

Réjean Houle lors d'une altercation avec un joueur du St. Louis.

Rejean Houle in a dispute with a St. Louis player.

WILLIE DAGENAIS

Guy Lafleur en action contre Colorado, 1978.

Guy Lafleur moves into the action against Colorado, 1978.
M. PONOMAREFF

THE BELIVEAU YEARS

No one could have been more different from Richard than Jean Beliveau, the team's next superstar. Whereas Richard throbbed with the militance and wrath of an ancient tribal chieftain, Beliveau was the mildest of men. His unrambunctious nature was all the more conspicuous since he was a very big man, particularly for a center: he stood six feet three and weighed two hundred and five pounds. During Beliveau's first two years in the NHL, the tough-guy "intimidators" on the other teams jumped all over him, and his reluctance to retaliate set up doubts in many minds as to whether he would survive long in the league. In his third season, Beliveau changed his policy. When an opposing player tried to belt him around, he waded in and demonstrated past any doubt that he was essentially as tough as the tough guys and a better fighter than most of them. They left him alone after that. Beliveau was an unusually handsome young man. There was a look of nobility in his facial expressions as well as in the dignity with which he comported himself. He reminded one of the characters that Gary Cooper played, and just as Cooper in real life was as honest and decent as he seemed on the screen, so was Beliveau off the ice.

Beliveau was born in Trois Rivières, on the north bank of the St. Lawrence, but grew up in Victoriaville, a town about forty miles south of the river. In a typically large French-Canadian family, he was the eldest of seven children. His parents—his father worked for Hydro-Quebec—were gentle people, and the household had an old-fashioned, quiet-voiced atmosphere based on implicit respect. Jean got his size early: at fifteen, he was a slim six-footer. People who shoot up fast are often gangling and awkward, but Beliveau was an exception. A well-coördinated athlete, he had quick reflexes and was an effortless, graceful skater. At seventeen, he was the best Junior player in the country. He played his last two years of Junior hockey in Quebec City for a team called the Citadelles. When he turned twenty, he chose to stay in Quebec City and play Senior amateur hockey with the Quebec Aces rather than turn professional and go up with the Canadiens, who owned the rights to him. Considering the circumstances, his decision was understandable. Quebec City and Montreal are old rivals, and the former, well aware that in Beliveau it had a star whose capability and charisma were unmatched by any player his age in the NHL, could not do enough for him. Beliveau received such a high salary and so much subsidiary income from commercial endorsements that it became a cliché to say that he could not afford to turn pro. For his part, he loved Quebec City, where, from his Junior days on, he was able to live as he wanted to. He roomed in a nice old house run by three elderly women—"the beautiful, white-haired McKenna sisters," as he likes to describe them—and they made his home life comfortable and pleasant.

After two seasons with the Aces, Beliveau joined the Canadiens at the start of the 1953-54 season, when he was twenty-two. Frank J. Selke, then the managing director of the Canadiens, had offered him a contract calling for a total payment of approximately a hundred thousand dollars over five years—by far the most money ever waved before a young hockey player. Like Richard, who was his teammate for seven seasons, Beliveau put in eighteen years with Montreal, retiring a few months before his fortieth birthday. He was a wonderful all-around player. A superlative stickhandler—stickhandling is roughly the equivalent of dribbling in basketball—he elicited roars of rapture from the Forum regulars as he sifted his way through a cluster of defenders with a combination of quick feints and quicker changes of direction. He was an excellent player in a league in which, surprisingly, few players can lead a teammate with an accurate pass slid ahead at the correct speed. He was no less adept at receiving a pass; he took the puck with a little momentary give of the blade of his stick and had the puck so surely under control that it seemed as if the blade were sticky with fresh black tape. He could build plays. He could shoot. He could battle for the puck along the boards. He could back-check efficiently. He could do just about everything, and, like all the great players, he could do it when it mattered. Some statistics are relevant here. Beliveau holds the Canadiens' record for most points scored: twelve hundred and nineteen, on five hundred and seven goals and seven hundred and twelve assists. He also holds the NHL record for most total points in Stanley Cup play: a hundred and seventy-six, on seventy-nine goals and ninety-seven assists. During his career, Montreal made the playoffs seventeen times and won the Cup ten times. In 1970-71—his last season—after the team had defeated the Chicago Black Hawks in Chicago in the seventh and deciding game of the final series, Beliveau, as the Canadiens' captain, was presented with the Stanley Cup. Raising the three-foot trophy high above his head, he skated around the perimeter of the rink a couple of times. The Black Hawk fans, despite their disappointment at the loss of a very close series, perceived almost instantly that they were looking at no conquering foe but at a rare gentleman whose manner as he displayed the Cup unmistakably said, "I am not merely celebrating the Canadiens' triumph. I am celebrating the superb game of ice hockey and what it means to all of us." In previous years, the captain of the winning team had sometimes exhibited the Stanley Cup with a flourish, but Beliveau brought a whole new meaning to the ceremony, and since that time the circling of the rink with the huge trophy held aloft has come to be regarded as the perfect climax to the long, long season, which now begins in early October and stretches well into May.

CONTINUING THE TRADITION: GUY LAFLEUR

Many Canadian boys who watched Jean Beliveau on television, or occasionally in person, were so admiring of him, both as a hockey player and as a man, that they made up their minds to model themselves after him. One who did is the current Montreal hero, Guy Lafleur, the high-scoring right wing on the team's first line. A native of the town of Thurso, in western Quebec, where his father works as a welder in a pulp mill, Lafleur is one of five children. (The others are girls—Suzanne, Giselle, Lise, and Lucie.) Like Beliveau, Lafleur played his Junior hockey in Quebec City, for a team called Les Remparts. Last year, he led the NHL in scoring for the third straight season—he had sixty goals and seventy-two assists—and he was voted the league's Most Valuable Player for the second straight season. A swift, darting skater with a blazing shot, Lafleur has matured into a rugged two-way player and a clever, imaginative playmaker. For example, when an offensive sortie has gone sour and there is no Canadien free, while the men on both teams are milling around inchoately in front of the opposition's net, Lafleur has the knack of finding open ice, which he often does by taking the puck to the back of the attacking zone and stickhandling laterally across the rink. This has the effect of unclogging the situation: sooner or later, an opposing player has to come out to cover him,

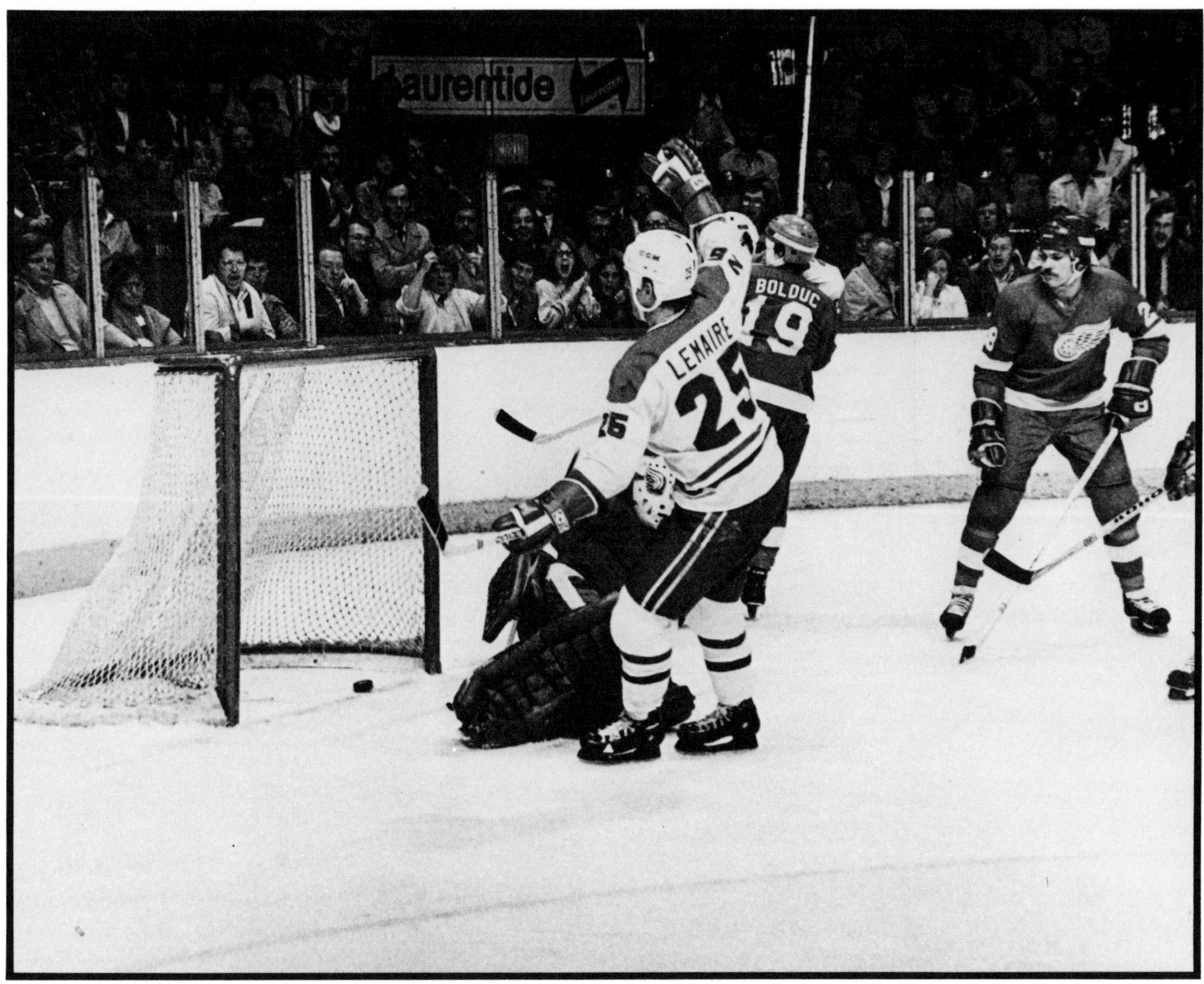

Jacques Lemaire nets one against the Red Wings.
JEAN-GUY PARADIS

and this frequently allows one of the Canadiens to work himself into position to receive a pass; the moment he does, Lafleur whips the puck to him and kindles a new play. A sandy-haired young man with the sharply arched eyebrows and chiselled features of a matinée idol, Lafleur conducts himself with the modesty of a Beliveau. He is almost always the first player to arrive for the practice sessions. He always wears a tie, even to practices. Like Beliveau and most other Canadiens past and present, he thrives on the family atmosphere that has long made the team a genuine team and not merely a group of individuals. It should be brought out that if there has usually been a Richard, a Beliveau, a Lafleur, or some other star of French ancestry up front, so has there also been a Morenz, an Elmer Lach, and a Dickie Moore on the forward lines; that if there have been stalwart defensemen like Sylvio Mantha and Emile (Butch) Bouchard, there has also been a Sprague Cleghorn, a Doug Harvey, and currently, a Larry Robinson; and that if Georges Vezina and Jacques

Plante have performed wonders in the goal for the Canadiens, so have George Hainsworth, Bill Durnan, and Ken Dryden. The best players on the squad, regardless of their background, are the ones who play. However, if a young man of English descent and a young man of French descent are battling for an open spot on the team and there is little or no difference in their abilities, the job usually goes to the French Canadian, which is certainly understandable, considering that over sixty-five per cent of the city's population—and over eighty per cent of the province's—is of French stock. Just before this season got under way, many of the Canadiens' fans were predictably upset when the front office sent Pierre Bouchard to the Washington Capitals. He refused to report, and retired from hockey. During his eight seasons with the Canadiens, Pierre, the son of the revered Butch Bouchard, was a fairly efficient defenseman, but nothing like the player his father had been. "We always knew Pierre had his limitations," a representative Canadiens rooter explained to me. "Nevertheless, in Montreal—and the front office should have known this—you just don't get rid of a Bouchard."

MONTREAL, THE PARIS OF HOCKEY

Montreal may not be Paris, but one thinks of it as the Paris of hockey, because the Canadiens have played the game down through the years with an artistry and verve that no other NHL team has come close to. As a result, while the upper-stratum patrons of most of the other long-established teams in the league lost interest in them years ago and stopped attending their games, all of Montreal continues to follow the Canadiens ardently, and the red, white, and blue seats in the Forum are still filled by people from every walk of life, including college professors, doctors, business leaders, lawyers, and judges. (I am told that this is true in only one other city in the league—Toronto.) Quite a number of the Canadiens' perennial season-ticket holders value their tickets so highly that they have stipulated in their wills to whom their seats are to go. Another index of the fervor with which Montrealers take their hockey is the improbable coverage the game receives in both the French and English daily newspapers. Two French tabloids, *Métro Matin* and *Journal de Montreal,* are well out in front. In their sports sections, which often run to twenty or more pages, it is not uncommon for at least fifteen pages to be devoted to hockey. What with this rampant enthusiasm, watching a Canadiens game in the Forum can be one of the most vivid experiences in contemporary sports, and ever since my first winter trip to Montreal, in 1954, I have made it a point not to let too many years slip by between visits.

Early in the winter of 1978-79, I thought it was time to go up again. For one thing, I wanted to get a clearer idea as to whether the present team is just a good, sound team in an over-expanded league filled with thin teams or if, as its record would suggest, it is one of the great Canadiens teams of all times: During regular-season play in 1975-76, 1976-77, and 1977-78, it lost a total of only twenty-nine of the two hundred and forty games it played, and it won the Stanley Cup each of those three years. On the other hand, the standard of hockey the Canadiens exhibited in the final series of the Stanley Cup playoffs last year against the Boston Bruins was decidedly disappointing. With the series tied at two games each, they resorted to roughhousing all over the ice to wear down the Bruins and gain command of the play. These tactics are well

The intensity of the game: Boston's Brad Park battles Jacques Lemaire and Yvon Lambert.
JEAN-GUY PARADIS

and good for lesser teams, but they are utterly alien to the Canadiens' traditional style of play, and one was put off by them. Was this the handwriting on the wall or merely a momentary fall from grace? During my stay in Montreal, I learned some of the answers I was seeking—with so much of its strength concentrated in its defense corps and its goaltenders, this is an enigmatic Canadiens team—but as I walked down Sherbrooke, Maisonneuve, Ste. Catherine, and other streets in downtown Montreal, thinking hockey every step of the way, I realized that foremost in my mind was a much more profound appreciation of the exceptional achievements of the Canadiens since the beginning of the era of modern sport, at the close of the First World War. In a word, the Canadiens have constituted one of the two most remarkable dynasties in sport over those sixty years. The only comparable dynasty has been the New York Yankees. The special mystique of the Canadiens is not easy to describe, but it strikes me that an effective way of getting it across would be to put together a string of glimpses of people—players, ad-

The 1951 All-Star game in Toronto. Doug Harvey (left) and Gordie Howe (right) move into the action around Gerry McNeil.
HOCKEY HALL OF FAME, TORONTO

ministrators, fans—I talked to on my visit this winter who have either been close to the team in the past or are close to it at the moment, with the idea that these glimpses might fuse like the parts of a mosaic and produce an image of the unique personality of Le Club de Hockey Canadien.

THE CANADIENS' FRONT OFFICE

One of the oldest members of the Canadiens' front office in point of service is Camil DesRoches, a diminutive man with a cheerful disposition and a perky black mustache. The youngest of nineteen children of a tailor (eighteen of them boys), DesRoches grew up in a pocket of northeast Montreal populated by people of all nationalities. He picked up his English on the street. When he finished school, he went to work as a cub reporter for *Le Petit Journal*, a weekly publication. Likable and industrious, he moved up in 1938 and became the sports editor of a minor daily called *Le Canada.* At this time, Tommy Gorman, the general manager of the Canadiens, hired him to translate into French the daily press releases that Gorman wrote about the team

Action around the Ranger net during the Stanley Cup final in Montreal, 1979, as Pierre Mondou heads for the ice.
JEAN-GUY PARADIS

and to deliver the whole batch to the various Montreal papers. It took DesRoches from two until five in the afternoon to discharge these duties, after which he hurried to the offices of *Le Canada* and worked on the sports section until three in the morning. He maintained this backbreaking schedule until 1946, when Gorman left the Canadiens and Frank Selke was brought in as the managing director. Gorman had always paid him in cash, but Selke, after talking with DesRoches, asked him to join the Canadiens on a staff basis as a public-relations man. (During Selke's regime, the team had two public-relations men, one working with the French media, the other with the English.) DesRoches accepted the offer, and has been with the organization ever since. In recent years, he has been the Forum's director of special events, which include everything from ice shows to rock concerts, but he remains very much a part of the Canadiens' inner family. As Claude Mouton, the current director of public relations, has expressed it, "If we need to know a particular piece of information about the early days of Montreal hockey—or, for that matter, the not so early days—we call for Camil."

On one of my visits to Montreal in the

nineteen-sixties, I asked DesRoches if he could tell me anything about Howie Morenz's death. Along with most hockey fans, I had been stunned by the news of it. On January 28, 1937, Morenz, who was then thirty-four and enjoying a very good season, was the victim of a freak accident. As he went careening into the boards after being checked, his skate got caught in the wood, and his ankle was twisted grotesquely; when a defenseman then fell heavily across him, Morenz's leg was severely fractured. For some reason—perhaps because Morenz had become deeply depressed at the thought that his hockey career might be over—the hospital, instead of facilitating his recovery by treating him as a patient, allowed groups of his friends to drop in on him and attempt to raise his spirits with a succession of parties. His condition suddenly took a turn for the worse, and on March 8th he suffered a fatal heart attack. It was hard to believe that this comparatively young man, who had been flying over the ice only weeks before, had died—there had been nothing quite like it before in sports. As DesRoches told me, "After the initial shock of this tragedy, the men who ran the Club de Hockey arranged for Morenz's casket to lie in state at center ice in the Forum for a day and a night so that the fans who loved him could pay their respects to him. I was just a kid of twenty-two, working for *Le Petit Journal.* I'll never forget what a sorrowful occasion it was. An endless line of grieving people filed slowly by the casket, thousands and thousands of them. The funeral service was held in the Forum on March 11th. Close to fifteen thousand people jammed every inch of space in the building, and thousands more filled the nearby streets. The streetcars had to stop blocks away. I don't think we had any conception till then how much Howie Morenz meant to all of us. It was as if a beloved president or prime minister had died. It really wasn't until Morenz's death that many of us—this was true of me, I know— became aware that he had made the Canadiens an inseparable part of our lives."

FRANK SELKE

Frank Selke, who directed the Canadiens organization from 1946 through 1964, is now eighty-seven. He continues to attend all of the team's home games. He would feel cut off

Lorne (Gump) Worsley, inducted into the Hall of Fame in 1980, is shown here in action during the 1979 Old Timers game.
JEAN-GUY PARADIS

from life if he didn't. He comes in the forty-six miles from his hundred-and-sixty-eight-acre farm in Rigaud, where the Ottawa River flows twenty feet from his door. Until two years ago, he ran a working farm, raising Belted Galloway cattle and more than a hundred varieties of poultry, among them White Plymouth Rocks, Buff Wyandottes, and Golden Pencilled Hamburgs, some of which won prizes in the leading Canadian and American shows. Selke, who stands only five feet two but has always seemed much taller to me, looks very well. His short-cropped hair is now silver and his step a little slow, but I noticed few other effects of the advancing years. A warm, percipient man with an instinctive feeling for hockey, Selke has struck me from our first meeting as one of the ablest executives in sports. When he took over as managing director in Montreal, there was no restriction on the number of young prospects an NHL team could sign and try to develop, and Selke had the foresight to set up an incomparable farm system that stretched from Edmonton and Regina in the west to Halifax in the east. Under his leadership, the Canadiens won six Stanley Cups. This included a record five in a row, from 1956 to 1960. When

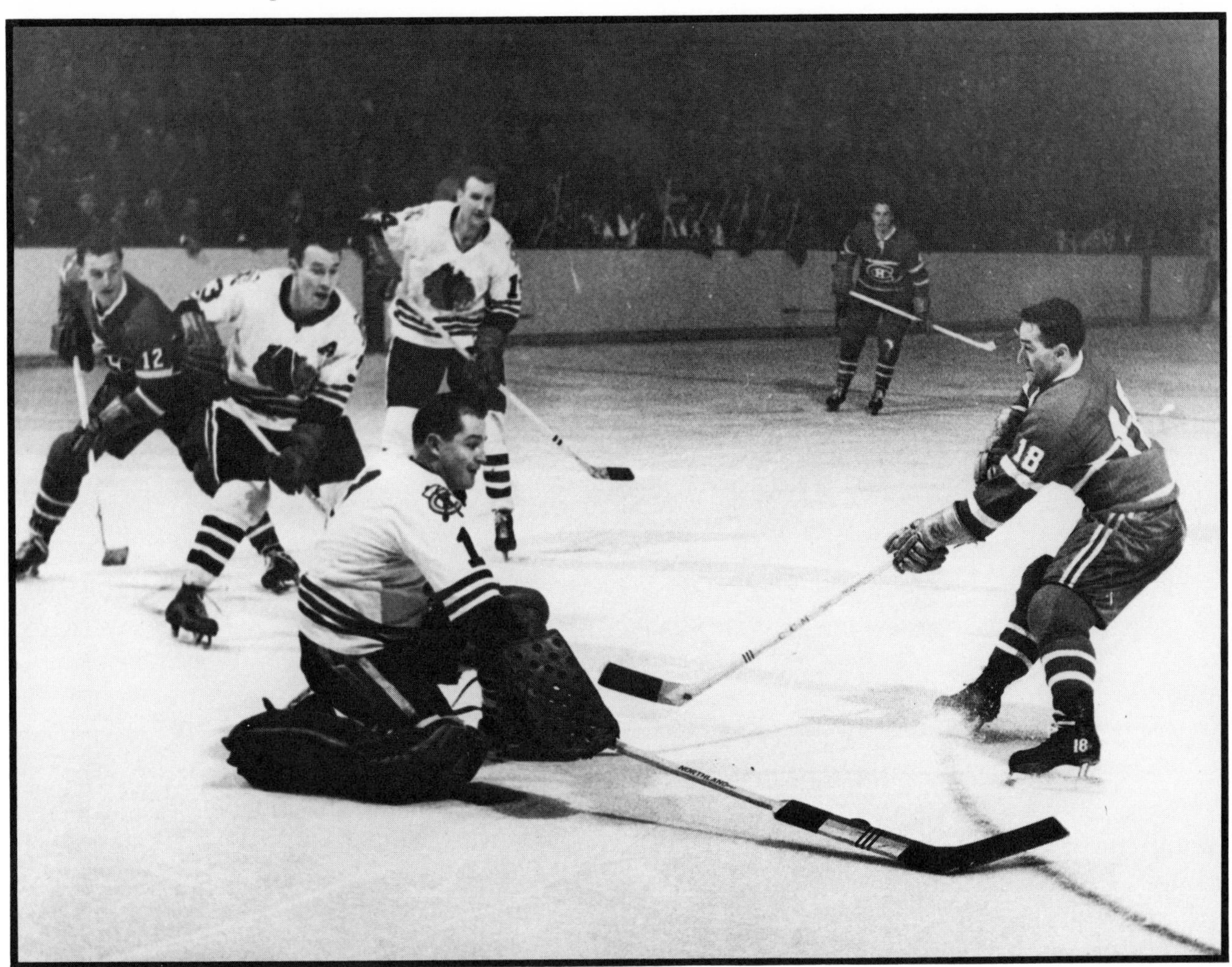

Action in the 1960's, as Dickie Moore, Pierre Pilote, Glen Skov, Marcel Bonin and Jean Beliveau converge on Glenn Hall.
HOCKEY HALL OF FAME, TORONTO

Dickie Moore scores against Al Rollins of Toronto, 1952.
HOCKEY HALL OF FAME, TORONTO

Selke retired in 1964, he was succeeded by Sam Pollock, who had served as his director of farm personnel. A first-class administrator in his own right, Pollock had to operate during the difficult expansion period in the nineteen-sixties and nineteen-seventies, when the Canadiens and the five other long-established teams could no longer protect for their own use the players on the minor-league teams they sponsored—any of the twelve new expansion teams could now grab them in the annual Amateur Draft. Nevertheless, by astutely trading surplus players on the Canadiens' roster to expansion teams in exchange for future draft picks Pollock kept the Canadiens the premier team in professional hockey. They won the Stanley Cup nine times during the fourteen years of his stewardship, which ended last summer when he stepped down after the team was sold to Molson Breweries by Peter and Edward Bronfman, who are closely related to the family that runs the Seagram Company.

To return to Frank Selke. Like most architects of winning teams, he was exceedingly proficient at appraising the potential of teenage players who were still years away from the first bloom of maturity. He had another

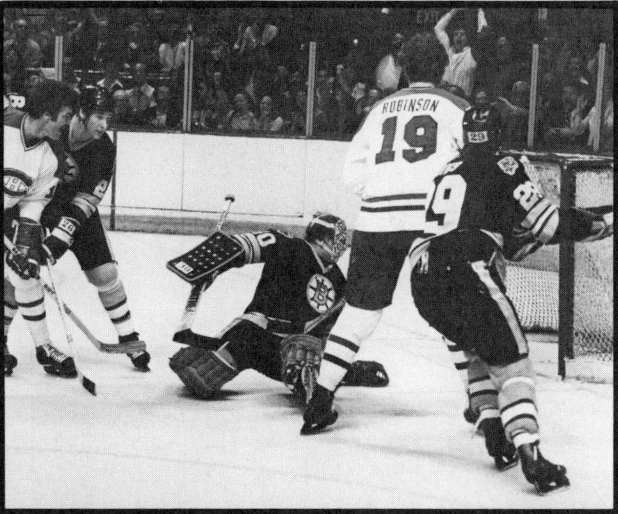

Upper left, John Davidson of the Rangers and Steve Shutt of Montreal bat at the puck while Ron Greschner (#4) ducks.
JEAN-GUY PARADIS

Upper right, Gerry Cheevers watches the puck slide into the net from the stick of Larry Robinson.
JEAN-GUY PARADIS

Middle left, Rejean Houle misses against Boston.
JEAN-GUY PARADIS

Middle right, Mario Tremblay has Jimmy Rutherford of the Wings going in the wrong direction.
JEAN-GUY PARADIS

Lower left, action around the Washington Capitals' net.
JEAN-GUY PARADIS

important attribute: he understood people well and could reach his players and often help them. The classic case was the tempestuous Maurice Richard. Selke was able to get through to Richard on many troublous occasions, for he was convinced that Richard was a man of integrity and high standards who, once the situation had been explained to him, would never fail to do the right thing. He was not mistaken. During his long career, the Rocket never entirely lost the primitive intensity that set him apart from other players, but he learned to control it much better and to avoid incidents that might have truncated his career had there been no friend like Selke to guide him.

The way that Selke went about building the Canadiens into one of the finest teams of all time is a fascinating story, but I have always found myself more interested in his early years in hockey. He was born in 1893, in Berlin, Ontario (which adroitly changed its name to Kitchener during the First World War), the son of a Polish immigrant who worked as a laborer for the provincial Department of Public Works. As a boy, he did not let his small size deter him from making the school and neighborhood hockey teams. He discovered that he could check the top players on the opposing teams if he skated hard and stuck with them closely. At the same time, accepting the fact that he could not expect to have much of a future as a player, he started to prepare himself for the jobs in hockey that might enable him to make a life for himself in the game. At thirteen, he managed his first team. (At that time, incidentally, a team was made up of seven men, and games were divided into two thirty-minute periods. In Berlin, the games were usually played on the natural ice of artificial ponds that had been created when the local brick factory had excavated an area known to contain clayey soil). Selke left school at an early age and went to work, first in a furniture factory and then, in 1911, as an electrician. He always found the extra time to continue in hockey. At the age of twenty, he managed and coached a Berlin team, the Union Jacks, that went all the way to the semifinals of the Junior Ontario Hockey Association championship. Several years later, after moving to Toronto, he continued his double life, working as an electrician at the University of Toronto and coaching hockey teams in his off-hours. In 1924, he scored a signal triumph: he reorganized the Junior Marlboros, a famous team that had stopped operation, and led them to the JOHA playoffs that very first year. He entered professional hockey shortly after the NHL franchise in Toronto had been purchased by a syndicate headed by Conn Smythe, a brave and brilliant, if at times impossibly egotistical, man. When Smythe became the general manager of the Maple Leafs, he appointed Selke his assistant. At the outbreak of war in 1939, Smythe, who had fought in the First World War, volunteered for service, although he was well over military age, and ultimately he was in the thick of the action in the Normandy invasion. In his absence, Selke ran the team and ran it well. However, during the 1945-46 season the Leafs did not make the playoffs, and Smythe, who by then was back in Toronto, publicly flayed Selke for their failure, charging him with having selected the wrong reserve players. Selke resigned his post with the Leafs that spring, and a few months later was signed by the Canadiens as their managing director. He soon came to be regarded as the top executive in the game.

During my visit to Montreal, I had a wonderfully enjoyable chat with Selke one afternoon when he came in from Rigaud for a game between the Canadiens and the Detroit Red Wings. He made a number of wise and tren-

Paul Mulvey of Washington scores against Bunny Larocque.
JEAN-GUY PARADIS

chant comments as he roved through his many years in hockey. Here are a few I remember:

"Strong defense, good physical condition, and teamwork are the elements that make for a winning hockey team. I think I began to realize this when I was fourteen and had a year of managing behind me. . . .

"I am frequently given too much credit for the renaissance of the Canadiens. Several years before I came to Montreal, Dick Irvin, who had been brought in as the coach, got the team back on the right track. He saw to it that there was discipline both in the dressing room and on the ice. He knew the value of pride and dignity. . . .

"When you keep the game on a high plane, the money will take care of itself."

LES JUNIORS DE MONTREAL

The evening before my meeting with Selke, I went out to the Paul Sauvé Arena, in the north end of the French section of the city, to look in on a practice session of Les Juniors de Montreal, a team that has an informal connection with the Canadiens. This was my first expedition to that part of town, and I discovered that street after street is lined with carefully maintained two-story houses and that the streets themselves are so clean that, to the eyes of a visitor from New York City, they practically sparkle. Inside the arena, some sixteen or so players were moving around the rink, working on whatever they wished to—ragging the puck, zinging their slap shots, practicing standard skating exercises like starts and stops, and so on. I asked one of them where I could find Roger Bédard, the coach, and learned that he wasn't on hand; the team had played a game the night before, and this was an optional practice: the players who wanted to work out could. He suggested I talk to the team captain, Réal Paiement. A stocky defenseman, Paiement is a pleasant, well-spoken young man of nineteen who grew up in the suburb of Dollard-des-Ormeaux, in the west end of Greater Montreal. He finished junior college last year and is now concentrating solely on his hockey while supporting himself on the fifty dollars a week plus board which the members of Les Juniors de Montreal and other Junior teams receive, even though they are technically considered amateurs. (A player who does not reach his

The Richard brothers—Number 9, the Rocket and Number 16, Henri.

twentieth birthday until the first of January that season is eligible to play Junior hockey.) It is not the easiest of lives. The teams in the Quebec Junior Major Hockey League play a schedule of seventy-two games, travel by bus on their road trips, and practice most days when no game is scheduled. It requires the same kind of dedication that minor-league baseball does.

Paiement thought that I might like to talk with one of the two Americans on the team, and called over Clint Campbell, a native of Rochester, New York, who stands well over six feet but despite his size is a forward and not a defenseman. He is eighteen and attends Rosemount High School, in Montreal—he finds he can combine school and hockey satisfactorily. Five years ago, when the Bruins installed a farm team in Rochester, Campbell became seriously interested in the game. He developed into a standout player in high school and was drafted by the Hull team of the Junior Quebec League. Early this year, Hull traded him to Les Juniors de Montreal in exchange for two players. When we finished our chat, Campbell skated away, and I let my eyes wander around the rink. In front of me, two energetic giants were engaged in a friendly stand-up wrestling match, each trying to pull the other's jersey over his head—a tactic frequently used in brawls on the ice. At one end, a goalie was testing his reflexes as three men peppered him with shots at close range. When I turned my attention to the opposite end, I saw that Campbell was positioned just to one side of an untended goal, standing with his back to it. Two players a yard or so inside the blue line were taking turns firing low, hard shots, and Campbell, handling his stick dexterously, was practicing deflecting the puck into the near and far corners of the goal. He looked pretty good to me.

Paiement came over at the end of practice. "Every Junior has the same ambition," he told me. "When he's twenty and eligible for the Amateur Draft, he hopes he'll be selected by one of the teams in the NHL. The fellows on our team naturally hope they'll be drafted by Montreal. We think there's no club like the Canadiens. Still, you've got to be practical. All the guys realize how tough it is to make the Canadiens, so they wouldn't be too downhearted if they ended up with, say, Atlanta or Buffalo, or even with one of the poorer NHL teams. The thing is to get drafted and get a chance to play in the big time."

As I was leaving the arena, I passed a succession of kids of about nine or ten, each carrying his hockey gear and wearing a smile of quiet pride at the prospect of playing on such a fine rink. Canadians start playing organized hockey at a very early age. The boys I saw were Atoms—the next-to-youngest class. The youngest are the Squirts, who are seven and eight. When the boys graduate from the Atoms, they become, successively, Mosquitoes, Pee-Wees, Bantams, Midgets, and Juniors, and a fortunate few will go all the way and become successful professionals.

THE RICHARD LEGEND

Maurice Richard hasn't changed much in appearance over the last twenty years. There are a few flecks of gray at the temples, and he has put on a few pounds around the middle, but that is the extent of it. "I should try to get rid of that stomach—I now weigh two-twenty," he said to me one morning when I called on him in his office at S. Albert & Company, a fuel-oil distributing outfit on Boulevard St. Laurent with which he has been connected for fifteen years. "But you know something?" he continued, puffing on a cigar. "I weighed over two hundred pounds my last five years with the Canadiens. Too much. The trouble was that if I went on a diet I lost weight too fast and didn't feel strong enough to play my best hockey." Anyhow, Richard is still recognized immediately wherever he goes in Canada. This is a happy state of affairs, for it is human nature, evidently, for the public to take pleasure in a popular entertainer, athlete, or any other celebrated person of an earlier period who looks more or less like his or her old self. For example, the fact that Joe DiMaggio still resembles the young Yankee Clipper has had a great deal to do with his success as a spokesman on television commercials for a savings bank and a coffee-making machine. In some ways, however, Richard has changed. Certainly his eyes are different. Within a few years after he retired in 1960, the Rocket's red glare was gradually replaced by a calm, relaxed expression—the heavy burden of not letting down himself, the team, his friends, the whole province had been lifted from his shoulders. He has become a man with a nice sense of humor and a basic ease of manner that no one would have

Referee Frank Udvari raises his hand for a penalty as Bower, Baun and Brewer of the Leafs battle the Richard brothers for the puck in 1959.
HOCKEY HALL OF FAME, TORONTO

dreamed possible when he wore No. 9 and, during those stretches when the goals were not coming, glowered for days on end.

In 1975, Maurice Richard, at fifty-four, gave up hockey. He had been a member of a team called the Old Timers, a group of ex-professionals in their fifties and sixties, which played teams made up of show-business favorites and other celebrities. Canadians continue to get a thrill from seeing the old lion. Today, he attends forty or fifty banquets each year, at which he says a few words and answers a few questions, and he referees around seventy-five exhibition games. When the warm weather comes, he plays a bit of tennis, a game he found a helpful off-season conditioner during his hockey days. His friends are agreed to a man that his happiest hours, unquestionably, are those he spends in the backcountry, away from the hubbub of Montreal. Fourteen years ago, he bought a small fishing-line company—its trade name is Clipper—and when the long Canadian winter at last breaks up he travels through Quebec selling his equipment at country stores and getting in some fishing on the side. In the summer, he spends a lot of time at three favorite fishing spots: St. Michel-des-Saints, a hundred miles north of Montreal, where there is good red trout; Mont-Laurier, a hundred and fifty miles north, which has gray trout and pickerel in addition to red trout; and Lac St. Jean, two hundred miles north of Quebec City, which has landlocked salmon. He doesn't do much deep-sea fishing, but a few years ago he did catch a nine-hundred-and-twenty-pound tuna off Caraquet, New Brunswick.

The Canadiens' front office has always seen to it that Richard receives two tickets to the team's home games. Most of the time, he gives them to one or another of his seven children. (The oldest three are married, and Richard has five grandchildren.) "Last year, with my wife, Lucille, I went to five games," he told me, in a matter-of-fact way. "I never stayed after the second period. It just happened I went to see the wrong games." As his spotty attendance intimates, Richard has not changed completely. While he thinks highly of some of the current players, he is critical of the style of hockey now in vogue and doesn't think it compares in skillfulness with the game played twenty-five years ago. "In my day, the Canadiens passed the puck up the ice and made plays," he said during our talk. "Then, when we were in the attacking zone, we worked to keep possession of the puck until we set someone up for a good shot. Now the teams simply shoot the puck into the attacking zone from way out, and then everyone chases it. No teamwork. No disciplined patterns."

I asked him if he didn't think defensemen today are more mobile than they used to be.

"Sure," he said. "That's because they have to run after the puck all the time."

One of the inconveniences a national figure like Richard has to put up with wherever he goes is people who ask him the same banal questions, such as who was his favorite center or what opposing players he respected the most. As I was leaving and we walked to the front door, I asked him just such a question: "When you made that unforgettable goal against the Bruins in the 1952 Stanley Cup playoffs, were you, as some people say, only semi-conscious?"

He lowered his head an instant to collect his thoughts. "I *was* dizzy," he answered. "I didn't know at which end of the ice the Bruins' net was. To be honest, I didn't remember too much about what I did once I started up the ice."

He smiled a light smile, and a moment later we stepped outside and he hailed a taxi for me.

Jean Beliveau and Eddie Shack, from the cover of the 1980 Old Timers Program.
ANDY DONATO, TORONTO SUN

HUGH MacLENNAN'S HOCKEY MEMORIES

Many people are of the opinion that Hugh MacLennan is the finest Canadian novelist of the post-Second World War period. He is probably best known for "Two Solitudes," published in 1945, a chronicle of the age-old breach between French Canadians and English Canadians, and for "The Watch That Ends the Night," a best-seller in the United States in 1959. MacLennan is also an accomplished essayist. No other essay on hockey I know of stands comparison with the one he wrote for *Holiday,* in 1954. Here is an excerpt that I particularly like:

In the little towns from which so many of those puck artists came, the kids were on the ponds or makeshift rinks as soon as school was out. Nobody skated without a stick in his hands, and if frostbitten feet had been a deterrent there would have been no hockey players. The boards of the rink were slapped together by the local carpenter, goals and scrapers made by the blacksmith, and the rink cleared of snow by the kids themselves. On clear afternoons when frigid air pinched the nostrils and made noses run, when the sky changed from deep blue through pale blue to aquamarine and rose, those rinks were a focus for the yells of all the kids in town. You could see their bright-colored jerseys weaving in and out, toques or peaked caps on their heads, and always there were one or two who would hold your eye. They were the ones who made their shoulders swerve one way while their feet went the other, who sliced through a mêlée with their heads up and the puck controlled as if their sticks were extensions of their arms.

Often there was a shack nearby where skates could be changed and hands warmed beside a hot stove. The stove was tended by a bad-tempered old man in galluses who sold chocolate bars and soft drinks. The air was hot and foul, and the old man's perpetual refrain was, "Shut thet door—and keep it shut!" To this day there are millions of Canadians who can't see a potbellied, rusty old stove without feeling nostalgia for a happy youth. It reminds a man of ice in the hair of his temples, of rime in his eyebrows, and of the lovely swollen feeling of throbbing feet after supper when he pretended to do his lessons.

MacLennan was born on Cape Breton Island, in Nova Scotia, and grew up in the provincial capital, Halifax, where he attended Dalhousie University. He went on to Oriel College at Oxford as a Rhodes Scholar, and did graduate work in classical studies at Princeton. He taught school in Montreal, starting at twenty-five dollars a week, before settling down in the nineteen-fifties at McGill, the top-ranked Canadian university, which was founded in 1829 and occupies part of the beautiful southern slope of Mount Royal, in the heart of Montreal. At the present time, he gives two courses of lectures, "The Twentieth-Century English Novel" and "The Evolution of English Prose Expression." MacLennan is starting into his seventies, but with his slim, athletic physique, light-brown hair, pink cheeks, and animated manner he seems many years younger. We had lunch at the McGill Faculty Club. Since boyhood, he has followed sports closely—and played many of them well—but at lunch we talked mainly about hockey. Over coffee, he leaned back a little in his chair and let one fond recollection follow another: How he used to stand in the Millionaires Section before the war, and how one night Morenz hit the goalpost with an angled shot and, when the rebound came back to him twenty feet out, shot again and scored; how he was at the Forum the night, in 1936, when the Montreal Maroons (who were dis-

Jacques Plante covers up, while Tom Johnson takes Carl Brewer out of the play.
HOCKEY HALL OF FAME, TORONTO

banded in 1938) met the Detroit Red Wings in a Stanley Cup clash that turned out to be the longest hockey game in history—it was two-twenty-five in the morning and sixteen minutes into the sixth overtime period when Modère (Mud) Bruneteau, of the Red Wings, finally won the game with the only goal scored during the hundred and seventy-six minutes that the teams had gone at it; the pleasure he derived from watching cool, savvy defensemen, such as Bucko McDonald (later a member of Parliament), Bob Goldham, Marcel Pronovost, and Doug Harvey, thwart the offensive paragons by sensing their moves in advance and shrewdly countering them; the traumatic shock that swept the country in 1972 when the Russians invaded Canada and demonstrated that the Dominion was no longer in a class by itself as a hockey power—"It was a masterly con job. We should have known that the Russians would never have come over unless they were darn sure that their teams were about as good as ours, and in some respects superior." I think he could have gone on for hours.

As we broke up after lunch—MacLennan went up McTavish Street and I went down it—he said, thoughtfully and slowly, "Canadians never get completely away from hockey. In the summer, I go down to North Hatley, a very pleasant village twenty-six miles from the Vermont border. One of my neighbors there is Sam Pollock, who used to be the general manager of the Canadiens. We talk as much hockey in the summer as we do baseball. I think we probably would even if Sam had never been connected with the Canadiens. It's in your blood up here."

THE GROWTH OF A STAR

Over the years, a number of young hockey players who appeared to be headed for stardom because of their flashing speed have quickly vanished from the scene when they decided they wanted no further part of the physical pounding they were subjected to in the NHL by opposing teams that were out to slow them down. A case in point is Leo Gravelle, who came up with the Canadiens just after the war. He was one of the fastest skaters ever seen in the league, but he lasted only a few years—he did not choose to spend his life being banged around. There was a time when it seemed to some observers that Guy Lafleur might perhaps be a fringe member of the same species. Lafleur, a muscular six-footer, was the No. 1 over-all choice in the Amateur Draft in 1971, and was acquired by the Canadiens thanks to Pollock's deft wheel-

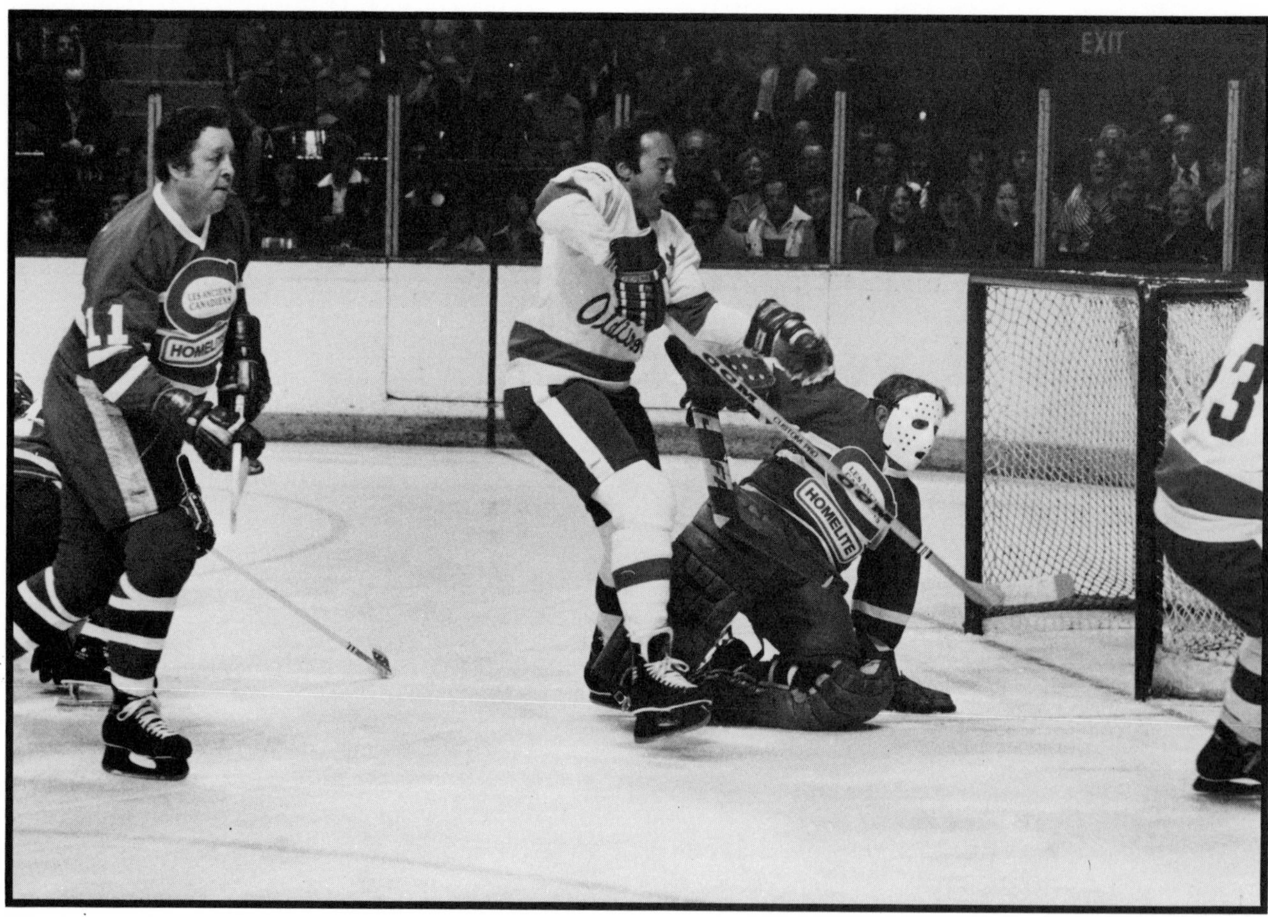

The action centers around Jean Gauthier, Frank Mahovlich and Gump Worsley during the 1979 Old Timers game in Montreal.
JEAN-GUY PARADIS

ing and dealing. In his first three professional seasons, his scoring figures were respectable, but he did not display the poise and the panache expected of a player with his imposing credentials, possibly because the other teams gave him the extra physical attention a flashy skater always receives. In the 1974-75 season, a marked change took place. Lafleur began to play with a new confidence, which deepened as the season progressed. He appeared to be far less concerned with what the men checking him were up to, and, unharried and unhurried, started to make the spontaneously imaginative moves that only the best players are capable of. Along with this, he became more aggressive physically. When the situation demanded it, he threw his weight around, and he backed away from no one.

That season, he was named to the NHL All-Star Team. The last three seasons, he has also gained that distinction, as well as the distinction of leading the league in total points —that is, goals and assists. The past two seasons, Lafleur was voted the league's Most Valuable Player. Furthermore, he showed that he could do his stuff when it counted: in 1975, he scored twelve goals in Stanley Cup play, and last year he scored ten. As the new hero of Montreal and of Quebec Province, he has earned a million-dollar contract, as well as considerable subsidiary income from his endorsements for General Motors of Canada and

Ken Dryden in heavy action around the Montreal net.
JEAN-GUY PARADIS

such products as Bauer skates, Koho hockey equipment for boys, and Yoplait yogurt. He has it coming to him. No one else brings the crowd at the Forum to its feet today the way Lafleur does when, flying at top speed—and thinking equally fast about what variations of maneuver are possible as the positioning of the attacking and defending players changes each instant—he sets up a goal for one of his line mates with a perfectly timed pass or himself scores with a lightning irruption. Fame and fortune have not changed him a whit.

One day I had a ten-minute chat with Lafleur before a Canadiens practice session—at which, as usual, he was the first player to arrive. Never having heard him speak before, I was particularly impressed by his intelligence and by the fluency with which he expressed himself in his soft, lightly accented English. Here are a few of his answers to questions I asked. Lafleur on why so many French Canadians are such outstanding skaters: "To skate well is the ideal, is it not? It is one of the skills a player sets out to achieve. It takes hard work, but a hockey player knows he must make his talent better and better." On why he suddenly blossomed into such a fine all-around player during the 1974-75 season: "First, I was given the chance to play more. This strengthened my confidence. In addition, I was used much more in critical games, and that also helped my confidence. The more you play, the more you want to play." On how he learned to shake off the stiff checks, the ganging-up in the corners, and the physical punishment in general, and to keep playing hard and well: "Desire is the main thing. The desire to outplay the other team, to beat the other team. That is your responsibility. If you feel great inside, you can push yourself to play very aggressive hockey, and nothing will happen to you. If anything, quite the opposite. You enjoy the feeling of health."

At the conclusion of our talk, I found myself asking Lafleur if he had ever thought of going to college. "Yes, I think I might have qualified," he said. "I preferred to try for a career in hockey. My father thought I should think seriously about going to the university. 'What if something happens to you?' he said. I told him I would take my chances."

JEAN BELIVEAU TODAY

Jean Beliveau is currently a member of the five-man board of directors of Le Club de Hockey Canadien and the senior vice-president in charge of corporate affairs. He has actually functioned as a director of the Canadiens since 1972, when, shortly after retiring as an active player, he was made a director of Carena Bancorp, the company that then owned the team. When his retirement was only weeks away, Sam Pollock, the general manager, and David Molson, representing the owners, spoke to him and proposed a Jean Beliveau Night to honour him for his incalculable contributions to Montreal hockey. Beliveau said he would agree to this under certain conditions. "I don't need a car," he told Pollock and Molson. "I don't need carts full of gifts. I will accept souvenirs from my teammates, from the club management, and from the team we'll be playing that night." Molson and Pollock understood and consented. The next day, a close friend of Beliveau's, who knew of his impending retirement, told him he had been approached by a number of companies and individuals who wanted to show in some tangible way their appreciation of what Beliveau had done over the years. He asked Beliveau how he would feel if contributions could be made to set up a foundation whose purpose would be to disburse money to small organizations that could make good use of it —Beliveau would act as the disburser. After thinking it over, Beliveau told his friend that nothing would give him greater pleasure, and not long afterward the Jean Beliveau Foundation, with total assets of a hundred and fifty-five thousand dollars, was established. Over the past seven years, the funds have more than doubled. The foundation has meanwhile given away approximately a hundred and forty thousand dollars. "They haven't been large gifts," Beliveau explained when I called on him in his office in the Forum. "For instance, we sent a check last week to a minor hockey association in Nicolet that needed sweaters for its Midget team. We sent another check to a small swimming club that needed some stopwatches. Being able to help out in this way gives me a very good feeling."

Today, at forty-seven, Beliveau weighs two hundred and five pounds, his old playing weight. He keeps it there by watching his diet and by jogging ten to twelve miles a week. He exercises nearly every working day, changing at midday from his conservative business suit into a sweatsuit and loping a mile or two around the oval walkway behind the top row of the white seats of the Forum. A few gray hairs have infiltrated, but otherwise he looks much as he did during his playing days, except when he puts on his gold-rimmed reading glasses. Then he looks like a judge or a college president. Aside from his administrative duties with the Canadiens, there is a lot to keep him busy. He receives forty to seventy personal letters a week, and, as you would expect of a man of his conscientiousness, answers them all. Civic organizations continually seek his participation, and he works with the Chamber of Commerce, the Easter Seal Society, and several others. From time to time, he serves on special city committees, such as one that welcomed a Russian delegation early this winter. He makes a good many appearances at sports functions, but a year ago started to cut down on the amount of

Action sequence, as Bunny Larocque thwarts a Washington breakaway.
JEAN-GUY PARADIS

CLUB DE HOCKEY CANADIEN

Ken Dryden during his rookie year (1971) when he helped the Blue, White and Red to yet another Cup victory.

Two great captains of the Canadiens:
Henri Richard and Jean Béliveau.

travelling he does and the number of speeches he undertakes. Nevertheless, he flew out to San Diego last September to tape a television show with Tom Seaver, a man he holds in the highest esteem. Beliveau is on the board of six corporations, including Dominion Textiles and Carena Bancorp. Since 1969, when he incorporated himself, he has been extremely selective about the products he endorses and the firms with which he chooses to be affiliated. Two of the latter are RCA and the Bank of Nova Scotia.

Beliveau, in brief, is one of the most admired and sought-after men in Canada. His long and memorable career, his distinguished appearance, and his capability all contribute to this, of course, but the quality that sets him apart—and always has—is his genuineness. He never means to be dramatic, but when he tells you that for twenty summers he and a friend used to fish for red trout in the Murray River but that he hasn't got around to doing any fishing to speak of since his friend's death, you are moved. So are you when he says, "Not counting the foundation, I suppose the thing I've helped with that I'm proudest of is the student-exchange program that the Canadiens set up eight years ago. On weekends during the hockey season, a team from a school outside Montreal comes to the city to play a team from one of our local schools. The visiting players arrive on Friday and stay with families in Montreal. The two teams play on Saturday afternoon, and that night they go to the Canadiens game together. Over three thousand youngsters have played here under this program."

Beliveau lives with his wife and their daughter, Hélène, south of the city across the Jacques Cartier Bridge, in a modest house he bought twenty-three years ago. On evenings at home, he invariably finds the time to do some reading—biographies, for the most part. On hockey nights, he is at the Forum. When I saw him there one night, his eyes alight like a young man's at the expectation of watching a first-rate game, it brought to mind something he had said to me earlier: "As a player, I felt that when the day arrived that coming to the Forum for a game or a practice became a chore, it would be time to retire. It never beame a chore. I enjoyed every minute on the ice."

SCOTTY BOWMAN AND THE STANLEY CUP

One morning when the floor of the Forum was being set up for a rock concert, the Canadiens' practice was shifted to the arena in Verdun, a suburb situated across the Lachine Canal. Scotty Bowman, the Canadiens' coach, was driven out to the practice by two boyhood friends who are now Montreal firemen. I went along with them. During a game, as he paces behind the players' bench, Bowman wears one set expression—his jaw juts up at about the same angle that Mussolini's did, and it gives him an air of arrogance. It is misleading. Bowman is a likable, direct man who goes at his job assiduously and without theatricality and who is himself at all times.

The practice that morning was extremely instructive. To begin with, each of the four forward lines and the three sets of defensemen were dressed in different-colored uniforms, so that they could keep track of each other more easily and work in combination more smoothly during their turns on the ice. (Bowman adopted this wrinkle after watching a practice session of the Czechoslovakian team that toured Canada and the United States in 1976.) The Canadiens use a practice drill I had never seen before. The three men in a forward line did not immediately try to score when they came on the ice. Instead, they skated toward the goal at one end, pass-

Yvan Cournoyer slips the puck past Gerry Cheevers, with help from Lapointe and Lambert. DENIS BRODEUR, MONTREAL

ing the puck as they would when setting up a play; then they turned and skated toward the goal at the other end, passing the puck as they went; then they turned once more, and this time as they came down the ice they tried to score against the two defensemen who moved out to frustrate their efforts. (Bowman picked up this drill from Doug Harvey, one of the best defensemen of all time, who played for him when Bowman coached the St. Louis Blues. Harvey felt that little benefit resulted if during a practice session the forwards tried to score when they were fresh, inasmuch as they rarely operate under these conditions in a game.) The Canadiens devoted a good deal of time to two other drills as well: clearing the puck out of the defensive zone—a standard drill all teams emphasize—and working the defensemen so cohesively into the attack that they take half the shots.

On the ride back to the Forum after the practice, while Bowman and his two friends were chatting, I began to reflect, and not for the first time, on how his life in hockey reads like a tale from an old-time storybook. Bowman was born in Verdun in 1933, the son of a blacksmith who had emigrated from Forfar in Scotland. In 1951, when he was eighteen and one of the brightest lights on the Junior Canadiens, he suffered a serious head injury that ended his playing career. He spent the next sixteen years in the Canadiens organization, scouting, trouble-shooting throughout the farm system, and coaching both amateur and minor-league professional teams. It was assumed in many quarters that whenever Toe Blake chose to terminate his long and successful tenure as the Canadiens' coach the job would probably go to Bowman. However, when the league expanded, in 1967, Bowman left the Canadiens to become the assistant coach of the St. Louis Blues, one of the six new teams that came into being that year. Shortly after the season got under way, he was moved up to head coach. He did a magnificent job in St. Louis. The first three of his four years there, he drove his gallimaufry of aged veterans, castoffs, and green kids all the way to the Stanley Cup final series. The fourth year, the Blues had to settle for second place in the West Division, but that spring—1971—Bowman was offered the opportunity he had long dreamed of: the chance to coach the Canadiens. He did well. During seven seasons under Bowman, the team won the Stanley Cup four times—in 1973 and successively in 1976, 1977, and 1978. The triumph in 1976 was undoubtedly the sweetest. In the final series, the Canadiens whipped the Philadelphia Flyers, the rough-and-tough Broad Street Bullies, who had won the Cup the two previous years. What is more, they did it by sweeping four straight games. The key to their triumph was the strategy Bowman devised for containing Bobby Clarke, the Flyers' resourceful center, who was the heart of the team. Since there was no one player on the Canadiens who could handle Clarke, Bowman used a corps of three centers on him, substituting a fresh man every twenty-five seconds or so. Slowly but surely, the trio wore Clarke down in each game and blunted the Flyers' offense. Bowman's ambition is to win a total of seven hundred games in regular-season NHL play, which would make him the winningest coach in league history. During his first eleven seasons in the NHL, his teams won four hundred and seventy-seven (out of seven hundred and ninety-two) games, so at the start of the 1978-79 season, he had two hundred and twenty-three victories to go.

A coach with a record like that is well worth listening to when he discusses how he has gone about running his team. Bowman believes that in hockey, as in nearly all sports, you must first build a sturdy defense: a team with a low goals-against average is bound to finish near the top. No one knows better than he that the Canadiens' success in recent years has depended on having a pair of excellent goalies, Ken Dryden and Michel (Bunny) Larocque, and three of the best defensemen in the league: Larry Robinson, Guy Lapointe, and Serge Savard. What has occupied Bowman primarily is putting together the right blend of forward lines to complement this rear-guard strength. "You have to have skillful forwards of all kinds these days," he says. "The ones who are offensive specialists must be able to check acceptably. You need a good many defensive specialists. If they can get you a few goals now and then, that helps. And you also need some grinders—aggressive guys who are tough and big and can handle the other teams' power lines. Of course, you've got to have specialists who are proficient at killing off penalties for you. Things like that. When you play an eighty-game schedule, you have to be able to utilize your full bench, and you can't afford to have one selfish player on your team."

This approach is Bowman's legacy to the Canadiens. Now that Claude Ruel is the team's coach, it seems likely that the Canadiens will capitalize on the years of Bowman leadership while continuing the team's tradition of winning.

DRYDEN IN GOAL

The high point of the montage of dynamic hockey action that used to introduce one of the network telecasts of NHL games was a sequence that showed a player—a Boston Bruin, I believe—drilling the puck from about fifteen feet out on a low line toward the unprotected left half of the net for what looked like a sure goal until, at the last second, a long padded leg suddenly appeared from nowhere to block the shot in midair and deflect it wide of the goal. The long padded leg belonged to Ken Dryden, and this was just one of the many spectacular saves he made in the 1971 playoffs, when, having seen action in only six NHL games after being called up from the Canadiens' top farm club, the Montreal Voyageurs, of the American Hockey League, he played all twenty games in the quarterfinal, semifinal, and final rounds of a prolonged Stanley Cup elimination series, which the Canadiens at last won. Had Dryden, then twenty-three, slipped back to the minors the next year, never to be heard of again, he would have earned for himself a permanent niche in hockey history because of that performance. As it turned out, his dramatic début was only the first exploit of an astonishing career during which, through the 1977-78 season, he has been named to the All-Star Team four times, has twice won the Vezina Trophy (for the lowest goals-against average), and has twice more shared the trophy with Larocque, who has been the Canadiens' second goalie the last half-dozen years. At six feet four, Dryden is one of the tallest men ever to tend goal in the NHL, but he has the agility of a much smaller man, and his technique is exemplary. One is aware of his size only when a long leg shoots out at the last second or when, during those moments when the play is confined to the other end of the rink, he stands up straight in front of the goal and, with his hands and arms resting on his stick in a way that suggests Cincinnatus at his plow, surveys the distant proceedings.

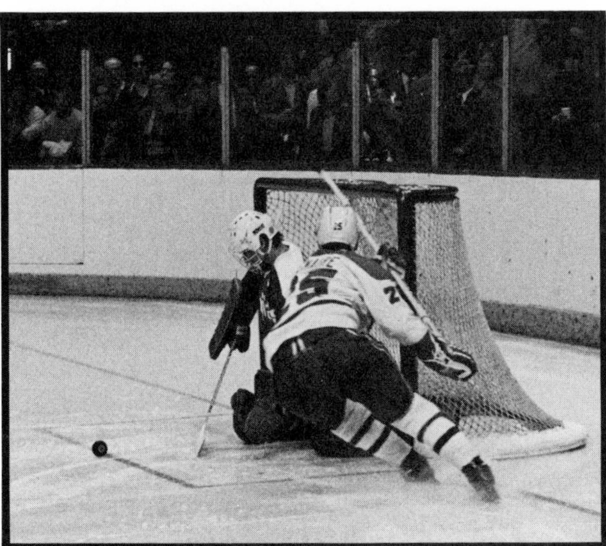

Jacques Lemaire wheels in for a rebound against the Washington Capitals.
JEAN-GUY PARADIS

Dryden, however, is much more than a goaltender *par excellence*. One gets a brief intimation of his other talents when a microphone is thrust in his face only minutes after he has been in the heat of the fray in a rather wild and angry game and he then proceeds to analyze calmly and precisely why the game was won or lost. "Oh, I think the goalie happens to be in a perfect position to have a good over-all view of a game," he once explained in an offhand way when he was complimented on a post-game recapitulation. There is some truth in this, I suppose, but the principal reason is that Dryden is a very intelligent man. A number of famous athletes have been authentic intellectuals—Bobby Jones, René Lacoste, Barry Wood, Byron (Whizzer) White, and Bill Bradley, for starters—and Dryden belongs in that special company. He is the only active player in hockey who is a lawyer, and while this may help to explain his articulateness, it is far from being the whole story.

Dryden, who comes from Hamilton, Ontario, is the second of three children of a building-materials broker who is now retired. His sister, who is four years younger, is a public-health nurse, and his brother, Dave, who is six years older, is at present the goalie for the Edmonton Oilers of the World Hockey Association, after earlier tours of duty with the New York Rangers, the Chicago Black Hawks, and the Buffalo Sabres of the NHL, as well as with the now defunct Chicago Cougars of the WHA. "We grew up in what seemed an average type of atmosphere at home," he said when I asked him about his boyhood. "We were deep into sports, but there was a good deal of emphasis on other things. What we thought and did in our family was quite understated but clearly understood." Possibly because his older brother had led the way, Dryden, a fairly good skater who might have played other positions, set out to become a goalie, and in his early days as a Junior began to attract attention. "You pretty much develop your own style," he told me. "You watch other goalies. They make an impression on you. Jacques Plante, naturally, would be one who did. He was responsible for two remarkable innovations; the protective mask for the goalie, and the practice whereby the goalie leaves the cage to help clear the puck out of trouble. Nearly all of us do that now."

Dryden wanted to go to college in the United States, and after looking into Princeton and Cornell—he had friends at both—elected to attend Cornell and to major in history. College hockey at that time was considered a dead-end street, but the Canadiens, who had acquired the rights to Dryden from the Bruins (who had drafted him at sixteen), kept an eye on his progress. In 1969, he graduated from Cornell—where, incidentally, he met a fellow history major who later became his wife. He wished to continue in hockey but also to study law, and in pursuit of those two ambitions he joined the Canadian National Team—an amateur team—in the autumn of 1969, because it was based in Winnipeg, which was also the home of the Universiy of Manitoba Law School. Around Christmastime, the National Team was summarily disbanded. After thinking the situation over, Dryden decided that the best parlay for him would be to enter McGill Law School and join the Montreal Voyageurs as a part-time goalie. The following season, 1970-71, he posted a 2.68 goals-against average in thirty-three games with the Voyageurs before being called up by the Canadiens and astounding the hockey world with his wonderful play in the Stanley Cup. In 1971-72, he made the second NHL All-Star Team, and the year after that the first All-Star Team. Then, when he and the Canadiens' management were unable to come to terms on an appropriate salary, Dryden made a surprising move. He left the team before the start of the 1973-74 season and spent the year in Toronto, where he broadcast the home games of the Toros, Toronto's entry in the WHA, and worked for a law firm. (He had received his law degree in 1973, but in Canada in order to be recognized as a lawyer it is mandatory to practice law for a year.) In Dryden's absence, the Canadiens, rotating three goalies, went through a rather dismal season, and Dryden's agent was able to negotiate with the team's management the richest contract for a goalie in history. Dryden was slightly disappointing his first year back, but after that he regained his old form and played a large part in the team's three straight championship seasons.

What lies ahead for Dryden when he hangs up to the tools of ignorance? (That term has long been used to describe a baseball catcher's paraphernalia, but it would seem to apply no less aptly to a hockey goalies' gear.)

"I don't know whether or not I'm going to practice law," Dryden said as we were ending our talk. "I'm leaning more toward working in public affairs, though from a non-governmental direction—somewhat along the lines of Ralph Nader's group or John Gardner's Common Cause. I find the realm of public affairs absorbing—you know, helping to found citizens-lobby groups, which can be more effective than they have been in the past, establishing a different set of priorities than the present interest groups, the whole matter of decision-making." Dryden did retire at the end of the 1979 season, and what is a great loss to the Canadiens may well turn out to be a great gain for public affairs.

THE FORUM

The Forum was the first large, covered arena designed expressly for hockey. There are no balconies. The sections of red, white, and blue seats, in that order, rise upward from the rink in an unbroken sweep. When it was opened, in 1924, the Forum accommodated around nine thousand spectators. Today, two "modernizations" later, its capacity has been expanded to over sixteen thousand. Besides being one of the most diligently maintained sports centers I know of, the Forum is without a doubt the best place in the world to watch a hockey game. The sight lines are right. The spectators, informed and vibrant, are always on top of the play, and several times during the course of a game they make the call, in concert, on some technical infraction, such as an offside, well before the linesman gets around to blowing his whistle. The Montreal fans come out not to watch fights, the main attraction for the majority of fans in many cities, but to watch good hockey. Their reaction to an elegant play by either team is instantaneous, but, to be sure, it is louder and more heartfelt, and is sustained longer, if it is the Canadiens who have executed the play. And, finally, the

A rebound flys loose from the Boston goalie as Steve Shutt and Jacques Lemaire battle for the puck.
JEAN-GUY PARADIS

Bob Pulford, Bud McPherson, Gerry McNeil, Paul Meger and Dollard St. Laurent renew the old Toronto-Montreal rivalry.
HOCKEY HALL OF FAME, TORONTO

intricate importance and complex character of the city of Montreal give the Forum a matchless ambience. When the Canadiens are playing a team from an American city, Roger Doucet, The Forums' resident vocalist, sings "The Star-Spangled Banner" in English, then sings "O Canada!" in French until he reaches the last twelve bars, when he switches to the English lyrics. Throughout the game, the announcements over the public-address system are made first in French, then in English. High above the ice, on one of the two steel catwalks that run the length of the rink, are the booths of the two television announcers, René Lecavalier, who does the play-by-play on the French telecast, and Danny Gallivan, who does the play-by-play on the English telecast. Both are bilingual. Lecavalier pronounces the names of the players who are not of French descent the way an English Canadian would, and, conversely, Gallivan pronounces the names of the players of French descent the way a Québécois would. Both men are now in their twenty-sixth year at their jobs. Throughout the game, the Forum organist fills in during the intervals when a stoppage in the action occurs. The tune he plays most often at these times is "Envoyons d'l'Avant," an old Habitant lumberjack song with a spirited tempo that gradually accelerates.

At a game with the Detroit Red Wings that I attended, just about the whole family of Le Club de Hockey Canadien was on hand. Frank Selke was in his regular box, deep in contemplation. Sam Pollock was in his regular box, and his successor as general manager, Irving Grundman, back in town after a trip to Nova Scotia to look over the Voyageurs, was in his. (Halifax has been the Voyageurs' home since 1971-72 season.) In the private snack bar, situated on the level of the catwalks, a conglomeration of hockey writers, radio and television people, members of the club's front office, former stars, and assorted specialists

Mario Tremblay challenges Gerry Cheevers as Doug Risebrough looks on.
JEAN-GUY PARADIS

from the Montreal NHL headquarters were trading opinions as they ate hamburgers. Camil DesRoches, who was there, introduced me to Roger Bédard, the coach of Les Juniors de Montreal, and, subsequently, to Eric Taylor, of the Canadiens' scouting staff, who gamely tried to explain to me the subtler effects that the Amateur Draft will have on the Canadiens in the years ahead. Red Fisher, who is now in his twenty-fifth year writing hockey for the Montreal *Star*, told me that he thought that the Canadiens' rooters are just as intense today as they were during Maurice Richard's era, though he knows that many people think otherwise. However, he feels that the quality of the players' talent has declined. I had a nice catch-up talk with Dick Irvin, Jr., the son of the former Canadiens coach, who has fared well as a hockey announcer; he does the play-by-play of the Canadiens' games for a Montreal English-language radio station and does the "color" whenever "Hockey Night in Canada," which is televised on Saturdays over the Canadian Broadcasting Corporation's network, emanates from the Forum. I had a word or two with Beliveau as he seasoned his hamburger meticulously, and a few with Toe Blake, a charming and well-founded man who, now that he is no longer playing or coaching, devotes his major attention to his tavern, one of the most popular in the city for over a quarter of a century. (In Montreal, a tavern sells only beer or ale, and it is open only to men. If a man wants to buy a brew for a woman, they go to a *brasserie*.) Between periods, this small army returned to the snack bar from their stations on the catwalks to refresh themselves with banter and soft drinks. The Canadiens won the game easily, 8-3, but their play was lacklustre after the opening ten minutes. I walked up Boulevard Maisonneuve to my hotel at a leisurely pace, slowly savoring the evening.

THE 1978-79 SEASON

On the sixth of January, the Canadiens reached the halfway mark in the 1978-79 sea-

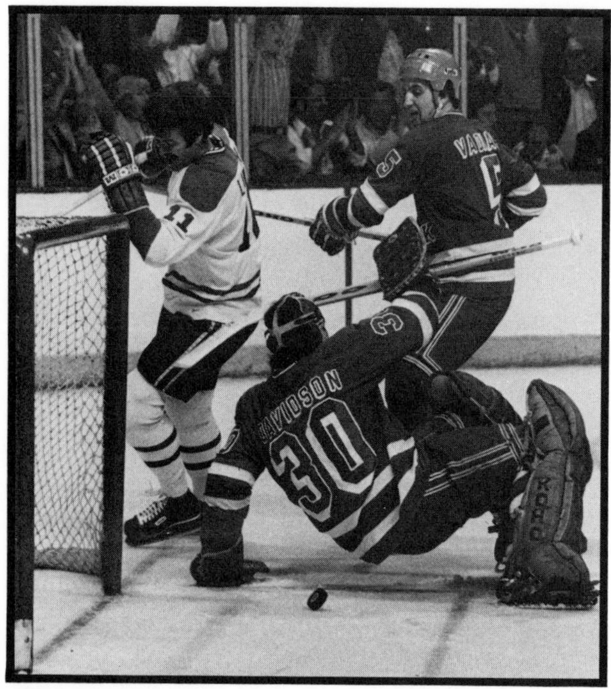

The fans cheer as Yvon Lambert scores against the Rangers.
JEAN-GUY PARADIS

son. On that date, they had won twenty-seven of their first forty games while tying five and losing eight. The NHL is divided into four divisions—named for patriarchs of the league—and the Canadiens' record put them well out in front in theirs, the Norris Division, and as much as guaranteed them a spot in the Stanley Cup playoffs. (This year, the final games of the regular season take place on April 8th, and the preliminary rounds of the playoffs commence the next week.) However, on January 6th two other teams had better records than the Canadiens. (One reason this is worth noting is that the team that compiles the highest number of points during the regular season—a victory is worth two points, a tie is worth one—earns the right in the complex playoffs system to play the first, second, fifth, and seventh games of the best-of-seven quarter-final, semifinal, and final series on its home ice, and this is a valuable advantage.)

After forty games, the Boston Bruins, the leaders of the Adams Division, had won twenty-seven tied seven, and lost six, and the New York Islanders, way out in front in the Patrick Division after thirty-eight games, had travelled at an even faster pace: twenty-six wins, seven ties, and only five losses. These strong performances by the Bruins, and Islanders did not come as a surprise. Before the start of the 1978-79 season, the general feeling was that they were the two teams that stood the best chance of contesting the Canadiens' domination of the league. The Bruins boast a large number of boisterous, stubborn young players who buzz around tirelessly on offense, and check vigorously on defense, and, under the coaching of Don Cherry, they have fused nicely with the core of veterans. The Bruins are not slick, but they play good, scrappy team hockey, and they can be dangerous if the opposing team relaxes and allows them to dictate the tempo and texture of play. The Islanders, an expansion team that received its franchise only in 1972, are quite a story. Well coached by Al Arbour, who wound up his career as a defenseman under Bowman in St. Louis, the Islanders stress position play. From the outset, they have had unusual success in the Amateur Draft, thanks to the ability of their general manager, Bill Torrey to judge talent (Torrey, by the way, grew up a block from the Forum.) The last couple of years, Torrey has been shopping for players who can skate, because he knows that speed is a requisite for any team that would stay with the Canadiens. The Islanders still have their weaknesses, but at the moment their first line of Clark Gillies, Bryan Trottier, and Mike Bossy is the highest-scoring forward line in the league. In Denis Potvin they have an All-Star defenseman, and they are well fixed in goal. It should be mentioned that there have been stretches throughout the season when the New York Rangers, the Atlanta Flames, and the belligerent old Philadelphia Flyers have played very sound hockey, but the percentages would indicate that if the Canadiens run into trouble in the playoffs, the Islanders or the Bruins are probably the teams that will provide it.

As for the Canadiens, they were a terribly difficult team to assess in 1978-79. During the first half of the season, they had a couple of streaks in which they went for weeks without dropping a game, but over all their play was not as commanding as their record implied. For example, they did not look sharp against the weak teams. The fast-breaking, head-manning offense that for years has been synonymous with the Canadiens was sometimes nowhere to be seen. During the last three weeks of January and throughout February, the Canadiens travelled at a fairly fast pace, losing only four games. By March 1st, they had opened up a fourteen-point lead on the badly faltering Bruins, but by that date they were leading the Islanders by only four points, and the Islanders had a game in hand. A significant game during this stretch took place on February 27th at the Nassau Coloseum, the Islanders' home arena, in Long Island. A victory would have given the Canadiens a six-point bulge, but an inspired Islander team blew them out of the rink, 7-3. This game underlined some typical failings of the Canadiens, even in victory, during 1978-79. Their defense has been diffident and spotty, and their attack has all but begun and ended with Lafleur's quick-silver forays. It is true that Jacques Lemaire, the team's best two-way center, was sidelined for ten weeks with a shoulder separation and that two other centers have suffered minor injuries, but this does not explain, really, why the team has not been able to move the puck this season with the flair one has long associated with the

Risebrough and Nilsson one-on-one in front of the Ranger goal.
JEAN-GUY PARADIS

Canadiens. Maybe this is the inevitable result of the system that was introduced when the league expanded in the nineteen-sixties. The premise was to bring the new teams up to the level of the older ones as soon as possible, by giving the teams that finished lowest in the league standings each year the first crack at the players available in the Amateur Draft. Among other things, this ended, once and for all, the old convention whereby nearly all the best young French-Canadian players spawned on the rinks and ponds of Quebec ended up wearing the *bleu, blanc, et rouge*. Even the most vital dynasty cannot remain at the top unless it has a reasonable chance to renew its talent. The recent renaissance of the Yankee dynasty has depended almost entirely on their being both rich and smart enough to pick up a great many first-class players in the newly instituted free-agent market. In hockey, there are no free agents.

THE RUSSIANS VERSUS THE ALL-STARS

In midwinter during the 1978-79 season the league race was not the topic of conversation on every hockey lover's lips. They scarcely paid it any attention, because of their absorption in the three-game Challenge Cup series between the Russian national team and the NHL All-Stars, which was held in Madison Square Garden on February 8th, 10th, and 11th. A good many informed fans thought that Russia might win this short series. The Russian team had practiced together for many months this year—some sources said from July on—and a number of the older players on the team had been through prolonged training sessions and tournaments in many previous winters. As a result, the Russians had learned each other's habits—when to expect this or that linemate to drop a backhand pass behind as he skated by, when to expect this or that defenseman to cross the blue line and buttress the attack, and so on. On the other hand, the NHL players, with only a few days to practice together, were relatively unacquainted with the moves and idiosyncrasies of the players from the other teams. Then, too, the Russians, because of the intensely Spartan nature of their training, were bound to be in better physical condition than the NHL players.

The first game turned out to be a surprise. The NHL All-Stars scored within sixteen seconds of the opening face-off and held the upper hand throughout the game, winning 4-2. Scotty Bowman, the coach of the All-Stars, knowing that the Russians like to set up quick-breaking plays down the middle of the ice, had instituted a defense that completely nullified this favorite Russian maneuver. (Seven Canadiens, by the way, had been selected for the twenty-five-man NHL squad: Dryden; Robinson, Savard, and Lapointe on defense; and Lafleur, Steve Shutt, and Bob Gainey on the forward lines.) Unable to get an offense started in this first game, the Russians, both as skaters and hockey players, looked decidely inferior to the Russian teams that had been sent to this country in 1972 and 1976. The second game was a different story. By bringing the puck up along the sides of the rink, the Russians met with far more success on offense. However, their celebrated goaltender, Vladislav Tretyak, had a very bad day. He failed to handle two stoppable shots in the first period and two more easy shots in the first five minutes of the second. Trailing 4-2 at this point, the Russians came to life. They fore-checked and back-checked more assiduously, and, slowly but surely, took control of the game, beating the All-Stars to the puck, constantly harrying them in their defensive zone, and, on the attack, setting up good shots on the goal with some of the brilliant precision passing that had astounded us during their first visit in 1972. They scored twice in the second period, to tie the game, and once more in the third period, to win it. The third game proved to be a disaster for the All-Stars. During the first ten minutes of play, it was evident that their game plan was to gain the upper hand by intimidating the Russians with punishing body checks and general rough-house tactics. This strategy may have been based on the success they had enjoyed in 1972, when they came back to defeat the Russians in an eight-game series, played half in Canada and half in Russia, after discovering that the Russian defensemen did not know how to clear the belligerent Canadian forwards, who had camped right in front of Tretyak, out of that vital area. Well, this time the Russians knew how to deal with this and with the chronic overaggressiveness of the NHL players, who attempted to awe the Russians by "taking the body" to them, to use the strange current phrase. The Russians absorbed the elbowing and charging and the rest of the uncalled infractions with hardly a flicker of expression, and kept going. After the opening ten minutes, which were scoreless, the NHL Stars slowed down to a walk, or maybe is just seemed so as the tireless Russians began to skate faster and more purposefully, swarming all over the ice and preventing the All-Stars from getting well-organized attacks started. What was particularly mystifying was the ease with which they were able to take the puck away from such stars as Larry Robinson and Bobby Clarke, who are seldom subjected to this indignity. (Lafleur was the only All-Star whom they couldn't contain.) The explanation that makes most sense is that when the Russians check a player they first give him a quick nudge to slow him down and then, instead of trying to knock the player to the ice or into the boards—a not uncommon practice in the NHL—they concentrate on making a fast jab with their stick to poke the puck away. The Russians are always on the move, and the moment a teammate checks an opposing player a second Russian is usually on hand to add a second check and to help gain control of the puck. The Russians can handle their sticks and they can skate, skate, skate. By the end of the second period, they led 2-0. By the end of the game, it was Russia 6, NHL All-Stars 0. During the last ninety-four minutes of play—more than half of the second game and all of the third—the Russians scored nine goals and the All-Stars none.

Throughout Canada, the Challenge Cup series was regarded as nothing less than a national humiliation. It was as if the great Japanese baseball team the Yomiuri Giants has come over to New York and routed the Yankees in a series for the world championship. After all, hockey is a Canadian game—they invented it. The Russians did not begin to play it until after the Second World War. The best one could do to explain what had happened in the Challenge Cup series was to point out that the Russian national team, having played together for a long time, necessarily had a considerable advantage over a collection of stars brought together for a one-week stand. Nevertheless, a number of Canadian hockey fans, looking the issue squarely in the eye, have come to some arresting conclusions: At the top level, the Russians are playing a better type of hockey than is currently being played in the NHL. They skate better, because they practice harder and longer. They handle their sticks more adroitly for that same reason. As the Russians have improved over the last dozen years, simultaneously the standard of play over here has declined in many significant respects. Young players eager for a professional career don't work on the fine points the way their fathers and grandfathers did. They work on their slap shots, since the high scorers are the men who reap the big contracts in this overly commercial age, and the hefty, bruising young men work on becoming "intimidators" and "enforcers," as they are called, because they know there is always a high-salary job open for a brawler. And they're right. When the Philadelphia Flyers climaxed their rise to power by winning the Stanley Cup in 1974 and 1975, their roster was an amalgam of talented players and outright goons, like Dave Schultz and Don Saleski, who had only a modicum of hockey ability but who were pretty capable hooligans. If an opposing star—a Lafleur, say—was causing the Flyers too much trouble, someone like Schultz purposely charged into him, rammed him against the boards, and started to pummel him, hoping that the other player would retaliate and that the referee would call a double penalty, which would be far more costly for the other team than for Philadelphia. A player who was so openly attacked couldn't ignore it and just skate away—that was out of the question. By

Paul Meger scoring against the Black Hawks in 1953.

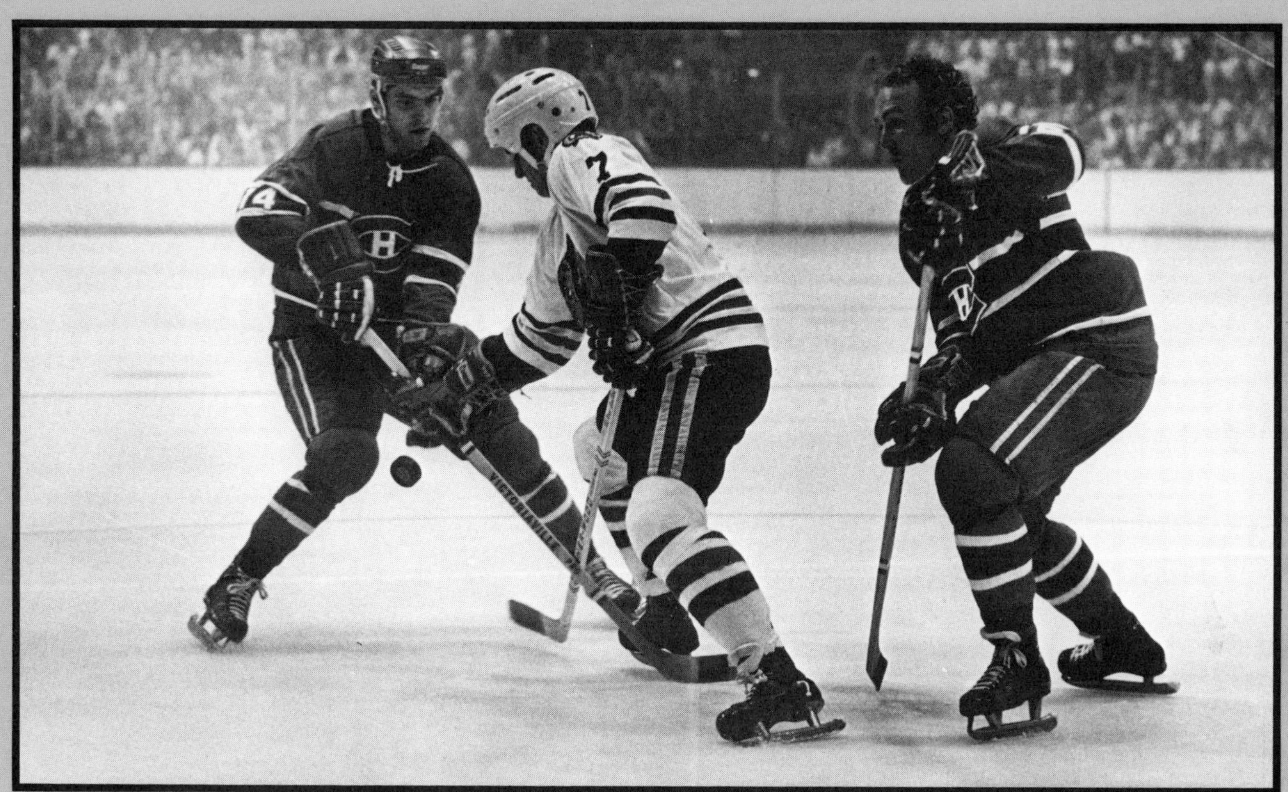

A young Réjean Houle battling for the puck with Chicago's Pit Martin in 1971.

Bob Gainey taking a graceful fall caused by a well-placed stick.

refusing to act to control this ugly trend, the NHL in effect sanctioned the calculated assaults of the goons and made it imperative for the other teams to marshal their own goon squads. One was forced to reach the conclusion that the NHL tolerated this burgeoning violence because the league thought it sold tickets. Anyhow, the point has now been reached where teams composed of kids in their early teens have their enforcers and their intimidators, as if hockey couldn't be played without them. Little wonder that, in this period when the game's atmosphere has changed so radically, only a small percentage of the players work from boyhood on to develop more finesse, which, as the Russians reminded us, is where the beauty of the game eventually resides. Quite a few Canadians have now reached the point where they are beginning to regard the Russian victory as a blessing in disguise. They feel it is bound to awaken us to a greater awareness that while clean, hard checking is an intrinsic part of hockey, violence isn't, and that when all is said and done there is no substitute for skill. Furthermore, to be able to keep pace with the Russians, aspiring young Canadian and American players are going to have to work diligently on their passing, their puck carrying, their defensive play, and all the other niceties of the game which have been more or less neglected. They are also going to have to find ways to become better and stronger skaters. Today, the roads in most parts of Canada are plowed down to the dirt or the asphalt or the concrete after a snowfall. As late as the Richard era, when it was not uncommon in many country districts for the snow left on the streets to get packed down hard until it practically gained the consistency of ice, Canadian boys skated to school down the roads, skated home down the roads, played hockey until it was time for dinner, and after dinner went out and played some more hockey if a pond in the vicinity happened to be lit up by street lamp. You can see how a routine like that would develop marvellous skaters.

THE YEARS AHEAD

It should be added, I think, that the Stanley Cup playoffs are something altogether different from the end-of-the-season-series that decide the year's championship in most other professional team sports. Some World Series are enthralling, but at least an equal number are anticlimactic. The 1979 Super Bowl game was very well played, but most of the Super Bowls have been plain dull. By the time one gets to the last round of the National Basketball Association playoffs, it is an effort to remember who is playing whom. On the other hand, Stanley Cup competition is like a second season of hockey. The players go all out, holding nothing in reserve. They skate with more abandon. They check more severely. However, since penalties can be disastrous, they check cleanly. At times, the pace during these games can become so high-pitched that I have known sophisticated hockey fans to gasp wordlessly as they gazed in disbelief at the dervishes on the ice. When people assert that hockey action at its best is as exciting as anything in sports, it is the Stanley Cup windup they have in mind.

The 1978-79 playoffs were more thought-provoking than usual. Whether they discussed it or not, most fans were comparing the hockey played by the contending teams with the hockey the Russians showed us, and they were wondering what steps must be taken if Canada—nearly all the players in the NHL are Canadian—is to regain its birthright. Since Le Club de Hockey Canadien has been associated for so long with the best expression of the game on this continent and has been *the* force in its development, fans will also be watching the standard of play that the team produces at this critical juncture in hockey history.

14

A TRADITION OF WINNING

CLAUDE MOUTON

There is the list of names on a plaque in the dressing room of the Montreal Forum, staring down at you as though silently issuing a command to excel. "It all started right here," says Noel Price, "right there in the room. That was the psychology of hanging those names there." Tradition best sums up the Montreal Canadiens. A tradition of winning. "They teach their people to play and win," adds Price, a former Atlanta Flames defenseman. "It's not just play but play to win." At that moment there were seven Atlanta Flames who either started or played during their careers with the Canadiens' organization. Three more in the front office were involved with Montreal.

Phil Myre was a goalie for the Canadiens. Price, Ray Comeau, Keith McCreary, Leon Rochefort, Chuck Arnason and Bob Murray all spent time on that hallowed ice. Flames general manager Cliff Fletcher started his road to the top in the Montreal chain. Boom Boom Geoffrion, of course, is in the Hockey Hall of Fame wearing a Canadiens sweater. Young Bobby Stewart, the assistant trainer, worked in the Canadiens' locker room for four years before coming to Atlanta. To a man, they felt the tradition when they were there. "Let's face it," says Fletcher, who grew up in Montreal, "Ninety-nine per cent of the Montreal kids dream of playing with the Canadiens. I idolized and worshipped the Canadiens organization when I was coming up. When I had a chance to work with them in 1956, well, it was a great honor. It hasn't changed that much for me. I still respect and admire them for being one of the dominant forces in hockey. But I guess I look at them a little differently now that I'm in competition."

Former Flames captain Keith McCreary came up through the Montreal organization as a youth. "The first game I ever played for them was in the playoffs against Chicago, I was really awe-struck. I mean, there were two million kids waiting to play for them and Montreal was such a tough team to crack. Just to be there, sitting in that locker room was very inspiring. When I started out there, shoot, there was Rocket Richard and the Boomer and all the great names I'd grown up idolizing. Sitting right there in the same locker room. It took me a long time to get used to that. A long time to adjust."

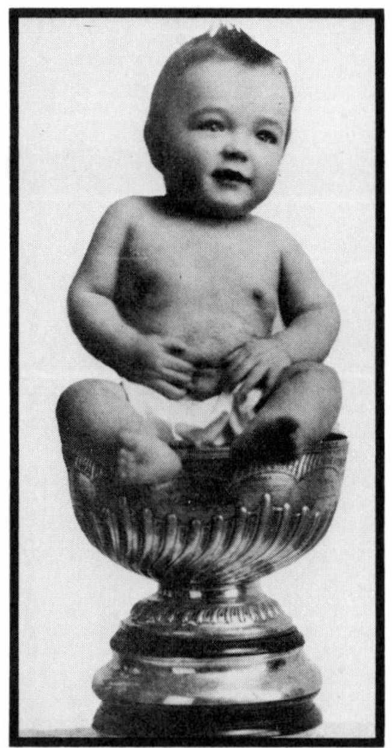

Marcel Stanley Vezina, son of goalie Georges Vezina, poses in the Stanley Cup, March, 1916.
MONTREAL MUNICIPAL ARCHIVES

Montreal was not just a name to its players. Not just a plaque on the wall. The name Montreal Canadiens meant much, much more to the players wearing Montreal sweaters. "You knew, you just knew, that to play for Montreal was to win," says McCreary. "That's just the way it worked. You knew when you stepped out on the ice you were going to win. And you usually did in those days. The other teams knew it, too, and that was half the battle."

Price grew up in the Toronto organization, another of the traditionally great clubs. But he, too, felt the inspiration when he went to Montreal in the mid-1960s. "They are winners

Henri Richard's last Stanley Cup before he retired.
DENIS BRODEUR, MONTREAL

and always have been," says Price. "I should have been brought up that way. Like I said, they teach their people to win, not just to play. And I'll tell you it was a real honor to put on one of their sweaters."

Bobby Stewart (former Flames' assistant trainer) perhaps typifies the Montreal feeling more than anyone. "I was a rink rat in those days," he laughs, "just hanging around, hoping to catch a glimpse of the stars I'd idolized all my life. I caught on with the junior team there as stick boy, just to be close. Then one day they asked me if I'd like to be stick boy for the Canadiens, and I almost croaked. What a thrill that was! I was 14 years old then and that was it for me. It was really something to be in the locker room with the big guns. I couldn't believe how lucky I was."

Montreal, perhaps more than any other club in hockey, is almost dominated by tradition. The Canadiens have been the best in their business for so long now that even the fans don't like second place. "We lost 10 games last season," says Canadiens' captain Henri Richard, "Ten games. That's a record. And yet every one of those 10 were disasters as far as

Ken Dryden.
DENIS BRODEUR, MONTREAL

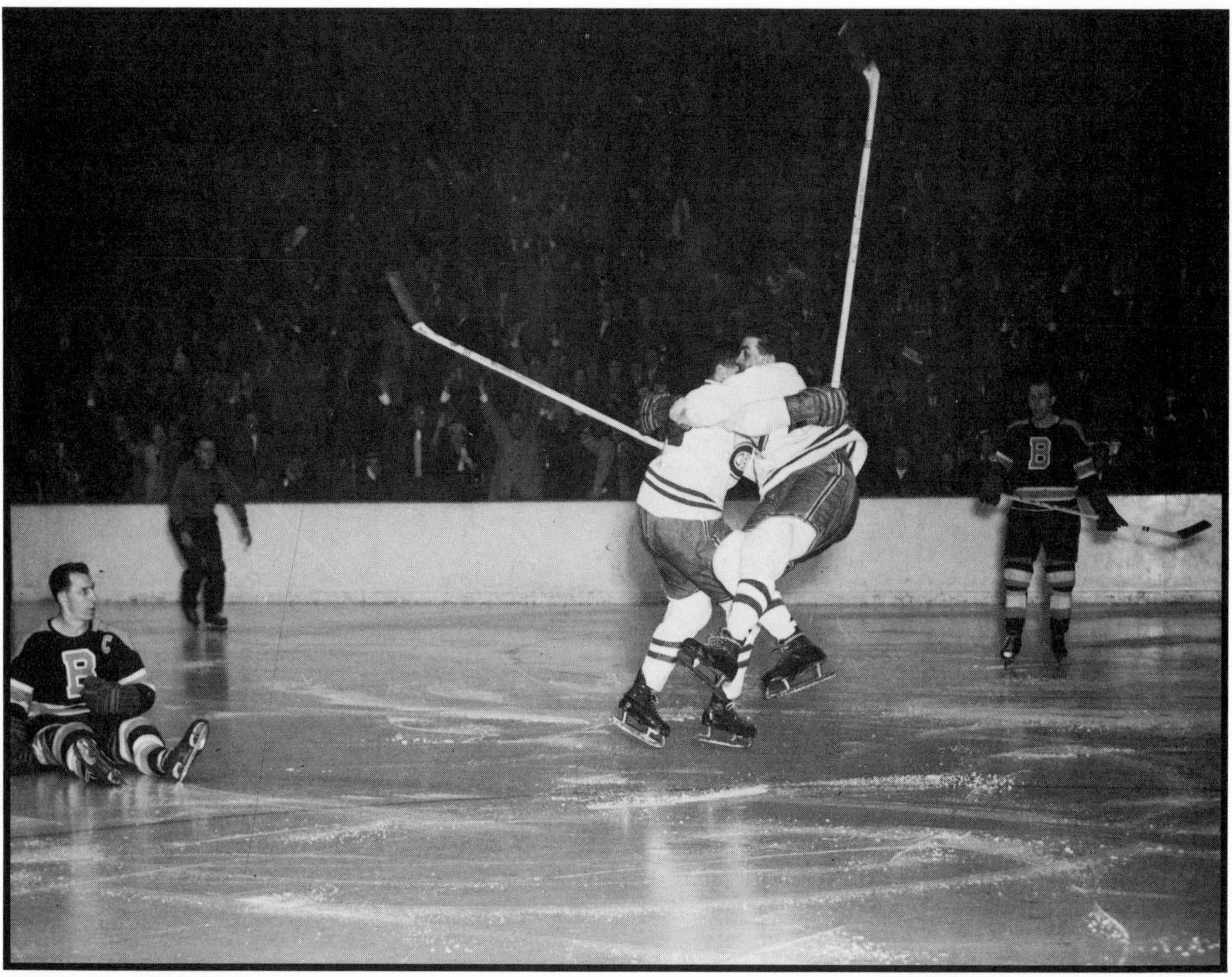

Elmer Lach and Maurice Richard embrace after Lach's winning goal at 1:22 of overtime in the 1953 Stanley Cup final. Boston's Milt Schmidt (sitting) and Joe Klukay look on. LA PRESSE

the fans were concerned. Remember, when you're the Canadiens, you cannot make mistakes. And certainly never excuses. If you finish first and do not win the Stanley Cup, these people . . . they forget you finished in first place."

Because of this tradition, some players would rather not play in a Canadiens uniform. Tom Lysiak, the Flames number one draft choice, publicly stated he'd rather not face the pressure of the Montreal fans, and the winning tradition. Others have said basically the same thing. "One of our disadvantages here," says Fletcher of Atlanta, "is that we don't have tradition yet. But after all, it takes a long time. How long did it take Montreal to build theirs? A long, long time. In 30 years or so, we'll have tradition here."

The plaque still hangs in the home locker room, and some of the names staring down are: Maurice Richard, Toe Blake, Bernie Geoffrion, Dickie Moore, Jean Béliveau, Jacques Plante, Doug Harvey, Howie Morenz . . . it goes on and on. Atlanta has started on the right track. Winning helps tradition take root faster than anything else. Perhaps someday, who knows, there may be a list in the home dressing room of the Omni.

Guy Lafleur, Yvon Lambert and Jacques Lemaire after a Lafleur goal in the 1979 playoffs against Toronto.
JEAN-GUY PARADIS

Andre Pronovost and Toe Blake watching the action during the 1960 playoffs.
HOCKEY HALL OF FAME, TORONTO

A 1950's training camp publicity shot. From the left, Bonin, Geoffrion, Goyette, Henri Richard, Moore and Beliveau.
HOCKEY HALL OF FAME, TORONTO

4

NINE GLORIOUS EPOCHS

CAMIL DESROCHES

To write about the Montreal Canadiens is really to write about the sport of ice hockey itself. The Canadiens is the oldest professional team, the one with the most players and builders in the Hall of Fame and the club that has won twenty-two Stanley Cups, more than any other team. It is mentioned elsewhere in this book that hockey fans usually have two favorites, their home team and the Canadiens. At least one reason for this is that many of these fans would say that the Canadiens is the most spectacular and consistent team to watch year after year. Another reason may be that the team has had some of the greatest players in the history of the sport, breaking more records over the years than any other club.

In 1893, the Stanley Cup was put at stake for the first time, soon to become emblematic of the world championship. From 1893 to about 1907, the Cup was contested by amateur clubs since no professional teams had yet been formed. In fact, between 1893 and 1899 there

The Montreal Shamrocks, 1899.
HOCKEY HALL OF FAME, TORONTO

was only one amateur league. Its headquarters were located in Montreal, and it included five teams: Montreal, Victoria and the Crystals (all from Montreal), as well as Quebec and Ottawa. There was little change from 1899 to 1903, except that the league became known as the "Canadian Amateur Hockey League."

Things were totally different between 1903 and 1910. It was an era of great change, or rather great turbulence, as the large local league changed names several times. In 1907-08, the Ontario Professional Hockey League was formed, leading eventually to the National League as we know it today. The various team owners fought doggedly for the services of the best players, and the war was on between the East and the West, where professional hockey had also appeared.

THE FIRST FRENCH-SPEAKING PLAYERS

There were enough French-speaking players by 1903-04 to form a club. Actually, there were two clubs: the Nationals and the Montagnards (two well known Montreal organizations with a high degree of proficiency in lacrosse). These were the predecessors of the "Club de Hockey Canadien." The National team was admitted to the Federal League in 1903, and with aces like Jack Laviolette and Didier Pitre did fairly well during the first season. The following year, however, the team lost its two stars to the West and to Ontario and decided to leave the Federal League to try its luck in the "big" local league, the Canadian Amateur Hockey League. The result was disastrous. The French-Canadian team played four games, lost them all, and defaulted on the next six, ending the season with a dismal 0-10 record. The Nationals halted operations at this point, returning only in 1909-10.

The Montagnards replaced the Nationals in the Federal League. Although the team was very popular and attracted large crowds wherever it played, it could not get the players it wanted because of the warlike competition among owners from Montreal, Ontario and the West. Like the Nationals, the Montagnards faced disaster. The team did not win a single game during its first season (1904-05). The next season was even worse, losing four times in regular play and four more times by default. Probably the worst of these defeats came on February 2, 1906 when the Montagnards were crushed 26-0 at a game played in Brockville.

By the 1906-07 season the schedule had been expanded from eight to twelve games, and the Montagnards were finally able to play successfully, losing only one regular season game. They finished the year in first place thanks to the brilliant play of Jack Marshall and Alphonse Prevost (the stars), as well as W. Viau, Strike, Lannon, Dostaler, Millard, Leblanc, T. Viau and others. On March 1, 1907, towards the end of the regular schedule, the Montagnards beat Cornwall 7-3, but Cornwall protested the game. The management of the league ordered the Montagnards to repeat the game, but the victors refused and simply quit hockey for good. This decision was the end of the so-called French-speaking teams until the 1909-10 season when the Nationals returned to play a few games. The Montagnards were popular, though, and a song was dedicated to them: "Halte-là, halte-là, halte-là, les Montagnards sont là." As we shall see, this became an important war chant for the Canadiens in later years.

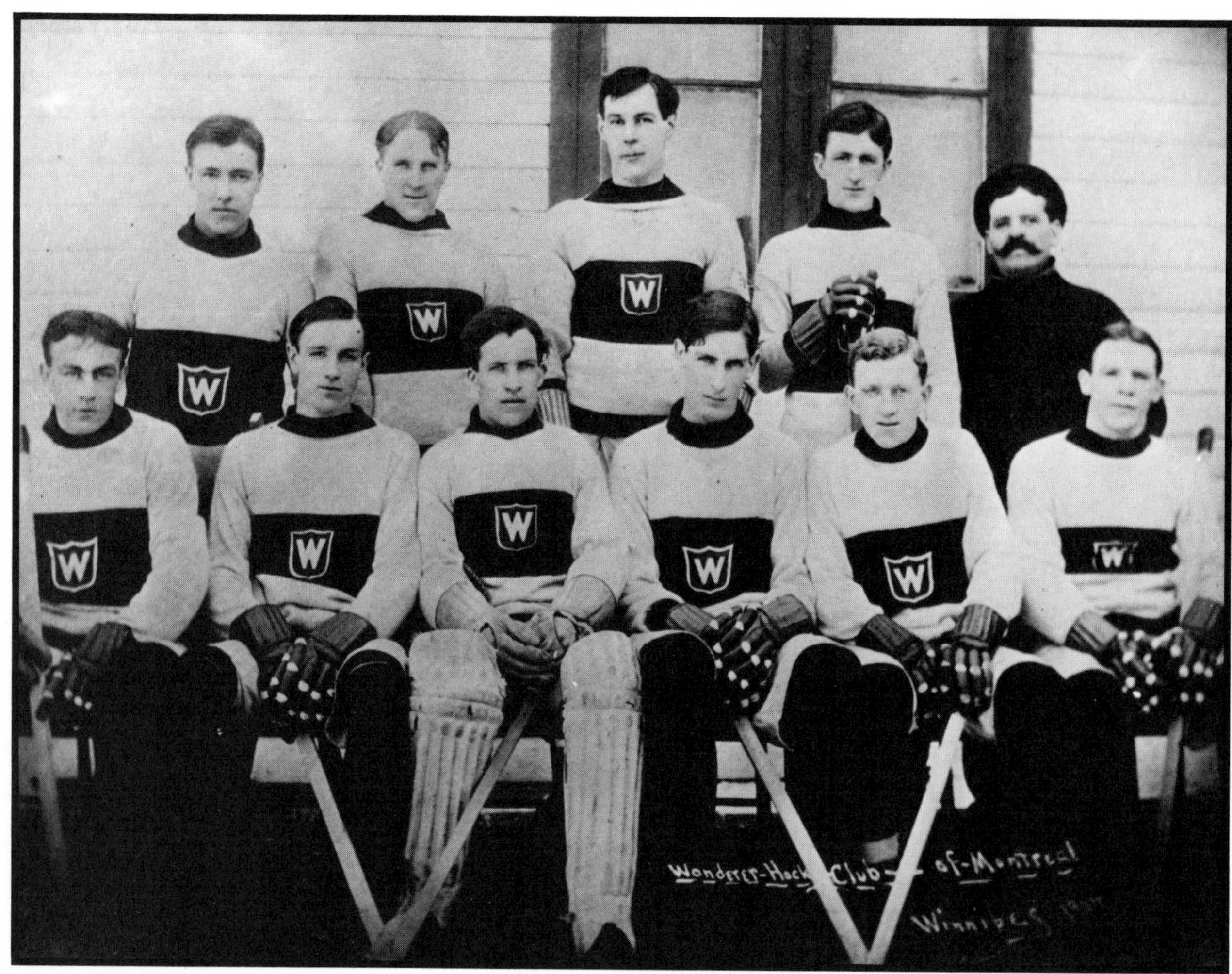

The Montreal Wanderers, 1907, known as the "Little Men of Iron."
HOCKEY HALL OF FAME, TORONTO

THE BIRTH OF THE CANADIENS

J. Ambrose O'Brien, of Ottawa and also Renfrew and Cobalt in northern Ontario, was responsible for the creation of the "Club de Hockey Canadien." The 1909-10 season was expected to be the most tumultuous ever, since the leagues decided to fight it out in Montreal. To start with, the Eastern Canadian Hockey Association decided to change its name on November 25th, calling itself the Canadian Hockey Association. One week later, a circuit called the National Hockey Association of Canada was born after a meeting held in Montreal at the Windsor hotel. The Montreal Wanderers and a team from Renfrew had been expelled from the CHA the week before, and along with teams from Cobalt and Haileybury they were to form the new NHA.

Two weeks later (December 4th) the members of each league met again, but unknowingly in the same place, the Windsor Hotel, to draw up their respective 1909-10 schedules. As fate would have it the meetings were held in nearly adjacent rooms (129 and 135). Acting on a rumor that the Shamrocks, the Nationals

The first Canadiens hockey club, 1909. Their sweaters were blue then.
WILLIE DAGENAIS

and the Ottawa team were ready to join the NHA, the hotel hallways were paced by hordes of newsmen, but no such decision was announced.

Instead the announcement was made that a franchise had been given to a new club which would be called the Canadiens and would have in its lineup only French-Canadian players The owner would be J. Ambrose O'Brien, with T. C. Hare of Cobalt as a silent partner. Jack Laviolette, the famous hockey and lacrosse player, would be the manager, and he was given the job of providing a lineup.

The Canadian Hockey Association was the first to start playing, beginning the season on December 30th. It should be noted here that seventy years ago the seasons started much later than they do today, because there was no such thing as artificial ice. It soon became apparent that it would be next to impossible for any professional team to be successful at the box office, simply because there were no fewer than five such teams in Montreal alone. The game between the Nationals and the Shamrocks in early January, for example, attracted only 800 spectators, and the crowd was even smaller for the Ottawa-All Montreal game two days later.

There was some talk about a merger between the two leagues to solve this problem, but at an important joint meeting held on January 5, 1910 this was not discussed as predicted. To everyone's surprise it was announced that the Shamrocks and the Ottawa team had been admitted to the NHA. An offer had also been made to buy the Nationals' franchise, but the owners of the team, Adolphe Lecours and Napoléon Dorval, insulted because their team had not been invited to join the NHA, absolutely refused to sell. The Nationals, returning to hockey after a four year hiatus, failed again at the beginning of the season, losing four times in as many games and giving up fifty goals in the process. There is no doubt why the NHA refrained from inviting the Nationals into the league.

The Nationals disappeared again, this time for good, and it was also the end of the Canadian Hockey Association. However, the Canadiens had been born. The team won its first game 7-6 against Cobalt on January 5, 1910, at Montreal's Jubilee Rink, thanks to a goal by "Skinner" Poulin after five and a half minutes of sudden-death play. The Canadiens started small, winning only twice and losing ten times during the first season, but the popularity and success of the team grew steadily over the next years.

THE "CLUB ATHLÉTIQUE CANADIEN"

George Kennedy appeared on the scene for the 1910-11 season, and he was the man who transformed the Canadiens into the spectacular team that earned the nickname "The Flying Frenchmen." Kennedy (his real name was Georges Kendall) was a true-blue Montrealer who was French-Canadian on his mother's side. He was very successful, but he had the help of the team's "Three Musketeers," Georges Vezina in goal, Jack Laviolette and Didre Pitre. This was the club that all the fans wanted to see, and the one that won its first Stanley Cup in 1915-16.

Kennedy was the owner of the "Club Athlétique Canadien" in Montreal, a French-Canadian sports club very popular in those days. One month before the annual meeting of the NHA he announced that he was going to ask for a franchise in that league, because he held the rights, by registration and incorporation, to the name "Canadien." If the franchise was refused, he warned, he would not permit any NHA team to use the name. He said, finally, that he had been opposed to the use of the name by O'Brien's team during the preceding season. He had tolerated it, but according to him his rights were being abused.

An NHA meeting was held on November 12, 1910, where it was decided that Kennedy could obtain the Hailybury franchise and that Quebec could have the Cobalt franchise, since both clubs were ceasing operations. So far as the previous season's franchise to O'Brien was concerned, it was decided that it would probably go to a Toronto club one or two seasons later.

The "Canadiens" officially became "Le Club Athlétique Canadien," and Kennedy started working hard, hacking away day and night, to build the team that was to become so famous in less than ten years and so renowned today.

During the 1910-11 season the games were split into three 20 minute periods instead of two 30 minute periods as in the past. Only the Canadiens could use French-speaking players, a rule that continued into the next season. This was the season, 1911-12, that the game was first played with six men instead of seven, the rover position was eliminated, and

A 1934 Turofsky cartoon on a game with the Leafs.
HOCKEY HALL OF FAME, TORONTO

the first season that official programs displaying the players' numbers were sold to the spectators.

The following season, 1912-13, the Canadiens team was permitted to hire two English-speaking players, while the other teams (Quebec, Wanderers, Ottawa, Toronto and Tecumsehs) could sign up two French-speaking players. The Canadiens jumped at the chance and hired Donald Smith and Harry Scott. With these players and such men as Vezina, Lalonde, Laviolette, Pitre and Berlinquette, the "Tricolore" became one of the best professional teams of the day. The team finished first in the 1913-14 season, and by 1915-16 was able to win the Stanley Cup. This was the last season that the team was known as the "Club Athlétique Canadien."

DANDURAND, CATTARINICH AND LETOURNEAU

George Kennedy died in 1921 at the age of 41, a victim of an influenza epidemic. The trio of Dandurand, Cattarinich and Letourneau bought the team in November of that year. It was Dandurand, "m'sieu Leo" (Mister Leo) as he was known everywhere, who made the team very popular during these early days with a lineup of such aces as Newsy Lalonde, the immortal Howie Morenz, the unique Georges Vezina, George Hainsworth, the prolific scorer Joe Malone, the atom Aurèle Joliat, Sylvio Mantha, Pit Lepine, the Cleghorn brothers, Sprague and Odie, Johnny Gagnon, the always smiling Albert Leduc, Wildor Larochelle and Lorne Chabot. He was assisted during his reign by very capable coaches: the well known Cecil Hart (seven years) and Newsy Lalonde (three years), Dandurand himself acting as coach for five seasons.

It was during the Dandurand era that hockey became international with the arrival of the Boston Bruins in 1924, the New York Americans and the Pittsburgh Pirates in 1925, the New York Rangers, the Chicago Black Hawks and the Detroit Cougars in 1926. Despite this change, Dandurand's Canadiens, just like those of Kennedy before him, would bring in the largest crowds in the league, the American fans were eager to see those astonishing "Flying Frenchmen" skate. Dandurand piloted the Canadiens for fourteen seasons, and the Canadiens were able to win the Stanley Cup three times: 1923-24, 1929-30 and 1930-31.

It was also with Dandurand that the team moved permanently to the Forum, which had originally been built for the Montreal Maroons. The contract was signed on October 26, 1926, and the team relocated even before the lease had expired on the Mount Royal Arena where they had been playing since January 10, 1920. Previously, even before George Kennedy owned the team, it had played at the Jubilee Rink at the corner of Moreau and St. Catherine streets in the eastern part of Montreal. When Kennedy arrived, the decision was made to play on the same rink used by the Wanderers, the Westmount Arena, which stood at the corner of Wood Street and St. Catherine West, near the site of the present Forum.

Like the Forum after it, the Westmount Arena had the distinct advantage of artificial ice, and the Canadiens played their first game there in December of 1914. This rink, commonly called "l'aréna Montreal," burned to the ground on the evening of January 2, 1918, and the Canadiens had to return to the Jubilee rink until moving to the Mount Royal Arena.

THE SLOW-DOWN, 1935 TO 1940

When Dandurand and his partners bought the club in 1921 the price was $11,500. On September 17, 1935, the team was sold to a syndicate composed of Ernest Savard, Col. Maurice Forget and Louis Gelinas. These three men indirectly represented the Canadian Arena Company (The Forum), which already owned the Montreal Maroons. A cash payment of $65,000 was made to Dandurand and Cattarinich (Louis Letourneau had left three years earlier), and the balance of $100,000 took the form of four annual payments. The large profit made in this sale proved the extraordinary popularity that the Canadiens had attained since Dandurand had been with the team. It is even more extraordinary when one considers that the team was bought for $11,500 during a very prosperous time and sold for much, much more during the worst economic depression the world has ever known.

After the 1935 sale, the Canadiens entered what could be called their ordinary period. Between 1935 and 1940, Sylvio Mantha, Cecil Hart, Jules Dugal, Babe Seibert and Alfred "Pit" Lepine successively coached the team but with little success. During one five-year period (1936-1940), the Habs failed twice to qualify for the playoffs, a very rare occurrence in their history up to that point. The team was going through a very bad time, marked by the deaths of Howie Morenz (1937), Babe Seibert (1939) and Cecil Hart (1940), three men whose individual roles were vital to the success of the team over more than twenty years. Towards the end of 1937-38, the Maroons ceased operations, because the lingering effects of the Great Depression made it impossible for Montreal to support two professional teams. The same conditions caused the Canadiens to change hands once more.

SENATOR RAYMOND

On May 11th, 1940, a meeting of the National League was held in New York where it was announced that the Canadian Arena Company was officially and directly assuming ownership of the Canadiens. The president of the company, Senator Donat Raymond, and the vice-president, William Northey, had been totally devoted to hockey for nearly 40 years, and since they were also the owners of the Forum it was logical that once the Maroons disappeared they would try to maintain the Blue, White and Red as the best hockey club in the world.

Raymond was fortunate to hire Dick Irvin, who had quit his position as coach for Toronto the previous year, and successively entrusted Frank Patrick and Tommy Gorman, two well known hockey men, with the job of building a team that would quickly become champion. Aces like Toe Blake, Ray Getliffe and Charlie Sands were retained from the old team, of course, but they brought in new players like goaltender Herb Gardiner, defensemen Ken Reardon and Jack Portland, and forwards Murph Chamberlain, Johnny Quilty, Joseph Benoit and Elmer Lach.

The fiery-eyed Maurice Richard, considered one of the game's best players.
F. DUPUIS

Success eluded the team at first, managing only to finish in sixth place of the seven team league during the 1940-41 and 1941-42 seasons. The Canadiens certainly didn't break any records, with only sixteen wins in 50 games in 1940-41. The situation changed dramatically with the arrival of a young local player, Maurice Richard, in 1942. He played only sixteen games during his first season, because of a broken ankle, but in the following year he came back with a vengeance. This was the beginning of his absolutely fantastic career of eighteen seasons. When the fiery Richard was on the ice, there were never any leftover tickets at the Forum box office, nor anywhere else for that matter.

With goaltender Bill Durnan and the famous "Punch Line" of Toe Blake, Elmer Lach and Maurice Richard, the Canadiens quickly showed the opposition what playing hockey was all about. In fact, the Blue, White and Red had a nearly perfect season in 1943-44, with 38 wins, seven ties and only five losses in 50 games. Irvin's team did not lose a single game on home ice. A year later "Rocket" Richard contributed 50 goals in 50 games, a record that has yet to be equalled.

During the seventeen years that Raymond owned the team and during the managing directorship of Tommy Gorman and then Frank J. Selke (he assumed this post on August 1, 1946), the Canadiens made it to the playoffs every year except 1948. Dick Irvin and the Canadiens won the Stanley Cup three times as well in 1944, 1946 and 1953.

SENATOR MOLSON

Donat Raymond had just celebrated his 75th birthday when he decided to sell the Canadiens. It was not an easy decision, especially because he wanted to entrust the team to someone who would insure that the now famous club would retain its family character, its tradition and its Quebec soul. He certainly could not have found a better candidate than Hartland de M. Molson, who was a friend of the family and a senator like himself. As a result, Senator Molson and his brother Tom acquired the "Club de Hockey Canadien" and the Canadian Arena Company on September 24, 1957.

Molson ownership continued for eleven years, a glorious period when the Canadiens enjoyed an extraordinary wave of popularity and success that has lasted up to the present day. Frank Selke was managing director until 1964, and the unforgettable Toe Blake was a remarkably successful coach, winning eight Stanley Cups in thirteen years, including five in a row from 1956 to 1960. This new and wonderful era of the Blue, White and Red continued when the young Sam Pollock succeeded Selke as managing director.

As a result, the Molsons rewarded the fans and the team by presenting them with a magnificent new Forum on Saturday, November 2nd, 1968. It was fitting that Jean Beliveau scored the first goal during the opening game. The Canadiens went on to beat the Detroit Red Wings 2-1 in front of a record crowd of 18,114, as well as more than three million excited fans across Canada who were watching the game on TV.

DAVID, WILLIAM AND PETER

Senator Molson turned over active presidency of the Canadiens and the Forum to his young cousin, David, on May 15, 1964. It was David who directed the enormous project of building the new Forum. As soon as the building was inaugurated, the Senator and his brother sold it and the team to David and his two brothers, William and Peter. During the seven years they managed the team, the Canadiens had several fruitful seasons. With Sam Pollock and Toe Blake at the controls, later with Claude Ruel and Al MacNeil as coaches, the team won the impressive number of five Stanley Cups: in 1965, 1966 and 1968 under Pollock and Blake; in 1969 under Pollock and Ruel; and finally in 1971 under Pollock and MacNeil. Surprisingly, the Blue, White and Red did not participate in the 1970 playoffs—for the first time in 22 years.

1978 in Boston, and the Canadiens win another Cup.
DENIS BRODEUR, MONTREAL

THE BRONFMANS

The Molson brothers continued with the team until December 30, 1971, when they surprised the fans by announcing that they were quitting hockey and selling the club and the Forum to a company specifically set up for the purpose called Placements Rondelles Ltée. The owners were Peter and Edward Bronfman, and sportsman E. Jacques Courtois was president.

With the help of Courtois and Jean Beliveau as vice-president, success kept coming during the Bronfmans' reign. This was to be yet another seven year period, and the team won the coveted cup four more times: 1973, 1976, 1977 and 1978. Sam Pollock continued to be master of masters, but he had the able assistance of the well known coach, Scotty Bowman, who continued to build his already impressive reputation.

THE NINTH EPOCH

In 1978 the Canadiens changed hands for the ninth time in 70 years. The Bronfman brothers sold the team, but not the Forum, to the "Brasserie Molson du Canada Ltée." on August 4th, 1978.

Morgan McCammon became president, and a few changes were made in the team's management. Sam Pollock decided to leave hockey and recommended Irving Grundman as his successor. Grundman had been president of the Forum during the Bronfman years, and no doubt he had benefited greatly from Pollock's example and advice. With Scotty Bowman as coach, Grundman continued the good work of his predecessors, and in his first year saw the Canadiens win yet another Stanley Cup.

This was the fourth consecutive Stanley Cup victory, the fifth championship in seven years for Scotty Bowman and the 22nd Stanley Cup for the team during its illustrious history. The record is truly unbelievable; fifteen of these victories have come in the last 25 years.

It is difficult to ask for better. The fans have really been spoiled by the caliber of Canadiens' hockey since 1924. In the years to come, with Irving Grundman and Claude Ruel at the helm, and the indefatigable Ron Caron and his scouts searching out promising new players, the Blue, White and Red will continue to do credit to its several million fans—preparing to spoil them even more.

THE BLUE, WHITE AND RED

CAMIL DESROCHES

The Canadiens' sweater has not really changed over the last 60 years, but before this time the team had three different sweaters during its first three seasons. By the 1915-16 season a sweater had been designed which was the basis of the one we know so well. This was the season that the Canadiens won their first Stanley Cup. Finally, in 1921-22, the team adopted the sweater which is still proudly worn today.

The club was born in 1909, and the very first sweater was dark blue with only a narrow white trimming around the collar, the wrists and the hem. In the center was a large white "C" about six inches high. The pants were white and the stockings red.

George Kennedy owned the team in 1910-11, and the club was called "Club Athletique Canadien." At this point, the sweater color was changed to red with a large, white gothic "C" in the middle which was about four inches high and superimposed on a green maple leaf about six inches high. The trimmings were white and blue at the collar, the wrists and bottom.

The look of the sweater was completely altered for the 1911-12 season. Instead of wearing only one color as in the first two seasons, the Canadiens now wore the so-called "barber stripe" sweater. The blue, white and red colors were displayed in two-inch wide stripes repeated four times. In the center was the outline of a rather small maple leaf (about three inches high) with the letters "C.A.C." The collar, the wrists and the hem of the sweater were trimmed in red. For the first time the players wore numbers on their backs, and because the games were played in rinks that were not very well heated, some of the players added toques to their uniforms.

Three wide bands of blue, white and red appeared on the sweaters used in 1915-16. The bands were about ten inches high, a red one at the top and bottom with a blue one in between. Two white stripes, one inch wide, separated the blue from the red. On the blue band were two fairly large letters (about eight inches high), one large "C" with a smaller "A" inside it. There was also a three-inch wide stripe at the collar, the wrists and the bottom edge of the sweater. This was the last season when the letters "C/A" were used. George Kennedy adopted the familiar large "C" with a smaller "H" inside it.

The trio of Dandurand, Cattarinich and Letourneau owned the team by 1921-22. Dandurand, the driving force among them, had new uniforms made up which were almost the same as those used in 1915-16. This became the official uniform of the "Club de Hockey Canadien," and has continued in use for the past 60 seasons. The sweater is red with a blue band about eight inches high in the center and on the sleeves. White stripes about one inch high separate the red from the blue. One large "C" with a smaller "H" inside is set on a blue background. There is a narrow white stripe at the collar and at the wrists, as well as one white and one blue band at the hem. The socks are also red with blue stripes. It has only been for about the last fifteen years that numbers have been worn on the sleeves and on the back.

There has been one season in the Canadiens' history when none of the letters "C," "C.A.C." or "C.H." appeared. This was during the 1924-25 season, the year following the team's second Stanley Cup win. The letters "C.H." were replaced (for one season only) by a map of the world to signify that the Canadiens were supreme in the sport.

It is often asked when the white sweater was first used and when the players started wearing it regularly for all the games played at the Forum. Around 1944-45, at the end of

This was the sweater worn during the 1915-16 season; a narrow white stripe separated the wider red and blue bands. The letters were red.

The altered sweater designed by Dandurand, Catterinich and Letourneau. The wide red bands at top and bottom are separated from the blue field by two narrow white stripes.

During the 1924-25 season the team wore sweaters displaying a map of the world to indicate they had won their second Stanley Cup in 1923-24.

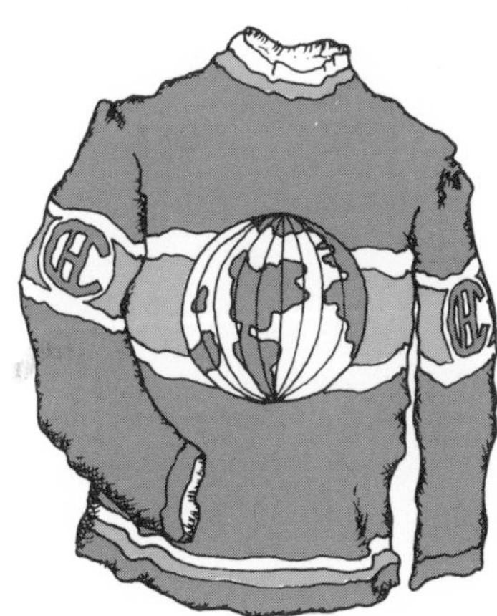

This is the original white home sweater first worn in 1945. The "C" is red on a blue band.

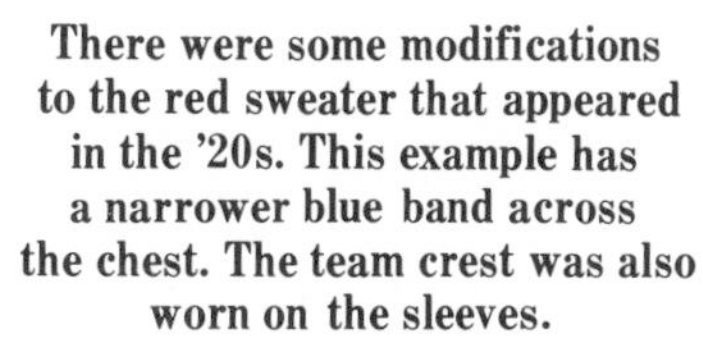

There were some modifications to the red sweater that appeared in the '20s. This example has a narrower blue band across the chest. The team crest was also worn on the sleeves.

The familiar Blue, White and Red as it's worn today.

John Ferguson, Yvan Cournoyer, Charlie Hodge and Claude Provost.

the war, the fans first saw the Canadiens jump on Forum ice wearing the white sweater instead of the traditional red uniform. The reason for the change was that for some years the Detroit Red Wings, the Chicago Black Hawks and the New York Rangers were wearing predominantly red sweaters as the Canadiens were, and this caused confusion among the players. Coach Dick Irvin got the idea to have the Canadiens wear the white sweater when playing any of these teams. On the other hand, when playing Boston or Toronto, the players kept wearing the red sweater. Around 1955, the Red Wings, the Black Hawks and the Rangers also started to use a white sweater, and the Canadiens returned to wearing red sweaters when playing at the Forum, reserving the white one for the games played away from home ice.

A few years later, when TV became a permanent part of the game, first in Canada then in the United States, and following the 1967-68 expansion, the National League required that all teams wear a white uniform on home ice and a dark one away. The Canadiens wore the red sweater at the Forum for the last time on May 11, 1968, against the St. Louis Blues. Dick Duff scored during the third period to give the Canadiens a 3-2 victory and the Stanley Cup.

The white sweater has been modified a few times. At first there was a wide blue band in the middle and on the sleeves (exactly the opposite of the red sweater). The crest was the same as today's. Fifteen years ago, the blue band was replaced by a wide red band on the shoulders, as well as two narrower bands, red and blue, at the bottom of the sweater and a red stripe at the wrist. The "C" is red with a blue stripe around it, and inside it is a smaller white "H". The number on the back is blue with a red stripe around it, as are the sleeve numbers. The pants, with either sweater, are blue with a one inch vertical red stripe between two narrower white stripes on each leg.

JARVIS

THE SUPERSTARS

CLAUDE MOUTON

Georges Vezina.
HOCKEY HALL OF FAME, TORONTO

Over the years many great players have worn the Montreal Canadiens' uniform, but the club has usually been known more for its outstanding teams than single, electrifying players. It is precisely this group effort that has led the Tricolore to so many successful seasons and so many Stanley Cups. There are many players who could legitimately appear on a list of Canadiens' stars, both past and present, but there are very, very few who can honestly be called superstars. The nine men whose biographies appear here attained the highest achievements in hockey; they are the immortals whose names are indelibly marked on the history of the Blue, White and Red. They are the superstars of the past; the future will bring us more.

GEORGES VEZINA

There is no possible comparison between the goaltenders of Georges Vezina's days and those of modern times. Vezina played at a time when the goalies were forbidden to throw themselves on the ice to stop the puck, and during fifteen seasons he never broke that rule. From 1910 to 1925, he enjoyed a more than glorious career.

This excellent goaltender, who started playing at Lac St. Jean, was born in Chicoutimi, Quebec, in 1887. He was 23 when the management of the Canadiens showed a strong interest in his services. At the time, Vezina was playing with a Chicoutimi amateur team.

The story began in February 1910, when the Canadiens were on a province-wide tour playing exhibition games. One game had been scheduled between the powerful Blue, White and Red and an amateur team from Chicoutimi whose leader was its young goalie, Georges Vezina. That night, Vezina certainly did not play like an amateur, because he beat the Canadiens by himself, registering a shutout. By the following fall, Vezina had become the Canadiens' goaltender.

Vezina quickly became the favorite of the Montreal public, as he was becoming the star of his team. With Georges in the net, the Canadiens won the NHA championship twice, crowned champion of the National League three times, as well as having won the Stanley Cup twice (1916 and 1924).

According to those who followed his adventures as a goalie, Vezina's trademark was his extraordinary coolness. In a short period of time, he was nicknamed the "Chicoutimi Cucumber" in every city of the National

League. Even when the opposing players were buzzing around his cage, Vezina would always be stoically calm and radiate a disconcerting dignity. During a championship game against Ottawa, which made history, Vezina stopped 78 of the 79 pucks shot at him.

Also nicknamed "l'Habitant silencieux," the "Silent Habitant," Vezina talked very little and never complained. Father of 22 children, Georges loved the family atmosphere. He complained so little that nobody realized on the night of November 28, 1925 that he was fighting for his life while at his post in the Canadiens' net. Pittsburgh was playing against the Canadiens that night at the old Mount Royal arena in Montreal. After a scoreless first period, Vezina left the rink bleeding from the mouth. After falling unconscious in the locker room, he returned in the net for the second period, but after a few minutes, he fell again and had to leave the game. It was at that moment that the members of his family learned he had tuberculosis. Vezina died four months later at the age of 39.

The memory of Georges Vezina, the man who exuded peace and tranquillity, has been perpetuated by the creation of the trophy that bears his name. This trophy is given year after year to the best goaltender of the NHL. Member of the Hall of Fame, Georges Vezina will always be recognized as one of the greatest goaltenders in the history of our national sport.

HOWIE MORENZ

Aces like Babe Ruth, Bobby Jones, Bill Tilden and Jack Dempsey were the athletes who dominated the golden years of sport in America in the early 20s. Canada also had its hero: Howie Morenz. He played for the Canadiens and was without a doubt the best hockey player of his time. The Francophones called him "l'homme éclair," while the Anglophones nick-named him "The Stratford Streak."

This sensational center wore the colors of the Blue, White and Red during twelve seasons. He then played for the Chicago Black Hawks and the New York Rangers before coming back to Montreal and the Canadiens,

Howie Morenz

where he played until the end of his career. He was a high-scorer and in one fantastic season in particular, he scored 40 times in 44 games. In those days, it was really an achievement. During his entire career in the NHL, he totalled 270 goals and was one of the very first players to be elected to the Hall of Fame in 1945.

His large eyes overlooked a tough beard. He was remarkably light hearted and represented the typical hero of the 20s. This proud man was colorful and charming. He was considered to be the fastest man on skates, and he was a born competitor. "Toe" Blake was only a rookie when Morenz's career was nearing its end, but he still remembers this extraordinary athlete. "He was an inspiration for all of us," said "Toe," and he added: "his skill was truly remarkable. Howie loved hockey and it was his whole life. He used to work and laugh wholeheartedly."

Morenz was both fast and crafty, and these two qualities were his trademark. One of his friends, Ott Heller, a brilliant player for the New York Rangers, often said: "When Howie was skating at full speed as only he knew how, the other players of both teams seemed to be skating backwards. His shot was not to be disregarded since he would always shoot without warning."

Even though he never weighed more than 170 pounds, Morenz would always hit with all his heart and might . . . like a giant. He was a complete hockey player. Of German descent, Howie was born in the small village of Mitchell, Ontario, and fourteen years later, he came to Stratford with his parents.

It was during an amateur game played at Montreal in 1922, where he scored nine goals, that he attracted the attention of the Canadiens' management. Leo Dandurand, the popular sportsman and co-owner of the team, offered him a $1,000 bonus the following year, and Morenz moved to Montreal to wear the Blue, White and Red uniform.

Morenz maintained a fast and jovial demeanor even outside the rink. Although he loved to sing, he also played the ukelele, a very popular instrument in those days. A real fashion follower, he would change clothes two or three times a day. For Howie Morenz, Montreal was paradise.

However, youth does not last forever, and after spending eleven seasons with the Canadiens, Howie was traded to the Chicago Black Hawks in 1934, and then played with the New York Rangers the following year. In 1936, the Canadiens bought his contract back to allow him to finish his career wearing the uniform he defended so well.

Howie felt perfectly at home wearing the Canadiens' jersey, and he was making an excellent comeback when he met with a tragic accident. During a game against the Chicago Black Hawks at the Forum on the night of 28 January 1937, Morenz broke four bones in his left leg and ankle. He seemed to be totally cured five weeks later and was going to leave the hospital to go home when he suffered a relapse. He died from an embolism. His funeral was held in the Forum in front of more than 12,000 people, while almost as many were outside the building to pay their respects to their hero.

MAURICE RICHARD

Even though Maurice Richard retired from active competition in 1960, there are several goalies who would like to be able to play against him still, because of the mark he has left in everybody's memory. Glen Hall, who was a star goaltender with the Detroit Red Wings and the Chicago Black Hawks before joining the St. Louis Blues, has kept a special memory of the legendary Number 9: "His eyes were terrifying, and when he was roaring towards me with the puck, they would sparkle, crackle like a pin-ball machine."

Maurice Richard, known also as the "Rocket," was a constant menace to goalies like Hall for eighteen seasons. During that time, the Rocket scored at least 544 goals in regular season play. Only Gordie Howe is ahead of him in that department. Richard was the first player in history to score 50 goals in one season and is still the only man to have ever scored 50 goals in as many games.

Maurice Richard.
FRANK PRAZAK

Nothing was more dramatic and spectacular than a goal by the Rocket. Maurice did not slide on the ice. He was so anxious to score that he seemed to be running. He used his backhand shot as well as his wrist shot to outmaneuver the opposing goaltenders. Richard had a major trump in his hand. He was ambidextrous, and this is why he could shoot correctly and powerfully when he would leave his right wing position to move on the enemy's net.

Frank Selke, who was managing director of the Canadiens during the Rocket's best seasons, used to say: "Not only was he endowed with phenomenal strength, but the Rocket possessed an unparalleled instinct. He was the most opportunistic player I have ever seen."

Bill Chadwick, an ex-referee and member of the Hall of Fame, is one of Maurice Richard's numerous fans. He has said: "From the blue line to the net, he was unequalled. He was the best scorer without a doubt. He possessed Herculean strength, and once I saw him score with a defenseman on his back."

Maurice Richard learned about hockey when he was a boy playing at Lafontaine Park during the years prior to World War II. Even at that age, he was a prolific scorer. There were doubts, however, about his future as a hockey player, because he seemed to get hurt easily. After breaking his ankle when he was still playing for the seniors (amateurs), Maurice then broke his wrist in 1942 when he was making his debut with the Canadiens. He could not complete the season because of another broken ankle which made Tommy Gorman, the manager of the Canadiens at that time, say: "We have here a very fragile player." Gorman even thought of letting the Rocket go unconditionally, but Richard stayed and became stronger and more resistant as he matured. After that, he avoided being injured, and he looked like a small ox on skates. At the apex of his career, Richard was a little under six feet tall and weighed 180 pounds without and ounce of fat. Several formations in the National League even used two players to take care of this right-winger and his fiery temperament. Richard considered that as a compliment—when opposing players stood in his way, he simply knocked them down then gave them a withering look.

Richard was well known in the NHL for his temper, and because of it was involved in a great number of quarrels with officials as well as players of other teams. He was suspended in March 1955 by President Clarence Campbell, following an altercation with a linesman and a player of the Boston Bruins, and that caused a riot at the Forum.

Everything was forgiven when the Rocket was elected to the Hall of Fame in 1961. This honor is usually granted to a player at least five years after he has announced his retirement. Maurice Richard was chosen as an immortal of hockey only nine months after he hung up his skates.

Two of the greatest—Gordie Howe and Maurice Richard.
DENIS BRODEUR, MONTREAL

BILL DURNAN

Bill Durnan's career in the National Hockey League did not last very long. However, those short years were filled with glory, sparkle and great personal satisfaction.

It was in 1943, when he was 29, that Bill Durnan made his debut in the National Hockey League with the Canadiens. After seven glorious seasons, he had to leave the Canadiens and hockey in the middle of the 1950 playoffs, following a nervous breakdown. During that short period of time, however, he managed to establish records that still hold today.

During the 1948-49 season, Durnan established a modern record, preventing opposing teams from scoring during 309 minutes and 21

Bill Durnan and Mike McMahon. HOCKEY HALL OF FAME, TORONTO seconds—more than five complete games—and he was also the first goaltender to win the Vezina trophy four years in a row, from 1944 to 1947. Toronto's "Turk" Broda interrupted Durnan's series of successes in 1948, but Durnan came right back and got the Vezina trophy the following two years, which meant he had won it six times in seven seasons. Durnan was chosen for the First All-Star team six times, including his first season with the NHL. He stopped making the All-Star teams in 1948 when Broda was chosen.

Bill Durnan possessed one unique characteristic which gave him quite an advantage over the other goaltenders in the league. He was ambidextrous. "This unequalled capability," he would say, "I owe to Steve Faulkner, a coach for whom I played in my younger days in Toronto. He taught me how to change my stick from one hand to the other. That was not easy I assure you, especially in the beginning because, being young, the stick was quite heavy. But Steve always urged me to keep practising with the result that, with time it became a routine for me."

This skill to grab the puck with either hand and clear his territory without difficulty to the right or to the left, he developed during his long stay in the amateur ranks. He then moved up to the Blue, White and Red. He was the type of goalie who hardly ever gave returns.

During his very first season with the Canadiens, Durnan gave up only 109 goals to the enemy in 50 games. That was also the great year that Maurice Richard scored 32 goals in 46 games, and the Canadiens, as a result of Durnan's and Richard's sparkling performances, amongst other things, lost only five games during the 1943-44 campaign. Durnan never lost a game at the Forum during the regular season, and the Canadiens ended the season with the greatest honor, that is by winning the prestigious Stanley Cup.

Bill Durnan, a six foot two-inch tall colossus weighing more than 200 pounds, also became a victim of the great pressure which seemed to eventually overcome every professional goaltender, and Bill said a few years later: "I felt so bad that I could not sleep on the eve of a game. I could not even digest my food. This type of agony is unequalled."

Wounds, as we know, are generally tied to the job of goaltender. Bill Durnan did not avoid this rule, and towards the end of the 1949-50 season he suffered a deep cut to the scalp as a result of a blow from an opposing player's skate during a game against the Black Hawks at Chicago. Durnan missed several games, but he came back at the beginning of the series against the New York Rangers, and it was in the middle of that series that he asked to be replaced.

Bill had just played his last game with the Canadiens and the National League. Durnan did not play for very long in the NHL, but this did not prevent him from performing great exploits and winning several trophies. His greatest dream came true in 1964 when he was elected to the Hockey Hall of Fame. He deserved it.

DOUG HARVEY

Most players are happy when they can master a couple of sides of our national sport. This was not the case for Doug Harvey, a marvelous defense player who mastered almost all aspects of the game during his best years with the Blue, White and Red.

Whether the game was rough or fast, his rare talent would let him adapt to all kinds of plays and all kinds of situations. When the Canadiens had to "kill time," either when they were one man short on the ice or towards the end of the game, they would invariably call on Doug Harvey. The crafty defenseman could control the puck at will and would make skillful passes to his teammates without ever losing his calm, even in critical situations.

For Harvey, everything looked easy. He never appeared tense or tired and was without doubt a leader and an undisputed hero with the Canadiens during most of his illustrious career. When Montreal won five consecutive Stanley Cups, from 1956 to 1960, Harvey was one of the main sparkplugs of the team.

Doug Harvey.

Originally from Montreal, Doug decided to become a professional hockey player after having rejected alluring offers from major football and baseball teams. His was a wise choice for himself as well as for the Canadiens. During his thirteen seasons with the Blue, White and Red, Harvey was chosen for the first All-Star team nine times and once for the second All-Star team. He also won the Norris Trophy six times.

Experts could find only one thing wrong with the style of play of this wonderful athlete. He did not shoot often enough, and therefore his highest scoring total for one season was nine goals. Doug gave the following explanation about his low scoring totals: "I would not get any bonus for scoring a certain number of goals during one season; so why not help those who were paid for scoring since they were receiving bonuses." As we know, Harvey would constantly feed his teammates with skillful passes, and he would himself produce slap-shots from the point. Doug was a very intelligent player whose play was subtle and precise.

Hero of the Montreal youth, Harvey began not to get along too well with the Canadiens' management when he decided to belong to the National League Players Association. In June 1961, he was traded to the New York Rangers where he became player-coach. He managed then to lead the unfortunate Rangers to the playoffs for the first time in four years. That year, he won the Norris Trophy for the seventh time and was chosen for the NHL All-Star team.

The following year, Doug quit his coaching post, because he hated the responsibilities that came with the job. He kept playing with the Rangers for eighteen months, and used to say: "When I was coach I could not belong to the players' group and live like they did. I was not one of them. Now I can go for a beer with my teammates without a second thought."

After that, Doug Harvey roamed in the minor leagues and played successively for Baltimore, St. Paul, Quebec, Pittsburgh and Kansas City. He returned to the National League in 1968 wearing the St. Louis Blues' uniform. He even played against his old team, the Canadiens, when the Blues played Montreal in the Stanley Cup final that year.

Even at the age of 45, Harvey stayed with St. Louis during the 1968-69 season and held both jobs of defenseman and assistant-coach. He then became defensive coach for the Los Angeles Kings before definitely retiring and returning home to Montreal.

BERNARD GEOFFRION

A lot of players in the history of the National Hockey League have impressed their coaches right from the start in an organized league, at the age of 15 or 16, but Bernard "BoomBoom" Geoffrion was certainly not one of these. He still remembers the pitiful day in 1945, when he was trying for a spot on a junior team in Montreal. "I was only 14 then," he said, "and the assistant-coach picked up my gear after a practice session and threw it outside the locker room while saying that I could never hope to play in the National League. I was furious and I had to prove something to this

Bernie "Boom Boom" Geoffrion.
FRANK PRAZAK

Bernie Geoffrion, Jean Beliveau and Bert Olmstead.
HOCKEY HALL OF FAME, TORONTO

man and that is exactly what I did."

Luckily, Geoffrion got a second chance with that team, and we now know how he proved what he could do during his great career of sixteen seasons in the major leagues. During fourteen of these years, he patrolled with great spirit at right wing for the Canadiens before leaving the active game in 1964 and becoming a coach for the Quebec Aces of the American League. The "Boomer" could not stay inactive, however, and he returned to the game as a player in 1966, wearing this time the New York Rangers' colors. After two seasons, he became a coach for the "Blue Shirts," but his stay with the Rangers was short-lived since he had to quit six months later for health reasons.

His perseverance and his thundering shot contributed to make him one of the highest scorers in the history of the league, and he ended his career with a total of 393 goals, being preceded only by Gordie Howe, Maurice Richard, Bobby Hull, Jean Beliveau, Phil Esposito and six or seven other famous scorers.

Unlike the majority of players in his day, Geoffrion never played in the minor leagues. He jumped directly from the juniors to the Canadiens in 1951, and he made his debut in the National League at a time when competition was very strong at right wing, since Maurice Richard and Gordie Howe, amongst others, were continuously struggling against each other.

In 1961, Geoffrion became the second player to score 50 goals during one season. Crowned champion scorer twice, the "Boomer" distinguished himself by winning the Hart Trophy in 1961 for being his team's most useful player.

Most of his exploits can be attributed to his thundering shot. Goaltenders trembled when facing one of his powerful and fast shots. Al Rollins, the Chicago Black Hawks' goalie, said after a game against the Canadiens and Geoffrion: "One of his cannonballs hit my leg pads below the knees, and that shot was so powerful that I thought that my toes were paralysed."

Bernard Geoffrion came close to losing his life in 1958, during a team practice at the Forum. Following a collision with a teammate, Bernard suffered a perforation of the intestine. He was rushed to hospital, and a few days later he was told by his doctors to forget about hockey until the end of the current season. The "Boomer" ignored the advice and returned to the game six weeks later, when he played against the Boston Bruins in the finals for the Stanley Cup. This was the sixth game—and was to be the last of the Series —and Bernard not only scored the first and the winning goals, but also got one assist on the second. The sensational playing of Geoffrion permitted the Blue, White and Red to win a third Stanley Cup in a row.

The Canadiens' ex-number 5 has always been a proud man, and this is probably the reason he has never forgotten his beginnings with the juniors. He does not hesitate to say: "I never was a good skater, and I always had to furnish an extra effort to be able to keep up with the others . . . but I proved to this man [the assistant-coach mentioned above] that he had made a mistake when he threw me out of the dressing room."

Bill Nyrop à la défense contre Rick Middleton des Bruins de Boston.

Bill Nyrop defending against Boston's Rick Middleton.
WILLIE DAGENAIS

Doug Jarvis, un des meilleurs à la mise en jeu.

Doug Jarvis, one of the best face-off men in the game.

Peter Mahovlich fait des pieds et des mains pour s'emparer de la rondelle devant le filet des Islanders.

Peter Mahovlich in a scramble for the puck in front of the Islanders' net.

Bob Gainey lutte pour la possession de la rondelle.

Bob Gainey battles for the puck.

WILLIE DAGENAIS

La partie est terminée et on se félicite mutuellement à la suite d'une autre victoire.

The game's over, and the team congratulate each other for another victory.

WILLIE DAGENAIS

Au centre de la patinoire du Forum, "Toe" Blake reçoit un trophée spécial coulé dans l'argent de la coupe Stanley.

"Toe" Blake on center ice at the Forum receiving a special trophy made of silver from the Stanley Cup.

Guy Lapointe brille également à la balle molle.

Guy Lapointe in an exhibition softball game.

WILLIE DAGENAIS

Montréal pendant le défilé de la coupe Stanley.
Downtown Montreal during a Stanley Cup parade.

Yvan Cournoyer et Serge Savard avec la coupe Stanley durant le défilé de 1979.

Yvan Cournoyer and Serge Savard with the Stanley Cup during the 1979 parade.

Larry Robinson — un virtuose au maniement du bâton.

Larry Robinson — a great stick-handler.

Larry Robinson et sa fille Rachèle.

Larry Robinson and his daughter, Rachele.

Guy Lafleur compte contre les Russes en 1979.

Guy Lafleur scores against the Russians, 1979.

M. PONOMAREFF

Réjean Houle lève son bâton indiquant qu'un but vient d'être compté lors des séries hors concours contre les Russes.

Rejean Houle raises his stick to signify a goal during the 1979 exhibition series with the Russians.

WILLIE DAGESNAIS

MONTREAL
FORUM
SPORTS MAGAZINE
10¢
R. HUGGINS

MONTREAL
FORUM
SPORTS MAGAZINE
Murph Chamberlain
15¢

LA REVUE SPORTIVE du **Forum** SPORTS MAGAZINE

25¢

Boom-Boom Geoffrion

TEX

1960 L'ORGANE OFFICIEL des CANADIENS et and ROYALS OFFICIAL PUBLICATION 1961

Maurice Richard, que l'on voit entre M. Jacques Allard (à gauche), président de la Brasserie Molson Ltée (Québec) et M. Irving Grundman, vice-président exécutif et directeur de gestion du Club de Hockey Canadien, est revenu aux Canadiens en juillet 1980 pour occuper un poste dans les relations publiques.

Maurice Richard pictured between Mr Jacques Allard (left), President of Molson Brewery Ltd. (Quebec) and Mr. Irving Grundman, Executive Vice-President and Managing Director of the Canadiens hockey club, returned to the Canadiens in July, 1980, in a public relations position.

JEAN BELIVEAU

Believe it or not, the Canadiens had to buy a whole hockey league to make Beliveau one of their players. This was happening in 1953 when Beliveau was completing his second season with the Quebec Aces of the Quebec Senior Hockey League. Even though this was an amateur league, the players did receive a small salary. Small was the word, but there was an exception: Jean Beliveau, since his annual salary was $20,000, which in those days, a quarter of a century ago, was an astronomical sum.

Beliveau, like several amateur tennis aces of those days, would declare that he was not interested in becoming a professional player. This situation was more than embarrassing for the Canadiens who owned the rights to the young star. In Montreal, the Blue, White and Red fans kept demanding the transfer of "Le Gros Bill"—that was the nickname given to Beliveau in Quebec—but he would not leave the ancient city.

The Canadiens then used an unconventional method to ensure the services of the famous young athlete. They simply bought the whole Quebec Senior League! In doing so, the Montreal team acquired every player in the league, and the new owners made a professional league out of it and named it *la Ligue Senior Professionnelle du Québec.* Beliveau did not have any other choice but to join the Canadiens, and the athlete from Victoriaville, who was then 23 years old, received a $20,000 bonus when he signed his first contract on October 3, 1953. Moreover, "Grand Jean" was assured of a $105,000 salary, spread over a period of five years.

Jean Beliveau.
DAVID BIER

The young colossus who played at center was worth his weight in gold. He became the most prolific center in the history of the National League with a total of 1219 points during his eighteen seasons with the league. The Canadiens ex-number 4 turned the red light on no less than 507 times, and during his last season, in 1970-71, he lead his team to the conquest of the prestigious Stanley Cup. For the "Gros Bill" that was his tenth cup in eighteen years!

MISTER ELEGANCE

There is no doubt that Jean Beliveau had a very graceful style and, at the same time, everything seemed so easy for him. He was THE elegance. The "Grand Jean" did not seem to skate very fast, but very few could follow him. His movements were instinctive. His shot was not only powerful but also ex-

Ceremonial face-off for the 1962 All Star game. From left, George Armstrong, Clarence Campbell, Frank Udvari and Jean Beliveau. HOCKEY HALL OF FAME, TORONTO

tremely precise . . . which made him doubly dangerous.

Players on other teams were slightly intimidated by Jean's size and strength when he made his debut in the National League. Bill Ezinicki, a tough and cunning player during his best years with Toronto and Boston, remembers very well his first confrontation with Beliveau. "It was as if I was trying to hit and move an oak. I simply bounced back . . . and found myself stretched out on the ice. There was nothing I could do!" said the "badman" of those days.

At the time, the experts could find only one thing wrong with Beliveau. He was too mild to earn a living in such a rough sport. Everywhere in the National League, attempts were made to demolish him, but he never tried to retaliate. All Jean wanted was to play hockey. Beliveau kept that attitude during his first two seasons with the Blue, White and Red, but the third year, he changed his policy and fought back. As a result, he became one of the most penalized players in the league that year. However, he was not proud to be categorized with the "tough" of the NHL, but his discontentment died down when he was crowned top scorer of the league and winner of the Art Ross Trophy that same year.

Jean Beliveau has always been well respected as an individual and a player by everyone in the National League. He has been honored several times and not only has he been chosen for the First and Second All-Star teams on no less than ten occasions, but he has also won the Hart Trophy twice which is emblematic of the most useful player in the best league in the world.

Hector "Toe" Blake, who coached Jean Beliveau for thirteen seasons, inexhaustibly praises this marvelous player. "Ever since Beliveau has been associated with hockey," he said, "I have never heard any derogatory comments about him. As a hockey player and a gentleman, Jean Beliveau is unbeatable. . . . He has no equal," concluded the most illustrious coach of the history of the *Club de Hockey Canadien*.

JACQUES PLANTE

Not only did Jacques Plante travel a lot, but he also lived a large number of adventures during his career of 20 years. From the 50 cents earned for each game he was playing with a manufacturer's team, Jacques became one of the best paid goaltenders of modern times.

It all started at Shawinigan, Quebec, where Plante was born. "At the age of fifteen, I was playing for fun," he said, "until my father suggested I ask for a salary of 50 cents per game from my coach. He agreed but asked me not to tell anybody. That little amount of money represented a lot for me at the time. I was the oldest of a family of eleven children and we could not afford anything superfluous, not even a radio set. The only time of the year when we had soft drinks was at Christmas."

Jacques left his native city to go to Quebec City where he played with a junior team. He was then earning $85 a week. One year later, Plante made his debut with the professionals, playing for the Royals of the Quebec Professional Senior League. The following year he began with the Canadiens in dramatic circumstances: he had to step in, in the middle of the Stanley Cup series. The Canadiens were playing the Chicago Black Hawks at Chicago and were in a very bad position, close to being eliminated.

This first game will stay forever engraved on his mind. "I was so nervous," he said later, "that I couldn't even tie up my skates." Nevertheless, Plante shut out the Hawks 3-0. A brilliant career was starting, and Plante was to become one of the best goalies in professional hockey.

Toe Blake and Jacques Plante.
HOCKEY HALL OF FAME, TORONTO

During the ten seasons he spent with the Canadiens, Plante helped his team win the Stanley Cup five years in a row, from 1956 to 1960. He also tied Bill Durnan's record by winning the Vezina trophy six times, five of them in succession. The colorful goaltender was also chosen to be on the First All-Star team six times, and in 1962 Jacques became the fourth goalie in NHL history to win the Hart Trophy.

Plante loved drama; every save looked difficult. He was an innovative player, the first goaltender to leave his net, either to clear the puck from his territory or to freeze it. "At one time," he often explained, "I was playing with such a weak team that I had to leave my cage in order to keep control of the puck behind our net." Plante perfected this art while playing for the Blue, White and Red.

Jacques Plante was the first goalie to wear a mask regularly, and he made it popular all over North America. It began on November 1st, 1959, when the Canadiens were playing the New York Rangers at New York. During the first period, Plante was hit in the face by a powerful shot from Andy Bathgate. After spending 20 minutes at the first-aid clinic where he received several stitches, he insisted he wanted to go back to the game. His sweater soaked with blood, he came back on the ice of the Garden wearing a cream colored mask. Several seasons later, every goaltender had imitated Jacques and was wearing a mask.

In 1963, Plante was traded to the New York Rangers, where he played during one and a half seasons. He then retired and became a representative for a Montreal brewery. In 1968, the St. Louis Blues offered the ex-Canadiens goaltender no less than $35,000 to play for them. The elegant goalie could not resist this enticing offer and went with the Blues.

At St. Louis, Plante shared the work with another veteran, Glen Hall, then 37 years old. This excellent duo played so well that they won the Vezina trophy and led the Blues to two consecutive championships of the West Division. Plante's contract was bought by the Toronto Maple Leafs in 1970, and he played well with the Torontonians during three seasons. In March 1973, he was traded to the Boston Bruins who were in trouble on the eve of the Stanley Cup Series, but Plante, then 44 years old, unfortunately could not help the Bruins win the Cup.

HECTOR "TOE" BLAKE

It's 1944; Thursday, April 13th to be exact. The Canadiens are playing host to the Chicago Black Hawks for the fourth game of the Stanley Cup Finals. Dick Irvin's team had not lost once on Forum ice in twenty-five games, until Toronto beat them at home 3-1 during a semi-final game. The situation was quickly remedied, though, through the efforts of the famous "Punch Line." Maurice Richard scored five goals in one game, and "Toe" Blake and Elmer Lach added goals and assists to take the Tricolore to four consecutive semi-final wins and the right to face the Black Hawks.

On April 13th, the Canadiens are ahead in the Stanley Cup Series three games to none. The fans, more than 15,000 of them in the old Forum, where it was permitted to stand around the walkway, expect nothing less than another victory and the Stanley Cup, the first for the team since 1931.

Things are not happening as planned, however, and with less than ten minutes to play in the third period the Black Hawks are leading 4 to 1. The crowd begins to wonder what is going on, what is happening to the team who seemed, since the beginning of the season, to be able to win at will. A fan, probably feeling he is being cheated of a victory or possibly because he is on the losing end of a large bet, suddenly begins to shout: "Fake! Fake! Fake!" Half the crowd, tired of the Hawks' ultra-defensive play, takes up the chant and soon the whole building resonates with "Fake! Fake! Fake!"

It doesn't take long for Blake, Richard, Lach and the rest of the team to get the message. The insulting chant heats them up to the point where they tie the score 4–4 with the help of Lach's one goal and Richard's two, forcing the teams into sudden-death play. "Toe" was to keep the sweetest victory of all for himself. He had not scored in the series yet, but he had tied a National League record, twice in three weeks, by contributing three assists in one period. In fact, a few days earlier (March 24th), when the Canadiens, or rather Maurice Richard, defeated the Maple Leafs 5 to 1 on five Richard goals, the always reliable "Toe" went in with five assists, including three in the second period on three of the "Rocket's" goals. On April 13th, Blake added three more assists in one period on the three goals that permitted the Canadiens to tie the score. Best of all for "Toe" and the Canadiens, after nine minutes and twelve seconds of sudden-death play Blake outmanoeuvred the skillful defensemen and Mike Karakas, moved in on the net and scored. This goal brought victory for the Canadiens and the first Stanley Cup in thirteen years.

During his career, Blake also scored another Cup-winning goal, two years later against the Boston Bruins in the fifth game of a final that the Tricolore won four games to one. Throughout the history of the National League, only five players have scored the Cup-winning goal twice. For statistics lovers, four of the five were Canadiens: Jean Beliveau, Henri Richard, Jacques Lemaire and "Toe" Blake. The other player was Boston's Bobby Orr.

It seems that thirteen was Blake's lucky number. He scored against the Black Hawks on April 13th; after playing for thirteen seasons on the ice, Blake reigned supreme as the Canadiens' coach for thirteen more seasons.

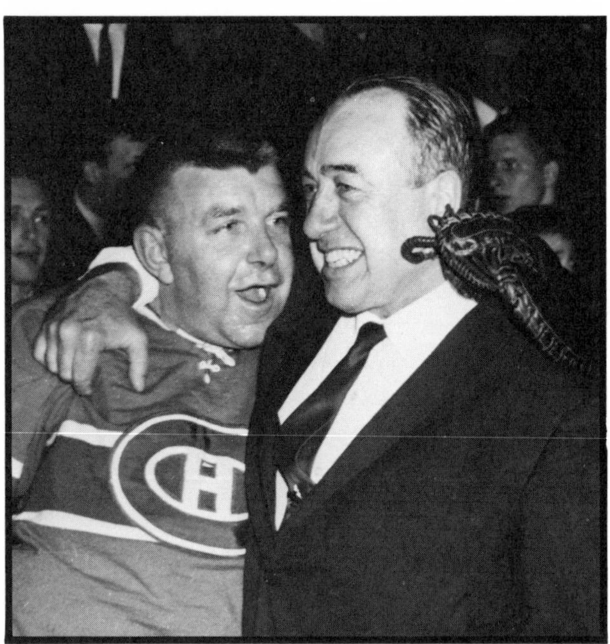

Lorne "Gump" Worsley and Toe Blake.
DENIS BRODEUR, MONTREAL

Both as player and coach he proved to be a real master.

Blake was one of the greatest left wingers the Canadiens and major hockey ever had. During his thirteen seasons, he played 577 games, scored 235 goals and 292 assists for a total of 527 points. With the excellent average of .913, he is in twenty-sixth position among the best scorers in the history of hockey. Only two players, Boston's Bill Cowley and Chicago's Doug Bentley, both aces of his era (1935 to 1946), had a better average: .995 and .959 respectively. Blake was the best goal scorer among them, however, with 235, while Bentley recorded 219 and Cowley 195.

Blake's greatest qualities as a player were his courage, determination and tenacity. For those who are too young to remember having seen him play, Bob Gainey, the current team's marvellous left winger, plays a very similar game. Just like thoroughbred bulldogs, "Toe" and Bob never let go.

"Toe" was even better during the end-of-the-season series. He played 57 of these games in ten years, and he distinguished himself with twenty-five goals and thirty-seven assists for a total of 62 points and a truly remarkable average of 1.087 points per game. He was also chosen three times for the first All-Star Team and twice for the second. He picked up the Hart Trophy in 1938-39. Even though he was known as a tough player, he surprised everybody during the 1945-46 season when he won the Lady Byng Trophy, because he had visited the penalty box only once, and that for two minutes, in 50 games. He could hardly believe it himself.

"Toe" Blake was a great player, but he was an even better coach. In fact, he became the best coach in National League history as a result of his successes over thirteen seasons with the Blue, White and Red.

He was very hard to please and very strict, but he was also very humane. He had the knack of getting his players to do exactly what he wanted; he could extract the very last ounce of energy whether during the regular season or during the very important games of the end-of-season series.

Blake piloted the Canadiens from 1955 to 1968. Right after his nomination to the post on June 5, 1955, he started working resolutely towards building the team he had always dreamt about as a player. He had the good luck to enlist several superstars, whom he directed with an "iron fist in a velvet glove", and he led his team to the Stanley Cup at the end of his very first season. His players were so inspired that they repeated the 1955-56 exploit in 1957, 1958, 1959 and 1960; five Stanley Cups, an unequalled record in the National League.

The Canadiens never missed the playoffs while he was coach, and during the thirteen seasons he was at his post the Canadiens picked up the circuit championship (the Prince of Wales Trophy) no fewer than nine times. Blake's teams won the Stanley Cup an amazing eight times; the five consecutive Cups mentioned above and in 1965, 1966 and 1968. Under Blake's guidance, the Canadiens participated in 119 playoff games, won 82 of them and lost only 27, for an average of .689, giving "Toe" his title of best coach of all time.

He was at his post for the last time on Saturday night, May 11, 1968, when his Canadiens defeated the St. Louis Blues to win yet another Stanley Cup in four consecutive games. After the game he announced to the assembled journalists that he would not be back next season, and he kept his word. This marked the end of another glorious epoch for the Blue, White and Red. One interesting footnote that has never been mentioned before is that when Blake left the Forum around midnight on the 11th workers were already taking one of the Forum walls down to prepare for the construction of the superb building we now know. The new Forum opened its doors a mere five and a half months later. Blake and the old Forum, both justifiably famous, ended their brilliant careers at the same time and left together with all their marvellous memories.

Four years after Blake retired, the management of the "Club de Hockey Canadien" decided to give him special homage—he certainly deserved it—at a huge banquet served at a Montreal hotel. The banquet organizers sent out exactly 319 invitations, and not one guest failed to appear. All of them came to pay their respects to a friend and hero. A few hours later, on the ice at the Forum, Blake was given a trophy made in part of silver from the very first Stanley Cup. "Toe"—Mister Stanley Cup—really deserved nothing less than that.

Hector "Toe" Blake leaving the Forum on Saturday, May 11th, 1968, after the Canadiens had just won an eighth Stanley Cup in thirteen seasons by eliminating the St. Louis Blues in four straight games. Blake officially announced his retirement the next day.

LEMAIRE
25

7

THE FORUM

CAMIL DESROCHES

The Montreal Forum, the best known hockey rink in the world and one of the most famous sports and entertainment centers in America, is celebrating its 56th anniversary this year.

Home of the celebrated Montreal Canadiens, the first Forum was built at a cost of $1,500,000. and opened its doors on November 29, 1924. Its initial capacity was 9,000 seats but this was raised to 12,500 in 1949. In 1968, a magnificent new Forum, modern, fully air-conditioned and equipped with 16,500 seats, was completed in 5½ months at a cost of $10,000,000. This is in fact the existing building and it was inaugurated with a Gala Premiere on Saturday, November 2 of that year.

During the 56 wonderful years of the Forum's existence, more than 77 million enthusiastic fans have watched their beloved Canadiens win the Stanley Cup no fewer than 20 times, finish in first place 25 times and in second place 12 times. The Montreal Maroons (two Stanley Cups), the Senior Royals (1947 Allan Cup), the Junior Canadiens (Memorial Cup in 1950, 1969 and 1970) have also been a great credit to the Forum.

Wrestling, boxing and tennis were also very popular throughout the more than half century, while in the entertainment world, audiences have acclaimed the most famous artists from the four corners of the earth during ice revues, musical comedies, concerts, opera performances, rodeos, circuses and exhibitions, not to mention numerous rallies and conventions.

The Forum in 1924.

If hockey fans have been spoiled by the consistently brilliant performances of the Canadiens since 1924, Montrealers have been royally served by the wide variety of shows which our famous sports arena has hosted during its 56 years of existence.

THE SPECTACULARS

Professional tennis with the world's leading aces from 1935 through 1965; the "Skating Vanities" with the sparkling Gloria Nord and the "Dancing Waters"; the Bolshoi and Moiseyev Ballets; the "Aqua Parade" extravaganza with Tarzan himself, the more than likeable Buster Crabbe; the Harlem Globetrotters who have been visiting us yearly since 1952 with such athletes as ace players and irrepressible comedians, Goose Tatum, Meadowlark Lemon and Geese Ausbie; The Moscow and Shriners Circuses; Bob Dylan (36,500 persons in two evenings, January '74); Gene Autry (17,000 spectators in '51); Lawrence Welk (16,500 August '74) and the magnificent Lipizzan Stallions of Vienna (55,000 persons during four shows in 1964); and the beautiful Ice Follies and Ice Capades, each of which has drawn more than four mil-

Hockey night, with Boston and Montreal playing to a full house.
DAVID BIER

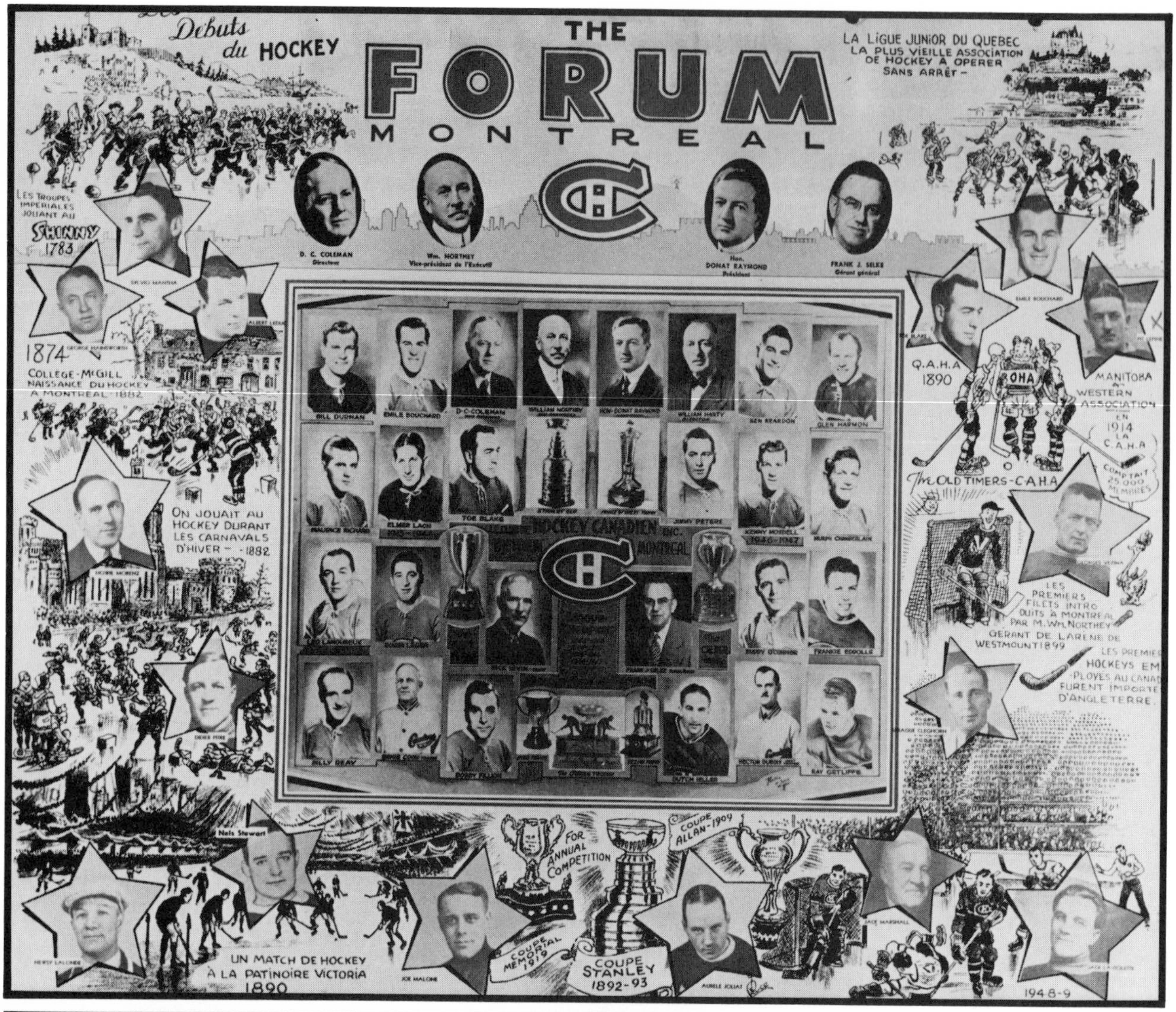

Top.
WILLIE DAGENAIS

Bottom, The Forum in 1949, with 1800-seat terraces added.
DAVID BIER

The new Forum, opened on November 2, 1968. DAVID BIER

lion spectators over forty years.

It would take an entire book to list the titles of all the shows and their stars whose names have appeared on the program of the old and the new Forum. We have merely attempted to give you a broad outline. We should not close, however, without mentioning that in addition to the above-mentioned shows, the Forum has, over the years, hosted almost every conceivable type of attraction, including The Passion in 1931; a visit by evangelist Aimée McPherson in 1934; symphony orchestras from all over the world; military tattoos; even the famous bands of Philip Souza and Creatore; the Midnight Mass, which was attended by more than 15,000 persons in 1951, '52 and '53 and—what a wonderful souvenir it brings to us all—the finals of boxing, basketball, volleyball and handball and the entire gymnastic events of the 1976 Olympics with Nadia Comaneci and the others when more than 300,000 people applauded the superb athletes that came from the four corners of the globe.

Bob Gainey attacks against Vancouver.
BOB FISHER

FORUM FACTS

Seating Capacity *16,109*

Capacity Including Standees *18,409*

Largest Professional Hockey Crowd *19,040—January 7, 1974. (Philadelphia) regular season.—For playoffs, May 8, 1973, 19,005 vs Chicago.*

Record Crowd at a Junior Hockey Game *18,838, February 23, 1969. Oshawa: 2—Junior Canadiens: 9.*

Dimensions of Rink *200 feet by 85 feet. Entire surface, other than players' benches enclosed with Herculite glass.*

Club Colours *Blue, White and Red. Two sets of uniforms: white base with red and blue trim worn at home; red base with blue and white trim worn on the road.*

Location of Press Box *suspended above ice along west side.*

Location of Radio and TV Booth *suspended above ice along east side.*

Maloney and Anderson of the Leafs against the Montreal defence.
JEAN GUY PARADIS

A BRIEF NHL HISTORY

The 1980-81 season is the 65th in the history of the National Hockey League. The chronological history of the League is as follows:

1917

The National Hockey League was organized in Montreal on November 22. Delegates representing Montreal Canadiens, Montreal Wanderers, Ottawa and Quebec were present. These four teams along with the Toronto Arenas were admitted into the League. Quebec held a franchise but decided not to operate it that season. Frank Calder was elected President and Secretary-Treasurer. First games in this new League were played December 19, 1917. Toronto was the only city that had artificial ice.

1917-18

Clubs played a 22-game schedule.

1918

When the Westmount Arena, home of the Wanderers, burned down, the team dropped out of the League.

1918-19

Clubs played an 18-game schedule.

1919

Quebec Bulldogs operated their franchise in the League. Toronto Arenas changed their name to Toronto St. Patricks.

1919-20

Clubs played a 24-game schedule.

1920

Hamilton Tigers replaced Quebec.

1924

Boston Bruins became first American Club to join the League and Montreal Maroons entered the ever-expanding circuit, giving Montreal two teams.

1924-25

Clubs play a 30-game schedule.

1925

Hamilton Tigers' franchise was sold to New York Americans for $75,000. The third United States Club, the Pittsburgh Pirates, entered the League.

1925-26

Schedule increased to 36 games per club.

1926

Three new United States teams, New York Rangers, Chicago Black Hawks and Detroit Cougars were admitted into the League. It was now a 10-club circuit, and was divided into two sections; Canadian Division had Toronto Maple Leafs (changed name from St. Pats to Maple Leafs), Ottawa Senators, Montreal Canadiens, Montreal Maroons and New York Americans. American Division consisted of Boston Bruins, New York Rangers, Chicago Black Hawks, Detroit Cougars and Pittsburgh Pirates. The Stanley Cup, most coveted prize in hockey, came into the exclusive control of the National Hockey League.

1926-27

Schedule increased to 44 games per club.

1930

Pittsburgh franchise was transferred to Philadelphia where a team known as the Quakers operated for one season. Detroit changed team's name from Cougars to Falcons.

1931

Philadelphia dropped out of League. Ottawa retired from League for one year.

1931-32

Schedule increased to 48 games per club.

1932

Ottawa resumed play for two seasons.

1933

Detroit changed nickname from Falcons to Red Wings.

1934

Ottawa franchise transferred to St. Louis. Team was called St. Louis Eagles and consisted of most of the Ottawa players of the previous season.

1935

St. Louis dropped out of the League, leaving the membership at eight teams.

1938

Montreal Maroons retired from the NHL.

1941

New York Americans changed name to Brooklyn Americans.

1942

Brooklyn Americans retired from League. This left the present six East Division teams in the League.

1942-43

Schedule increased to 50 games per club.

1943

Frank Calder, President of League since its inception, died in Montreal in February. Mervyn "Red" Dutton, former manager of New York Americans, succeeded him as president.

1946

Dutton retired as President of League prior to opening of 1946-47 season and was succeeded by Clarence S. Campbell.

1946-47

Players' Bonuses and Playoff Guarantees, 60-game schedule.

1947

New Constitutional Agreement entered into by all Member Clubs to continue in perpetuity.

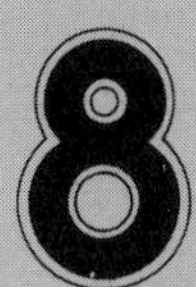

1947

First Annual All-Star Game played in Toronto, and former All-Stars recognized.

1948

National Hockey League Pension Society formed.

1949-50

70-game schedule introduced.

1954

Inter-league draft modified to provide effective means of assuring availability of players

1957

First 10 years of Pension Plan completed and Plan revised with greatly increased benefits. Players Playoff awards substantially increased. Owner-Player Council established.

1960

Arrangements completed with Canadian National Exhibition and City of Toronto for construction of Hockey Hall of Fame at C.N.E.

1961

Hockey Hall of Fame officially opened on August 26 by Prime Minister John Diefenbaker and U.S. Ambassador Livingston T. Merchant.

1967

Biggest single year in history of NHL. Six new United States teams were added, making the League a 12-team, two-division circuit. The new teams were California Seals, Los Angeles Kings, Minnesota North Stars, Philadelphia Flyers, Pittsburgh Penguins and St. Louis Blues, all operating in the West Division. Midway through season, California Seals changed name to Oakland Seals.

1967-68

Schedule increased to 74 games per club.

1968-69

Schedule increased to 76 games per club.

1969-70

NHL expanded to 14 teams with Buffalo Sabres and Vancouver Canucks joining the East Division and Chicago Black Hawks moving to the West Division.

1970-71

Schedule increased to 78 games per club. Oakland Seals changed name to California Golden Seals.

1971-72

NHL voted to expand to 16 teams for following season. New teams were to be located in Long Island and Atlanta.

1972-73

New York Islanders added to East Division and Atlanta Flames added to West Division.

1973-74

NHL franchises awarded to Washington and Kansas City, play commencing with the 1974-75 season.

1974-75

NHL splits into four divisions. New York Islanders to play in division with New York Rangers, Atlanta Flames, Philadelphia Flyers. Schedule increased to 80 games.

1975-76

NHL names Divisions for famous hockey stars. Clarence Campbell Conference: Lester Patrick Division and Conn Smythe Division. Prince of Wales Conference: James Norris Division and Charles Adams Division.

1976-77

For the first time since 1934, NHL franchises were shifted. The Cleveland Barons, formerly the California Seals, to play in the Adams Division, while the Colorado Rockies, late of Kansas City, to play in Smythe Division.

1977-78

Clarence S. Campbell, President of the League since 1946, retired; John A. Ziegler, Jr. elected President.

1978-79

The first time two NHL franchises merged. The Cleveland Barons ceased operations and merged with the Minnesota North Stars with the North Stars moving to the Prince of Wales Conference and playing in the Adams Division. Intra-Divisional play increased from six to eight games. The 1978-79 NHL All-Star team to play the Soviet All-Stars at mid-season.

1979-1980

The NHL expands to 21 teams with the addition of four WHA teams. The new franchises are: Hartford Whalers; Quebec Nordiques; Winnipeg Jets and Edmonton Oilers.

9

RECORDS AND HONORS

NHL Team Records—Regular Season

Most points one season 132
Canadiens, 1976-77 (80 game schedule).

Fewest points, one season 65
Canadiens, 1950-51 (70 game schedule).

Most goals against, one season 240
Canadiens, 1973-74 (78 game schedule).

Fewest goals against, one season 131
Canadiens, 1955-56 (70 game schedule).

Longest winning streak 12
Canadiens, 1967-68.

Longest undefeated streak 28
Canadiens, 1977-78

Fewest losses, one season 5
Canadiens, 1943-44 (50 game schedule).

Canadiens, 1972-73 (78 game schedule), **10**

Canadiens, 1976-77 (80 game schedule), **8**

Canadiens, 1977-78 (80 game schedule), **10**

Most wins in one season 60
Canadiens, 1976-77.

Fewest wins, one season 25
Canadiens, 1950-51 (70 game schedule).

Most defeats, one season 33
Canadiens, 1939-40 (48 game schedule).

Fewest losses, one season 8
Canadiens, 1976-77 (80 game schedule).

Fewest home losses, one season 0
Canadiens, 1943-44 (25 game schedule).

Fewest home losses, one season (minimum 70 game schedule) 1
Canadiens, 1976-77 (80 game schedule).

Most wins on the road, one season 27
Canadiens, 1976-77—1977-78.

Fewest road losses, one season 3
Canadiens, 1928-29 (22 games)

Fewest road losses, one season (new game schedule) 6
Canadiens, 1972-73 (39 games)
Canadiens, 1974-75 (40 games)
Canadiens, 1977-78 (40 games)

Longest undefeated road record 23
Canadiens, Nov. 27, 1974 to March 12, 1975 (14-0-9)

Longest losing streak 10

Longest winless streak 12
Canadiens, 1935.

Most tie games, one season 23
Canadiens, 1962-63 (70 game schedule).

Fewest ties, one season 8
Canadiens, 1965-66 (70 game schedule).

Fewest home ties, one season 0
Canadiens, 1936-37 (24 game schedule).
Canadiens, 1955-56 (35 game schedule), **1**
Canadiens, 1965-66 (35 game schedule), **1**

Fewest road ties, one season 0
Canadiens, 1926-27 (22 game schedule).
Canadiens, 1939-40 (24 game schedule).

Longest road winning record
Canadiens, 1977-78, **8**

Longest undefeated home record 34
Canadiens from Nov. 1, 1976 to April 3, 1977: 28 wins, 6 ties.

Most shutouts, one season 22
Canadiens, 1928-29 (44 game schedule), **22**

Most penalty minutes, one season 1271
Canadiens, 1970-71 (78 game schedule).

Most goals, one season 387
Canadiens, 1976-77 (80 game schedule).

Fewest goals, one season 155
Canadiens, 1952-53 (70 game schedule).

Most goals against, one season 240
Canadiens, 1973-74 (78 game schedule).
Canadiens, 1979-80 (80 game schedule).

Fewest goals against, one season (Minimum 70-game schedule) 131
Canadiens, 1955-56.

Most goals, both teams, one game 21
Canadiens, Toronto St-Patricks, at Montreal, Jan. 10, 1920. Montreal won 14-7.

Most goals, one team, one game 16
Canadiens, March 3, 1920, at Montreal, defeated Quebec Bulldogs 16-3.

Most goals, one game, one player 6
Newsy Lalonde, January 10, 1920.

Fastest six goals, both teams 3 min. 15 sec.
Canadiens, Toronto Maple Leafs, at Montreal, Jan. 4, 1944, first period Montreal scored 4 goals, Toronto 2. Montreal won the game 6-3.

Fastest four goals, both teams 1 min. 5 sec.
Canadiens, Toronto Maple Leafs, at Toronto, March 16, 1966, second period. Scorers were: Jean Beliveau (Montreal) 5:00; Dave Keon (Toronto) 5:21; Jean Beliveau, 5:43; Ralph Backstrom (Montreal) 6:05. Montreal won the game 7-2.

Fastest three goals, both teams 18 sec.
Canadiens, New York Rangers, at Montreal, Dec. 12, 1963, first period. Scorers were: Dave Balon (Montreal) 0:58; Gilles Tremblay (Montreal) 1:04; Camille Henry (New York) 1:16. Montreal won the game 6-4.

Fastest three goals from start of game and period, both teams 1 min. 16 sec.
Canadiens, New York Rangers, at Montreal, Dec. 12, 1963, first period. Scorers were: Dave Balon (Montreal) 0:58; Gilles Tremblay (Montreal) 1:04; Camille Henry (New York) 1:16. Montreal the won game 6-4.

Highest goal per game average, one season 5.38
In 1919-20, 129 goals in 24 games.

Lowest goals against average, one season 0.98
In 1928-29, 43 goals allowed in 44 games.

The most points between a champion team and a second-place team, regular season 51
Canadiens 1977-78 (80 games).

Most power play goals, one season 92
Canadiens, 1974-75 (80 games).

The most 40 goal scorers, one season 3
1979-80 (record equalled).
Guy Lafleur: 50
Pierre Larouche: 50
Steve Shutt: 47

The most 50 goal scorers, one season 2
1976-77 (record equalled).
Guy Lafleur: 56
Steve Shutt: 60
1979-80 (record equalled).
Guy Lafleur: 50
Pierre Larouche: 50

NHL Team Records—Playoffs

Most Stanley Cup championships 22
Canadiens: 1916, 1924, 1930, 1931, 1944, 1946, 1953, 1956, 1957, 1958, 1959, 1960, 1965, 1966, 1968, 1969, 1971, 1973, 1976, 1977, 1978, 1979.

Most final series appearances 26

Most years in playoffs 50

Most consecutive Stanley Cup championships 5
Canadiens: 1956, 1957, 1958, 1959, 1960.

Most consecutive final series appearances 10
Canadiens, 1951-1960, inclusive.

Most consecutive playoff appearances 21
Canadiens, 1949-1969, inclusive.

Most goals, both teams, six-game series 56
Canadiens vs Chicago in 1973 final. Canadiens won best-of-seven series 4-2, outscoring Chicago 33-23.

Most goals, one team, six-game series 33
Canadiens in 1973 final. Canadiens defeated Chicago 4-2 in best-of-seven series, outscoring Chicago 33-23.

Most goals, one team, in a 3-game series 18
The Canadiens in 1980 preliminary round. Canadiens defeated the Hartford Whalers 3-0 in best-of-five series, outscoring Hartford 18-8.

Fewest goals, one team, four-game series 2
Canadiens in 1952 final outscored by Detroit Red Wings 11-2. Detroit won best-of-seven series 4-0.

Most goals, both teams, one game 15
Canadiens and Chicago at Montreal, May 8, 1973. Chicago 8, Canadiens 7. Canadiens won best-of-seven final 4-2.

Most goals, one team, one game 11
Canadiens at Montreal, March 30, 1944. Canadiens 11, Toronto 0. Canadiens won best-of-seven semi-final 4-1.

Most goals, both teams, one period 8
Canadiens vs Chicago at Montreal, May 8, 1973, in 2nd period. Canadiens scored 3 goals and Chicago 5.

Most goals, one team, one period 7
Canadiens, March 30, 1944, at Montreal in third period against Toronto during 11-0 win.

Most overtime games, final series 5
Toronto and Canadiens in 1951. Toronto defeated Canadiens 4-1 in best-of-seven series.

Most consecutive playoff game victories 11
Canadiens: Streak began April 16, 1959, at Toronto, with 3-2 win in fourth game of final series, won by Canadiens 4-1, and March 23, 1961, when Chicago defeated Canadiens 4-3 in second game of semi-final series. Included in streak were eight straight victories in 1960.
Canadiens: Streak began April 28, 1968, at Montreal, with 4-3 win in fifth game of semi-final series, won by Canadiens 4-1, and ended April 17, 1969, at Boston, when Bruins defeated them 5-0 in third game of semi-final series. Included in the streak were four straight wins over New York in a 1969 quarter-final series.
Canadiens: Streak started May 6, 1976, at Montreal, with 5-2 win in fifth game of semi-final against New York Islanders won by Montreal 4-1. It continued with a 4-game victory against Philadelphia in the 1976 finals and a 4-game win against St. Louis in the 1977 quarter-final. Canadiens then won first 2 games of the 1977 semi-final against the Islanders; the streak ended April 28th in Uniondale by a 5-3 loss.

Most consecutive wins final series games (1977-78) 11
Those 11 wins are:
May 8, 1973, 1 game.
May 1976, 4 games.
May 1977, 4 games
May 1978, 2 games.
The previous record (10) was held by the Toronto Maple Leafs.

Most power-play goals, one team, one playoff year 21
Canadiens in 1965. 11 against Toronto in best-of-seven semi-final series, won by Montreal 4-2. 10 against Chicago in best-of-seven final, won by Montreal 4-3.

Most power-play goals, both teams, one game 6
Detroit Red Wings, Canadiens, March 23, 1939, at Detroit. Detroit had four power-play goals, Montreal two. Detroit won the game 7-3.

Fastest two shorthanded goals, one game 24 sec.
April 23, 1978. Canadiens vs Detroit, in Detroit, Doug Risebrough and Bob Gainey scored.

Fastest three goals, both teams 38 sec.
Toronto and Montreal at Toronto, April 13, 1965, Red Kelly of Toronto scored at 3:11 of first period, John Ferguson of Montreal at 3:32 and Ron Ellis of Toronto at 3:49. Montreal won the game 4-3 in overtime, and best-of-seven semi-final series 4-2.

Fastest five goals, one team 3 min. 36 sec.
Canadiens at Montreal, March 30, 1944, against Toronto. Toe Blake scored at 7:58 of third period and 8:37, Maurice Richard at 9:17, Ray Getliffe at 10:33 and Buddy O'Connor at 11:34. Canadiens won the game 11-0, and best-of-seven semi-final 4-1.

Individual Records—Playoffs

Most goals in playoffs 82
Maurice Richard.

Most goals in final series 7
Jean Beliveau, in 1956, in 5 games against Detroit.

Most goals, one game 5
Maurice Richard, March 23, 1944, at Montreal. Final score: Canadiens 5, Toronto 1.

Most goals, one period 3
Maurice Richard, March 23, 1944, at Montreal against Toronto, second period. Final score: Canadiens 5, Toronto 1. March 29, 1945, at Montreal against Toronto, third period. Final score: Canadiens 10, Toronto 3. April 6, 1957, at Montreal against Boston, second period. Final score: Canadiens 5, Boston 1.
Jacques Lemaire, April 20, 1971, at Montreal against Minnesota, second period.
Final score: Montreal 7, Minnesota 2.

Most power-play goals, playoff career 26
Jean Beliveau, in 17 years.

Most power-play goals, one period 2
Maurice Richard, April 6, 1954, first period at Detroit in 3-1 win by Montreal.
Bernard Geoffrion, April 7, 1955, first period at Montreal in 4-2 win against Detroit Red Wings.
Gilles Tremblay, April 14, 1966, second period at Toronto in 4-1 win by Montreal.
Jean Beliveau, April 20, 1968, second period at Montreal in 4-1 win against Chicago Black Hawks.

Most three-goals-or-more games 7
Maurice Richard. Four games of three goals in each; two of four in each; one of five.

Most three-goal games, one playoff year 2
Maurice Richard, 1944. Five goals against Toronto, March 23, at Montreal. Montreal won 5-1. Three goals against Chicago, April 7, at Chicago. Montreal won 3-1.

Most points in playoffs 176
Jean Beliveau, 79 goals, 97 assists.

Most points in final series 12
Yvan Cournoyer, Jacques Lemaire, 1973.

Most points, one game 6
Guy Lafleur, on April 11, 1977, at Montreal, during 7-2 win over the St. Louis Blues. Lafleur had 3 goals and 3 assists.
Dickie Moore, March 25, 1954, at Montreal during 8-1 win over Boston. Moore had two goals, four assists.

Most points, one period 4
Maurice Richard, March 29, 1945, at Montreal against Toronto. Third period, three goals, one assist. Final score: Canadiens 10, Toronto 3.
Dickie Moore, March 25, 1954, at Montreal against Boston. First period, two goals, two assists. Final score: Canadiens 8, Boston 1.

Most assists in playoffs 97
Jean Beliveau.

Most assists in final series 9
Jacques Lemaire, in 1973 against Chicago.

Most assists, one game 5
Toe Blake, March 23, 1944, at Montreal. Final score: Canadiens 5, Toronto 1.
Maurice Richard, March 27, 1956, at Montreal. Final score: Canadiens 7, Rangers 0.
Bert Olmstead, March 30, 1957, at Montreal. Final score: Canadiens 8, Rangers 3.

Most assists, one period 3
Toe Blake, March 23, 1944, at Montreal against Toronto, second period. Final score: Canadiens 5, Toronto 1. April 13, 1944, at Montreal against Chicago, third period. Final score: Canadiens 5, Chicago 4.
Elmer Lach, March 30, 1944, at Montreal against Toronto, third period. Final score: Canadiens 11, Toronto 0.
Jean Beliveau, March 25, 1954, at Montreal against Boston, first period. Final score: Canadiens 8, Boston 1.
Maurice Richard, March 27, 1956, at Montreal against Rangers, second period. Final score: Canadiens 7, Rangers 0.
Doug Harvey, April 6, 1957, at Montreal against Boston, second period. Final score: Canadiens 5, Boston 1. April 2, 1959, at Montreal against Chicago, first period. Final score: Canadiens 4, Chicago 2.
Dickie Moore, April 2, 1959, at Montreal against Chicago, first period. Final score: Canadiens 4, Chicago 2.
Henri Richard, April 7, 1960, at Montreal against Toronto, first period. Final score: Canadiens 4, Toronto 2.
Robert Rousseau, May 1, 1965, at Montreal against Chicago, first period. Final score: Canadiens 4, Chicago 1.
Jean Beliveau, April 27, 1971, at Montreal against Minnesota, third period. Final score: Montreal 6, Minnesota 1.

Most game-winning goals 18
Maurice Richard, in 15 playoff years.

Most overtime goals 6
Maurice Richard, 1 in 1946, 3 in 1951, 1 in 1957, 1 in 1958.

Most overtime goals, one playoff year 3
Maurice Richard, in 1951. He scored two against Detroit in semi-final, won by Montreal 4-2, and one against Toronto in final, won by Toronto 4-1.

Canadiens—All-Time Records

	At MONTREAL							AWAY			
OPPONENT	**GP**	**W**	**L**	**T**	**GF**	**GA**	**PTS**	**GP**	**W**	**L**	**T**
Atlanta	17	11	2	4	56	28	26	17	12	2	3
Boston	255	145	71	39	855	565	329	256	93	117	46
Buffalo	25	16	5	4	117	75	36	25	8	9	8
Chicago	247	153	47	47	956	574	353	247	117	82	48
Colorado	12	10	1	1	64	31	21	12	11	1	0
Detroit	253	152	60	41	871	557	345	254	88	117	49
Edmonton	2	2	0	0	9	7	4	2	1	1	0
Hartford	2	0	0	2	9	9	2	2	1	0	1
Los Angeles	37	24	5	8	169	91	56	37	24	7	6
Minnesota	31	22	4	5	140	76	49	31	20	7	4
N.Y. Islanders	17	11	3	3	70	52	25	18	9	7	2
N.Y. Rangers	248	165	51	32	970	558	362	247	99	101	47
Philadelphia	31	20	5	6	113	74	46	31	15	9	7
Pittsburgh	37	33	1	3	203	87	69	37	21	9	7
Québec	2	2	0	0	8	2	4	2	0	1	1
St. Louis	31	24	5	2	140	70	50	31	17	6	8
Toronto	294	179	79	36	1037	710	394	294	100	150	44
Vancouver	24	21	2	1	125	55	43	23	16	1	6
Washington	18	18	0	0	113	27	36	18	14	1	3
Winnipeg	2	2	0	0	10	0	4	2	1	1	0
Clubs défunts Defunct clubs	231	148	58	25	779	469	321	230	98	97	35
TOTALS	1816	1158	399	259	6814	4117	2575	1816	765	726	32[illegible]

GF	GA	PTS	TOTAL GP	W	L	T	GF	GA	PTS
67	43	27	34	23	4	7	123	71	53
59	741	232	511	238	188	85	1514	1306	561
70	62	24	50	24	14	12	187	137	60
80	651	282	494	270	129	95	1636	1225	635
60	27	22	24	21	2	1	124	58	43
37	711	225	507	240	177	90	1508	1268	570
10	8	2	4	3	1	0	19	15	6
12	7	3	4	1	0	3	21	16	5
145	102	54	74	48	12	14	314	193	110
15	68	44	62	42	11	9	255	144	93
58	54	20	35	20	10	5	128	106	45
713	712	245	495	264	152	79	1683	1270	607
96	70	37	62	35	14	13	209	144	83
140	103	49	74	54	10	10	343	190	118
8	9	1	4	2	1	1	16	11	5
116	82	42	62	41	11	10	256	152	92
734	876	244	588	279	229	80	1771	1586	638
95	51	38	47	37	3	7	220	106	81
89	34	31	36	32	1	3	202	61	67
6	9	2	4	3	1	0	16	9	6
586	606	231	461	246	155	60	1365	1075	552
5096	5026	1855	3632	1923	1125	584	11910	9143	4430

Most short-handed goals, one playoff series 2
Serge Savard, in 1968 final series against St. Louis, won by Montreal 4-0.

Most playoff games appeared in by a goaltender, one playoff year 20
Ken Dryden, 1971.

Most times on Stanley Cup winning team 11
Henri Richard in 1956, 1957, 1958, 1959, 1960, 1965, 1966, 1968, 1969, 1971, 1973.

Most playoff games career 180
Henri Richard.

Most consecutive years in playoffs 16
Jean Beliveau (1954 to 1969 inclusive).

Individual Records—Regular Season

CENTER

Most goals, career 507
Jean Beliveau, from 1950-51 to 1970-71

Most goals, one season 50
Pierre Larouche, 1979-80

Most assists, career, including playoffs 809
Jean Beliveau, from 1950-51 to 1970-71, 712 season, 97 playoffs.

Most assists, one season 82
Peter Mahovlich, 1974-75

Most assists, one game 6
Elmer Lach, February 6, 1943, at Montreal. Montreal 8, Boston 3.

Most assists, one period 4
Buddy O'Connor, November 8, 1942, at Montreal, third period.

Most points, career, including playoffs 1395
Jean Beliveau, from 1950-51 to 1970-71, 1219 season, 176 playoffs.

Most points, one season 117
Peter Mahovlich, 1974-75.

Most seasons with the team 20
Henri Richard.

Most games with the team 1256
Henri Richard

Most consecutive games streak 400
Doug Jarvis

Most penalty minutes, career 1029
Jean Béliveau, from 1950-51 to 1970-71.

Most penalty minutes, one season 198
Doug Risebrough, 1974-75

RIGHT WING

Most goals, career, including playoffs 626
Maurice Richard, from 1942-43 to 1959-60, 544 season, 82 playoffs.

Most goals in one season 60
Guy Lafleur, 1977-78.

Most assists, career 536
Guy Lafleur, from 1971-72 to 1979-80.

Most assists in one season 80
Guy Lafleur, 1976-77.

Most points, career 965
Maurice Richard, from 1942-43 to 1959-60.

Most points, one season including playoffs 162
Guy Lafleur, 1976-77, 136 season, 26 playoffs.

Most points, one game 8
Maurice Richard, December 28, 1944, at Montreal, 5 goals, 3 assists.
Montreal 9, Detroit 1.

Most consecutive 20 or more goal seasons 14
Maurice Richard, from 1943-44 to 1956-57.

Most 50 or more goals season 6
Guv Lafleur, 1974-75 to 1979-80.

Most consecutive 50 or more goals seasons 6
Guy Lafleur, 1974-75 to 1979-80.

Most 100 or more points seasons 6
Guy Lafleur, 1974-75 to 1979-80 (record equalled).

Most consecutive 100 or more points seasons 6
Guy Lafleur, 1974-75 to 1979-80 (record equalled).

Longest consecutive point scoring streak 28
Guy Lafleur, 1976-77.

Fastest goal from start of period 4 sec.
Claude Provost, Nov. 9, 1957, at Montreal, second period, Montreal 4, Boston 2.

Most penalty minutes, career, including playoffs 1473
Maurice Richard, from 1942-43 to 1959-60, 1285 season, 188 playoffs.

Most penalty minutes, one season 125
Maurice Richard, 1954-55.

Most goals by a player in his first NHL game 3
Alex Smart, Jan. 14, 1943.

LEFT WING

Highest goals per game average, one season 2.20
Joe Malone, 1917-18, 44 goals in 20 games.

Longest consecutive goal-scoring streak 14
Joe Malone, 1917-18 (35 goals in that streak).

Most goals, career 291
Steve Shutt, from 1972-73 to 1979-80.

Most goals in one season 60
Steve Shutt, 1976-77.

Most assists, career 340
Dickie Moore, from 1951-52 to 1962-63.

Most assists, one season 56
Bert Olmstead, 1955-56.

Most points, career 594
Dickie Moore, from 1951-52 to 1962-63.

Most points, one season 105
Steve Shutt, 1976-77.

Most points, one game 8
Bert Olmstead, January 9, 1954, at Montreal, 4 goals, 4 assists. Montreal 12, Chicago 1.

Most penalty minutes, career 1214
John Ferguson, from 1963-64 to 1970-71.

Most penalty minutes, one season 185
John Ferguson, 1968-69.

DEFENSEMEN

Most goals, career 164
Guy Lapointe, from 1970-71 to 1979-80.

Most goals, one season 28
Guy Lapointe, 1974-75.

Most goals, one game, by a defenseman 4
Sprague Cleghorn, January 14, 1922, at Montreal. Montreal 10, Hamilton Tigers 6.
Newsy Lalonde, January 11, 1919, at Montreal. Montreal 13, Toronto Arenas 4.
Newsy Lalonde, March 3, 1920, at Quebec. Canadiens 16, Quebec Bulldogs 3.
Harry Cameron, March 3, 1920. Canadiens 16, Quebec Bulldogs 3.

Most assists, career 378
Guy Lapointe, 1970-71 to 1979-80.

Most assists, one season 66
Larry Robinson, 1976-77.

Most assists, one period 4
Phil Watson, March 18, 1944, at Montreal, third period. Montreal 11, New York Rangers 2.
Jean-Claude Tremblay, December 29, 1962, at Montreal, second period. Montreal 5, Detroit 1.

Most points, career 542
Guy Lapointe, 1970-71 to 1979-80.

Most points, one season 85
Larry Robinson, 1976-77.

Most penalty minutes, career 1042
Doug Harvey, from 1947-48 to 1960-61.

Most penalty minutes, one season 167
Lou Fontinato, 1961-62.

GOALTENDERS

Most shutouts, career 75
George Hainsworth, from 1926-27 to 1932-33.

Most shutouts, one season 22
George Hainsworth, 1928-29.

Longest shutout sequence 309 min. 21 sec.
Bill Durnan, 1948-49 (Feb. 24 to March 9, 1949).

Most assists by a goaltender, one season 4
Ken Dryden, 1972-73.
Michel Larocque, 1977-78.

Bert Olmstead scores against Harry Lumley of the Leafs as Ted Kennedy looks on, 1951.
HOCKEY HALL OF FAME, TORONTO

Bert Olmstead déjoue Harry Lumley des Leafs sous l'oeil désappointé de Ted Kennedy, en 1951.
TEMPLE DE LA RENOMMÉE, TORONTO

Les Meneurs Pour Les Points

Career Point Leaders

	PJ GP	B G	A A	PTS PTS
1. Jean BELIVEAU	1125	507	712	1219
2. Henri RICHARD	1256	358	688	1046
3. Maurice RICHARD	978	544	421	965
* 4. Guy LAFLEUR	677	405	536	941
5. Yvan COURNOYER	968	428	435	863
6. Jacques LEMAIRE	853	366	469	835
7. Bernard GEOFFRION	766	371	388	759
8. Elmer LACH	664	215	408	623
9. Dickie MOORE	654	254	340	594
10. Claude PROVOST	1005	254	335	589
11. Peter MAHOVLICH	581	223	346	569
*12. Steve SHUTT	586	291	261	552
*13. Guy LAPOINTE	697	164	378	542
14. Hector "Toe" BLAKE	577	235	292	527
15. Robert ROUSSEAU	643	200	322	522
16. Ralph BACKSTROM	844	215	287	502
17. Aurèle JOLIAT	654	269	190	459
18. Doug HARVEY	890	76	371	447
*19. Larry ROBINSON	570	94	325	419
20. Howie MORENZ	550	256	156	412
*21. Serge SAVARD	840	96	299	395
22. Bert OLMSTEAD	507	105	281	386
23. Jean-Claude TREMBLAY	794	57	306	363
*24. Yvon LAMBERT	533	159	202	361
25. Gilles TREMBLAY	509	168	162	330
26. Frank MAHOVLICH	263	129	181	310
27. John FERGUSON	500	145	158	303
*28. Réjean HOULE	491	121	181	302
29. Ken MOSDELL	627	132	155	287
30. Jacques LAPERRIERE	691	40	242	282
31. Billy REAY	475	103	162	265
32. Johnny GAGNON	—	120	141	261
33. Don MARSHALL	585	114	140	254
34. Jean-Guy TALBOT	791	36	209	245

*Actif/active

Les Meneurs Pour Les Buts

Career Goal Leaders

	1. Maurice RICHARD	544
	2. Jean BELIVEAU	507
	3. Yvan COURNOYER	428
*	4. Guy LAFLEUR	405
	5. Bernard GEOFFRION	371
	6. Jacques LEMAIRE	366
	7. Henri RICHARD	358
*	8. Steve SHUTT	291
	9. Aurèle JOLIAT	269
	10. Howie MORENZ	256
	11. Dickie MOORE	254
	12. Claude PROVOST	254
	13. Hector "Toe" BLAKE	235
	14. Peter MAHOVLICH	223
	15. Elmer LACH	215
	16. Ralph BACKSTROM	215
	17. Robert ROUSSEAU	200
	18. Gilles TREMBLAY	168
*	19. Guy LAPOINTE	164
*	20. Yvon LAMBERT	159
	21. John FERGUSON	145
	22. Alfred "Pit" LEPINE	143
	23. Ken MOSDELL	132
	24. Frank MAHOVLICH	129
	25. Ed "Newsy" LALONDE	124
*	26. Réjean HOULE	121
	27. Johnny GAGNON	120
	28. Claude LAROSE	117
	29. Don MARSHALL	114
*	30. Mario TREMBLAY	106
	31. Bert OLMSTEAD	105
	32. Floyd CURRY	105

*Actif/active

Les Meneurs Pour Les Assistances

Career Assist Leaders

	1. Jean BELIVEAU	712
	2. Henri RICHARD	688
*	3. Guy LAFLEUR	536
	4. Jacques LEMAIRE	469
	5. Yvan COURNOYER	435
	6. Maurice RICHARD	421
	7. Elmer LACH	408
	8. Bernard GEOFFRION	388
*	9. Guy LAPOINTE	378
	10. Doug HARVEY	371
	11. Peter MAHOVLICH	346
	12. Dickie MOORE	340
	13. Claude PROVOST	335
*	14. Larry ROBINSON	325
	15. Robert ROUSSEAU	322
	16. J.-Claude TREMBLAY	306
*	17. Serge SAVARD	299
	18. Hector "Toe" BLAKE	292
	19. Ralph BACKSTROM	287
	20. Bert OLMSTEAD	281
*	21. Steve SHUTT	261
	22. Jacques LAPERRIERE	242
	23. Jean-Guy TALBOT	209
*	24. Yvon LAMBERT	202
	25. Aurèle JOLIAT	190
	26. Tom JOHNSON	183
	27. Frank MAHOVLICH	181
*	28. Réjean HOULE	181
	29. Billy REAY	162
	30. Gilles TREMBLAY	162
	31. John FERGUSON	158
	32. Howie MORENZ	156
	33. Buddy O'CONNOR	155
	34. Ken MOSDELL	155

*Actif/active

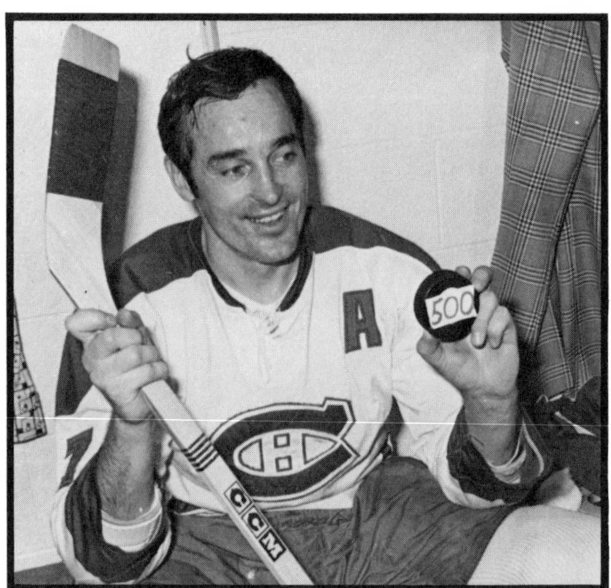

Frank Mahovlich, qui a marqué son cinq centième but pour les Canadiens.
DENIS BRODEUR, MONTRÉAL
Frank Mahovlich, who scored his 500th career goal with the Canadiens.
DENIS BRODEUR, MONTREAL

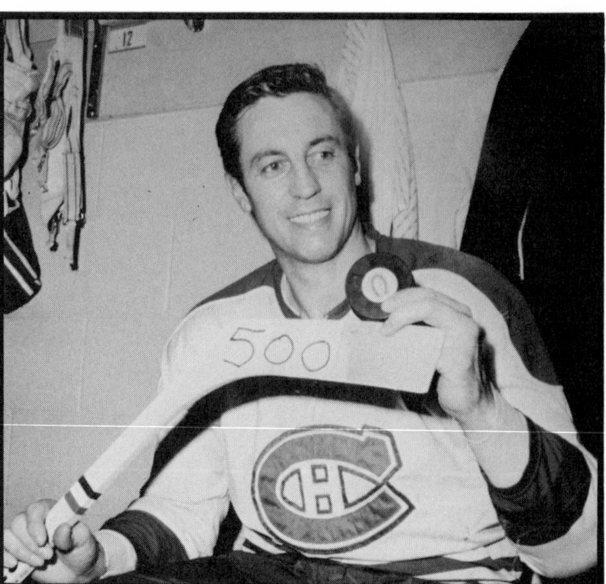

Jean Béliveau qui a marqué plus de 500 buts dans sa carrière.
FORUM DE MONTRÉAL
Jean Beliveau, who scored more than 500 goals in his career.
MONTREAL FORUM

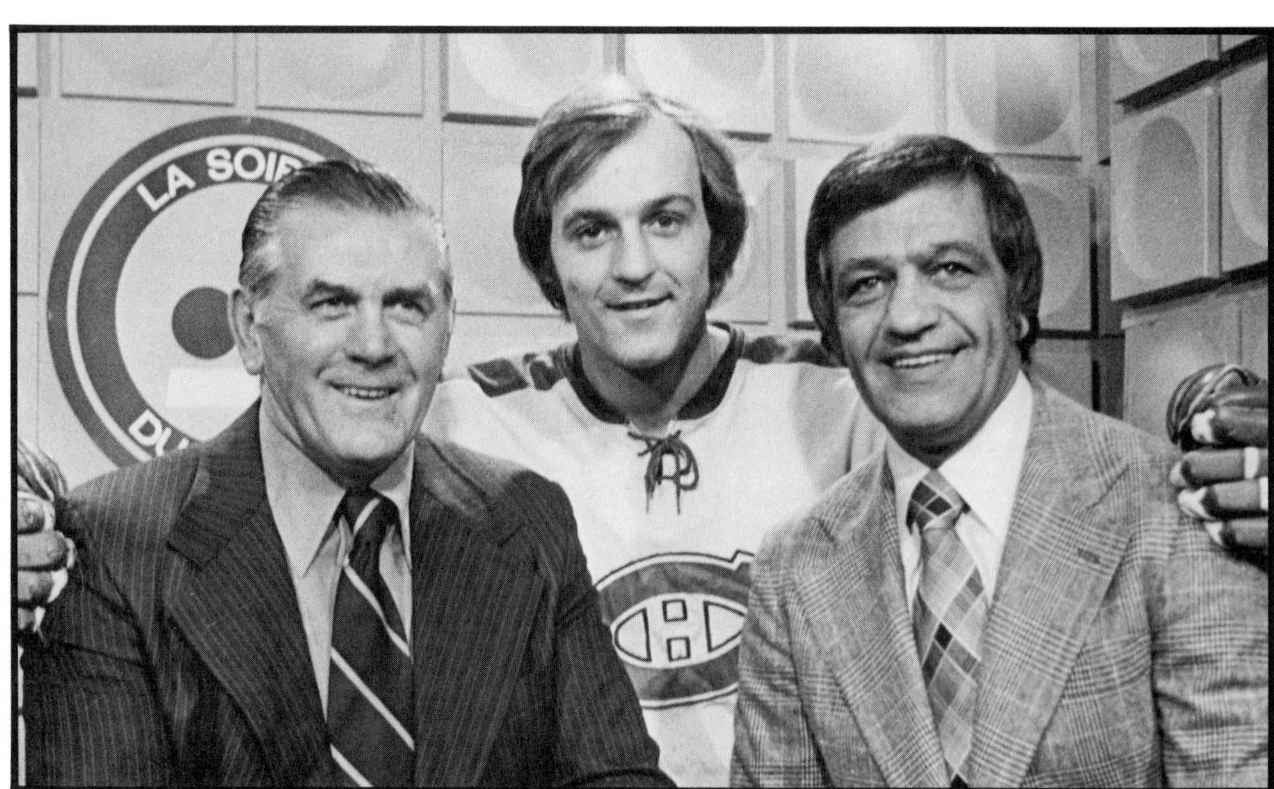

Maurice Richard, Guy Lafleur, Boom Boom Geoffrion, les trois premiers compteurs de cinquante buts du Canadien.
Maurice Richard, Guy Lafleur, Boom Boom Geoffrion, the first three Canadiens to score fifty goals.
DENIS BRODEUR, MONTRÉAL DENIS BRODEUR, MONTREAL

Les Meneurs Pour Les Points en Series Éliminatoires

Career Playoff Point Leaders

	PJ GP	B G	A A	PTS PTS
1. Jean BELIVEAU	162	79	97	176
2. Jacques LEMAIRE	145	61	78	139
3. Henri RICHARD	180	49	80	129
4. Yvan COURNOYER	147	64	63	127
5. Maurice RICHARD	133	82	44	126
* 6. Guy LAFLEUR	101	55	69	124
7. Bernard GEOFFRION	127	56	59	115
8. Dickie MOORE	112	38	56	94
* 9. Steve SHUTT	79	40	45	85
10. Peter MAHOVLICH	86	30	41	71
*11. Larry ROBINSON	96	16	52	68
*12. Guy LAPOINTE	111	25	43	68
*13. Serge SAVARD	120	19	49	68
14. Doug HARVEY	123	8	59	67
15. J.-Claude TREMBLAY	108	14	51	65
16. Elmer LACH	79	19	45	64
17. Claude PROVOST	126	25	38	63
18. Hector "Toe" BLAKE	57	25	37	62
19. Frank MAHOVLICH	49	27	31	58
20. Ralph BACKSTROM	100	22	26	48
*21. Yvon LAMBERT	83	24	22	46
22. Robert ROUSSEAU	78	16	29	45
*23. Réjean HOULE	83	13	30	43
24. Dick DUFF	60	16	26	42
*25. Bob GAINEY	85	16	26	42
26. Bert OLMSTEAD	86	8	33	41
27. Floyd CURRY	91	23	17	40
28. John FERGUSON	85	20	18	38
29. Emile BOUCHARD	113	11	21	32
30. Jacques LAPERRIERE	88	9	22	31
31. Aurèle JOLIAT	—	13	17	30
*32. Doug JARVIS	64	10	20	30
33. Ken MOSDELL	79	16	13	29
34. Billy REAY	63	13	16	29
35. Claude LAROSE	82	11	16	27
*36. Doug RISEBROUGH	66	8	19	27

*Actif/active

Les Meneurs Pour Les Points en Series Éliminatoires

Career Playoff Point Leaders

	PJ GP	B G	A A	PTS PTS
37. Phil GOYETTE	52	12	14	26
*38. Mario TREMBLAY	65	8	18	26
39. Buddy O'CONNOR	35	10	15	25
*40. Pierre MONDOU	39	7	17	24
41. Howie MORENZ	45	14	9	23
42. Johnny GAGNON	—	12	11	23
43. Gilles TREMBLAY	48	9	14	23
44. Tom JOHNSON	111	8	15	23
45. Murph CHAMBERLAIN	42	11	11	22
46. Marc TARDIF	40	11	10	21
47. Murray WILSON	52	5	14	19
48. Jean-Guy TALBOT	105	3	16	19
49. Jim ROBERTS	101	11	7	18
50. Calum MACKAY	38	5	13	18
51. Don MARSHALL	78	5	13	18
52. Ed "Newsy" LALONDE	—	16	1	17
53. Terry HARPER	94	4	12	16
54. Dollard ST. LAURENT	59	2	14	16
55. Glen HARMON	53	5	10	15
*56. Pierre LAROUCHE	20	4	11	15
57. Ray GETLIFFE	—	6	7	13
*58. Mark NAPIER	22	5	8	13
59. Pierre BOUCHARD	76	3	10	13
60. Ted HARRIS	62	1	12	13
61. Alfred "Pit" LEPINE	—	7	5	12
62. Bob FILLION	28	7	4	11
*63. Rick CHARTRAW	51	7	4	11
64. Albert LEDUC	31	5	6	11
65. Paul MEGER	35	3	8	11
66. Wildor LAROCHELLE	—	6	4	10

*Actif/active

Instructeur Dick Irvin.
TEMPLE DE LA RENOMMÉE, TORONTO
Coach Dick Irvin.
HOCKEY HALL OF FAME, TORONTO

Les Canadiens au Temple de la Renommée

Canadiens in the Hall of Fame

AURÈLE JOLIAT
Avril/April 1945

HOWIE MORENZ
Avril/April 1945

GEORGES VÉZINA
Avril/April 1945

NEWSY LALONDE
Juin/June 1950

JOE MALONE
Juin/June 1950

SPRAGUE CLEGHORN
Avril/April 1958

HERB GARDINER
Avril/April 1958

SYLVIO MANTHA
Sept./Sept. 1960

JOE HALL
Juin/June 1961

GEORGE HAINSWORTH
Juin/June 1961

MAURICE RICHARD
Juin/June 1961

JACK LAVIOLETTE
Août/August 1962

DIDIER PITRE
Août/August 1962

BILL DURNAN
Juin/June 1964

BABE SEIBERT
Juin/June 1964

HECTOR "TOE" BLAKE
Juin/June 1966

EMILE BOUCHARD
Juin/June 1966

ELMER LACH
Juin/June 1966

KENNY REARDON
Juin/June 1966

TOM JOHNSON
Juin/June 1970

JEAN BÉLIVEAU
Juin/June 1972

BERNARD GEOFFRION
Juin/June 1972

DOUGLAS HARVEY
Juin/June 1973

DICKIE MOORE
Juin/June 1974

JACQUES PLANTE
Juin/June 1978

HENRI RICHARD
Juin/June 1979

LORNE WORSLEY
Juin/June 1980

BATISSEURS/Builders

WILLIAM NORTHEY
Avril/April 1945

HON. DONAT RAYMOND
Avril/April 1958

FRANK SELKE
Sept./Sept. 1960

J. AMBROSE O'BRIEN
Juin/June 1962

LÉO DANDURAND
Avril/April 1963

TOMMY GORMAN
Avril/April 1963

HON. HARTLAND DE M. MOLSON
Juin/June 1973

JOS CATTARINICH
Août/August 1977

SAM POLLOCK
Août/August 1978

Aurèle Joliat
TEMPLE DE LA RENOMMÉE, TORONTO
HOCKEY HALL OF FAME, TORONTO

Howie Morenz

Newsy Lalonde
TEMPLE DE LA RENOMMÉE, TORONTO
HOCKEY HALL OF FAME, TORONTO

Joe Malone
TEMPLE DE LA RENOMMÉE, TORONTO
HOCKEY HALL OF FAME, TORONTO

Sprague Cleghorn
TEMPLE DE LA RENOMMÉE, TORONTO
HOCKEY HALL OF FAME, TORONTO

Herb Gardiner
TEMPLE DE LA RENOMMÉE, TORONTO
HOCKEY HALL OF FAME, TORONTO

Sylvio Mantha
TEMPLE DE LA RENOMMÉE, TORONTO
HOCKEY HALL OF FAME, TORONTO

Joe Hall
TEMPLE DE LA RENOMMÉE, TORONTO
HOCKEY HALL OF FAME, TORONTO

George Hainsworth
TEMPLE DE LA RENOMMÉE, TORONTO
HOCKEY HALL OF FAME, TORONTO

Jack Laviolette
TEMPLE DE LA RENOMMÉE, TORONTO
HOCKEY HALL OF FAME, TORONTO

Didier Pitre
TEMPLE DE LA RENOMMÉE, TORONTO
HOCKEY HALL OF FAME, TORONTO

Bill Durnan
TEMPLE DE LA RENOMMÉE, TORONTO
HOCKEY HALL OF FAME, TORONTO

Babe Seibert
TEMPLE DE LA RENOMMÉE, TORONTO
HOCKEY HALL OF FAME, TORONTO

Toe Blake
F. DUPUIS

Emile Bouchard
TEMPLE DE LA RENOMMÉE, TORONTO
HOCKEY HALL OF FAME, TORONTO

Elmer Lach
F. DUPUIS

Kenny Reardon
F. DUPUIS

Bernard Geoffrion

Lorne Worsley
DAVID BIER

William Northey
TEMPLE DE LA RENOMMÉE, TORONTO
HOCKEY HALL OF FAME, TORONTO

Donat Raymond
DAVID BIER

Frank Selke
TEMPLE DE LA RENOMMÉE, TORONTO
HOCKEY HALL OF FAME, TORONTO

J. Ambrose O'Brien
TEMPLE DE LA RENOMMÉE, TORONTO
HOCKEY HALL OF FAME, TORONTO

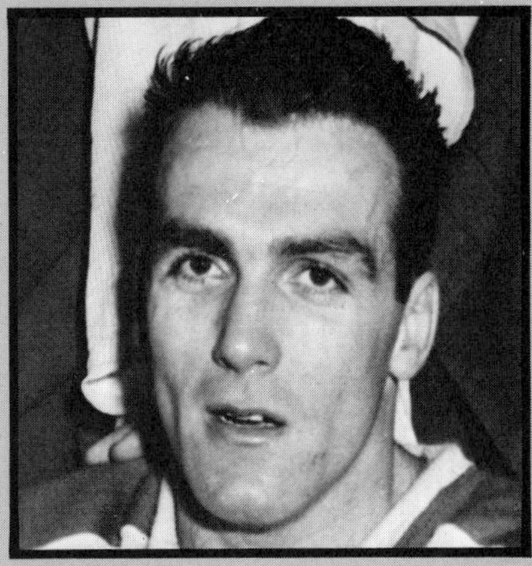

Henri Richard
TEMPLE DE LA RENOMMÉE, TORONTO
HOCKEY HALL OF FAME, TORONTO

Tommy Gorman
TEMPLE DE LA RENOMMÉE, TORONTO
HOCKEY HALL OF FAME, TORONTO

Hartland de M. Molson
TEMPLE DE LA RENOMMÉE, TORONTO
HOCKEY HALL OF FAME, TORONTO

Sam Pollock
DAVID BIER

LEMAIRE
25

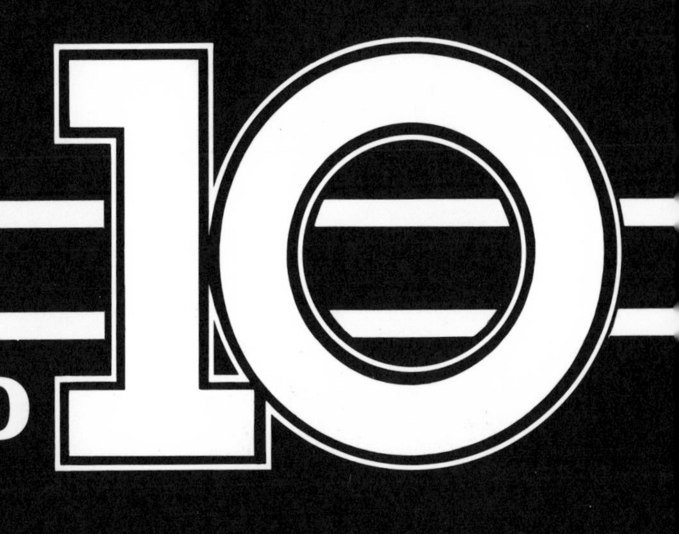

ROSTERS AND PERSONNEL

1915-16, l'année où les Canadiens remportèrent leur première coupe Stanley, deux ans avant la fondation de la LNH.

TEMPLE DE LA RENOMMÉE, TORONTO

1915-16, the year the Canadiens first won the Stanley Cup, two years before the founding of the NHL.

HOCKEY HALL OF FAME, TORONTO

Tous les efforts ont été tentés pour découvrir les numéros des chandails portés par tous les joueurs, mais dans certains cas cela s'est avéré impossible, étant donné que la Ligue Nationale ne possède pas tous les renseignements nécessaires. Les joueurs qui ont porté plus d'un numéro sont indiqués à l'aide d'un astérisque.

Every attempt has been made here to ascertain the sweater numbers worn by all players, but in some cases this has proved impossible due to the fact that the National Hockey League does not have the pertinent information. Players that wore more than one number are indicated by an asterisk.

1917-18

INSTRUCTEUR/COACH: George Kennedy
CAPITAINE/CAPTAIN: Newsy Lalonde

NO.	NOMS/NAMES
•	Joe Malone
•	Newsy Lalonde
•	Didier Pitre
•	Jack McDonald
•	Bert Corbeau
•	Joe Hall
•	Louis Berlinguette
•	Jack Laviolette
•	Bill Coutu
•	Bill Bell
•	Georges Vézina
•	Payer

1918-19

INSTRUCTEUR/COACH: George Kennedy
CAPITAINE/CAPTAIN: Newsy Lalonde

NO.	NOMS/NAMES
1	Georges Vézina
2	Bert Corbeau
3	Joe Hall
4	Newsy Lalonde
5	Didier Pitre
6	Odie Cleghorn
8	Louis Berlinguette
9	Bill Coutu
10	Jack McDonald
•	Joe Malone
•	Bill Bell
•	Amos Arbour
•	Fred Doherty

1919-20

INSTRUCTEUR/COACH: George Kennedy
CAPITAINE/CAPTAIN: Newsy Lalonde

NO.	NOMS/NAMES
•	Newsy Lalonde
•	Amos Arbour
•	Odie Cleghorn
•	Harry Cameron
•	Didier Pitre
•	Bert Corbeau
•	Louis Berlinguette
•	Bill Coutu
•	Howie McNamara
•	Don Smith
•	Jack Coughlin
•	Georges Vézina

TEMPLE DE LA RENOMMÉE, TORONTO
HOCKEY HALL OF FAME, TORONTO

1920-21

INSTRUCTEUR/COACH: Léo Dandurand
CAPITAINE/CAPTAIN: Newsy Lalonde

NO.	NOMS/NAMES
•	Newsy Lalonde
•	Didier Pitre
•	Harry Mummery
•	Amos Arbour
•	Bert Corbeau
•	Louis Berlinguette
•	Cully Wilson
•	Odie Cleghorn
•	Jack McDonald
•	Dave Ritchie
•	Bill Bell
•	Georges Vézina
•	Dave Campbell

1921-22

INSTRUCTEUR/COACH: Léo Dandurand
CAPITAINE/CAPTAIN: Sprague Cleghorn

NO.	NOMS/NAMES
•	Odie Cleghorn
•	Bill Boucher
•	Sprague Cleghorn
•	Louis Berlinguette
•	Newsy Lalonde
•	Bill Coutu
•	Bert Corbeau
•	Bill Bell
•	Didier Pitre
•	Edmond Bouchard
•	Jack McDonald
•	Phil Stephens

1922-23

INSTRUCTEUR/COACH: Léo Dandurand
CAPITAINE/CAPTAIN: Sprague Cleghorn

NO.	NOMS/NAMES
1	Georges Vézina
2	Sprague Cleghorn
3	Bill Coutu* Bert Corbeau
4	Aurèle Joliat Newsy Lalonde
5	Bill Boucher* Didier Pitre*
6	Louis Berlinguette
7	Odie Cleghorn
9	Bill Bell Bill Coutu*
10	Didier Pitre*
11	Edmond Bouchard Joe Malone
12	Marchand
13	Bill Boucher*

1923-24

INSTRUCTEUR/COACH: Léo Dandurand
CAPITAINE/CAPTAIN: Sprague Cleghorn

NO.	NOMS/NAMES
1	Georges Vézina
2	Sprague Cleghorn
3	Bill Coutu

NO.	NOMS/NAMES
4	Aurèle Joliat
5	Bill Boucher
6	Odie Cleghorn
7	Howie Morenz
8	Bill Cameron
9	Sylvio Mantha
10	Robert Boucher
11	Bill Bell
•	Charles Fortier

1924-25

INSTRUCTEUR/COACH: Léo Dandurand
CAPITAINE/CAPTAIN: Sprague Cleghorn

NO.	NOMS/NAMES
1	Georges Vézina
2	Sprague Cleghorn
3	Bill Coutu
4	Aurèle Joliat
5	Bill Boucher
6	Odie Cleghorn
7	Howie Morenz
8	Sylvio Mantha
9	John Matz
10	Fern Headley
11	Dave Ritchie
•	René Lafleur
•	René Joliat

TEMPLE DE LA RENOMMÉE, TORONTO
HOCKEY HALL OF FAME, TORONTO

1925-26

INSTRUCTEUR/COACH: Cecil Hart
CAPITAINE/CAPTAIN: Bill Coutu

NO.	NOMS/NAMES
•	Howie Morenz
•	Aurèle Joliat
•	Alfred "Pit" Lépine
•	Albert Leduc
•	Bill Boucher
•	Hector Lépine
•	Sylvio Mantha
•	Bill Coutu
•	Wildor Larochelle
•	Jean Matte
•	Rolland Paulhus
•	Georges Vézina
•	Bill Holmes
•	John McKinnon
•	Dave Ritchie
•	Alphonse Lacroix
•	Bill Taugher
•	Herb Rheaume

1926-27

INSTRUCTEUR/COACH: Cecil Hart
CAPITAINE/CAPTAIN: Sylvio Mantha

NO.	NOMS/NAMES
1	Herb Gardiner
2	Sylvio Mantha
3	Ambrose Moran A. Gauthier*
4	Aurèle Joliat
5	Carson Cooper A. Gauthier*
6	Arthur Gagné
7	Howie Morenz
8	Albert Leduc
9	Alfred "Pit" Lépine
10	Wildor Larochelle
11	Gizzy Hart Léo Lafrance Lachance
12	George Hainsworth*
14	George Hainsworth* Palangio Lacroix

1927-28

INSTRUCTEUR/COACH: Cecil Hart
CAPITAINE/CAPTAIN: Sylvio Mantha

NO.	NOMS/NAMES
1	Herb Gardiner
2	Sylvio Mantha George Hainsworth
3	Charles Langlois Marty Burke
4	Aurèle Joliat
5	George Patterson Léo Lafrance
6	Arthur Gagné
7	Howie Morenz
8	Albert Leduc
9	Alfred "Pit" Lépine
10	Wildor Larochelle
11	Gizzy Hart
14	Léo Gaudreault

1928-29

INSTRUCTEUR/COACH: Cecil Hart
CAPITAINE/CAPTAIN: Sylvio Mantha

NO.	NOMS/NAMES
1	Marty Burke
2	Sylvio Mantha
3	Gerry Carson* Herb Gardiner
4	Aurèle Joliat
5	Armand Mondou Léo Gaudreault
6	Arthur Gagné
7	Howie Morenz
8	Albert Leduc
9	Alfred "Pit" Lépine
10	George Patterson* Georges Mantha* Arthur Lesieur* Wildor Larochelle
11	George Patterson* Georges Mantha*
12	George Hainsworth
14	Gerry Carson* R. Palangio Arthur Lesieur*

George Hainsworth.

1929-30

INSTRUCTEUR/COACH: Cecil Hart
CAPITAINE/CAPTAIN: Sylvio Mantha

NO.	NOMS/NAMES
1	George Hainsworth Roy Worters Tom Murray
2	Sylvio Mantha
3	Marty Burke
4	Aurèle Joliat
5	Armand Mondou
6	Nick Wasnie
7	Howie Morenz
8	Albert Leduc
9	Alfred "Pit" Lépine
10	Wildor Larochelle
11	Bert McCaffrey Gord Fraser
12	Georges Mantha
14	Gerry Carson
15	Desrivières*
16	Gus Rivers Desrivières*

TEMPLE DE LA RENOMMÉE, TORONTO
HOCKEY HALL OF FAME, TORONTO

1930-31

INSTRUCTEUR/COACH: Cecil Hart
CAPITAINE/CAPTAIN: Sylvio Mantha

NO.	NOMS/NAMES
1	George Hainsworth
2	Sylvio Mantha
3	Marty Burke
4	Aurèle Joliat
5	Armand Mondou
6	Nick Wasnie
7	Howie Morenz
8	Albert Leduc
9	Alfred "Pit" Lépine
10	Wildor Larochelle
11	Bert McCaffrey Arthur Lesieur
12	Georges Mantha
14	John Gagnon
15	Gus Rivers

TEMPLE DE LA RENOMMÉE, TORONTO
HOCKEY HALL OF FAME, TORONTO

1931-32

INSTRUCTEUR/COACH: Cecil Hart
CAPITAINE/CAPTAIN: Sylvio Mantha

NO.	NOMS/NAMES
1	George Hainsworth
2	Sylvio Mantha
3	Marty Burke
4	Aurèle Joliat
5	Armand Mondou
6	Nick Wasnie
7	Howie Morenz
8	Albert Leduc
9	Alfred "Pit" Lépine
10	Wildor Larochelle
11	Dunc Munro
12	Georges Mantha
14	John Gagnon
15	Arthur Lesieur Gus Rivers
16	Arthur Alexandre

1932-33

INSTRUCTEUR/COACH: Newsy Lalonde
CAPITAINE/CAPTAIN: George Hainsworth

NO.	NOMS/NAMES
1	George Hainsworth
2	Sylvio Mantha* Harold Starr*
3	Sylvio Mantha* Marty Burke Harold Starr*
4	Aurèle Joliat
5	Léo Bourgault* Armand Mondou Gizzy Hart* Leo Murray
6	Gerry Carson Léo Gaudreault Hago Harrington*
7	Howie Morenz
8	Albert Leduc
9	Alfred "Pit" Lépine
10	Wildor Larochelle* Hago Harrington*
11	John Gagnon
12	Georges Mantha Léonard Grosvenor
14	John Gagnon* Wildor Larochelle*
15	Arthur Giroux* Léo Bourgault* Paul-Marcel Raymond
16	Arthur Giroux* Gizzy Hart* R. McCartney

1933-34

INSTRUCTEUR/COACH: Newsy Lalonde
CAPITAINE/CAPTAIN: Sylvio Mantha

NO.	NOMS/NAMES
1	Lorne Chabot Wilf Cude
2	Sylvio Mantha
3	Gerry Carson
4	Aurèle Joliat
5	John Gagnon
6	Georges Mantha
7	Howie Morenz
8	Wildor Larochelle
9	Alfred "Pit" Lépine
10	Marty Burke
11	Léo Bourgault
12	Armand Mondou
14	John Riley
15	Adélard Lafrance
16	Samuel Godin Paul-Marcel Raymond
17	John Portland

Première rangée: le gardien Lorne Chabot flanqué d'Aurèle Joliat (à gauche) et de Howie Morenz (à droite).
TEMPLE DE LA RENOMMÉE, TORONTO
Front row: Goalie Lorne Chabot flanked by Aurèle Joliat (left) and Howie Morenz (right).
HOCKEY HALL OF FAME, TORONTO

1934-35

INSTRUCTEURS/COACHES: Newsy Lalonde & Léo Dandurand
CAPITAINE/CAPTAIN: Sylvio Mantha

NO.	NOMS/NAMES
1	Wilf Cude
2	Sylvio Mantha
3	Gerry Carson*
4	Aurèle Joliat
5	Paul Runge Albert Leduc
6	Georges Mantha
8	Wildor Larochelle Gerry Carson*
9	Alfred "Pit" Lépine
12	Tony Savage B. McCully Léo Bourgault*
22	Nels Crutchfield
33	John Riley
48	John Gagnon Paul-Marcel Raymond Norm Collings
55	John McGill
64	Armand Mondou
75	Leroy Goldsworthy John Portland Desse Roche*
88	Roger Jenkins
99	Joe Lamb Léo Bourgault* Desse Roche*

1935-36

INSTRUCTEUR/COACH: Sylvio Mantha
CAPITAINE/CAPTAIN: Sylvio Mantha

NO.	NOMS/NAMES
1	Wilf Cude Abbie Cox
2	Sylvio Mantha
3	Walter Buswell
4	Aurèle Joliat
5	Armand Mondou
6	Georges Mantha
8	Wildor Larochelle Max Bennett Conrad Bourcier
9	Alfred "Pit" Lépine
10	Leroy Goldsworthy
11	John McGill
12	Paul Haynes
14	John Gagnon
15	G. Leroux Joffre Desilets
16	Arthur Lesieur
17	Cliff Goupille
18	Irving Frew
19	Bill Miller Jean-Louis Bourcier Paul Runge
20	Paul-Emile Drouin
21	Hector "Toe" Blake Rosario "Lolo" Couture Rodrigue Lorrain

1936-37

INSTRUCTEUR/COACH: Cecil Hart
CAPITAINE/CAPTAIN: Babe Seibert

NO.	NOMS/NAMES
1	Babe Seibert
2	Bill MacKenzie Gallagher
3	Walter Buswell
4	Aurèle Joliat
5	Rodrigue Lorrain
6	Bill Miller
8	George Brown Roger Jenkins
9	Alfred "Pit" Lépine
10	Paul Haynes
11	John McGill
12	Georges Mantha
14	John Gagnon
15	Joffre Desilets
16	Hector "Toe" Blake
17	Wilf Cude* George Hainsworth
18	Armand Mondou*
19	Paul Runge* Armand Mondou* Paul-Emile Drouin*
20	Paul Runge* Armand Mondou* Paul-Emile Drouin*
21	Armand Mondou* Wilf Cude*

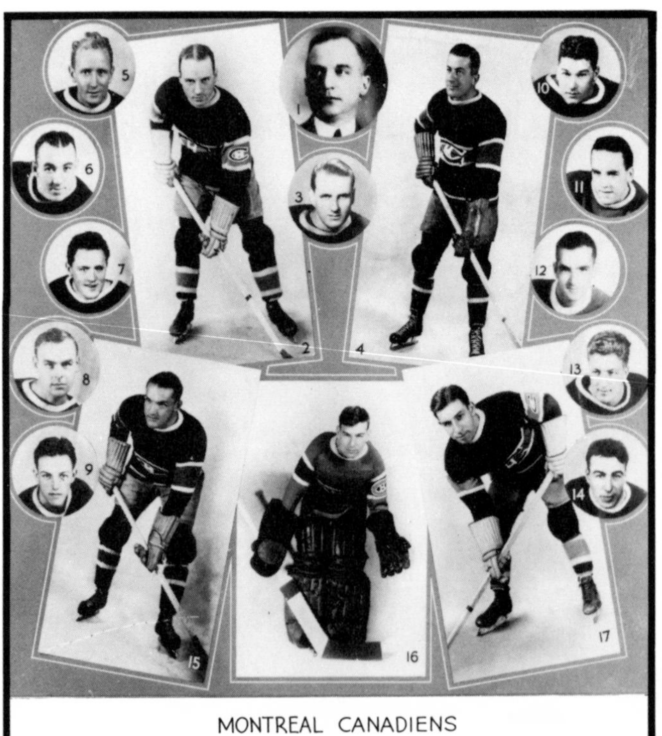

MONTREAL CANADIENS
1- Cecil Hart 2-Aurel Joliat. 3- George Brown. 4- Pit Lepine. 5- Jack McGill. 6-W. Buswell 7-A Mondou 8- Geo. Mantha. 9- Rod Lorrain. 10- W. McKenzie. 11-Paul Haynes 12- Bill Miller. 13- Joffre Desilets 14- Toe Blake. 15- Babe Siebert. 16. Wilf Cude. 17- Johnny Gagnon

TEMPLE DE LA RENOMMÉE, TORONTO

HOCKEY HALL OF FAME, TORONTO

1937-38

INSTRUCTEUR/COACH: Cecil Hart
CAPITAINE/CAPTAIN: Babe Seibert

NO.	NOMS/NAMES
1	Babe Seibert
2	Marty Burke Bill MacKenzie
3	Walter Buswell
4	Aurèle Joliat
5	Rodrigue Lorrain
6	Hector "Toe" Blake Antonio Demers*
8	Don Willson* Armand Mondou Ossie Asmundson
9	Alfred "Pit" Lépine
10	Paul Haynes
11	Cliff Goupille
12	Georges Mantha
14	John Gagnon
15	Joffre Desilets
16	Don Willson* George Brown Antonio Demers
17	Wilf Cude Paul Gauthier
18	Paul-Marcel Raymond
20	Paul-Emile Drouin Gus Mancuso Armand Raymond

1938-39

INSTRUCTEURS/COACHES: Cecil Hart & Jules Dugal
CAPITAINE/CAPTAIN: Babe Seibert

NO.	NOMS/NAMES
1	Babe Seibert
2	Marv "Cy" Wentworth
3	Walter Buswell
4	Paul-Emile Drouin Wilf Cude*
5	Rodrigue Lorrain Marcel Tremblay
6	Hector "Toe" Blake
8	Stuart Evans
9	Herb Cain
10	Paul Haynes
11	Bill Summerhill Bob Gracie
12	Georges Mantha
14	John Gagnon
15	George Brown Desse Smith
16	Jim Ward* Cliff Goupille
17	Armand Mondou Wilf Cude*
18	Jim Ward*
19	Claude Bourque
20	Louis Trudel
24	Wilf Cude*

Ace Bailey Benefit Game, Toronto, February 14, 1934.

Match bénéfice Ace Bailey, Toronto, 14 février, 1934.

TEMPLE DE LA RENOMMÉE, TORONTO
HOCKEY HALL OF FAME, TORONTO

Wilf Cude.
TEMPLE DE LA RENOMMÉE, TORONTO
HOCKEY HALL OF FAME, TORONTO

1939-40

INSTRUCTEURS/COACHES: Babe Seibert & Alfred "Pit" Lépine
CAPITAINE/CAPTAIN: Walter Buswell

NO.	NOMS/NAMES
1	Wilf Cude Claude Bourque Mike Karakas
2	Marv "Cy" Wentworth Rhys Thomson
3	Walter Buswell
4	Paul-Emile Drouin
5	Rodrigue Lorrain
6	Hector "Toe" Blake
8	Louis Trudel
9	Marty Barry
10	Paul Haynes Antonio Demers
11	Ray Getliffe
12	Georges Mantha
14	John Gagnon Gus Mancuso Gordon Poirier
15	Bill Summerhill Earl Robinson John Doran Armand Raymond
16	Cliff Goupille
17	Armand Mondou
18	Charlie Sands
19	Doug Young*
20	Doug Young*

1940-41

INSTRUCTEUR/COACH: Dick Irvin
CAPITAINE/CAPTAIN: Hector "Toe" Blake

NO.	NOMS/NAMES
1	Bert Gardiner Wilf Cude
2	Cliff Goupille
3	John Portland Doug Young
4	Ken Reardon
5	Joseph Benoît
6	Hector "Toe" Blake
8	Paul-Emile Drouin Louis Trudel* Stuart Smith
9	Charlie Sands
10	Louis Trudel* Alex Singbush* Georges Mantha Paul Haynes
11	Ray Getliffe
12	Murph Chamberlain
14	Elmer Lach Paul-Emile Bibeault
15	John Adams
16	John Quilty
17	Tony Graboski
18	Alex Singbush* "Peggy" O'Neil
19	Antonio Demers

1941-42

INSTRUCTEUR/COACH: Dick Irvin
CAPITAINE/CAPTAIN: Hector "Toe" Blake

NO.	NOMS/NAMES
1	Paul-Emile Bibeault Bert Gardiner
2	Cliffe Goupille
3	John Portland
4	Ken Reardon
5	Joseph Benoît
6	Hector Blake
8	Tony Graboski Léo Lamoureux
9	Charlie Sands
10	Elmer Lach Jim Haggerty
11	Ray Getliffe
12	Murph Chamberlain Red Heron
14	Terry Reardon
15	"Bunny" Dame
16	John Quilty
17	Emile Bouchard
18	Stuart Smith "Peggy" O'Neil Connie Tudin
19	Antonio Demers
20	Pierre Morin
21	Bud O'Connor
22	Gerry Heffernan Rodrigue Lorrain

1942-43

INSTRUCTEUR/COACH: Dick Irvin
CAPITAINE/CAPTAIN: Hector "Toe" Blake

NO.	NOMS/NAMES
0	Paul-Emile Bibeault*
1	Paul-Emile Bibeault* Tony Graboski*
2	Cliff Goupille
3	John Portland
4	Léo Lamoureux
5	Joseph Benoît
6	Hector "Toe" Blake
8	Glen Harmon Terry Reardon R. Lee John Mahaffey* Frank Mailley
9	Charlie Sands
10	Bud O'Connor
11	Ray Getliffe
12	Gord Drillon
14	Antonio Demers Charlie Phillips Ernest Laforce
15	Maurice Richard "Smiley" Meronek John Mahaffey* Irving McGibbon
16	Elmer Lach Paul-Emile Bibeault*
17	Emile Bouchard
18	"Dutch" Hiller* Alex Smart Tony Graboski*
19	Marcel Dheere*
20	"Dutch" Hiller*
21	Marcel Dheere*
22	Gerry Heffernan

1943-44

INSTRUCTEUR/COACH: Dick Irvin
CAPITAINE/CAPTAIN: Hector "Toe" Blake

NO.	NOMS/NAMES
1	Bill Durnan
2	Mike McMahon
3	Emile Bouchard
4	Léo Lamoureux
6	Hector "Toe" Blake
8	Glen Harmon
9	Maurice Richard
10	Bud O'Connor
11	Ray Getliffe
12	Murph Chamberlain
14	Phil Watson
16	Elmer Lach
17	Fernand Majeau
18	Gerry Heffernan
21	Robert Fillion
22	Jean-Claude Campeau Robert Walton

1944-45

INSTRUCTEUR/COACH: Dick Irvin
CAPITAINE/CAPTAIN: Hector "Toe" Blake

NO.	NOMS/NAMES
1	Bill Durnan
2	Frank Eddolls
3	Emile Bouchard
4	Léo Lamoureux
5	"Dutch" Hiller
6	Hector "Toe" Blake
8	Glen Harmon
9	Maurice Richard
10	Bud O'Connor
11	Ray Getliffe
12	Murph Chamberlain
14	Rolland Rossignol Rosario Joanette Ed Emberg (éliminatoires/playoffs) John Mahaffey (éliminatoires/playoffs)
15	Robert Fillion
16	Elmer Lach
17	Fernand Majeau Nils Tremblay
18	Ken Mosdell
19	Fernand Gauthier
22	Wilf Field Frank Stahan (éliminatoires/playoffs)

1945-46

INSTRUCTEUR/COACH: Dick Irvin
CAPITAINE/CAPTAIN: Hector "Toe" Blake

NO.	NOMS/NAMES
1	Bill Durnan Paul-Emile Bibeault*
2	Frank Eddolls
3	Emile Bouchard
4	Léo Lamoureux
5	"Dutch" Hiller
6	Hector "Toe" Blake
8	Glen Harmon
9	Maurice Richard
10	Bud O'Connor
11	Joseph Benoît
12	Murph Chamberlain
14	Bill Reay
15	Robert Fillion
16	Elmer Lach
17	Ken Reardon
18	Ken Mosdell Murdo MacKay
19	Jim Peters
20	Gérard Plamondon Moe White Mike McMahon
21	Lorrain Thibeault Paul-Emile Bibeault*
22	Vic Lynn

TEMPLE DE LA RENOMMÉE, TORONTO
HOCKEY HALL OF FAME, TORONTO

1946-47

INSTRUCTEUR/COACH: Dick Irvin
CAPITAINE/CAPTAIN: Hector "Toe" Blake

NO.	NOMS/NAMES
1	Bill Durnan
2	Frank Eddolls
3	Emile Bouchard
4	Léo Lamoureux
5	Robert Fillion
6	Hector "Toe" Blake
8	Glen Harmon
9	Maurice Richard
10	Bud O'Connor
11	Hubert Macey* Doug Lewis George Pargeter Joseph Benoît
12	Murph Chamberlain
14	Bill Reay
15	George Allen
16	Elmer Lach
17	Ken Reardon
18	Ken Mosdell
19	Jim Peters
20	Léo Gravelle
21	Roger Léger
22	John Quilty Hubert Macey*
23	Murdo MacKay (éliminatoires/playoffs)

G. Harmon, K. Reardon, E. Bouchard, R. Léger, L. Lamoureux, F. Eddolls, 1947.
TEMPLE DE LA RENOMMÉE, TORONTO
HOCKEY HALL OF FAME, TORONTO

1947-48

INSTRUCTEUR/COACH: Dick Irvin
CAPITAINES/CAPTAINS: Hector "Toe" Blake & Bill Durnan

NO.	NOMS/NAMES
1	Bill Durnan Gerry McNeil
2	Doug Harvey
3	Emile Bouchard
4	Howard Riopelle
5	Jacques Locas
6	Hector "Toe" Blake
8	Glen Harmon
9	Maurice Richard
10	Robert Fillion John Quilty
11	Jean-Claude Campeau
12	Murph Chamberlain
14	Bill Reay
15	Floyd Curry
16	Elmer Lach
17	Ken Reardon
18	Gérard Plamondon Ken Mosdell
19	Jim Peters Joe Carveth
20	Bob Carse George Robertson
21	Roger Léger
22	Normand Dussault Tom Johnson Léo Gravelle
23	Hal Laycoe Murdo MacKay

1948-49

INSTRUCTEUR/COACH: Dick Irvin
CAPITAINE/CAPTAIN: Emile Bouchard

NO.	NOMS/NAMES
1	Bill Durnan
2	Doug Harvey
3	Emile Bouchard
4	Howard Riopelle
5	Gérard Plamondon Jacques Locas
6	Jos Carveth
8	Glen Harmon
9	Maurice Richard
10	Robert Fillion
11	George Robertson Floyd Curry (éliminatoires/playoffs)
12	Murph Chamberlain
14	Bill Reay
15	Léo Gravelle Ed Dorohoy
16	Elmer Lach
17	Ken Reardon
18	Ken Mosdell
19	Murdo MacKay (éliminatoires/playoffs)
20	Jean-Claude Campeau
21	Roger Léger Jim MacPherson
22	Normand Dussault
23	Hal Laycoe

L'équipe des étoiles de 1949.
TEMPLE DE LA RENOMMÉE, TORONTO

The 1949 All Star team.
HOCKEY HALL OF FAME, TORONTO

1949-50

INSTRUCTEUR/COACH: Dick Irvin
CAPITAINE/CAPTAIN: Emile Bouchard

NO.	NOMS/NAMES
1	Bill Durnan Gerry McNeil*
2	Doug Harvey
3	Emile Bouchard
4	Howard Riopelle Gilles Dubé
5	Gérard Plamondon Bert Hirschfeld
6	Joe Carveth Floyd Curry
8	Glen Harmon
9	Maurice Richard
10	Robert Fillion
11	Calum MacKay
12	Grant Warwick Bob Fryday Gerry McNeil* Paul Meger (éliminatoires/playoffs)
14	Bill Reay
15	Léo Gravelle
16	Elmer Lach
17	Ken Reardon
18	Ken Mosdell
19	Louis "Lulu" Denis Bob Frampton
20	Tom Johnson (éliminatoires/playoffs)
21	Roger Léger
22	Normand Dussault
23	Hal Laycoe

1950-51

INSTRUCTEUR/COACH: Dick Irvin
CAPITAINE/CAPTAIN: Emile Bouchard

NO.	NOMS/NAMES
1	Gerry McNeil
2	Doug Harvey
3	Emile Bouchard
4	Claude Robert Ernie Roche Hugh Currie
5	Bert Hirschfeld* Bernard Geoffrion Gérard Desaulniers Louis "Lulu" Denis
6	Floyd Curry
8	Glen Harmon
9	Maurice Richard
10	Tom Johnson
11	Calum MacKay
12	Hal Laycoe Ed Mazur Fred Burchell Dollard St.Laurent Dick Gamble Syd McNabney (éliminatoires/playoffs)
14	Bill Reay
15	Léo Gravelle Bert Olmstead
16	Elmer Lach
17	Bob Dawes Jean Béliveau* Ross Lowe (éliminatoires/playoffs)
18	Ken Mosdell
19	Vern Kaiser Bert Hirschfeld* Gérard Plamondon
20	Paul Meger Frank King Tony Manastersky Jean Béliveau*
21	Jim MacPherson
22	Normand Dussault
23	Paul Masnick

DAVID BIER

1951-52

INSTRUCTEUR/COACH: Dick Irvin
CAPITAINE/CAPTAIN: Emile Bouchard

NO.	NOMS/NAMES
1	Gerry McNeil
2	Doug Harvey
3	Emile Bouchard
4	Ross Lowe
5	Bernard Geoffrion
6	Floyd Curry
8	Dick Gamble
9	Maurice Richard
10	Tom Johnson
11	Paul Masnick* Gene Achtymichuk Calum MacKay Lorne Davis
12	Dickie Moore Gérald Couture
14	Bill Reay
15	Bert Olmstead
16	Elmer Lach
17	John McCormack
18	Ken Mosdell
19	Dollard St. Laurent
20	Paul Meger
21	Jim MacPherson
23	Don Marshall Stan Long Paul Masnick* Bob Fryday Ed Mazur Garry Edmundson Cliff Malone

1952-53

INSTRUCTEUR/COACH: Dick Irvin
CAPITAINE/CAPTAIN: Emile Bouchard

NO.	NOMS/NAMES
1	Gerry McNeil Jacques Plante Hal Murphy
2	Doug Harvey
3	Emile Bouchard
4	Ed Litzenberger Reg Abbott Calum MacKay (éliminatoires/playoffs) Ivan Irwin
5	Bernard Geoffrion
6	Floyd Curry
8	Dick Gamble
9	Maurice Richard
10	Tom Johnson
11	Paul Masnick
12	Dickie Moore Jean Béliveau
14	Bill Reay
15	Bert Olmstead
16	Elmer Lach
17	John McCormack
18	Ken Mosdell
19	Dollard St.Laurent
20	Paul Meger
21	Jim MacPherson
22	Lorne Davis
23	Gaye Stewart Rolland Rousseau Ed Mazur (éliminatoires/playoffs) Doug Anderson (éliminatoires/playoffs) Gérard Desaulniers

1953-54

INSTRUCTEUR/COACH: Dick Irvin
CAPITAINE/CAPTAIN: Emile Bouchard

NO.	NOMS/NAMES
1	Gerry McNeil Jacques Plante
2	Doug Harvey
3	Emile Bouchard
4	Jean Béliveau
5	Bernard Geoffrion
6	Floyd Curry
8	Dick Gamble Paul Masnick*
9	Maurice Richard
10	Tom Johnson
11	Calum MacKay
12	Dickie Moore
14	André Corriveau Fred Burchell Lorne Davis*
15	Bert Olmstead
16	Elmer Lach
17	Gérard Desaulniers Ed Litzenberger* John McCormack
18	Ken Mosdell
19	Dollard St. Laurent
20	Paul Meger
21	Jim MacPherson
22	Lorne Davis* Paul Masnick* Ed Litzenberger*
23	Ed Mazur
24	Gaye Stewart

DWIGHT E. DOLAN

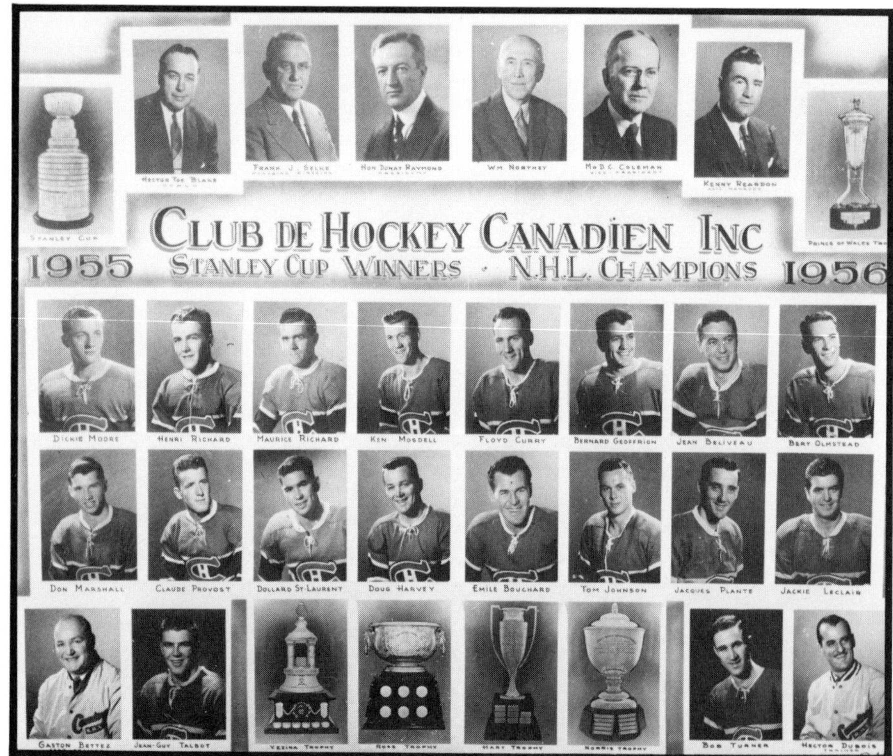

DAVID BIER

1954-55

INSTRUCTEUR/COACH: Dick Irvin
CAPITAINE/CAPTAIN: Emile Bouchard

NO.	NOMS/NAMES
1	Jacques Plante Charlie Hodge Claude Evans André Binette
2	Doug Harvey
3	Emile Bouchard
4	Jean Béliveau
5	Bernard Geoffrion
6	Floyd Curry
8	Jack LeClair
9	Maurice Richard
10	Tom Johnson
11	Calum MacKay
12	Dickie Moore
14	Paul Masnick* Paul Ronty
15	Bert Olmstead
17	Ed Litzenberger Garry Blaine Jean-Guy Talbot*
18	Ken Mosdell
19	Dollard St. Laurent
20	Paul Meger Jim Bartlett
21	Jim MacPherson
22	Paul Masnick* Don Marshall Orval Tessier
23	Jean-Guy Talbot* Jean-Paul Lamirande Ed Mazur George McAvoy (éliminatoires/playoffs)
24	Dick Gamble (éliminatoires/playoffs) Guy Rousseau

1955-56

INSTRUCTEUR/COACH: Hector "Toe" Blake
CAPITAINE/CAPTAIN: Emile Bouchard

NO.	NOMS/NAMES
1	Jacques Plante Robert Perreault
2	Doug Harvey
3	Emile Bouchard
4	Jean Béliveau
5	Bernard Geoffrion
6	Floyd Curry
8	Jack LeClair
9	Maurice Richard
10	Tom Johnson
12	Dickie Moore
14	Dick Gamble Connie Broden
15	Bert Olmstead
16	Henri Richard
17	Jean-Guy Talbot
18	Ken Mosdell
19	Dollard St. Laurent
21	Walter Clune Jacques Deslauriers
22	Don Marshall
23	Claude Provost
24	Bob Turner

ARNOTT & ROGERS

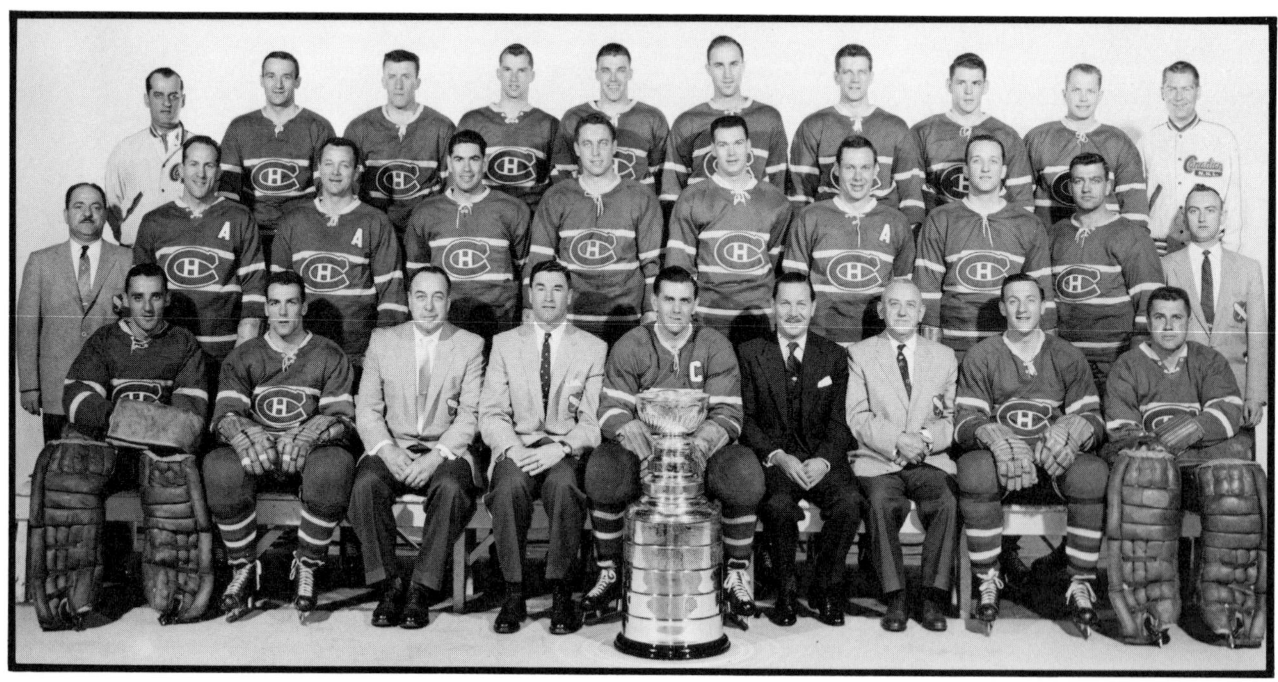

ARNOTT & ROGERS

1956-57

INSTRUCTEUR/COACH: Hector "Toe" Blake
CAPITAINE/CAPTAIN: Maurice Richard

NO.	NOMS/NAMES
1	Jacques Plante Gerry McNeil
2	Doug Harvey
4	Jean Béliveau
5	Bernard Geoffrion
6	Floyd Curry
8	Jack LeClair Stan Smrke
9	Maurice Richard
10	Tom Johnson
11	Bob Turner
12	Dickie Moore
14	Claude Provost
15	Bert Olmstead
16	Henri Richard
17	Jean-Guy Talbot
19	Dollard St.Laurent
20	Jerry Wilson Ralph Backstrom Philippe Goyette Allan Johnson Bronco Horvath Murray Balfour Glenn Cressman* Guy Rousseau
21	Jim MacPherson
22	Don Marshall
23	André Pronovost
24	Gene Achtymichuk Glenn Cressman*

1957-58

INSTRUCTEUR/COACH: Hector "Toe" Blake
CAPITAINE/CAPTAIN: Maurice Richard

NO.	NOMS/NAMES
1	Jacques Plante Charlie Hodge Len Broderick
2	Doug Harvey
4	Jean Béliveau
5	Bernard Geoffrion
6	Floyd Curry
8	Connie Broden Stan Smrke Ken Mosdell Bill Carter Ralph Backstrom Gene Achtymichuk Claude Laforge Murray Balfour
9	Maurice Richard
10	Tom Johnson
11	Bob Turner
12	Dickie Moore
14	Claude Provost
15	Bert Olmstead
16	Henri Richard
17	Jean-Guy Talbot
18	Marcel Bonin
19	Dollard St. Laurent
20	Philippe Goyette
21	Albert Langlois John Bownass
22	Don Marshall
23	André Pronovost
24	Ab McDonald (éliminatoires/playoffs)
25	Don Aiken

DAVID BIER

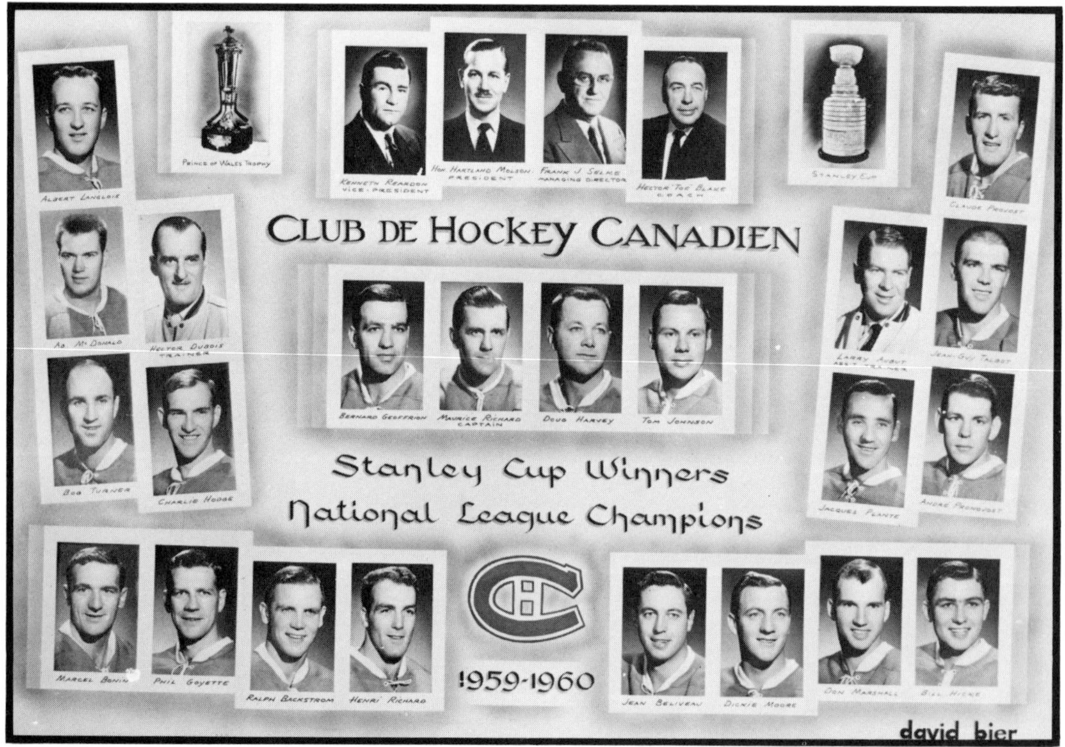

DAVID BIER

1958-59

INSTRUCTEUR/COACH: Hector "Toe" Blake
CAPITAINE/CAPTAIN: Maurice Richard

NO.	NOMS/NAMES
1	Jacques Plante Charlie Hodge Claude Pronovost Claude Cyr
2	Doug Harvey
4	Jean Béliveau
5	Bernard Geoffrion
6	Ralph Backstrom
8	Ken Mosdell (éliminatoires/playoffs) Bill Hicke (éliminatoires/playoffs)
9	Maurice Richard
10	Tom Johnson
11	Bob Turner
12	Dickie Moore
14	Claude Provost
15	Ab McDonald
16	Henri Richard
17	Jean-Guy Talbot
18	Marcel Bonin
19	Albert Langlois
20	Philippe Goyette
21	Ian Cushenan
22	Don Marshall
23	André Pronovost

1959-60

INSTRUCTEUR/COACH: Hector "Toe" Blake
CAPITAINE/CAPTAIN: Maurice Richard

NO.	NOMS/NAMES
1	Jacques Plante Charlie Hodge
2	Doug Harvey
4	Jean Béliveau
5	Bernard Geoffrion
6	Ralph Backstrom
8	Bill Hicke
9	Maurice Richard
10	Tom Johnson
11	Bob Turner
12	Dickie Moore
14	Claude Provost
15	Ab McDonald
16	Henri Richard
17	Jean-Guy Talbot
18	Marcel Bonin
19	Albert Langlois
20	Philippe Goyette
21	Jean-Claude Tremblay
22	Don Marshall
23	André Pronovost
24	Cecil Hoekstra Reg Fleming

1960-61

INSTRUCTEUR/COACH: Hector "Toe" Blake
CAPITAINE/CAPTAIN: Doug Harvey

NO.	NOMS/NAMES
1	Jacques Plante Charlie Hodge
2	Doug Harvey
3	Jean-Claude Tremblay Jean Gauthier*
4	Jean Béliveau
5	Bernard Geoffrion
6	Ralph Backstrom
8	Bill Hicke
10	Tom Johnson
11	Bob Turner
12	Dickie Moore
14	Claude Provost
15	Jean-Guy Gendron*
16	Henri Richard
17	Jean-Guy Talbot
18	Marcel Bonin
19	Albert Langlois
20	Philippe Goyette
21	Gilles Tremblay
22	Don Marshall
23	Jean-Guy Gendron* André Pronovost
24	Robert Rousseau Wayne Connelly
25	Cliff Pennington Jean Gauthier* Glen Skov

MOLSON

ARNOTT & ROGERS

1961-62

INSTRUCTEUR/COACH: Hector "Toe" Blake
CAPITAINE/CAPTAIN: Jean Béliveau

NO.	NOMS/NAMES
1	Jacques Plante
3	Jean-Claude Tremblay
4	Jean Béliveau
5	Bernard Geoffrion
6	Ralph Backstrom
8	Bill Hicke
10	Tom Johnson
11	Jean Gauthier
12	Dickie Moore
14	Claude Provost
15	Robert Rousseau
16	Henri Richard
17	Jean-Guy Talbot
18	Marcel Bonin
19	Lou Fontinato
20	Philippe Goyette
21	Gilles Tremblay
22	Don Marshall
23	Al MacNeil
24	Gord Berenson Charlie Hamilton
25	Bill Carter
26	Keith McCreary (éliminatoires/playoffs)

1962-63

INSTRUCTEUR/COACH: Hector "Toe" Blake
CAPITAINE/CAPTAIN: Jean Béliveau

NO.	NOMS/NAMES
1	Jacques Plante Cesare Maniago Ernie Wakely
3	Jean-Claude Tremblay
4	Jean Béliveau
5	Bernard Geoffrion
6	Ralph Backstrom
8	Bill Hicke
10	Tom Johnson
11	Jean Gauthier
12	Dickie Moore
14	Claude Provost
15	Robert Rousseau
16	Henri Richard
17	Jean-Guy Talbot
18	Gord Berenson*
19	Lou Fontinato
20	Philippe Goyette
21	Gilles Tremblay
22	Don Marshall
23	Bill McCreary Claude Larose*
24	Gord Berenson* Bill Sutherland (éliminatoires/playoffs)
25	Terry Harper Claude Larose*
26	Gérald Brisson Jacques Laperrière

1963-64

INSTRUCTEUR/COACH: Hector "Toe" Blake
CAPITAINE/CAPTAIN: Jean Béliveau

NO.	NOMS/NAMES
1	Charlie Hodge Lorne Worsley*
2	Jacques Laperrière
3	Jean-Claude Tremblay
4	Jean Béliveau
5	Bernard Geoffrion
6	Ralph Backstrom
8	Bill Hicke
10	Marc Rheaume
11	Ted Harris Wayne Hicks* Jean Gauthier
14	Claude Provost
15	Robert Rousseau
16	Henri Richard
17	Jean-Guy Talbot
18	Bryan Watson John Hanna
19	Terry Harper
20	Dave Balon
21	Gilles Tremblay
22	John Ferguson
23	André Boudrias* Yvan Cournoyer* Claude Larose
24	Gord Berenson
25	André Boudrias* Yvan Cournoyer* Wayne Hicks* Léon Rochefort* Terry Gray*
26	Jim Roberts Léon Rochefort* Terry Gray*
30	Lorne Worsley* Jean-Guy Morissette

1964-65

INSTRUCTEUR/COACH: Hector "Toe" Blake
CAPITAINE/CAPTAIN: Jean Béliveau

NO.	NOMS/NAMES
1	Charlie Hodge
2	Jacques Laperrière
3	Jean-Claude Tremblay
4	Jean Béliveau
6	Ralph Backstrom
8	Bill Hicke Dick Duff
10	Ted Harris
11	Claude Larose
12	Yvan Cournoyer
14	Claude Provost
15	Robert Rousseau
16	Henri Richard
17	Jean-Guy Talbot
18	Keith McCreary* Bryan Watson
19	Terry Harper
20	Dave Balon
21	Gilles Tremblay
22	John Ferguson
23	Gord Berenson Keith McCreary* Garry Peters*
24	Jean-Noël Picard* Garry Peters* André Boudrias Jean Gauthier (éliminatoires/playoffs)
25	Jean-Noël Picard* Léon Rochefort
26	Jim Roberts
30	Lorne Worsley

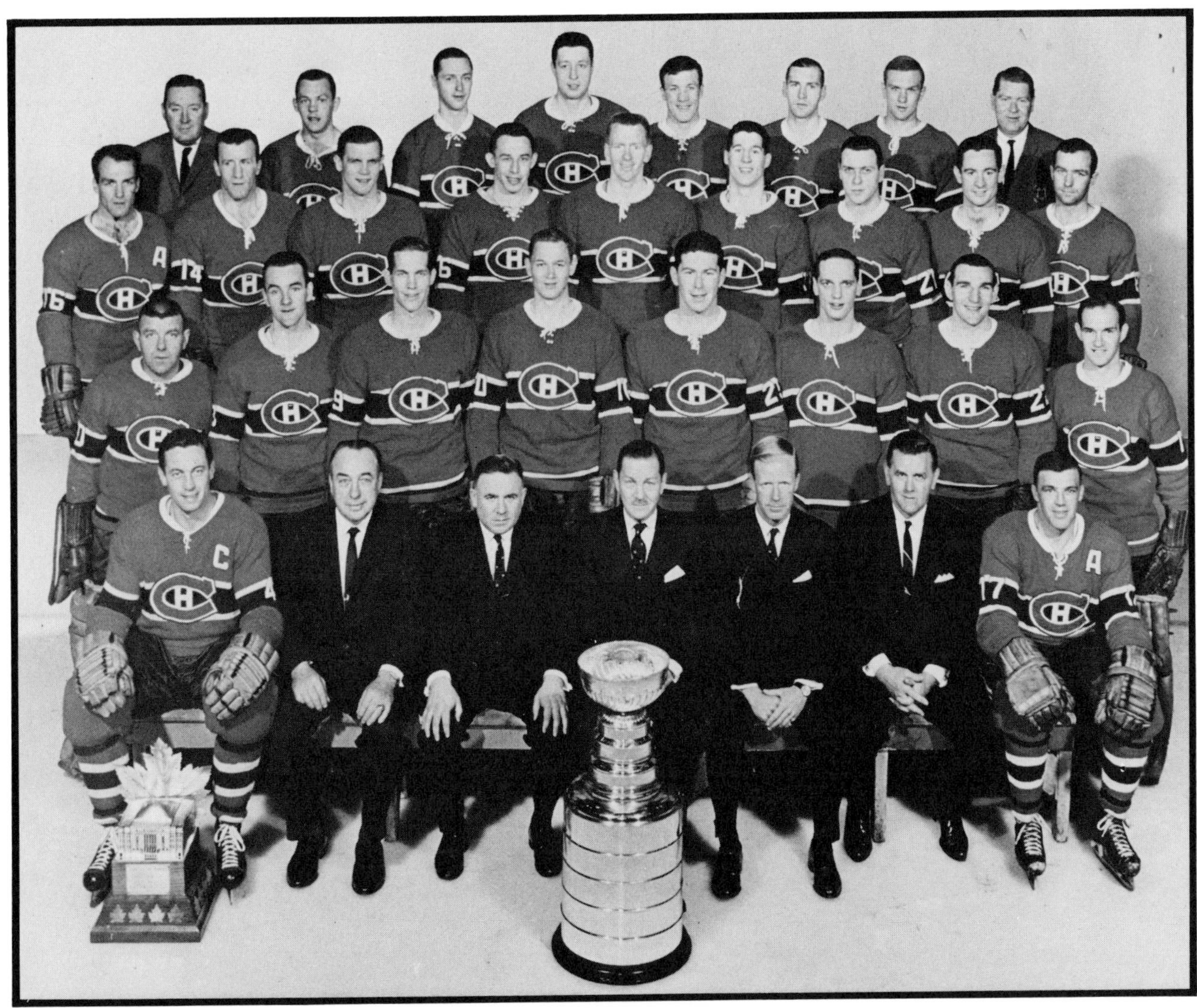

1965-66

INSTRUCTEUR/COACH: Hector "Toe" Blake
CAPITAINE/CAPTAIN: Jean Béliveau

NO.	NOMS/NAMES
1	Charlie Hodge
2	Jacques Laperrière
3	Jean-Claude Tremblay
4	Jean Béliveau
6	Ralph Backstrom
8	Dick Duff
10	Ted Harris
11	Claude Larose
12	Yvan Cournoyer
14	Claude Provost
15	Robert Rousseau
16	Henri Richard
17	Jean-Guy Talbot
18	Léon Rochefort Dan Grant
19	Terry Harper
20	Dave Balon
21	Gilles Tremblay
22	John Ferguson
23	Gord Berenson* Noel Price* Jean Gauthier*
24	Gord Berenson*
25	Noel Price* Don Johns Jean Gauthier*
26	Jim Roberts
30	Lorne Worsley

DENIS BRODEUR, MONTRÉAL

1966-67

INSTRUCTEUR/COACH: Hector "Toe" Blake
CAPITAINE/CAPTAIN: Jean Béliveau

NO.	NOMS/NAMES
1	Charlie Hodge
2	Jacques Laperrière
3	Jean-Claude Tremblay
4	Jean Béliveau
6	Ralph Backstrom
8	Dick Duff
10	Ted Harris
11	Claude Larose
12	Yvan Cournoyer
14	Claude Provost
15	Robert Rousseau
16	Henri Richard
17	Jean-Guy Talbot
18	André Boudrias Garry Peters
19	Terry Harper
20	Dave Balon
21	Gilles Tremblay
22	John Ferguson
23	Noel Price
24	Carol Vadnais Jean Gauthier Serge Savard
25	Léon Rochefort
26	Jim Roberts
29	Rogatien Vachon*
30	Rogatien Vachon* Lorne Worsley Garry Bauman

1967-68

INSTRUCTEUR/COACH: Hector "Toe" Blake
CAPITAINE/CAPTAIN: Jean Béliveau

NO.	NOMS/NAMES
1	Lorne Worsley
2	Jacques Laperrière
3	Jean-Claude Tremblay
4	Jean Béliveau
5	Gilles Tremblay
6	Ralph Backstrom
8	Dick Duff
10	Ted Harris
11	Claude Larose
12	Yvan Cournoyer
14	Claude Provost
15	Robert Rousseau
16	Henri Richard
17	Carol Vadnais
18	Serge Savard
19	Terry Harper
20	Garry Monahan
22	John Ferguson
23	Dan Grant
24	Mickey Redmond
25	Jacques Lemaire
26	Bryan Watson
30	Lorne Worsley

1968-69

INSTRUCTEUR/COACH: Claude Ruel
CAPITAINE/CAPTAIN: Jean Béliveau

NO.	NOMS/NAMES
1	Lorne Worsley Tony Esposito*
2	Jacques Laperrière
3	Jean-Claude Tremblay
4	Jean Béliveau
5	Gilles Tremblay
6	Ralph Backstrom
8	Dick Duff
10	Ted Harris
11	Jude Drouin Howie Glover
12	Yvan Cournoyer
14	Claude Provost
15	Robert Rousseau
16	Henri Richard
17	Larry Hillman Guy Lapointe
18	Serge Savard
19	Terry Harper
20	Garry Monahan* Lucien Grenier*
21	Lucien Grenier*
22	John Ferguson
23	Christian Bordeleau Alain Caron Bob Berry Garry Monahan*
24	Mickey Redmond
25	Jacques Lemaire
29	Tony Esposito* Ernie Wakely
30	Rogatien Vachon Tony Esposito*

1969-70

INSTRUCTEUR/COACH: Claude Ruel
CAPITAINE/CAPTAIN: Jean Béliveau

NO.	NOMS/NAMES
1	Rogatien Vachon* Lorne Worsley
2	Jacques Laperrière
3	Jean-Claude Tremblay
4	Jean Béliveau
5	Ted Harris*
6	Ralph Backstrom
8	Dick Duff Larry Mickey*
10	Ted Harris*
11	Bob Sheehan Jean Gauthier Phil Roberto Réjean Houle
12	Yvan Cournoyer
14	Claude Provost
15	Robert Rousseau
16	Henri Richard
17	Lucien Grenier Guy Lapointe
18	Serge Savard
19	Terry Harper
20	Peter Mahovlich
21	Ted Harris* Larry Mickey* Marc Tardif Fran Huck Guy Charron
22	John Ferguson
23	Christian Bordeleau
24	Mickey Redmond
25	Jacques Lemaire
26	Larry Pleau Paul Curtis Jude Drouin
29	Philippe Myre
30	Rogatien Vachon*

ARNOTT & ROGERS

1970-71

INSTRUCTEURS/COACHES: Claude Ruel & Al MacNeil
CAPITAINE/CAPTAIN: Jean Béliveau

NO.	NOMS/NAMES
1	Rogatien Vachon
2	Jacques Laperrière
3	Jean-Claude Tremblay
4	Jean Béliveau*
5	Guy Lapointe
6	Ralph Backstrom Fran Huck* Charles Lefley
8	Jean Béliveau* Phil Roberto* Larry Pleau Charles Lefley
10	Frank Mahovlich* Bill Collins
11	Marc Tardif
12	Yvan Cournoyer Fran Huck*
14	Réjean Houle*
15	Claude Larose
16	Henri Richard
17	Phil Roberto*
18	Serge Savard
19	Terry Harper
20	Peter Mahovlich
21	Réjean Houle* Léon Rochefort
22	John Ferguson
23	Guy Charron Bob Murdoch
24	Mickey Redmond Bob Sheehan
25	Jacques Lemaire
26	Pierre Bouchard
27	Frank Mahovlich*
29	Ken Dryden
30	Philippe Myre

DAVID BIER

1971-72

INSTRUCTEUR/COACH: Scott Bowman
CAPITAINE/CAPTAIN: Henri Richard

NO.	NOMS/NAMES
1	Denis Dejordy Rogatien Vachon
2	Jacques Laperrière
3	Jean-Claude Tremblay
5	Guy Lapointe
6	Jim Roberts Dale Hoganson*
8	Larry Pleau* Reynald Comeau
10	Guy Lafleur
11	Marc Tardif
12	Yvan Cournoyer
14	Réjean Houle
15	Claude Larose
16	Henri Richard
17	Larry Pleau* Phil Roberto
18	Serge Savard
19	Terry Harper
20	Peter Mahovlich
21	Charles Lefley
23	Bob Murdoch Germain Gagnon
24	Charles Arnason Dale Hoganson*
25	Jacques Lemaire
26	Pierre Bouchard
27	Frank Mahovlich
29	Ken Dryden
30	Philippe Myre

DAVID BIER

1972-73

INSTRUCTEUR/COACH: Scott Bowman
CAPITAINE/CAPTAIN: Henri Richard

NO.	NOMS/NAMES
1	Michel Plasse
2	Jacques Laperrière
3	Dale Hoganson
5	Guy Lapointe
6	Jim Roberts
8	Charles Arnason
10	Guy Lafleur
11	Marc Tardif
12	Yvan Cournoyer
14	Réjean Houle
15	Claude Larose
16	Henri Richard
17	Murray Wilson
18	Serge Savard
19	Larry Robinson
20	Peter Mahovlich
21	Randy Rota Dave Gardner Yvon Lambert
22	Steve Shutt
23	Bob Murdoch
24	Charles Lefley
25	Jacques Lemaire
26	Pierre Bouchard
27	Frank Mahovlich
29	Ken Dryden
30	Wayne Thomas

DAVID BIER

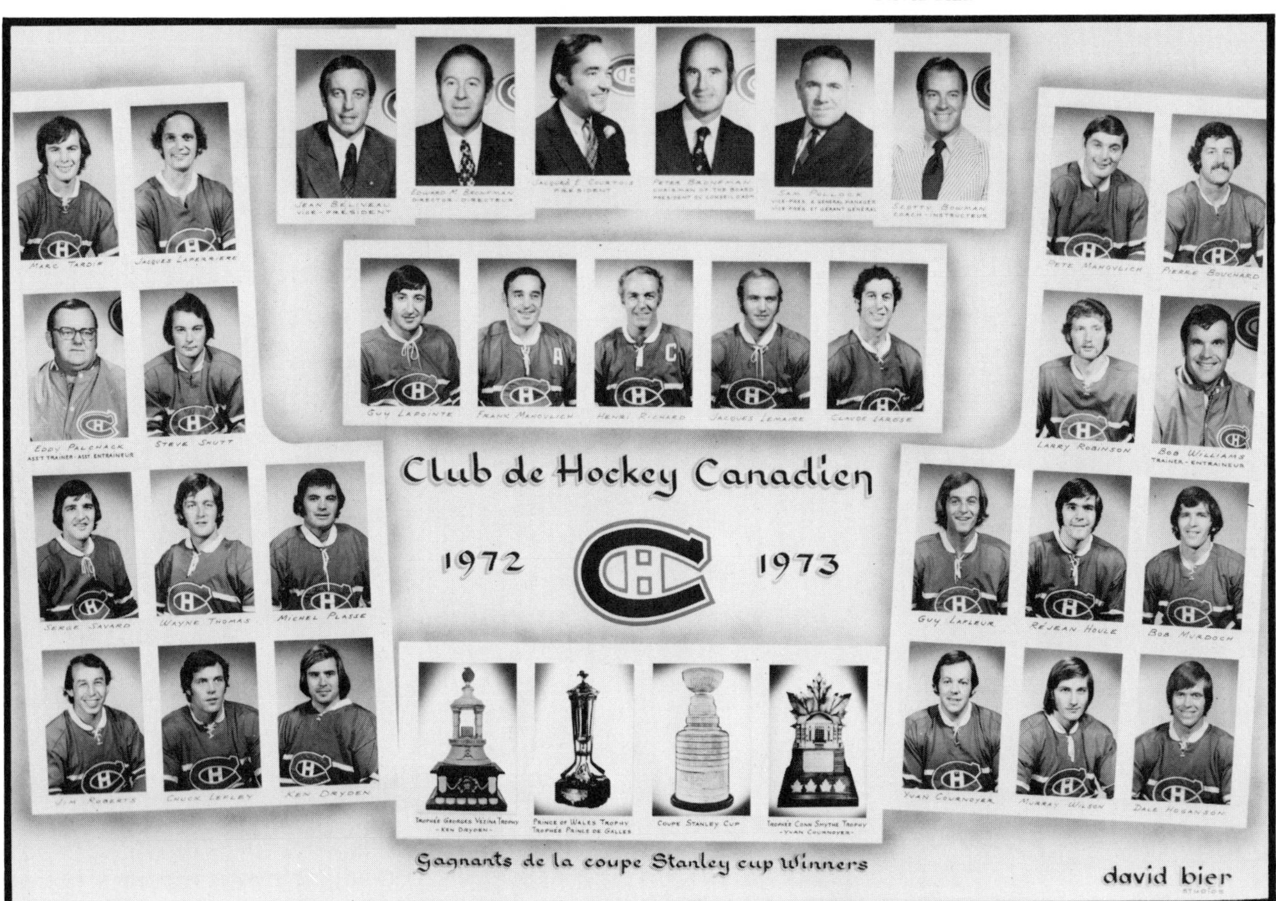

1973-74

INSTRUCTEUR/COACH: Scott Bowman
CAPITAINE/CAPTAIN: Henri Richard

NO.	NOMS/NAMES
1	Michel Plasse
2	Jacques Laperrière
3	Rick Wilson
5	Guy Lapointe
6	Jim Roberts
8	John Van Boxmeer
10	Guy Lafleur
11	Yvon Lambert
12	Yvan Cournoyer
14	Glenn Goldup
15	Claude Larose*
16	Henri Richard
17	Murray Wilson Claude Larose*
18	Serge Savard
19	Larry Robinson
20	Peter Mahovlich
22	Steve Shutt
23	Bob Gainey
24	Charles Lefley
25	Jacques Lemaire
26	Pierre Bouchard
27	Frank Mahovlich
30	Wayne Thomas
31	Michel Larocque

1974-75

INSTRUCTEUR/COACH: Scott Bowman
CAPITAINE/CAPTAIN: Henri Richard

NO.	NOMS/NAMES
1	Michel Larocque
3	John Van Boxmeer
5	Guy Lapointe
6	Jim Roberts
8	Doug Risebrough
10	Guy Lafleur
11	Yvon Lambert
12	Yvan Cournoyer
14	Glenn Goldup* Mario Tremblay
15	Claude Larose Ron Andruff Glenn Goldup*
16	Henri Richard
17	Murray Wilson
18	Serge Savard
19	Larry Robinson
20	Peter Mahovlich
21	Glen Sather
22	Steve Shutt
23	Bob Gainey
24	Charles Lefley Don Awrey
25	Jacques Lemaire
26	Pierre Bouchard
27	Rick Chartraw
29	Ken Dryden

DAVID BIER

1975-76

INSTRUCTEUR/COACH: Scott Bowman
CAPITAINE/CAPTAIN: Yvan Cournoyer

NO.	NOMS/NAMES
1	Michel Larocque
3	John Van Boxmeer*
5	Guy Lapointe
6	Jim Roberts
8	Doug Risebrough
10	Guy Lafleur
11	Yvon Lambert
12	Yvan Cournoyer
14	Mario Tremblay
15	Glenn Goldup Ron Andruff
17	Murray Wilson
18	Serge Savard
19	Larry Robinson
20	Peter Mahovlich
21	Doug Jarvis
22	Steve Shutt
23	Bob Gainey
24	Don Awrey
25	Jacques Lemaire
26	Pierre Bouchard
27	John Van Boxmeer* Sean Shanahan Rick Chartraw*
29	Ken Dryden

DAVID BIER

1976-77

INSTRUCTEUR/COACH: Scott Bowman
CAPITAINE/CAPTAIN: Yvan Cournoyer

NO.	NOMS/NAMES
1	Michel Larocque
2	Bill Nyrop Brian Engblom (éliminatoires/playoffs)
3	John Van Boxmeer
5	Guy Lapointe
6	Jim Roberts
8	Doug Risebrough
10	Guy Lafleur
11	Yvon Lambert
12	Yvan Cournoyer
14	Mario Tremblay
15	Réjean Houle
17	Murray Wilson
18	Serge Savard
19	Larry Robinson
20	Peter Mahovlich
21	Doug Jarvis
22	Steve Shutt
23	Bob Gainey
24	Pierre Mondou (éliminatoires/playoffs)
25	Jacques Lemaire
26	Pierre Bouchard
27	Rick Chartraw
28	Mike Polich (éliminatoires/playoffs)
29	Ken Dryden

1977-78

INSTRUCTEUR/COACH: Scott Bowman
CAPITAINE/CAPTAIN: Yvan Cournoyer

NO.	NOMS/NAMES
1	Michel Larocque
2	Bill Nyrop
3	Brian Engblom
5	Guy Lapointe
6	Pierre Mondou
8	Doug Risebrough
10	Guy Lafleur
11	Yvon Lambert
12	Yvan Cournoyer
14	Mario Tremblay
15	Réjean Houle
17	Murray Wilson Mike Polich
18	Serge Savard
19	Larry Robinson
20	Peter Mahovlich
21	Doug Jarvis
22	Steve Shutt
23	Bob Gainey
24	Gilles Lupien
25	Jacques Lemaire
26	Pierre Bouchard
27	Rich Chartraw
28	Pierre Larouche
29	Ken Dryden
30	Rodney Schutt
31	Pat Hughes

DAVID BIER

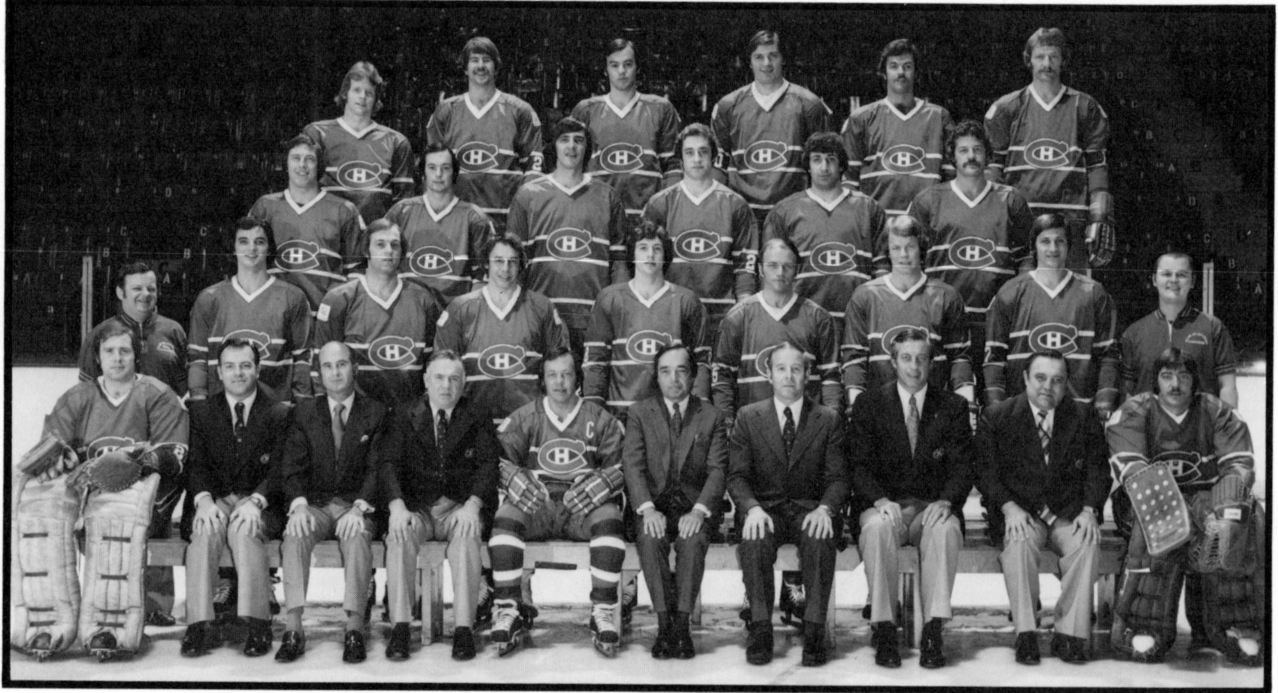

1978-79

INSTRUCTEUR/COACH: Scott Bowman
CAPITAINE/CAPTAIN: Serge Savard

NO.	NOMS/NAMES
1	Michel Larocque
3	Brian Engblom
5	Guy Lapointe
6	Pierre Mondou
8	Doug Risebrough
10	Guy Lafleur
11	Yvon Lambert
12	Yvan Cournoyer
14	Mario Tremblay
15	Réjean Houle
17	Rod Langway
18	Serge Savard
19	Larry Robinson
20	Cam Connor
21	Doug Jarvis
22	Steve Shutt
23	Bob Gainey
24	Gilles Lupien
25	Jacques Lemaire
26	Dan Newman
27	Rick Chartraw
28	Pierre Larouche
29	Ken Dryden
30	Pat Hughes
31	Mark Napier
32	David Lumley

DAVID BIER

1979-80

INSTRUCTEURS/COACHES: Bernard Geoffrion & Claude Ruel
CAPITAINE/CAPTAIN: Serge Savard

NO.	NOMS/NAMES
1	Michel Larocque
2	Gaston Gingras Moe Robinson
3	Brian Engblom
5	Guy Lapointe
6	Pierre Mondou
8	Doug Risebrough
10	Guy Lafleur
11	Yvon Lambert
14	Mario Tremblay
15	Réjean Houle
17	Rod Langway
18	Serge Savard
19	Larry Robinson
20	Danny Geoffrion
21	Doug Jarvis
22	Steve Shutt
23	Bob Gainey
24	Gilles Lupien
25	Yvan Joly (eliminatoires/playoffs)
26	Normand DuPont
27	Rick Chartraw
28	Pierre Larouche
30	Chris Nilan Keith Acton Rick Meagher
31	Mark Napier
32	Denis Herron
33	Richard Sevigny

DAVID BIER

1980-81

INSTRUCTEUR/COACH: Claude Ruel
CAPITAINE/CAPTAIN: Serge Savard

Player Personnel, automne/fall 1980

NO.	NOMS/NAMES
1	Michel Larocque
2	Gaston Gingras
3	Brian Engblom
5	Guy Lapointe
6	Pierre Mondou
8	Doug Risebrough
10	Guy Lafleur
11	Yvon Lambert
12	Keith Acton
14	Mario Tremblay
15	Réjean Houle
17	Rod Langway
18	Serge Savard
19	Larry Robinson
20	Danny Geoffrion
21	Doug Jarvis
22	Steve Shutt
23	Bob Gainey
24	Gilles Lupien
25	Doug Wickenheiser
26	Normand DuPont
27	Rick Chartraw
28	Pierre Larouche
30	Chris Nilan
31	Mark Napier
32	Denis Herron
33	Richard Sevigny

Pour Montréal, gagner était de mise, dès le début — trois équipes gagnantes de la coupe Stanley: en 1900, les Shamrocks (en haut); en 1897, les Victorias (en haut, à droite); en 1911, les Wanderers (en bas, à droite).

TEMPLE DE LA RENOMMÉE, TORONTO

Montreal's winning tradition—three early Stanley Cup teams: the 1900 Montreal Shamrocks (above), the 1897 Montreal Victorias (upper right) and the 1911 Montreal Wanderers (lower right).

HOCKEY HALL OF FAME, TORONTO

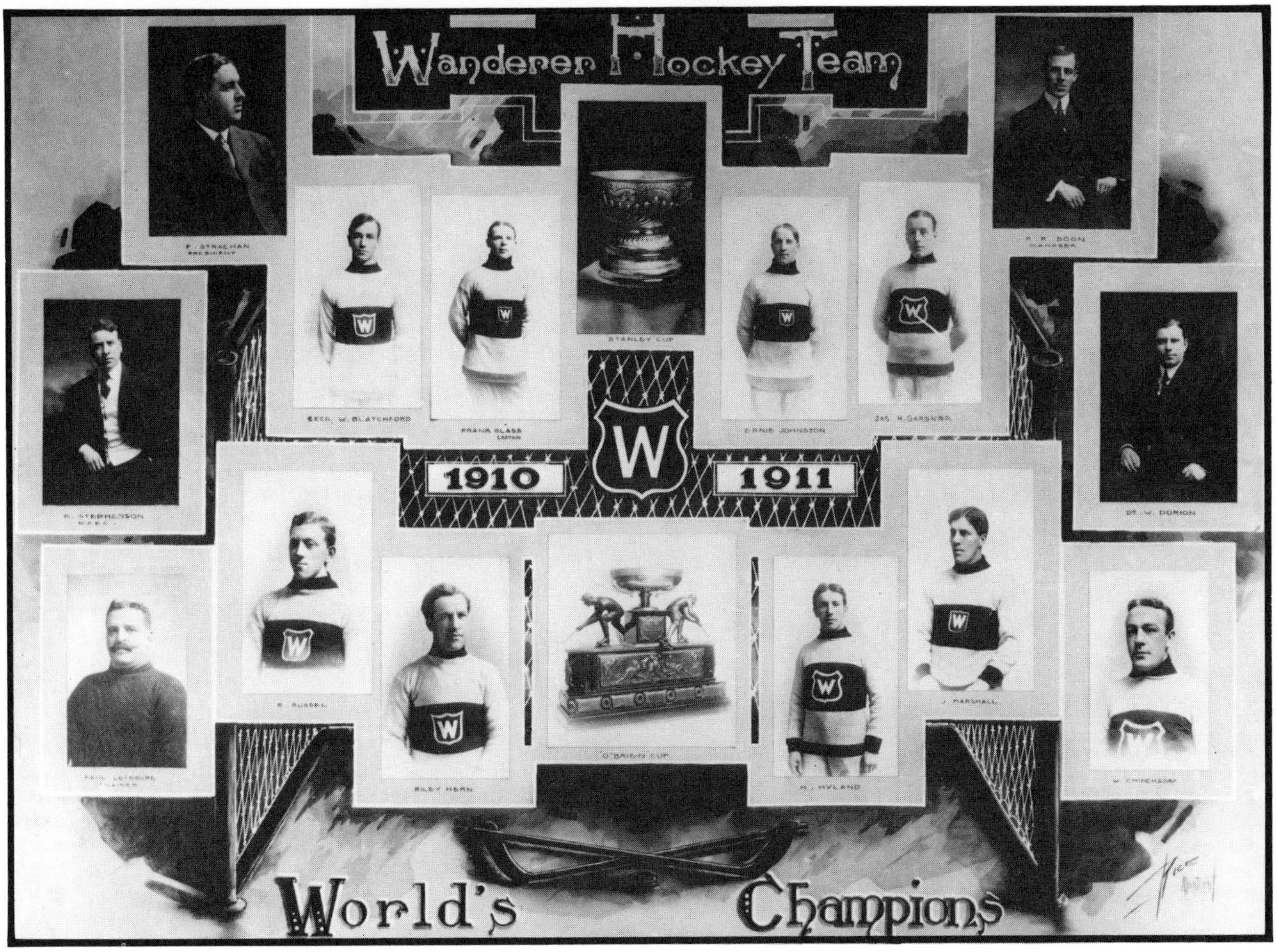

Wanderer Hockey Team
F. Strachan
President
Cecil W. Blatchford
Frank Glass
Captain
Stanley Cup
Ernie Johnston
Jas. R. Gardner
Dr. W. Dorion
1910
1911
E. Russel
Riley Hern
O'Brien Cup
H. Hyland
J. Marshall
Paul Lefebvre
Trainer
World's Champions

Les Instructeurs
Coaches

George Kennedy	1917-18 — 1919-20
Léo Dandurand	1920-21 — 1924-25
Cecil Hart	1925-26 — 1931-32
Newsy Lalonde	1932-33 — 1933-34
Newsy Lalonde & Léo Dandurand	1934-35
Sylvio Mantha	1935-36
Cecil Hart	1936-37 — 1937-38
Cecil Hart & Jules Dugal	1938-39
Babe Seibert*	1939
Pit Lépine	1939-40
Dick Irvin	1950-51 — 1954-55
Toe Blake	1955-56 — 1967-68
Claude Ruel	1968-69 — 1969-70
Claude Ruel & Al MacNeil	1970-71
Scott Bowman	1971-72 — 1978-79
Bernard Geoffrion & Claude Ruel	1979-80
Claude Ruel	1980-

*Nommé instructeur au cours de l'été mais décéda avant le commencement de la saison.
*Named coach during the summer but died before beginning of the season.

Les Capitaines
Captains

Newsy Lalonde	1917-21
Sprague Cleghorn	1921-25
Bill Coutu	1925-26
Sylvio Mantha	1926-32
Babe Seibert	1936-39
Walter Buswell	1939-40
Hector "Toe" Blake	1940-48
Bill Durnan	1948 (jan.-avr.)/(Jan.-Apr.)
Emile Bouchard	1948-56
Maurice "Rocket" Richard	1956-60
Doug Harvey	1960-61
Jean Béliveau	1961-71
Henri Richard	1971-75
Yvan Cournoyer	1975-79
Serge Savard	1979-81

Le Repêchage Amateur par les Canadiens

Amateur Draft Picks 1963-1980

			CHOIX/CHOICE	
1963	1	Garry MONAHAN	1	St. Michaels Juveniles
	2	Rodney PRESSWOOD	7	Georgetown Midgets
	3	Roy PUGH	13	Aurora Jr. "C"
	4	Glen SHIRTON	18	Port Colborne Midgets
1964	1	Claude CHAGNON	6	Comité des Jeunes, Rosemont
	2	Guy ALLEN	12	Stamford Jr. "B"
	3	Paul REID	18	Kingston Midgets
	4	Michel JACQUES	24	Juniors "B" de Mégantic
1965	1	Pierre BOUCHARD	5	St-Vincent de Paul Jr "B"
1966	1	Phil MYRE	5	Shawinigan Jrs.
	2	Maurice ST-JACQUES	11	London Nationals
	3	Jude DROUIN	17	Maple Leafs de Verdun
	4	Bob PATE	23	Canadiens jrs de Montréal
1967	1	Elgin McCANN	8	Weyburn Red Wings
1968	1	Michel PLASSE	1	Rangers de Drummondville
	2	Roger BELISLE	2	Montreal North Beavers
	3	Jim PRITCHARD	3	Winnipeg Jets
	4	Don GRIERSON	23	North Bay Trappers
1969	1	Réjean HOULE	1	Canadiens jrs de Montréal
	2	Marc TARDIF	2	Canadiens jrs de Montréal
	3	Bob SHEEHAN	32	St. Catharines Black Hawks
	4	Murray ANDERSON	44	Flin Flon Bombers
	5	Garry DOYLE	56	Ottawa 67's
	6	Guy DELPARTE	63	London Knights
	7	Lynn POWIS	68	University of Denver
	8	Ian WILKIE	74	Edmonton Oil Kings
	9	Dale POWER	75	Peterborough Petes
	10	Frank HAMILL	79	Toronto Marlboros
	11	Gilles DROLET	83	As de Québec
	12	Darrel KNIBBS	84	Lethbridge Sugar Kings

Year		Player	Pick	Team
1970	1	Ray MARTINUIK	5	Flin Flon Bombers
	2	Chuck LEFLEY	6	Canadian National Team
	3	Steve CARLYLE	31	Red Deer Rustlers
	4	Cal HAMMOND	45	Flin Flon Bombers
	5	John FRENCH	52	Toronto Marlboros
	6	Richard WILSON	66	University of North Dakota
	7	Robert BROWN	80	Boston University
	8	Bob FOWLER	93	Estevan Bruins
	9	Rick JORDAN	105	Boston University
1971	1	Guy LAFLEUR	1	Remparts de Québec
	2	Chuck ARNASON	7	Flin Flon Bombers
	3	Murray WILSON	11	Ottawa 67's
	4	Larry ROBINSON	20	Kitchener Rangers
	5	Michel DEGUISE	24	Eperviers de Sorel
	6	Terry FRENCH	25	Ottawa 67's
	7	Jim CAHOON	31	North Dakota University
	8	Ed SIDEBOTTOM	45	Estevan Bruins
	9	Greg HUBICK	53	Duluth University
	10	Mike BUSNIUCK	67	Denver University
	11	Ross BUTLER	81	Winnipeg Jets
	12	Peter SULLIVAN	95	Oshawa Generals
1972	1	Steve SHUTT	4	Toronto Marlboros
	2	Michel LAROCQUE	6	Ottawa 67's
	3	Dave GARDNER	8	Toronto Marlboros
	4	John VAN BOXMEER	14	Guelph Jrs.
	5	Edward GILBERT	46	Hamilton Red Wings
	6	Dave ELENBAAS	62	Cornell University
	7	Bill NYROP	66	University of Notre Dame
	8	D'Arcy RYAN	94	Yale University
	9	Yves ARCHAMBAULT	110	Eperviers de Sorel
	10	Graham PARSONS	126	Red Deer Rustlers
	11	Edward BUMBACCO	142	University of Notre Dame
	12	Fred RIGGALL	151	University of Dartmouth
	13	Ron LEBLANC	152	Moncton University

Year		Player	Pick	Team
1973	1	Bob GAINEY	8	Peterborough Petes
	2	Glenn GOLDUP	17	Toronto Marlboros
	3	Peter MARRIN	22	Toronto Marlboros
	4	Ron ANDRUFF	32	Flin Flon Bombers
	5	Ed HAMPHREYS	37	Saskatoon
	6	Alan HANGSLEBEN	56	North Dakota University
	7	Richard LATULIPPE	64	Remparts de Québec
	8	Gerry GIBBONS	80	St. Mary's University
	9	Denis PATRY	96	Drummondville
	10	Michel BELISLE	112	Canadiens jrs de Montréal
	11	Mario DESJARDINS	128	Sherbrooke
	12	Bob WRIGHT	143	Pembroke
	13	Alain LABRECQUE	158	Trois-Rivières
	14	Gord HALLIDAY	166	Pennsylvania University
	15	Cap RAEDER	167	New Hampshire University
	16	Louis CHIASSON	168	Trois-Rivières
1974	1	Cam CONNOR	5	Flin Flon Bombers
	2	Doug RISEBROUGH	7	Kitchener Rangers
	3	Rick CHARTRAW	10	Kitchener Rangers
	4	Mario TREMBLAY	12	Canadiens jrs de Montréal
	5	Gordon McTAVISH	15	Sudbury Wolves
	6	Gary MacGREGOR	30	Cornwall Royals
	7	Gilles LUPIEN	33	Canadiens jrs de Montréal
	8	Marty HOWE	51	Houston Aeros
	9	Barry LEGGE	61	Winnipeg Jets
	10	Mike McKEGNEY	69	Kitchener Rangers
	11	John STEWART	105	Bowling Green University
	12	Joe MICHELETTI	123	Minnesota University
	13	Jamie HISLOP	140	New Hampshire University
	14	Gordon STEWART	157	Kamloops Chiefs
	15	Charles LUKSA	172	Kitchener Rangers
	16	Clifford COX	187	New Hampshire University
	17	David LUMLEY	199	New Hampshire University
	18	Michael HOBIN	209	Hamilton Red Wings

1975	1	Robin SADLER	9	Edmonton Oil Kings
	2	Pierre MONDOU	15	Canadiens jrs de Montréal
	3	Brian ENGBLOM	22	Wisconsin University
	4	Kelly GREENBANK	34	Winnipeg - WCHL
	5	Paul WOODS	51	Sault Ste. Marie
	6	Pat HUGHES	52	Michigan University
	7	Dave GORMAN	70	Phoenix Roadrunners (WHA)
	8	Jim TURKIEWICZ	88	Toronto Toros (WHA)
	9	Michel LACHANCE	106	Canadiens jrs de Montréal
	10	Tim BURKE	124	New Hampshire University
	11	Craig NORWICH	142	Wisconsin University
	12	Paul CLARKE	158	University of Notre Dame
	13	Robert FERRITER	173	Boston College
	14	David BELL	187	Harvard University
	15	Carl JACKSON	198	Pennsylvania University
	16	Michel BRISEBOIS	204	Castors de Sherbrooke
	17	Roger BOURQUE	208	University of Notre Dame
	18	Jim LUNDQUIST	211	Brown University
	19	Don MADSON	214	Fargo Junior
	20	Bob BAIN	215	New Hampshire University
1976	1	Peter LEE	12	Ottawa 67's
	2	Rod SCHUTT	13	Sudbury Wolves
	3	Bruce BAKER	18	Ottawa 67's
	4	Barry MELROSE	36	Kamloops Chiefs
	5	Bill BAKER	54	Minnesota University
	6	Ed CLAREY	72	Cornwall Royals
	7	Maurice BARRETTE	90	Remparts de Québec
	8	Pierre BRASSARD	108	Cornwall Royals
	9	Richard GOSSELIN	118	Flin Flon Bombers
	10	John GREGORY	123	Wisconsin University
	11	Bruce HORSCH	125	Michigan Tech. University
	12	John TAVELLA	127	Sault Ste. Marie
	13	Mark DAVIDSON	129	Flin Flon Bombers
	14	Bill WELLS	131	Cornwall Royals
	15	Ron WILSON	133	St. Catharines Black Hawks

1977	1	Mark NAPIER	10	Birmingham Bulls
	2	Normand DUPONT	18	Canadiens jrs de Montréal
	3	Rod LANGWAY	36	New Hampshire University
	4	Alain COTE	43	Saguenées de Chicoutimi
	5	Pierre LAGACE	46	Remparts de Québec
	6	Moe ROBINSON	49	Kingston Canadiens
	7	Gordie ROBERTS	54	New England Whalers
	8	Robert HOLLAND	64	Junior de Montréal
	9	Gaétan ROCHETTE	90	Dynamos de Shawinigan
	10	Bill HIMMELRIGHT	108	North Dakota University
	11	Richard SEVIGNY	124	Castors de Sherbrooke
	12	Keith HENDRICKSON	137	Minnesota Duluth University
	13	Mike REILLY	140	Colorado College
	14	Barry BORRETT	152	Cornwall Royals
	15	Syd TANCHAK	154	Clarkson College
	16	Mark HOLDEN	160	Brown University
	17	Craig LAUGHLIN	162	Clarkson College
	18	Daniel POULIN	166	Saguenéens de Chicoutimi
	19	Tom McDONNEL	169	Ottawa 67's
	20	Cary FARELLI	173	Toronto Marlboros
	21	Carey WALKER	174	New Westminster Bruins
	22	Mark WELLS	176	Bowling Green University
	23	Stan PALMER	177	Minnesota Duluth University
	24	Jean BELISLE	179	Saguenéens de Chicoutimi
	25	Bob DALY	180	Ottawa 67's
	26	Bob BOILEAU	182	Boston University
	27	John COSTELLO	183	Lowell Technical College
1978	1	Dan GEOFFRION	8	Cornwall Royals
	2	Dave HUNTER	17	Sudbury Wolves
	3	Dale YAKIWCHUK	30	Portland Winter Hawks
	4	Ron CARTER	36	Castors de Sherbrooke
	5	Richard DAVID	42	Draveurs de Trois-Rivières
	6	Kevin REEVES	69	Junior de Montréal
	7	Mike BOYD	86	Sault Ste. Marie Greyhounds
	8	Keith ACTON	103	Peterborough Petes

	9	Jim LAWSON	120	Brown University
	10	Larry LANDON	137	Rensselaer Polytechnic Institute
	11	Kevin CONSTANTINE	154	Rensselaer Polytechnic Institute
	12	John SWAN	171	McGill University
	13	Daniel METIVIER	186	Olympiques de Hull
	14	Vjacheslav FEDISOV	201	U.S.S.R.
	15	Jeff MARS	212	Michigan University
	16	George GOULAKOS	225	St. Lawrence University
	17	Ken MOODIE	227	Colgate University
	18	Serge LEBLANC	229	Vermont University
	19	Bob MAGNUSON	230	Merrimack College
	20	Chris NILAN	231	North Eastern University
	21	Rick WILSON	232	St. Lawrence University
	22	Louis SLEIGHER	233	Saguenéens de Chicoutimi
	23	Doug ROBB	234	Billings Bighorns
1979	1	Gaston GINGRAS	27	Birmingham Bulls
	2	Nat NASLUND	37	Sweden
	3	Craig LEVIE	43	Edmonton Oil Kings
	4	Guy CARBONNEAU	44	Saguenéens de Chicoutimi
	5	Rick WAMSLEY	58	Brantford Alexanders
	6	Dave ORLESKI	79	New Westminster Bruins
	7	Yvan JOLY	100	Ottawa 67's
	8	Greg MOFFETT	121	University of New Hampshire
1980	1	Douglas WICKENHEISER	1	Regina Pats
	2	Rick NATTRESS	27	Brantford Alexanders
	3	John CHABOT	40	Olympiques de Hull
	4	John NEWBERRY	45	Nanaimo
	5	Craig LUDWIDG	61	University of North Dakota
	6	Jeff TEAL	82	University of Minnesota
	7	Rémi GAGNE	103	Saguenéens de Chicoutimi
	8	Mike McPHEE	124	Ryerson Polytech. Inst.
	9	Bill NORTON	145	Clarkson College
	10	Steve PENNY	166	Cataractes de Shawinigan Falls
	11	John SCHMIDT	187	University of Notre Dame
	12	Scott ROBINSON	208	University of Denver

JOUEURS SELON LE NUMÉRO

PLAYERS BY NUMBER

0

Paul-Emile Bibeault 1942-43

1

Georges Vézina 1918-25
Herb Gardiner 1926-28
Marty Burke 1928-29
George Hainsworth 1929-30
Roy Worters
Tom Murray
George Hainsworth 1930-33
Lorne Chabot 1933-34
Wilf Cude
Wilf Cude 1934-35
Wilf Cude 1935-36
Ab Cox
Babe Seibert 1936-39
Claude Bourque 1939-40
Mike Karakas
Wilf Cude
Bert Gardiner 1940-41
Wilf Cude
Bert Gardiner 1941-42
Paul-Emile Bibeault
Paul-Emile Bibeault 1942-43
Tony Graboski
Bill Durnan 1943-45
Bill Durnan 1945-46
Paul-Emile Bibeault
Bill Durnan 1946-47
Bill Durnan 1947-48
Gerry McNeil
Bill Durnan 1948-49
Bill Durnan 1949-50
Gerry McNeil
Gerry McNeil 1950-52
Gerry McNeil 1952-53
Jacques Plante
Hal Murphy
Gerry McNeil 1953-54
Jacques Plante
Jacques Plante 1954-55
Charlie Hodge
Claude Evans
André Binette
Jacques Plante 1955-56
Robert Perreault
Jacques Plante 1956-57
Jacques Plante 1957-58
Charlie Hodge
Len Broderick
Jacques Plante 1958-59
Charlie Hodge
Claude Pronovost
Claude Cyr
Jacques Plante 1959-60
Charlie Hodge
Jacques Plante 1960-61
Charlie Hodge
Jacques Plante 1961-62
Jacques Plante 1962-63
Cesare Maniago
Ernie Wakely
Charlie Hodge 1963-64
Lorne Worsley
Charlie Hodge 1964-67
Lorne Worsley 1967-68
Lorne Worsley 1968-69
Tony Esposito
Lorne Worsley 1969-70
Rogatien Vachon
Rogatien Vachon 1970-71
Rogatien Vachon 1971-72
Denis Dejordy
Michel Plasse 1972-74
Michel Larocque 1974-80

2

Bert Corbeau 1918-19
Sprague Cleghorn 1922-25
Sylvio Mantha 1926-27
Sylvio Mantha 1927-28
George Hainsworth
Sylvio Mantha 1928-32
Sylvio Mantha 1932-33
Harold Starr
Sylvio Mantha 1933-36
Bill MacKenzie 1936-37
Gallagher
Bill MacKenzie 1937-38
Marty Burke
Marv Wentworth 1938-39
Marv Wentworth 1939-40
Rhys Thomson
Cliff Goupille 1940-43
Mike McMahon 1943-44
Frank Eddolls 1944-47
Doug Harvey 1947-61
Jacques Laperrière 1963-74
Rich Chartraw 1975-76
Bill Nyrop 1975-78
Gaston Gingras 1979-80
Moe Robinson 1979-80

3

Joe Hall 1918-19
Bill Coutu 1922-23
Bert Corbeau
Bill Coutu 1923-25
Ambrose Moran 1926-27
Arthur Gauthier
Charles Langlois 1927-28
Marty Burke
Gerry Carson 1928-29
Herb Gardiner
Marty Burke 1929-32
Marty Burke 1932-33
Sylvio Mantha
Harold Starr
Gerry Carson 1933-35
Walt Buswell 1935-40
John Portland 1940-41
Doug Young
John Portland 1941-43
Emile "Butch" Bouchard 1943-56
Jean-Claude Tremblay 1960-61
Jean Gauthier
Jean-Claude Tremblay 1961-72
Dale Hoganson 1972-73
Rick Wilson 1973-74
John Van Boxmeer 1974-77
Brian Engblom 1976-77
(éliminatoires/playoffs)
1977-80

4

Newsy Lalonde 1918-19
Newsy Lalonde 1922-23
Aurèle Joliat
Aurèle Joliat 1923-38
Paul-Emile Drouin 1938-39
Wilf Cude
Paul-Emile Drouin 1939-40
Ken Reardon 1940-42
Léo Lamoureux 1942-47
Howard "Rip" Riopelle 1947-49
Howard "Rip" Riopelle 1949-50
Gilles Dubé
Claude Robert 1950-51
Hugh Currie
Ernie Roche
Ross Lowe 1951-52
Ed Litzenberger 1952-53
Reg Abbott
Calum MacKay
Ivan Irwin
*Jean Béliveau 1953-71

*Après la retraite de Jean Béliveau, le numéro 4 fut retiré de l'alignement, en l'honneur d'Aurèle Joliat et de Jean Béliveau.

*After Jean Beliveau retired, number 4 was also retired in honor of Aurele Joliat and Jean Beliveau.

5

Didier Pitre 1918-19
Didier Pitre 1922-23
Bill Boucher
Bill Boucher 1923-25
Carson Cooper 1926-27
Arthur Gauthier
George Patterson 1927-28
Léo Lafrance
Armand Mondou 1928-29
Léo Gaudreault
Armand Mondou 1929-32
Armand Mondou 1932-33
Léo Bourgault
Gizzy Hart
Leo Murray
John Gagnon 1933-34
Paul Runge 1934-35
Albert Leduc
Armand Mondou 1935-36
Rodrigue Lorrain 1936-38
Rodrigue Lorrain 1938-39
Marcel Tremblay
Rodrigue Lorrain 1939-40
Joseph Benoît 1940-43

"Dutch" Hiller 1944-46
Robert Fillion 1946-47
Jacques Locas 1947-48
Jacques Locas 1948-49
Gérard Plamondon
Gérard Plamondon 1949-50
Bert Hirschfeld
Bert Hirschfeld 1950-51
Gérard Desaulniers
Louis "Lulu" Denis
Bernard Geoffrion
Bernard Geoffrion 1951-64
Gilles Tremblay 1967-69
Ted Harris 1969-70
Guy Lapointe 1970-80

6

Odie Cleghorn 1918-19
Louis Berlinguette 1922-23
Odie Cleghorn 1923-25
Arthur Gagné 1926-29
Nick Wasnie 1929-32
Gerry Carson 1932-33
Léo Gaudreault
Hago Harrington
Georges Mantha 1933-36
Bill Miller 1936-37
Hector "Toe" Blake 1937-38
Antonio Demers
Hector "Toe" Blake 1938-48
Joe Carveth 1948-49
Joe Carveth 1949-50
Floyd Curry
Floyd Curry 1950-58
Ralph Backstrom 1958-70
Fran Huck 1970-71
Ralph Backstrom
Charles Lefley
Dale Hoganson 1971-72
Jim Roberts
Jim Roberts 1972-77
Pierre Mondou 1977-80

7

Odie Cleghorn 1922-23
*Howie Morenz 1923-34
*Après le décès d'Howie Morenz, suite à une blessure, le numéro 7 fut retiré de l'alignement en son honneur.
*After Howie Morenz died, number 7 was retired in his honor.

8

Louis Berlinguette 1918-19
Bill Cameron 1923-24
Sylvio Mantha 1924-25
Albert Leduc 1926-33
Wildor Larochelle 1933-34
Wildor Larochelle 1934-35
Gerry Carson
Wildor Larochelle 1935-36
Max Bennett
Conrad Bourcier
George Brown 1936-37
Roger Jenkins
Don Willson 1937-38
Armand Mondou
Ossie Asmundson
Stew Evans 1938-39
Louis Trudel 1939-40
Louis Trudel 1940-41
Paul-Emile Drouin
Stuart Smith
Tony Graboski 1941-42
Léo Lamoureux
Terry Reardon 1942-43
Glen Harmon
John Mahaffey
Frank Mailley
R. Lee
Glen Harmon 1943-51
Dick Gamble 1951-53
Dick Gamble 1953-54
Paul Masnick
Jack LeClair 1954-56
Jack LeClair 1956-57
Stan Smrke
Stan Smrke 1957-58
Connie Broden
Ken Mosdell
Bill Carter
Ralph Backstrom
Gene Achtymichuk
Claude Laforge
Murray Balfour
Ken Mosdell 1958-59
Bill Hicke
Bill Hicke 1959-64
Bill Hicke 1964-65
Dick Duff
Dick Duff 1965-69
Dick Duff 1969-70
Larry Mickey
Jean Béliveau 1970-71
Phil Roberto
Larry Pleau
Charles "Chuck" Lefley
Larry Pleau 1971-72
Reynald Comeau
Charles "Chuck" Arnason 1972-73
John Van Boxmeer 1973-74
Doug Risebrough 1974-80

9

Bill Coutu 1918-19
Bill Coutu 1922-23
Bill Bell
Sylvio Mantha 1923-24
John Matz 1924-25
Alfred "Pit" Lépine 1926-38
Herb Cain 1938-39
Marty Barry 1939-40
Charlie Sands 1940-43
*Maurice Richard 1943-60
*Après la retraite de Maurice "Rocket" Richard, le numéro 9 fut retiré de l'alignement en son honneur.
*After Maurice Richard retired, number 9 was also retired in his honor.

10

Jack McDonald 1918-19
Didier Pitre 1922-23
Robert Boucher 1923-24
Fern Headley 1924-25
Wildor Larochelle 1926-28
Wildor Larochelle 1928-29
George Patterson
Georges Mantha
Arthur Lesieur
Wildor Larochelle 1929-32
Wildor Larochelle 1932-33
Hago Harrington
Marty Burke 1933-34
Leroy Goldsworthy 1935-36
Paul Haynes 1936-39
Paul Haynes 1939-40
Antonio "Tony" Demers
Paul Haynes 1940-41
Louis Trudel
Alex Singbush
Georges Mantha
Elmer Lach 1941-42
Jim Haggerty
Bud O'Connor 1942-47
Robert Fillion 1947-48
John Quilty
Robert Fillion 1948-50
Tom Johnson 1950-63
Marc Rheaume
Ted Harris 1964-70
Bill Collins 1970-71
Frank Mahovlich
Guy Lafleur 1971-80

11

Edmond Bouchard 1922-23
Joe Malone
Bill Bell 1923-24
Dave Ritchie 1924-25
Gizzy Hart 1926-27
Léo Lafrance
Lachance
Gizzy Hart 1927-28
George Patterson 1928-29
Georges Mantha
Bert McCaffrey 1929-30
George Fraser
Bert McCaffrey 1930-31
Arthur Lesieur
Dunc Munro 1931-32
John Gagnon 1932-33
Léo Bourgault 1933-34
John McGill 1935-37
Cliff Goupille 1937-38
Bill Summerhill 1938-39
Bob Gracie
Ray Getliffe 1939-45
Joseph Benoît 1945-46
Joseph Benoît 1946-47
Hubert Macey
Doug Lewis
George Pargeter
Jean-Claude Campeau 1947-48
George Robertson 1948-49
Floyd Curry
Calum MacKay 1949-51
Calum MacKay 1951-52
Paul Masnick
Gene Achtymichuk
Lorne Davis
Paul Masnick 1952-53
Calum MacKay 1953-55
Bob Turner 1956-61
Jean Gauthier 1961-63
Jean Gauthier 1963-64
Ted Harris
Wayne Hicks
Claude Larose 1964-68
Jude Drouin 1968-69

Howie Glover
Jean Gauthier 1969-70
Bob Sheehan
Phil Roberto
Réjean Houle
Marc Tardif 1970-73
Yvon Lambert 1973-80

12

Marchand 1922-23
George Hainsworth 1926-29
Georges Mantha 1929-32
Georges Mantha 1932-33
Léonard Grosvenor
Armand Mondou 1933-34
Léo Bourgault 1934-35
Tony Savage
Bob McCully
Paul Haynes 1935-36
Georges Mantha 1936-40
Murph Chamberlain 1940-41
Murph Chamberlain 1941-42
Red Heron
Gord Drillon 1942-43
Murph Chamberlain 1943-49
Grant Warwick 1949-50
Bob Fryday
Gerry McNeil
Paul Meger
Hal Laycoe 1950-51
Ed Mazur
Fred "Skippy" Burchell
Dollard St. Laurent
Dick Gamble
Syd McNabney
Gérald "Gerry" Couture 1951-52
Dickie Moore
Dickie Moore 1952-53
Jean Béliveau
Dickie Moore 1953-63
Yvan Cournoyer 1964-70
Yvan Cournoyer 1970-71
Fran Huck
Yvan Cournoyer 1971-80

13

Bill Boucher 1922-23

14

George Hainsworth 1926-27
Pete Palangio
Lacroix
Armand Gaudreault 1927-28
Pete Palangio 1928-29
Gerry Carson
Arthur Lesieur
Gerry Carson 1929-30
John Gagnon 1930-32
John Gagnon 1932-33
Wildor Larochelle
John Gagnon 1935-39
John Gagnon 1939-40
Gus Mancuso
Gord Poirier
Elmer Lach 1940-41
Paul-Emile Bibeault
Terry Reardon 1941-42
Antonio Demers 1942-43
Charlie Phillips
Ernest Laforce
Phil Watson 1943-44
Rolland Rossignol 1944-45
Rosario "Kitoute" Joanette
Ed Emberg
John Mahaffey
Bill Reay 1945-53
André Corriveau 1953-54
Fred "Skippy" Burchell
Lorne Davis
Paul Masnick 1954-55
Paul Ronty
Dick Gamble 1955-56
Connie Broden
Claude Provost 1956-70
Réjean Houle 1970-73
Glenn Goldup 1973-74
Glenn Goldup 1974-75
Mario Tremblay
Mario Tremblay 1975-80

15

Desrivières 1929-30
Gus Rivers 1930-31
Gus Rivers 1931-32
Arthur Lesieur
Arthur Giroux 1932-33
Gizzy Hart
Ron McCartney
Léo Lafrance 1933-34
G. Leroux 1935-36
Joffre Desilets
Joffre Desilets 1936-38
George Brown 1938-39
Desse Smith
Bill Summerhill 1939-40
Earl Robinson
John "Red" Foran
Armand Raymond
John Adams 1940-41
"Bunny" Dame 1941-42
Maurice Richard 1942-43
"Smiley" Meronek
John Mahaffey
Irving McGibbon
Robert Fillion 1944-46
George Allen 1946-47
Floyd Curry 1947-48
Léo Gravelle 1948-49
Ed Dorohoy
Léo Gravelle 1949-50
Léo Gravelle 1950-51
Bert Olmstead
Bert Olmstead 1951-58
Ab McDonald 1958-60
Jean-Guy Gendron 1960-61
Robert Rousseau 1961-70
Claude Larose 1970-74
Claude Larose 1974-75
Ron Andruff
Glenn Goldup
Glenn Goldup 1975-76
Ron Andruff
Réjean Houle 1976-80

16

Gus Rivers 1929-30
Desrivières
Arthur Alexandre 1931-32
Arthur Giroux 1932-33
Gizzy Hart
Ron McCartney
Samuel Godin 1933-34
Paul-Marcel Raymond
Arthur Lesieur 1935-36
Hector "Toe" Blake 1936-37
Don Willson 1937-38
George Brown
Antonio "Tony" Demers
Jim Ward 1938-39
Cliff Goupille
Cliff Goupille 1939-40
John Quilty 1940-42
Paul-Emile Bibeault 1942-43
Elmer Lach
Elmer Lach 1943-54
*Henri Richard 1955-75

*Après la retraite d'Henri Richard. le numéro 16 fut retiré de l'alignement en l'honneur d'Elmer Lach et d'Henri Richard.

*After Henri Richard retired, number 16 wasalso retired in honor of Richard and Elmer Lach.

17

John Portland 1933-34
Cliff Goupille 1935-36
Wilf Cude 1936-37
George Hainsworth
Wilf Cude 1937-38
Paul Gauthier
Wilf Cude 1938-39
Armand Mondou
Armand Mondou 1939-40
Tony Graboski 1940-41
Emile Bouchard 1941-43
Fernand Majeau 1943-44
Fernand Majeau 1944-45
Nils Tremblay
Ken Reardon 1945-50
Bob Dawes 1950-51
Jean Béliveau
Ross Lowe
John McCormack 1951-53
John McCormack 1953-54
Ed Litzenberger
Gérard Desaulniers
Ed Litzenberger 1954-55
Garry Blaine
Jean-Guy Talbot
Jean-Guy Talbot 1955-67
Carol Vadnais 1967-68
Larry Hillman 1968-69
Guy Lapointe
Guy Lapointe 1969-70
Lucien Grenier
Phil Roberto 1970-71
Phil Roberto 1971-72
Larry Pleau
Murray Wilson 1972-73
Murray Wilson 1973-74
Claude Larose
Murray Wilson 1974-78
Mike Polich 1977-78
Rod Langway 1978-80

18

Irving Frew 1935-36
Armand Mondou 1936-37
Paul-Marcel Raymond 1937-38
Jim Ward 1938-39

Charlie Sands 1939-40

Alex Singbush 1940-41
"Peggy" O'Neil

"Peggy" O'Neil 1941-42
Desse Smith
Connie Tudin

"Dutch" Hiller 1942-43
Alex Smart
Tony Graboski

Gerry Heffernan 1943-44

Ken Mosdell 1944-45

Ken Mosdell 1945-46
Murdo MacKay

Ken Mosdell 1946-47

Ken Mosdell 1947-48
Gérard Plamondon

Ken Mosdell 1948-56

Marcel Bonin 1957-62

Gord "Red" Berenson 1962-63

Bryan Watson 1963-64
John Hanna

Bryan Watson 1964-65
Keith McCreary

Léon Rochefort 1965-66
Dan Grant

André Boudrias 1966-67
Garry Peters

Serge Savard 1967-80

19

Bill Miller 1935-36
Jean-Louis Bourcier
Paul Runge

Paul Runge 1936-37
Armand Mondou
Paul-Emile Drouin

Claude Bourque 1938-39

Doug Young 1939-40

Antonio Demers 1940-42

Marcel Dheere 1942-43

Fernand Gauthier 1944-45

Jim Peters 1945-47

Jim Peters 1947-48
Joe Carveth

Murdo MacKay 1948-49

Louis "Lulu" Denis 1949-50
Bob Frampton

Vern Kaiser 1950-51
Bert Hirschfeld
Gérard Plamondon

Dollard St.Laurent 1951-57

Albert "Junior" Langlois 1958

Lou Fontinato 1961-63

Terry Harper 1963-72

Larry Robinson 1972-80

20

Paul-Emile Drouin 1935-36

Paul-Emile Drouin 1936-37
Paul Runge
Armand Mondou

Paul-Emile Drouin 1937-38
Gus Mancuso
Armand Raymond

Louis Trudel 1938-39

Doug Young 1939-40

Pierre "Pete" Morin 1941-42

"Dutch" Hiller 1942-43

Gérard Plamondon 1945-46
Tony White
Mike McMahon

Léo Gravelle 1946-47

Bob Carse 1947-48
George Robertson

Jean-Claude Campeau 1948-49

Tom Johnson 1949-50

Paul Meger 1950-51
Frank King
Tony Manastersky
Jean Béliveau

Paul Meger 1951-54

Paul Meger 1954-55
Jim Bartlett

Jerry Wilson 1956-57
Ralph Backstrom
Allan Johnson
Bronco Horvath
Murray Balfour
Glen Cressman
Guy Rousseau
Philippe Goyette

Philippe Goyette 1957-63

Dave Balon 1963-67

Garry Monahan 1967-68

Garry Monahan 1968-69
Lucien Grenier

Peter Mahovlich 1969-78

Cam Connor 1978-79

Danny Geoffrion 1979-80

21

Hector "Toe" Blake 1935-36
Rosario "Lolo" Couture
Rodrigue Lorrain

Armand Mondou 1936-37
Wilf Cude

Bud O'Connor 1941-42

Marcel Dheere 1942-43

Robert Fillion 1943-44

Lorrain Thibeault 1945-46
Paul-Emile Bibeault

Roger Léger 1946-48

Roger Léger 1948-49
Jim "Bud" MacPherson

Roger Léger 1949-50

Jim "Bud" MacPherson 1950-55

Walter "Wally" Clune 1955-56
Jacques Deslauriers

Jim "Bud" MacPherson 1956-57

Albert "Junior" Langlois 1957-58
John "Jack" Bownass

Ian Cushenan 1958-59

Jean-Claude Tremblay 1959-60

Gilles Tremblay 1960-67

Lucien Grenier 1968-69

Ted Harris 1969-70
Larry Mickey
Marc Tardif
Fran Huck
Guy Charron

Réjean Houle 1970-71
Léon Rochefort

Charles "Chuck" Lefley 1971-72

Randy Rota 1972-73
Dave Gardner
Yvon Lambert

Glen Sather 1974-75

Doug Jarvis 1975-80

22

Nels Crutchfield 1934-35

Gerry Heffernan 1941-42
Rodrigue Lorrain

Gerry Heffernan 1942-43

Jean-Claude Campeau 1943-44
Bob Walton

Wilf Field 1944-45
Frank "Butch" Stahan

Vic Lynn 1945-46

John Quilty 1946-47
Hubert Macey

Normand Dussault 1947-48
Tom Johnson
Léo Gravelle

Normand Dussault 1948-51

Lorne Davis 1952-53

Lorne Davis 1953-54
Paul Masnick
Ed Litzenberger

Paul Masnick 1954-55
Orval Tessier
Don Marshall

Don Marshall 1955-63

John Ferguson 1963-71

Steve Shutt 1972-80

23

Murdo MacKay 1946-47

Murdo MacKay 1947-48
Hal Laycoe

Hal Laycoe 1948-50

Paul Masnick 1950-51

Paul Masnick 1951-52
Don Marshall
Stan Long
Bob Fryday
Ed Mazur
Garry Edmundson
Cliff Malone

Ed Mazur 1952-53
Gaye Stewart
Rolland Rousseau
Doug Anderson
Gérard Desaulniers

Ed Mazur 1953-54

Ed Mazur 1954-55
Jean-Guy Talbot
Jean-Paul Lamirande
George McAvoy

Claude Provost 1955-56

André Pronovost 1956-60

André Pronovost 1960-61
Jean-Guy Gendron

Al McNeil 1961-62

Bill McCreary 1962-63
Claude Larose

Claude Larose 1963-64
André Boudrias
Yvan Cournoyer

Keith McCreary 1964-65
Gord Berenson
Garry Peters

Gord Berenson 1965-66
Noel Price
Jean Gauthier

Noel Price 1966-67

Dan Grant 1967-68

Christian Bordeleau 1968-69
Alain Caron
Bob Berry
Garry Monahan

Christian Bordeleau 1969-70

Guy Charron 1970-71
Bob Murdoch

Bob Murdoch 1971-72
Germain Gagnon

Bob Murdoch 1972-73

Bob Gainey 1973-80

24

Wilf Cude 1938-39

Gaye Stewart 1953-54

Dick Gamble 1954-55
Guy Rousseau

Bob Turner 1955-56

Gene Achtymichuk 1956-57
Glenn Cressman

Ab McDonald 1957-58

Cecil Hoekstra 1959-60
Reg Fleming

Robert Rousseau 1960-61
Wayne Connelly

Gord Berenson 1961-62
Charles Hamilton

Gord Berenson 1962-63
Bill Sutherland

Gord Berenson 1963-64

Jean-Noël Picard 1964-65
Garry Peters
André Boudrias
Jean Gauthier

Gord Berenson 1965-66

Jean Gauthier 1966-67
Carol Vadnais
Serge Savard

Mickey Redmond 1967-70

Mickey Redmond 1970-71
Bob Sheehan

Charles "Chuck" Arnason 1971-72
Dale Hoganson

Charles "Chuck" Lefley 1972-74

Charles "Chuck" Lefley 1974-75
Don Awrey

Don Awrey 1975-76

Pierre Mondou 1976-77

Gilles Lupien 1977-80

25

Don Aiken 1957-58

Cliff Pennington 1960-61
Jean Gauthier
Glen Skov

Bill Carter 1961-62

Terry Harper 1962-63
Claude Larose

André Boudrias 1963-64
Yvan Cournoyer
Wayne Hicks
Léon Rochefort
Terry Gray

Léon Rochefort 1964-65
Jean-Noël Picard

Jean Gauthier 1965-66
Noel Price
Don Johns

Léon Rochefort 1966-67

Jacques Lemaire 1967-79

Yvan Joly 1979-80

26

Keith McCreary 1961-62

Gérald Brisson 1962-63
Jacques Laperrière

Léon Rochefort 1963-64
Terry Gray
Jim Roberts

Jim Roberts 1964-67

Bryan Watson 1967-68

Larry Pleau 1969-70
Paul Curtis
Jude Drouin

Pierre Bouchard 1970-78

Dan Newman 1978-79

Normand DuPont 1979-80

27

Frank Mahovlich 1970-74

Rick Chartraw 1974-75

Rick Chartraw 1975-76
Sean Shanahan
John Van Boxmeer

Rick Chartraw 1976-80

28

Mike Polich 1976-77

Pierre Larouche 1977-80

29

Rogatien Vachon 1966-67

Tony Esposito 1968-69
Ernie Wakely

Philippe Myre 1969-70

Ken Dryden 1970-79

30

Lorne Worsley 1963-64
Jean-Guy Morissette

Lorne Worsley 1964-66

Lorne Worsley 1966-67
Rogatien Vachon
Garry Bauman

Lorne Worsley 1967-68

Rogatien Vachon 1968-69
Tony Esposito

Rogatien Vachon 1969-70

Philippe Myre 1970-72

Wayne Thomas 1972-74

Rodney Schutt 1977-78

Pat Hughes 1978-79

Rick Meagher 1979-80
Keith Acton
Chris Nilan

31

Michel "Bunny" Larocque 1973-74

Pat Hughes 1977-78

Mark Napier 1978-80

32

Dave Lumley 1978-79

Denis Herron 1979-80

33

John Riley 1934-35

Richard Sévigny 1979-80

48

John Gagnon 1934-35
Paul-Marcel Raymond
Norm Collings

55

John McGill 1934-35

64

Armand Mondou 1934-35

75

Leroy Goldsworthy 1934-35
John Portland
Desse Roche

88

Roger Jenkins 1934-35

99

Joe Lamb 1934-35
Léo Bourgault
Desse Roche

PLAYER STATISTICS

(An asterisk indicates that during a single season a particular individual played for more than one team and that the statistics for that year are combined.)

ABBOTT, Reginald (Reg)

Born in Winnipeg, Manitoba, February 4th, 1930.
Center, left-hand shot.
5′11″, 155 lb.
Last amateur team: the Brandon Wheat Kings jrs.

SEASON	TEAM	GP	G	A	PTS	MIP
1952-53	Montreal Canadiens	3	0	0	0	0
	TOTALS	3	0	0	0	0

ACHTYMICHUK, Eugene Edward (Gene)

Born in Lamont, Alberta, September 7th, 1932.
Center, left-hand shot.
5′11″, 170 lb.
Last amateur team: the Crows Nest Pass jrs.

SEASON	TEAM	GP	G	A	PTS	MIP
1951-52	Montreal Canadiens	1	0	0	0	0
1956-57	Montreal Canadiens	3	0	0	0	0
1957-58	Montreal Canadiens	16	3	5	8	2
	TOTALS	20	3	5	8	2

Played with the team that won the Prince of Wales Trophy in 1956-57, 1957-58.

ACTON, Keith

Born in Peterborough, Ontario, April 15th, 1958.
Forward, right-hand shot.
5′8″, 167 lb.
Last amateur team: the Peterborough Petes jrs.

SEASON	TEAM	GP	G	A	PTS	MIP
1979-80	Montreal Canadiens	2	0	1	1	0
	TOTALS	2	0	1	1	0

ADAMS, John E. (Jack)

Born in Calgary, Alberta, May 5th, 1920.
Left-winger, left-hand shot.
5′10″, 163 lb.
Last amateur team: the Calgary K of C jrs.

SEASON	TEAM	GP	G	A	PTS	MIP
1940-41	Montreal Canadiens	42	6	12	18	11
	TOTALS	42	6	12	18	11

PLAYOFFS		GP	G	A	PTS	MIP
1940-41	Montreal Canadiens	3	0	0	0	0
	TOTALS	3	0	0	0	0

AIKEN, Donald (Don)

Born in Arlington, Massachusetts, January 1st, 1932.
Goaltender.

SEASON	TEAM	GP	GA	SO	AVE
1957-58	Montreal Canadiens	1	6	0	6.00
	TOTALS	1	6	0	6.00

Played with the team that won the Prince of Wales Trophy in 1957-58.
Substituted for Jacques Plante at 6:15 of the second period, March 13th, 1958.

ALEXANDRE, Arthur (Art)

Right-hand shot.

SEASON	TEAM	GP	G	A	PTS	MIP
1931-32	Montreal Canadiens	10	0	2	2	8
1932-33	Montreal Canadiens	1	0	0	0	0
	TOTALS	11	0	2	2	8

PLAYOFFS		GP	G	A	PTS	MIP
1931-32	Montreal Canadiens	4	0	0	0	0
	TOTALS	4	0	0	0	0

Died in 1976.

ALLEN, George Trenholme

Born in Bayfield, New Brunswick, July 27th, 1914.
Defenseman, left-hand shot, left-winger.
5′10″, 170 lb.
Last amateur team: the North Battleford Beavers.

SEASON	TEAM	GP	G	A	PTS	MIP
1946-47	Montreal Canadiens	49	7	14	21	12
	TOTALS	49	7	14	21	12

PLAYOFFS		GP	G	A	PTS	MIP
1946-47	Montreal Canadiens	11	1	3	4	6
	TOTALS	11	1	3	4	6

Played with the team that won the Prince of Wales Trophy in 1946-47.

ANDERSON, Douglas (Doug, Andy)

Born in Edmonton, Alberta, October 20th, 1927.
Center, left-hand shot.
5′7″, 157 lb.
Last amateur team: the Edmonton Flyers srs.

PLAYOFFS		GP	G	A	PTS	MIP
1952-53	Montreal Canadiens	2	0	0	0	0
	TOTALS	2	0	0	0	0

Played with the team that won the Stanley Cup in 1952-53.

ANDRUFF, Ronald Nicholas (Ron)

Born in Port Alberni, British Columbia, July 10th, 1953.
Center, right-hand shot.
6′, 185 lb.
Last amateur team: the Flin Flon Bombers jrs.

SEASON	TEAM	GP	G	A	PTS	MIP
1974-75	Montreal Canadiens	5	0	0	0	2
1975-76	Montreal Canadiens	1	0	0	0	0
	TOTALS	6	0	0	0	2

Played with the team that won the Prince of Wales Trophy in 1975-76.

ARBOUR, Amos

SEASON	TEAM	GP	G	A	PTS	MIP
1915-16	Montreal Canadiens	20	5	—	5	—
1918-19	Montreal Canadiens	1	0	0	0	0
1919-20	Montreal Canadiens	20	22	4	26	10
1920-21	Montreal Canadiens	22	14	3	17	40
	TOTALS	63	41	7	48	50

PLAYOFFS		GP	G	A	PTS	MIP
1915-16	Montreal Canadiens	4	3	—	3	—
	TOTALS	4	3	—	3	—

Played with the team that won the Stanley Cup in 1915-16.
Traded with Carol Wilson and Harry Mummery for Sprague Cleghorn and Bill Couture.

ARNASON, Ernest Charles (Chuck)

Born in Dauphin, Manitoba, July 15th, 1951.
Right-winger, right-hand shot.
5′10″, 185 lb.
Last amateur team: the Flin Flon Bombers jrs.

SEASON	TEAM	GP	G	A	PTS	MIP
1971-72	Montreal Canadiens	17	3	0	3	4
1972-73	Montreal Canadiens	19	1	1	2	2
	TOTALS	36	4	1	5	6

Played with the team that won the Prince of Wales Trophy in 1972-73.
Traded to the Atlanta Flames with Bob Murray and the rights to Dale Hoganson for a player named later and a future choice at the Draft in May, 1973.

ASMUNDSON, Oscar (Ossie)

Born in Red Deer, Alberta, November 17th, 1908.
Center, right-hand shot.
6′, 170 lb.

SEASON	TEAM	GP	G	A	PTS	MIP
1937-38	Montreal Canadiens	2	0	0	0	0
	TOTALS	2	0	0	0	0

AWREY, Donald William (Don, Elbows)

Born in Kitchener, Ontario, July 18th, 1943.
Defenseman, left-hand shot.
6′, 195 lb.
Last amateur team: the Niagara Falls Flyers jrs.

SEASON	TEAM	GP	G	A	PTS	MIP
1974-75	Montreal Canadiens	56	1	11	12	58
1975-76	Montreal Canadiens	72	0	12	12	29
	TOTALS	128	1	23	24	87

PLAYOFFS		GP	G	A	PTS	MIP
1974-75	Montreal Canadiens	11	0	6	6	12
	TOTALS	11	0	6	6	12

Obtained from the St. Louis Blues for Charles Lefley, November 28th, 1974.
Played with the team that won the Prince of Wales Trophy in 1975-76.
Traded to the Pittsburgh Penguins, August 11th, 1976, for the third Amateur Draft Choice of 1978 and other future considerations.

BACKSTROM, Ralph Gerald

Born in Kirkland Lake, Ontario September 18th, 1937.
Center, left-hand shot.
5′10″, 170 lb.
Last amateur team: the Hull-Ottawa Canadiens jrs.

SEASON	TEAM	GP	G	A	PTS	MIP
1956-57	Montreal Canadiens	3	0	0	0	0
1957-58	Montreal Canadiens	2	0	1	1	0
1958-59	Montreal Canadiens	64	18	22	40	19
1959-60	Montreal Canadiens	64	13	15	28	24
1960-61	Montreal Canadiens	69	12	20	32	44
1961-62	Montreal Canadiens	66	27	38	65	29
1962-63	Montreal Canadiens	70	23	12	35	51
1963-64	Montreal Canadiens	70	8	21	29	41
1964-65	Montreal Canadiens	70	25	30	55	41
1965-66	Montreal Canadiens	67	22	20	42	10
1966-67	Montreal Canadiens	69	14	27	41	39
1967-68	Montreal Canadiens	70	20	25	45	14
1968-69	Montreal Canadiens	70	20	25	45	14
1969-70	Montreal Canadiens	72	19	24	43	20
1970-71	Montreal Canadiens	16	1	4	5	0
	TOTALS	844	215	287	502	348

PLAYOFFS		GP	G	A	PTS	MIP
1958-59	Montreal Canadiens	11	3	5	8	12
1959-60	Montreal Canadiens	7	0	3	3	2
1960-61	Montreal Canadiens	5	0	0	0	4
1961-62	Montreal Canadiens	5	0	1	1	6
1962-63	Montreal Canadiens	5	0	0	0	2
1963-64	Montreal Canadiens	7	2	1	3	8
1964-65	Montreal Canadiens	13	2	3	5	10
1965-66	Montreal Canadiens	10	3	4	7	4
1966-67	Montreal Canadiens	10	5	2	7	6
1967-68	Montreal Canadiens	13	4	3	7	4
1968-69	Montreal Canadiens	14	3	4	7	10
	TOTALS	100	22	26	48	68

ALL-STAR GAMES		GP	G	A	PTS
1958	Montreal Canadiens	1	0	0	0
1959	Montreal Canadiens	1	0	1	1
1960	Montreal Canadiens	1	0	1	1
1962	NHL All-Stars	1	0	0	0
1965	Montreal Canadiens	1	0	1	1
1967	Montreal Canadiens	1	0	0	0
	TOTALS	6	0	3	3

Won the Calder Trophy (the best rookie) in 1958-59.
Played with the team that won the Prince of Wales Trophy in 1957-58, 1958-59, 1959-60, 1960-61, 1961-62, 1963-64, 1965-66, 1967-68, 1968-69.
Played with the team that won the Stanley Cup in 1958-59, 1959-60, 1964-65, 1965-66, 1967-68, 1968-69.
Traded to the Los Angeles Kings for Gord Labossière and Raymond Fortin, January 26th, 1971.

BALFOUR, Murray

Born in Regina, Saskatchewan, August 24th, 1936.
Right-winger, right-hand shot.
5'9", 178 lb.
Last amateur team: the Regina Pats jrs.

SEASON	TEAM	GP	G	A	PTS	MIP
1956-57	Montreal Canadiens	2	0	0	0	2
1957-58	Montreal Canadiens	3	1	1	2	4
	TOTALS	5	1	1	2	6

Played with the team that won the Prince of Wales Trophy in 1957-58.
Sold to the Chicago Black Hawks in June, 1959.

BALON, David Alexander (Dave)

Born in Wakaw, Saskatchewan, August 2nd, 1938.
Left-winger, left-hand shot.
5'11", 180 lb.
Last amateur team: the Prince Albert Mintos jrs.

SEASON	TEAM	GP	G	A	PTS	MIP
1963-64	Montreal Canadiens	70	24	18	42	80
1964-65	Montreal Canadiens	63	18	23	41	61
1965-66	Montreal Canadiens	45	3	7	10	24
1966-67	Montreal Canadiens	48	11	8	19	31
	TOTALS	226	56	56	112	196

PLAYOFFS		GP	G	A	PTS	MIP
1963-64	Montreal Canadiens	7	1	1	2	25
1964-65	Montreal Canadiens	10	0	0	0	10
1965-66	Montreal Canadiens	9	2	3	5	16
1966-67	Montreal Canadiens	9	0	2	2	6
	TOTALS	35	3	6	9	57

ALL-STAR GAMES		GP	G	A	PTS
1965	Montreal Canadiens	1	0	0	0
1966	Montreal Canadiens	1	0	0	0
	TOTALS	2	0	0	0

Obtained from the New York Rangers with Lorne Worsley, Leon Rochefort and Len Ronson for Jacques Plante, Don Marshall and Phil Goyette, June 4th. 1963.
Drafted by the Minnesota North Stars during the 1967 expansion, June 6th, 1967.
Played with the team that won the Prince of Wales Trophy in 1963-64, 1965-66.
Played with the team that won the Stanley Cup in 1964-65, 1965-66.

BARRY, Martin J.A. (Marty)

Born in Quebec, Quebec, December 8th, 1905.
Center, left-hand shot.
5'11", 175 lb.
Last amateur team: St. Anthony (Montreal).

SEASON	TEAM	GP	G	A	PTS	MIP
1939-40	Montreal Canadiens	30	4	10	14	2
	TOTALS	30	4	10	14	2

Bought from the Detroit Red Wings in 1939.
Hall of Fame member in June, 1965.
Died August 20th, 1969.

BARTLETT, James Baker (Jim)

Born in Verdun, Quebec, May 27th, 1932.
Left-winger, left-hand shot.
5'9", 165 lb.
Last amateur team: the Matane Red Rocks.

SEASON	TEAM	GP	G	A	PTS	MIP
1954-55	Montreal Canadiens	2	0	0	0	4
	TOTALS	2	0	0	0	4

BAUMAN, Garry Glenwood

Born in Innisfail, Alberta, July 21st, 1940.
Goaltender, left-hand shot.
5'11", 175 lb.
Last amateur team: Michigan Tech.

SEASON	TEAM	GP	GA	SO	AVE
1966-67	Montreal Canadiens	2	5	0	2.50
	TOTALS	2	5	0	2.50

OFFENSIVE RECORD		GP	G	A	PTS	MIP
1966-67	Montreal Canadiens	2	0	0	0	0
	TOTALS	2	0	0	0	0

Drafted by the Minnesota North Stars on June 6th, during the 1967 expansion.

BAWLF, Nick W.

Born in Winnipeg, Manitoba, in 1885.

SEASON	TEAM	GP	G	A	PTS	MIP
*1914-15	Montreal Canadiens/ Ontarios	15	9	—	9	—
	TOTALS	15	9	—	9	—

Obtained from the Ontarios in 1914-15.
Died June 6th, 1947.

BÉLIVEAU, Jean (Le Gros Bill)

Born in Trois-Rivières, Quebec, August 31st, 1931.
Center, left-hand shot.
6'3", 205 lb.
Last amateur team: the Quebec Aces srs.

SEASON	TEAM	GP	G	A	PTS	MIP
1950-51	Montreal Canadiens	2	1	1	2	0
1952-53	Montreal Canadiens	3	5	0	5	0
1953-54	Montreal Canadiens	44	13	21	34	22
1954-55	Montreal Canadiens	70	37	36	73	58
1955-56	Montreal Canadiens	70	47	41	88	143
1956-57	Montreal Canadiens	69	33	51	84	105
1957-58	Montreal Canadiens	55	27	32	59	93
1958-59	Montreal Canadiens	64	45	46	91	67
1959-60	Montreal Canadiens	60	34	40	74	57
1960-61	Montreal Canadiens	69	32	58	90	57
1961-62	Montreal Canadiens	43	18	23	41	36
1962-63	Montreal Canadiens	69	18	49	67	68
1963-64	Montreal Canadiens	68	28	50	78	42
1964-65	Montreal Canadiens	58	20	23	43	76
1965-66	Montreal Canadiens	67	29	48	77	50
1966-67	Montreal Canadiens	53	12	26	38	22
1967-68	Montreal Canadiens	59	31	37	68	28
1968-69	Montreal Canadiens	69	33	49	82	55
1969-70	Montreal Canadiens	63	19	30	49	10
1970-71	Montreal Canadiens	70	25	51	76	40
	TOTALS	1125	507	712	1219	1029

PLAYOFFS		GP	G	A	PTS	MIP
1953-54	Montreal Canadiens	10	2	8	10	4
1954-55	Montreal Canadiens	12	6	7	13	18
1955-56	Montreal Canadiens	10	12	7	19	22
1956-57	Montreal Canadiens	10	6	6	12	15
1957-58	Montreal Canadiens	10	4	8	12	10
1958-59	Montreal Canadiens	3	1	4	5	4
1959-60	Montreal Canadiens	8	5	2	7	6
1960-61	Montreal Canadiens	6	0	5	5	0
1961-62	Montreal Canadiens	6	2	1	3	4
1962-63	Montreal Canadiens	5	2	1	3	2
1963-64	Montreal Canadiens	5	2	0	2	18
1964-65	Montreal Canadiens	13	8	8	16	34
1965-66	Montreal Canadiens	10	5	5	10	6
1966-67	Montreal Canadiens	10	6	5	11	26
1967-68	Montreal Canadiens	10	7	4	11	6
1968-69	Montreal Canadiens	14	5	10	15	8
1970-71	Montreal Canadiens	20	6	16	22	28
	TOTALS	162	79	97	176	211

ALL-STAR GAMES		GP	G	A	PTS
1953	Montreal Canadiens	1	0	1	1
1954	NHL All-Stars	1	0	1	1
1955	NHL All-Stars	1	0	1	1
1956	Montreal Canadiens	1	0	0	0
1957	Montreal Canadiens	1	0	0	0
1958	Montreal Canadiens	1	0	0	0
1959	Montreal Canadiens	1	2	0	2
1960	Montreal Canadiens	1	0	0	0
1963	NHL All-Stars	1	0	0	0
1964	NHL All-Stars	1	1	0	1
1965	Montreal Canadiens	1	1	0	1
1968	NHL All-Stars	1	0	0	0
1969	NHL All-Stars (Div. East)	1	0	0	0
	TOTALS	13	4	3	7

Played with the team that won the Prince of Wales Trophy in 1955-56, 1957-58, 1958-59, 1959-60, 1960-61, 1961-62, 1963-64, 1965-66, 1967-68, 1968-69.
Played with the team that won the Stanley Cup in 1955-56, 1956-57, 1957-58, 1958-59, 1959-60, 1964-65, 1965-66, 1967-68, 1968-69, 1970-71.
Was selected for the first All-Star team in 1954-55, 1955-56, 1956-57, 1958-59, 1959-60, 1960-61.
Was selected for the second All-Star team in 1957-58, 1963-64, 1965-66, 1968-69.
Won the Art Ross Trophy in 1955-56.
Won the David A. Hart Trophy in 1955-56, 1963-64.
Won the Conn Smythe Trophy in 1964-65.
Became captain of the Canadiens in 1961 (1961-62 to 1970-71).
Became vice-president of the Canadiens in 1971.
Member of the Hall of Fame in June, 1972.

BÉLIVEAU, Marcil

SEASON	TEAM	GP	G	A	PTS	MIP
1914-15	Montreal Canadiens	1	0	—	0	—
	TOTALS	1	0	—	0	—

BELL, William (Bill)

Born in Lachine, Quebec, June 10th, 1891.
Defenseman, winger, center.

SEASON	TEAM	GP	G	A	PTS	MIP
*1917-18	Montreal Wanderers/ Montreal Canadiens	8	1	—	1	—
1918-19	Montreal Canadiens	1	0	0	0	0
1920-21	Montreal Canadiens	4	0	0	0	0
*1921-22	Montreal Canadiens/ Ottawa Senators	23	2	1	3	4
1922-23	Montreal Canadiens	15	0	0	0	0
1923-24	Montreal Canadiens	10	0	0	0	0
	TOTALS	61	3	1	4	4

PLAYOFFS		GP	G	A	PTS	MIP
1922-23	Montreal Canadiens	2	0	0	0	0
1923-24	Montreal Canadiens	5	0	0	0	0
	TOTALS	7	0	0	0	0

Drafted from the Montreal Red Bands Wanderers in 1917-18.
Played with the team that won the Stanley Cup in 1923-24.

BENNETT, Max

Born in Cobalt, Ontario, November 4th, 1912.
Right-winger, right-hand shot.
5'6", 157 lb.
Last amateur team: the Hamilton Tigers.

SEASON	TEAM	GP	G	A	PTS	MIP
1935-36	Montreal Canadiens	1	0	0	0	0
	TOTALS	1	0	0	0	0

BENOIT, Joseph (Joe)

Born in St. Albert, Alberta, February 27th, 1916.
Right-winger, right-hand shot.
5'9", 160 lb.
Last amateur team: the Trail Smoke Eaters.

SEASON	TEAM	GP	G	A	PTS	MIP
1940-41	Montreal Canadiens	45	16	16	32	32
1941-42	Montreal Canadiens	45	20	16	36	27
1942-43	Montreal Canadiens	49	30	27	57	23
1945-46	Montreal Canadiens	39	9	10	19	8
1946-47	Montreal Canadiens	6	0	0	0	4
	TOTALS	184	75	69	144	94

PLAYOFFS		GP	G	A	PTS	MIP
1940-41	Montreal Canadiens	3	4	0	4	2
1941-42	Montreal Canadiens	3	1	0	1	5
1942-43	Montreal Canadiens	5	1	3	4	4
	TOTALS	11	6	3	9	11

Played with the team that won the Prince of Wales Trophy in 1945-46, 1946-47.

BERENSON, Gordon Arthur (Red)

Born in Regina, Saskatchewan, December 8th, 1939.
Center, left-hand shot.
6′, 190 lb.
Last amateur team: Michigan University.

SEASON	TEAM	GP	G	A	PTS	MIP
1961-62	Montreal Canadiens	4	1	2	3	4
1962-63	Montreal Canadiens	37	2	6	8	15
1963-64	Montreal Canadiens	69	7	9	16	12
1964-65	Montreal Canadiens	3	1	2	3	0
1965-66	Montreal Canadiens	23	3	4	7	12
	TOTALS	136	14	23	37	43

PLAYOFFS		GP	G	A	PTS	MIP
1961-62	Montreal Canadiens	5	2	0	2	0
1962-63	Montreal Canadiens	5	0	0	0	0
1963-64	Montreal Canadiens	7	0	0	0	4
1964-65	Montreal Canadiens	9	0	1	1	2
	TOTALS	26	2	1	3	6

Played with the team that won the Prince of Wales Trophy in 1961-62, 1963-64, 1965-66.
Played with the team that won the Stanley Cup in 1964-65.
Traded to the New York Rangers for Ted Taylor and Garry Peters, June 13th, 1966.

BERLINGUETTE, Louis

SEASON	TEAM	GP	G	A	PTS	MIP
1911-12	Montreal Canadiens	4	0	—	0	—
1912-13	Montreal Canadiens	14	4	—	4	—
1913-14	Montreal Canadiens	20	4	—	4	—
1914-15	Montreal Canadiens	19	2	—	2	—
1915-16	Montreal Canadiens	19	2	—	2	—
1916-17	Montreal Canadiens	17	7	—	7	—
1917-18	Montreal Canadiens	20	2	—	2	—
1918-19	Montreal Canadiens	18	5	3	8	9
1919-20	Montreal Canadiens	24	7	7	14	36
1920-21	Montreal Canadiens	24	12	9	21	24
1921-22	Montreal Canadiens	24	12	5	17	8
1922-23	Montreal Canadiens	24	2	3	5	4
	TOTALS	227	59	27	86	81

PLAYOFFS		GP	G	A	PTS	MIP
1913-14	Montreal Canadiens	2	0	—	0	—
1915-16	Montreal Canadiens	1	0	—	0	—
1916-17	Montreal Canadiens	5	0	—	0	—
1917-18	Montreal Canadiens	2	0	—	0	—
1918-19	Montreal Canadiens	2	1	0	1	—
1922-23	Montreal Canadiens	2	0	1	1	—
	TOTALS	14	1	1	2	—

Drafted from the Professional Hockey League of Ontario in 1911.
Played with the team that won the Stanley Cup in 1915-16.
Traded to the Saskatoon Sheiks in 1923.
Died June 2nd, 1959.

BERNIER, Arthur (Art)

SEASON	TEAM	GP	G	A	PTS	MIP
1909-10	Montreal Canadiens	1	2	—	2	—
1910-11	Montreal Canadiens	3	1	—	1	—
	TOTALS	4	3	—	3	—

PLAYOFFS		GP	G	A	PTS	MIP
1909-10	Montreal Canadiens	12	11	—	11	—
	TOTALS	12	11	—	11	—

BERRY, Robert Victor (Bob)

Born in Montreal, Quebec, November 29th, 1943.
Left-winger, left-hand shot.
6′, 190 lb.
Last amateur team: Canada's National B Team.

SEASON	TEAM	GP	G	A	PTS	MIP
1968-69	Montreal Canadiens	2	0	0	0	0
	TOTALS	2	0	0	0	0

Played with the team that won the Prince of Wales Trophy in 1968-69.
Sold to the Los Angeles Kings, October 8th, 1970.

BERTRAND, Lorenzo

SEASON	TEAM	GP	G	A	PTS	MIP
1910-11	Montreal Canadiens	1	0	—	0	—
1913-14	Montreal Canadiens	1	0	—	0	—
	TOTALS	2	0	—	0	—

BIBEAULT, Paul-Emile (Paul)

Born in Montreal, Quebec, April 13th, 1919.
Goaltender, left-hand shot.
5′9″, 165 lb.
Last amateur team: the Montreal Canadiens srs.

SEASON	TEAM	GP	GA	SO	AVE
1940-41	Montreal Canadiens	3	15	0	5.00
1941-42	Montreal Canadiens	38	131	1	3.47
1942-43	Montreal Canadiens	50	191	1	3.82
1945-46	Montreal Canadiens	10	30	0	3.00
	TOTALS	101	367	2	3.63

PLAYOFFS		GP	GA	SO	AVE
1941-42	Montreal Canadiens	3	8	1	2.66
1942-43	Montreal Canadiens	5	15	1	3.00
	TOTALS	8	23	2	2.88

OFFENSIVE RECORD		GP	G	A	PTS	MIP
1940-41	Montreal Canadiens	3	0	0	0	0
1941-42	Montreal Canadiens	38	0	0	0	0
1942-43	Montreal Canadiens	50	0	0	0	0
1945-46	Montreal Canadiens	10	0	0	0	0
	TOTALS	101	0	0	0	0

PLAYOFFS		GP	G	A	PTS	MIP
1941-42	Montreal Canadiens	3	0	0	0	0
1942-43	Montreal Canadiens	5	0	0	0	0
	TOTALS	8	0	0	0	0

Played with the team that won the Prince of Wales Trophy in 1945-46.

BINETTE, André

Born in Montreal, Quebec, December 2nd, 1933.
Goaltender, left-hand shot.
5′7″, 165 lb.
Last amateur team: Trois-Rivières Reds jrs.

SEASON	TEAM	GP	GA	SO	AVE
1954-55	Montreal Canadiens	1	4	0	4.00
	TOTALS	1	4	0	4.00

OFFENSIVE RECORD		GP	G	A	PTS	MIP
1954-55	Montreal Canadiens	1	0	0	0	0
	TOTALS	1	0	0	0	0

BLAINE, Gary James

Born in St. Boniface, Manitoba, April 19th, 1933.
Right-winger, right-hand shot.
5′11″, 190 lb.
Last amateur team: the St. Boniface Canadiens jrs.

SEASON	TEAM	GP	G	A	PTS	MIP
1954-55	Montreal Canadiens	1	0	0	0	0
	TOTALS	1	0	0	0	0

BLAKE, Hector (Toe)

Born in Victoria Mines, Ontario, August 21st, 1912.
Left-winger, left-hand shot.
5′10″, 165 lb.
Last amateur team: the Hamilton Tigers

SEASON	TEAM	GP	G	A	PTS	MIP
1935-36	Montreal Canadiens	11	1	2	3	28
1936-37	Montreal Canadiens	43	10	12	22	12
1937-38	Montreal Canadiens	43	17	16	33	33
1938-39	Montreal Canadiens	48	24	23	47	10
1939-40	Montreal Canadiens	48	17	19	36	48
1940-41	Montreal Canadiens	48	12	20	32	49
1941-42	Montreal Canadiens	48	17	28	45	19
1942-43	Montreal Canadiens	48	23	36	59	26
1943-44	Montreal Canadiens	41	26	33	59	10
1944-45	Montreal Canadiens	49	29	38	67	35
1945-46	Montreal Canadiens	50	29	21	50	2
1946-47	Montreal Canadiens	60	21	29	50	6
1947-48	Montreal Canadiens	32	9	15	24	4
	TOTALS	569	235	292	527	272

PLAYOFFS		GP	G	A	PTS	MIP
1936-37	Montreal Canadiens	5	1	0	1	0
1937-38	Montreal Canadiens	3	3	1	4	2
1938-39	Montreal Canadiens	3	1	1	2	2
1940-41	Montreal Canadiens	3	0	3	3	5
1941-42	Montreal Canadiens	3	0	3	3	2
1942-43	Montreal Canadiens	5	4	3	7	0
1943-44	Montreal Canadiens	9	7	11	18	2
1944-45	Montreal Canadiens	6	0	2	2	5
1945-46	Montreal Canadiens	9	7	6	13	5
1946-47	Montreal Canadiens	11	2	7	9	0
	TOTALS	57	25	37	62	23

Played with the team that won the Prince of Wales Trophy in 1943-44, 1944-45, 1945-46, 1946-47.
Played with the team that won the Stanley Cup in 1943-44, 1945-46.
Won the scoring championship in 1938-39.
Won the Lady Byng Trophy in 1945-46.
Won the Hart Trophy in 1938-39.
Member of the first All-Star team in 1938-39, 1939-40, 1944-45.
Member of the second All-Star team in 1937-38, 1945-46.
Appointed coach of the Canadiens in 1955 (succeeded Dick Irvin), 1955-56 to 1967-68.
Member of the famous Punch Line with Maurice Richard at right wing and Elmer Lach at center.
Appointed captain of the Canadiens in 1940 (1940-41 to 1947-48).
Member of the Hall of Fame in June, 1966.

BONIN, Marcel

Born in Montreal, Quebec, September 12th, 1932.
Left-winger, left-hand shot.
5′9″, 175 lb.
Last amateur team: the Quebec Aces.

SEASON	TEAM	GP	G	A	PTS	MIP
1957-58	Montreal Canadiens	66	15	24	39	37
1958-59	Montreal Canadiens	57	13	30	43	38
1959-60	Montreal Canadiens	59	17	34	51	59
1960-61	Montreal Canadiens	65	16	35	51	45
1961-62	Montreal Canadiens	33	7	14	21	41
	TOTALS	280	68	137	205	220

PLAYOFFS		GP	G	A	PTS	MIP
1957-58	Montreal Canadiens	9	0	1	1	2
1958-59	Montreal Canadiens	11	10	5	15	4
1959-60	Montreal Canadiens	8	1	4	5	12
1960-61	Montreal Canadiens	6	0	1	1	29
	TOTALS	34	11	11	22	47

ALL-STAR GAMES		GP	G	A	PTS
1957	Montreal Canadiens	1	0	1	1
1958	Montreal Canadiens	1	0	0	0
1959	Montreal Canadiens	1	0	0	0
1960	Montreal Canadiens	1	0	0	0
	TOTALS	4	0	1	1

Drafted from the Boston Bruins in June, 1957.
Played with the team that won the Prince of Wales Trophy in 1957-58, 1958-59, 1959-60, 1960-61, 1961-62.
Played with the team that won the Stanley Cup in 1957-58, 1958-59, 1959-60.

BORDELEAU, Christian Gérard (Chris)

Born in Noranda, Quebec, September 23rd, 1947.
* Center, left-hand shot.
5′8″, 165 lb.
Last amateur team: the Montreal Canadiens jrs.

SEASON	TEAM	GP	G	A	PTS	MIP
1968-69	Montreal Canadiens	13	1	3	4	4
1969-70	Montreal Canadiens	48	2	13	15	18
	TOTALS	61	3	16	19	22

PLAYOFFS		GP	G	A	PTS	MIP
1968-69	Montreal Canadiens	6	1	0	1	0
	TOTALS	6	1	0	1	0

Played with the team that won the Prince of Wales Trophy in 1968-69.
Played with the team that won the Stanley Cup in 1968-69.
Brother of the Chicago Black Hawks' Jean-Pierre Bordeleau and the Quebec Nordiques' Paulin Bordeleau.
Sold to the St. Louis Blues, May 22nd, 1970.

BOUCHARD, Edmond

Born in Trois-Rivières, Quebec.

SEASON	TEAM	GP	G	A	PTS	MIP
1921-22	Montreal Canadiens	18	1	4	5	4
*1922-23	Montreal Canadiens/ Hamilton Tigers	24	6	0	6	2
	TOTALS	42	7	4	11	6

Traded with Albert Corbeau to the Hamilton Tigers for Joe Malone in 1922.

BOUCHARD, Émile Joseph (Butch)

Born in Montreal, Quebec, September 11th, 1920.
Defenseman, right-hand shot.
6′2″, 205 lb.
Last amateur team: the Montreal Canadiens srs.

SEASON	TEAM	GP	G	A	PTS	MIP
1941-42	Montreal Canadiens	44	0	6	6	38
1942-43	Montreal Canadiens	45	2	16	18	47
1943-44	Montreal Canadiens	39	5	14	19	52
1944-45	Montreal Canadiens	50	11	23	34	34
1945-46	Montreal Canadiens	45	7	10	17	52
1946-47	Montreal Canadiens	60	5	7	12	60
1947-48	Montreal Canadiens	60	4	6	10	78
1948-49	Montreal Canadiens	27	3	3	6	42
1949-50	Montreal Canadiens	69	1	7	8	88
1950-51	Montreal Canadiens	52	3	10	13	80
1951-52	Montreal Canadiens	60	3	9	12	45
1952-53	Montreal Canadiens	58	2	8	10	55
1953-54	Montreal Canadiens	70	1	10	11	89
1954-55	Montreal Canadiens	70	2	15	17	81
1955-56	Montreal Canadiens	36	0	0	0	22
	TOTALS	785	49	144	193	863

PLAYOFFS		GP	G	A	PTS	MIP
1941-42	Montreal Canadiens	3	1	1	2	0
1942-43	Montreal Canadiens	5	0	1	1	4
1943-44	Montreal Canadiens	9	1	3	4	4
1944-45	Montreal Canadiens	6	3	4	7	4
1945-46	Montreal Canadiens	9	2	1	3	17
1946-47	Montreal Canadiens	11	0	3	3	21
1948-49	Montreal Canadiens	7	0	0	0	6
1949-50	Montreal Canadiens	5	0	2	2	2
1950-51	Montreal Canadiens	11	1	1	2	2
1951-52	Montreal Canadiens	11	0	2	2	14
1952-53	Montreal Canadiens	12	1	1	2	6
1953-54	Montreal Canadiens	11	2	1	3	4
1954-55	Montreal Canadiens	12	0	1	1	37
1955-56	Montreal Canadiens	1	0	0	0	0
	TOTALS	113	11	21	32	121

ALL-STAR GAMES		GP	G	A	PTS
1947	NHL All-Stars	1	0	0	0
1948	NHL All-Stars	1	0	0	0
1950	NHL All-Stars	1	0	0	0
1951	NHL All-Stars	1	0	0	0
1952	NHL All-Stars	1	0	0	0
1953	NHL All-Stars	1	0	0	0
	TOTALS	6	0	0	0

Played with the team that won the Prince of Wales Trophy in 1943-44, 1944-45, 1945-46, 1946-47, 1955-56.
Played with the team that won the Stanley Cup in 1943-44, 1945-46, 1952-53, 1955-56.
Member of the first All-Star team in 1944-45, 1945-46, 1946-47.
Member of the second All-Star team in 1943-44.
Appointed captain of the Canadiens in 1948 (1948-49 to 1955-56).
Member of the Hall of Fame in June, 1966.

BOUCHARD, Pierre (Butch)

Born in Longueuil, Quebec, February 20th, 1948.
Defenseman, left-hand shot.
6′2″, 202 lb.
Last amateur team: the Montreal Canadiens jrs.

SEASON	TEAM	GP	G	A	PTS	MIP
1970-71	Montreal Canadiens	51	0	3	3	50
1971-72	Montreal Canadiens	60	3	5	8	39
1972-73	Montreal Canadiens	41	0	7	7	69
1973-74	Montreal Canadiens	60	1	14	15	25
1974-75	Montreal Canadiens	79	3	9	12	65
1975-76	Montreal Canadiens	66	1	11	12	50
1976-77	Montreal Canadiens	73	4	11	15	52
1977-78	Montreal Canadiens	59	4	6	10	29
	TOTALS	489	16	66	82	379

PLAYOFFS		GP	G	A	PTS	MIP
1970-71	Montreal Canadiens	13	0	1	1	10
1971-72	Montreal Canadiens	1	0	0	0	0
1972-73	Montreal Canadiens	17	1	3	4	13
1973-74	Montreal Canadiens	6	0	2	2	4
1974-75	Montreal Canadiens	10	0	2	2	10
1975-76	Montreal Canadiens	13	2	0	2	8
1976-77	Montreal Canadiens	6	0	1	1	6
1977-78	Montreal Canadiens	10	0	1	1	5
	TOTALS	76	3	10	13	56

Canadiens' first Amateur Draft choice in 1965.
Played with the team that won the Prince of Wales Trophy in 1972-73, 1975-76, 1977-78.
Played with the team that won the Stanley Cup in 1970-71, 1972-73, 1975-76, 1976-77, 1977-78.
Son of Emile Bouchard.
Drafted by the Washington Capitals in October 1978.

BOUCHER, Robert (Bob)

Born in Ottawa, Ontario.

SEASON	TEAM	GP	G	A	PTS	MIP
1923-24	Montreal Canadiens	12	0	0	0	0
	TOTALS	12	0	0	0	0

PLAYOFFS		GP	G	A	PTS	MIP
1923-24	Montreal Canadiens	5	0	0	0	0
	TOTALS	5	0	0	0	0

Brother of Frank, Bill and George Boucher.

BOUCHER, William (Bill)

Born in Ottawa, Ontario.
Right-winger.

SEASON	TEAM	GP	G	A	PTS	MIP
1921-22	Montreal Canadiens	24	17	5	22	18
1922-23	Montreal Canadiens	24	23	4	27	52
1923-24	Montreal Canadiens	23	16	6	22	33
1924-25	Montreal Canadiens	30	18	13	31	92
1925-26	Montreal Canadiens	34	8	5	13	112
*1926-27	Boston Bruins/ Montreal Canadiens	35	6	0	6	26
	TOTALS	170	88	33	121	303

PLAYOFFS		GP	G	A	PTS	MIP
1922-23	Montreal Canadiens	2	1	0	1	2
1923-24	Montreal Canadiens	6	6	2	8	14
1924-25	Montreal Canadiens	6	2	1	3	17
	TOTALS	14	9	3	12	33

Played with the team that won the Prince of Wales Trophy in 1924-25.
Played with the team that won the Stanley Cup in 1923-24.
Traded to the Boston Bruins for Carson Cooper in 1926.
Brother of Frank, George and Bob Boucher.

BOUDRIAS, André G.

Born in Montreal, Quebec, September 19th, 1943.
Center, left-hand shot.
5′8″, 165 lb.
Last amateur team: the Montreal Canadiens jrs.

SEASON	TEAM	GP	G	A	PTS	MIP
1963-64	Montreal Canadiens	4	1	4	5	2
1964-65	Montreal Canadiens	1	0	0	0	2
1966-67	Montreal Canadiens	2	0	1	1	2
	TOTALS	7	1	5	6	6

ALL-STAR GAMES		GP	G	A	PTS
1967	Montreal Canadiens	1	0	0	0
	TOTALS	1	0	0	0

Played with the team that won the Prince of Wales Trophy in 1963-64.
Traded to the Minnesota North Stars with Robert Charlebois and Bernard Côté for the first Amateur Draft of 1971 (C. Arnason), June 6th, 1967.

BOUGIE, J.

SEASON	TEAM	GP	G	A	PTS	MIP
1909-10	Montreal Canadiens	1	0	—	0	—
	TOTALS	1	0	—	0	—

BOURCIER, Conrad

Born in Montreal, Quebec, May 28th, 1916.
Center, left-hand shot.
5′7″, 145 lb.
Last amateur team: Verdun.

SEASON	TEAM	GP	G	A	PTS	MIP
1935-36	Montreal Canadiens	6	0	0	0	0
	TOTALS	6	0	0	0	0

Brother of Jean-Louis Bourcier.

BOURCIER, Jean-Louis

Born in Montreal, Quebec, January 3rd, 1912.
Left-winger, left-hand shot.
5′11″, 175 lb.
Last amateur team: Verdun.

SEASON	TEAM	GP	G	A	PTS	MIP
1935-36	Montreal Canadiens	9	0	1	1	0
	TOTALS	9	0	1	1	0

Brother of Conrad Bourcier.

BOURGEAULT, Léo A.

Born in Sturgeon Falls, Ontario, January 17th, 1903.
Defenseman, left-hand shot.
5'6", 165 lb.
Last amateur team: Guelph.

SEASON	TEAM	GP	G	A	PTS	MIP
*1932-33	Ottawa Senators/ Montreal Canadiens	50	2	2	4	27
1933-34	Montreal Canadiens	48	4	3	7	10
1934-35	Montreal Canadiens	4	0	0	0	0
	TOTALS	102	6	5	11	37

PLAYOFFS		GP	G	A	PTS	MIP
1932-33	Montreal Canadiens	2	0	0	0	0
1933-34	Montreal Canadiens	2	0	0	0	0
	TOTALS	4	0	0	0	0

Obtained from the Ottawa Senators (1932-33).

BOURQUE, Claude Hennessey

Born in Oxford, Nova Scotia, March 31st, 1915.
Goaltender.
5'6", 140 lb.
Last amateur team: Verdun.

SEASON	TEAM	GP	GA	SO	AVE
1938-39	Montreal Canadiens	25	69	2	2.76
*1939-40	Montreal Canadiens/ Detroit Red Wings	37	124	2	3.35
	TOTALS	62	193	4	3.05

PLAYOFFS		GP	GA	SO	AVE
1938-39	Montreal Canadiens	3	8	1	2.67
	TOTALS	3	8	1	2.67

OFFENSIVE RECORD		GP	G	A	PTS	MIP
1938-39	Montreal Canadiens	25	0	0	0	0
1939-40	Montreal Canadiens/ Detroit Red Wings	37	0	0	0	0
	TOTALS	62	0	0	0	0

PLAYOFFS		GP	G	A	PTS	MIP
1938-39	Montreal Canadiens	3	0	0	0	0
	TOTALS	3	0	0	0	0

BOWNASS, John (Jack, Red)

Born in Winnipeg, Manitoba, July 27th, 1930.
Defenseman, left-hand shot.
6'1", 200 lb.
Last amateur team: the Chicoutimi Sagueneens.

SEASON	TEAM	GP	G	A	PTS	MIP
1957-58	Montreal Canadiens	4	0	1	1	0
	TOTALS	4	0	1	1	0

Played with the team that won the Prince of Wales Trophy in 1957-58.

BRISSON, Gerald (Gerry)

Born in St. Boniface, Manitoba, September 3rd, 1937.
Right-winger, right-hand shot.
5'9", 155 lb.
Last amateur team: the Peterborough Petes jrs.

SEASON	TEAM	GP	G	A	PTS	MIP
1962-63	Montreal Canadiens	4	0	2	2	4
	TOTALS	4	0	2	2	4

BRODEN, Connell (Connie)

Born in Montreal, Quebec, April 6th, 1932.
Center, left-hand shot.
5'8", 160 lb.
Last amateur team: the Cincinnati Mohawks srs.

SEASON	TEAM	GP	G	A	PTS	MIP
1955-56	Montreal Canadiens	3	0	0	0	2
1957-58	Montreal Canadiens	3	2	1	3	0
	TOTALS	6	2	1	3	0

PLAYOFFS		GP	G	A	PTS	MIP
1956-57	Montreal Canadiens	6	0	1	1	0
1957-58	Montreal Canadiens	1	0	0	0	0
	TOTALS	7	0	1	1	0

Played with the team that won the Prince of Wales Trophy in 1955-56, 1957-58.
Played with the team that won the Stanley Cup in 1956-57, 1957-58.

BRODERICK, Len

Born in Toronto, Ontario, October 11th, 1930.
Goaltender.

SEASON	TEAM	GP	GA	SO	AVE
1957-58	Montreal Canadiens	1	2	0	2.00
	TOTALS	1	2	0	2.00

OFFENSIVE RECORD		GP	G	A	PTS	MIP
1957-58	Montreal Canadiens	1	0	0	0	0
	TOTALS	1	0	0	0	0

Played with the team that won the Prince of Wales Trophy in 1957-58.

BROOKS, ?

SEASON	TEAM	GP	G	A	PTS	MIP
1916-17	Montreal Canadiens	1	0	—	0	—
	TOTALS	1	0	—	0	—

BROWN, George Allan

Born in Winnipeg, Manitoba, May 17th, 1912.
Center, left-hand shot.
6', 185 lb.
Last amateur team: Verdun.

SEASON	TEAM	GP	G	A	PTS	MIP
1936-37	Montreal Canadiens	27	4	6	10	10
1937-38	Montreal Canadiens	34	1	7	8	14
1938-39	Montreal Canadiens	18	1	9	10	10
	TOTALS	79	6	22	28	34

PLAYOFFS		GP	G	A	PTS	MIP
1936-37	Montreal Canadiens	4	0	0	0	0
1937-38	Montreal Canadiens	3	0	0	0	2
	TOTALS	7	0	0	0	2

BURCHELL, Frederick (Skippy)

Born in Montreal, Quebec, January 9th, 1931.
Center, left-hand shot.
5'6", 145 lb.
Last amateur team: the Johnstown Jets.

SEASON	TEAM	GP	G	A	PTS	MIP
1950-51	Montreal Canadiens	2	0	0	0	0
1953-54	Montreal Canadiens	2	0	0	0	2
	TOTALS	4	0	0	0	2

BURKE, Martin Alphonsus (Marty)

Born in Toronto, Ontario, January 28th, 1906.
Defenseman, left-hand shot.
5'7", 160 lb.
Last amateur team: Port Arthur srs.

SEASON	TEAM	GP	G	A	PTS	MIP
*1927-28	Pittsburgh Pirates/ Montreal Canadiens	46	2	1	3	61
1928-29	Montreal Canadiens	44	4	2	6	68
1929-30	Montreal Canadiens	44	2	11	13	71
1930-31	Montreal Canadiens	44	2	5	7	91
1931-32	Montreal Canadiens	48	3	6	9	50
*1932-33	Montreal Canadiens/ Ottawa Senators	45	2	5	7	36
1933-34	Montreal Canadiens	45	1	4	5	28
*1937-38	Montreal Canadiens/ Chicago Black Hawks	50	0	5	5	39
	TOTALS	366	16	39	55	444

PLAYOFFS		GP	G	A	PTS	MIP
1928-29	Montreal Canadiens	3	0	0	0	8
1929-30	Montreal Canadiens	6	0	1	1	6
1930-31	Montreal Canadiens	10	1	2	3	10
1931-32	Montreal Canadiens	4	0	0	0	12
1933-34	Montreal Canadiens	2	0	1	1	2
	TOTALS	25	1	4	5	38

Obtained from the Pittsburgh Pirates for Charles Langlois in 1927-28.
Played with the team that won the Stanley Cup in 1929-30, 1930-31.
Traded to the Ottawa Senators for Leo Bourgeault and Harold Starr in 1932-33.
Traded from the Ottawa Senators for Albert Leduc in 1934.
Traded to the Chicago Black Hawks with Howie Morenz and Lorne Chabot for Lionel Conacher, Roger Jenkins and Leroy Goldsworthy in 1934.
Obtained from the Chicago Black Hawks for Bill MacKenzie in 1937-38.

BUSWELL, Walter Gerald Gerard (Walt)

Born in Montreal, Quebec, November 6th, 1907.
Defenseman, left-hand shot.
5'11", 170 lb.
Last amateur team: St. Francois Xavier jrs.

SEASON	TEAM	GP	G	A	PTS	MIP
1935-36	Montreal Canadiens	44	0	2	2	34
1936-37	Montreal Canadiens	44	0	4	4	30
1937-38	Montreal Canadiens	48	2	15	17	24
1938-39	Montreal Canadiens	46	3	7	10	10
1939-40	Montreal Canadiens	46	1	3	4	10
	TOTALS	228	6	31	37	108

PLAYOFFS		GP	G	A	PTS	MIP
1936-37	Montreal Canadiens	5	0	0	0	2
1937-38	Montreal Canadiens	3	0	0	0	0
1938-39	Montreal Canadiens	3	2	0	2	2
	TOTALS	11	2	0	2	4

Obtained from the Detroit Red Wings in 1935.
Appointed captain of the Canadiens in 1939-40.

CAIN, Herbert (Herb, Herbie)

Born in Newmarket, Ontario, December 24th, 1912.
Left-winger, left-hand shot.
5'11", 180 lb.
Last amateur team: the Hamilton Tigers.

SEASON	TEAM	GP	G	A	PTS	MIP
1938-39	Montreal Canadiens	45	13	14	27	26
	TOTALS	45	13	14	27	26

PLAYOFFS		GP	G	A	PTS	MIP
1938-39	Montreal Canadiens	3	0	0	0	2
	TOTALS	3	0	0	0	2

Traded to the Montreal Maroons for Nelson Crutchfield in 1934.
Drafted from the Montreal Maroons in 1938.
Traded to the Boston Bruins with Des Smith for Ray Getliffe and Charlie Sands in 1939.

CAMERON, Harold Hugh (Harry)

Born in Pembroke, Ontario, February 6th, 1890.
Defenseman.

SEASON	TEAM	GP	G	A	PTS	MIP
*1919-20	Toronto St. Patricks/ Montreal Canadiens	23	16	1	17	11
	TOTALS	23	16	1	17	11

Obtained from the Toronto St. Patricks and then returned to them during the 1919-20 season.
Member of the Hall of Fame in August, 1962.
Died October 20, 1953.

CAMERON, William (Bill)

Born in Timmins, Ontario in 1904.

SEASON	TEAM	GP	G	A	PTS	MIP
1923-24	Montreal Canadiens	18	0	0	0	2
	TOTALS	18	0	0	0	2

PLAYOFFS		GP	G	A	PTS	MIP
1923-24	Montreal Canadiens	6	0	0	0	0
	TOTALS	6	0	0	0	0

CAMPBELL, David (Dave)

Born in Lachute, Quebec, April 27th, 1896.
Defenseman.

SEASON	TEAM	GP	G	A	PTS	MIP
1920-21	Montreal Canadiens	3	0	0	0	—
	TOTALS	3	0	0	0	—

CAMPBELL, Herb

SEASON	TEAM	GP	G	A	PTS	MIP
1920-21	Montreal Canadiens	3	0	—	0	—
	TOTALS	3	0	—	0	—

CAMPEAU, Jean-Claude (Tod)

Born in St-Jerome, Quebec, June 4th, 1923.
Center, left-hand shot.
5'11", 175 lb.
Last amateur team: the Montreal Royals srs.

SEASON	TEAM	GP	G	A	PTS	MIP
1943-44	Montreal Canadiens	2	0	0	0	0
1947-48	Montreal Canadiens	14	2	2	4	4
1948-49	Montreal Canadiens	26	3	7	10	12
	TOTALS	42	5	9	14	16

PLAYOFFS		GP	G	A	PTS	MIP
1948-49	Montreal Canadiens	1	0	0	0	0
	TOTALS	1	0	0	0	0

Played with the team that won the Prince of Wales Trophy in 1943-44.

CARON, Alain Luc (Boom Boom)

Born in Dolbeau, Quebec, April 27th, 1938.
Right-winger, right-hand shot.
5'10", 175 lb.
Last amateur team: the Charlotte Checkers.

SEASON	TEAM	GP	G	A	PTS	MIP
1968-69	Montreal Canadiens	2	0	0	0	0
	TOTALS	2	0	0	0	0

Obtained from the Oakland Seals with Wally Boyer at the first Amateur Draft choice in 1968 (Jim Pritchard) and the first Amateur Draft choice in 1970 (Ray Martiniuk) for Norm Ferguson and Stan Fuller May 21, 1968.
Played with the team that won the Prince of Wales Trophy in 1968-69.

CARROLL, George

Defenseman.

SEASON	TEAM	GP	G	A	PTS	MIP
*1924-25	Montreal Canadiens/ Boston Bruins	15	0	0	0	9
	TOTALS	15	0	0	0	9

Played with the team that won the Prince of Wales Trophy in 1924-25.

CARSE, Robert Allison (Bob)

Born in Edmonton, Alberta, July 19th, 1919.
Left-winger, left-hand shot.
5'9", 160 lb.
Last amateur team: the Edmonton A.C. jrs.

SEASON	TEAM	GP	G	A	PTS	MIP
1947-48	Montreal Canadiens	22	3	3	6	16
	TOTALS	22	3	3	6	16

CARSON, Gerald (Gerry, Stub)

Born in Parry Sound, Ontario, October 10th, 1905.
Defenseman, left-hand shot.
5'10", 175 lb.
Last amateur team: The Grimsby Peach Kings.

SEASON	TEAM	GP	G	A	PTS	MIP
*1928-29	New York Rangers/ Montreal Canadiens	40	0	0	0	9
1929-30	Montreal Canadiens	35	1	0	1	8
1932-33	Montreal Canadiens	48	5	2	7	53
1933-34	Montreal Canadiens	48	5	1	6	51
1934-35	Montreal Canadiens	48	0	5	5	56
	TOTALS	219	11	8	19	177

PLAYOFFS		GP	G	A	PTS	MIP
1929-30	Montreal Canadiens	6	0	0	0	0
1932-33	Montreal Canadiens	2	0	0	0	2
1933-34	Montreal Canadiens	2	0	0	0	2
1934-35	Montreal Canadiens	2	0	0	0	4
	TOTALS	12	0	0	0	8

Obtained from the New York Rangers (1928-29).
Played with the team that won the Stanley Cup in 1929-30.

CARTER, William (Bill)

Born in Cornwall, Ontario, December 2nd, 1937.
Center, left-hand shot.
5'11", 155 lb.
Last amateur team: the Hull-Ottawa Canadiens jrs.

SEASON	TEAM	GP	G	A	PTS	MIP
1957-58	Montreal Canadiens	1	0	0	0	0
1961-62	Montreal Canadiens	7	0	0	0	1
	TOTALS	8	0	0	0	1

Played with the team that won the Prince of Wales Trophy in 1957-58, 1961-62.

CARVETH, Joseph Gordon (Jos, Joe)

Born in Regina, Saskatchewan, March 21st, 1918.
Right-winger, right-hand shot.
5'10", 175 lb.
Last amateur team: the Detroit Pontiacs.

SEASON	TEAM	GP	G	A	PTS	MIP
*1947-48	Montreal Canadiens/ Boston Bruins	57	9	19	28	8
1948-49	Montreal Canadiens	60	15	22	37	8
*1949-50	Montreal Canadiens/ Detroit Red Wings	71	14	18	32	15
	TOTALS	188	38	59	97	31

PLAYOFFS		GP	G	A	PTS	MIP
1948-49	Montreal Canadiens	7	0	1	1	8
	TOTALS	7	0	1	1	8

Obtained from the Boston Bruins for Jim Peters in 1948.
Traded to the Detroit Red Wings for Calum MacKay in 1950.

CATTARINICH, Joseph (Jos, Joe)

Goaltender.

SEASON	TEAM	GP	GA	SO	AVE
1909-10	Montreal Canadiens	1	6	0	6.00
	TOTALS	1	6	0	6.00

PLAYOFFS		GP	GA	SO	AVE
1909-10	Montreal Canadiens	3	23	0	7.66
	TOTALS	3	23	0	7.66

OFFENSIVE RECORD		GP	G	A	PTS	MIP
1909-10	Montreal Canadiens	1	0	—	0	7.66
	TOTALS	1	0	—	0	7.66

PLAYOFFS		GP	G	A	PTS	MIP
1909-10	Montreal Canadiens	3	0	—	0	—
	TOTALS	3	0	—	0	—

CHABOT, Lorne E.

Born in Montreal, Quebec, October 5th, 1900.
Goaltender, left-hand shot.
6'1", 185 lb.
Last amateur team: Port Arthur srs.

SEASON	TEAM	GP	GA	SO	AVE
1933-34	Montreal Canadiens	47	101	8	2.15
	TOTALS	47	101	8	2.15

PLAYOFFS		GP	GA	SO	AVE
1933-34	Montreal Canadiens	2	4	0	2.00
	TOTALS	2	4	0	2.00

OFFENSIVE RECORD		GP	G	A	PTS	MIP
1933-34	Montreal Canadiens	47	0	0	0	2
	TOTALS	47	0	0	0	2

PLAYOFFS		GP	G	A	PTS	MIP
1933-34	Montreal Canadiens	2	0	0	0	0
	TOTALS	2	0	0	0	0

Obtained from the Toronto Maple Leafs for George Hainsworth at the beginning of the 1933-34 season.
Traded to the Chicago Black Hawks with Howie Morenz and Martin Burke for Lionel Conacher, Roger Jenkins and Leroy Goldsworthy (1934).
Died October 10th, 1946.

CHAMBERLAIN, Erwin Groves (Murph)

Born in Shawville, Quebec, February 14th, 1915.
Left-winger, left-hand shot.
5'11", 170 lb.
Last amateur team: the Sudbury Frood Mines.

SEASON	TEAM	GP	G	A	PTS	MIP
1940-41	Montreal Canadiens	45	10	15	25	75
*1941-42	Montreal Canadiens/ New York Americans	36	12	12	24	46
1943-44	Montreal Canadiens	47	15	32	47	65
1944-45	Montreal Canadiens	32	2	12	14	38
1945-46	Montreal Canadiens	40	12	14	26	42
1946-47	Montreal Canadiens	49	10	10	20	97
1947-48	Montreal Canadiens	30	6	3	9	62
1948-49	Montreal Canadiens	54	5	8	13	111
	TOTALS	333	72	106	178	536

PLAYOFFS		GP	G	A	PTS	MIP
1940-41	Montreal Canadiens	3	0	2	2	11
1943-44	Montreal Canadiens	9	5	3	8	12
1944-45	Montreal Canadiens	6	1	1	2	10
1945-46	Montreal Canadiens	9	4	2	6	18
1946-47	Montreal Canadiens	11	1	3	4	19
1948-49	Montreal Canadiens	4	0	0	0	8
	TOTALS	42	11	11	22	78

Bought from the Toronto Maple Leafs in 1940.
Played with the team that won the Prince of Wales Trophy in 1943-44, 1944-45, 1945-46, 1946-47.
Played with the team that won the Stanley Cup in 1943-44, 1945-46.
Appointed assistant captain of the Canadiens in 1947.

CHARRON, Guy

Born in Verdun, Quebec, January 24th, 1949.
Left-winger, left-hand shot.
5'10", 175 lb.
Last amateur team: the Montreal Canadiens jrs.

SEASON	TEAM	GP	G	A	PTS	MIP
1969-70	Montreal Canadiens	5	0	0	0	0
1970-71	Montreal Canadiens	15	2	2	4	2
	TOTALS	20	2	2	4	2

Traded to the Detroit Red Wings with Mickey Redmond and Bill Collins for Frank Mahovlich, January 13, 1971.

CHARTRAW, Rick Raymond R.

Born in Caracas, Venezuela, July 13th, 1954.
Defenseman, right-winger, right-hand shot.
6'2", 210 lb.
Last amateur team: the Kitchener Rangers jrs.

SEASON	TEAM	GP	G	A	PTS	MIP
1974-75	Montreal Canadiens	12	0	0	0	6
1975-76	Montreal Canadiens	16	1	3	4	25
1976-77	Montreal Canadiens	43	3	4	7	59
1977-78	Montreal Canadiens	68	4	12	16	64
1978-79	Montreal Canadiens	62	5	11	16	29
1979-80	Montreal Canadiens	66	5	7	12	35
	TOTALS	267	18	37	55	218

PLAYOFFS		GP	G	A	PTS	MIP
1975-76	Montreal Canadiens	2	0	0	0	0
1976-77	Montreal Canadiens	13	2	1	3	17
1979-80	Montreal Canadiens	10	2	2	4	0
	TOTALS	25	4	3	7	17

Third Amateur Draft choice of the Canadiens in 1974.
Played with the team that won the Prince of Wales Trophy in 1975-76, 1976-77, 1977-78.
Played with the team that won the Stanley Cup in 1975-76, 1976-77, 1977-78, 1978-79.

CLEGHORN, Ogilvie (Odie)

Born in Montreal, Quebec, in 1891.
Center, defenseman.
Last amateur team: the Pittsburgh Yellow Jackets.

SEASON	TEAM	GP	G	A	PTS	MIP
1918-19	Montreal Canadiens	17	23	6	29	22
1919-20	Montreal Canadiens	21	19	3	22	30
1920-21	Montreal Canadiens	21	5	4	9	8
1921-22	Montreal Canadiens	23	21	3	24	26
1922-23	Montreal Canadiens	24	19	7	26	14
1923-24	Montreal Canadiens	22	3	3	6	14
1924-25	Montreal Canadiens	30	3	2	5	14
	TOTALS	158	93	28	121	128

PLAYOFFS		GP	G	A	PTS	MIP
1918-19	Montreal Canadiens	10	9	0	9	0
1922-23	Montreal Canadiens	2	0	0	0	2
1923-24	Montreal Canadiens	6	0	1	1	0
1924-25	Montreal Canadiens	5	0	1	1	0
	TOTALS	23	9	2	11	2

Signed up with the Canadiens in 1918.
Played with the team that won the Stanley Cup in 1923-24.
Played with the team that won the Prince of Wales Trophy in 1924-25.
Member of the Hall of Fame in April, 1958.
Brother of Sprague Cleghorn.
Died July 13, 1956.

CLEGHORN, Sprague

Born in Montreal, Quebec, in 1890.
Defenseman.

SEASON	TEAM	GP	G	A	PTS	MIP
1921-22	Montreal Canadiens	24	17	7	24	63
1922-23	Montreal Canadiens	24	9	4	13	34
1923-24	Montreal Canadiens	23	8	3	11	39
1924-25	Montreal Canadiens	27	8	1	9	82
	TOTALS	98	42	15	57	218

PLAYOFFS		GP	G	A	PTS	MIP
1922-23	Montreal Canadiens	1	0	0	0	0
1923-24	Montreal Canadiens	6	2	1	3	2
1924-25	Montreal Canadiens	6	1	2	3	4
	TOTALS	13	3	3	6	6

Obtained with Bill Couture (Coutu) for Harry Mummery, Carol Wilson and Amos Arbour in 1921.
Played with the team that won the Stanley Cup in 1923-24.
Played with the team that won the Prince of Wales Trophy in 1924-25.
Sold to the Boston Bruins for $5,000 in 1925.
Appointed captain of the Canadiens from 1921-22 to 1924-25.
Member of the Hall of Fame in April, 1958.
Brother of Ogilvie "Odie" Cleghorn.
Died July 12, 1956.

CLUNE, Walter James (Walt, Wally)

Born in Toronto, Ontario, February 20th, 1930.
Defenseman, right-hand shot.
5'9", 150 lb.
Last amateur team: the Montreal Royal srs.

SEASON	TEAM	GP	G	A	PTS	MIP
1955-56	Montreal Canadiens	5	0	0	0	6
	TOTALS	5	0	0	0	6

Played with the team that won the Prince of Wales Trophy in 1955-56.

CODERRE, Sam

Coderre played for two weeks with the Canadiens. He had been borrowed from the Ottawa Senators. We are not sure of the exact year, but it was between 1918 and 1921.
Incomplete record: See *The Flying Frenchmen, Hockey's Greatest Dynasty*, by Stan Fischler and Maurice Richard, pp. 33-34.

COLLINGS, Norman (Norm, Dodger)

Born in Bradford, Ontario.

SEASON	TEAM	GP	G	A	PTS	MIP
1934-35	Montreal Canadiens	1	0	1	1	0
	TOTALS	1	0	1	1	0

COLLINS, William Earl (Bill)

Born in Ottawa, Ontario, July 13th, 1943.
Right-winger, right-hand shot.
6', 178 lb.
Last amateur team: the Whitby Dunlops jrs.

SEASON	TEAM	GP	G	A	PTS	MIP
1970-71	Montreal Canadiens	40	6	2	8	39
	TOTALS	40	6	2	8	39

Obtained from the Minnesota North Stars for Jude Drouin, June 10th, 1970.
Traded to the Detroit Red Wings with Mickey Redmond and Guy Charron for Frank Mahovlich, January 13th,1971.

COMEAU, Reynald Xavier (Rey)

Born in Montreal, Quebec, October 25th, 1948.
Center, left-hand shot.
5'8", 170 lb.
Last amateur team: Verdun.

SEASON	TEAM	GP	G	A	PTS	MIP
1971-72	Montreal Canadiens	4	0	0	0	0
	TOTALS	4	0	0	0	0

Drafted from the Vancouver Canucks during the Inter-League Draft, June 1971.
Sold to the Atlanta Flames, June 16, 1972.

CONNELLY, Wayne Francis

Born in Rouyn, Quebec, December 16th, 1939.
Right-winger, right-hand shot.
5'10", 170 lb.
Last amateur team: the Peterborough Petes jrs.

SEASON	TEAM	GP	G	A	PTS	MIP
1960-61	Montreal Canadiens	3	0	0	0	0
	TOTALS	3	0	0	0	0

Played with the team that won the Prince of Wales Trophy in 1960-61.
Sold to the Boston Bruins June 10, 1961.

CONNOR, Cam

Born in Winnipeg, Manitoba, August 10th, 1954.
Left-winger, left-hand shot.
6'2", 200 lb.
Last amateur team: Flin Flon Bombers WCHL.

SEASON	TEAM	GP	G	A	PTS	MIP
1978-79	Montreal Canadiens	23	1	3	4	39
	TOTALS	23	1	3	4	39

PLAYOFFS		GP	G	A	PTS	MIP
1978-79	Montreal Canadiens	8	1	0	1	0
	TOTALS	8	1	0	1	0

COOPER, Carson E.

Born in Cornwall, Ontario.

SEASON	TEAM	GP	G	A	PTS	MIP
*1926-27	Montreal Canadiens/ Boston Bruins	24	9	3	12	16
	TOTALS	24	9	3	12	16

PLAYOFFS		GP	G	A	PTS	MIP
1926-27	Montreal Canadiens	3	0	0	0	0
	TOTALS	3	0	0	0	0

Obtained from the Boston Bruins for Bill Boucher in 1926-27.
Died April 7, 1955.

CORBEAU, Albert (Bert)

Point, defenseman.

SEASON	TEAM	GP	G	A	PTS	MIP
1914-15	Montreal Canadiens	18	1	—	1	—
1915-16	Montreal Canadiens	23	7	—	7	—
1916-17	Montreal Canadiens	19	7	—	7	—
1917-18	Montreal Canadiens	20	8	—	8	—
1918-19	Montreal Canadiens	16	2	1	3	51
1919-20	Montreal Canadiens	23	11	5	16	59
1920-21	Montreal Canadiens	24	12	1	13	86
1921-22	Montreal Canadiens	22	4	7	11	26
	TOTALS	165	52	14	66	222

PLAYOFFS		GP	G	A	PTS	MIP
1915-16	Montreal Canadiens	5	0	—	0	—
1916-17	Montreal Canadiens	6	4	—	4	—
1917-18	Montreal Canadiens	2	1	0	1	—
1918-19	Montreal Canadiens	10	1	0	1	—
	TOTALS	23	6	0	6	—

Played with the team that won the Stanley Cup in 1915-16.
Traded to the Hamilton Tigers with Edmond Bouchard for Joe Malone in 1922.
Died September 22, 1942.

CORMIER, Roger

SEASON	TEAM	GP	G	A	PTS	MIP
1925-26	Montreal Canadiens	—	0	0	0	—
	TOTALS	—	0	0	0	—

CORRIVEAU, Fred André (Dédé)

Born in Grand-Mère, Quebec, May 15th, 1928.
Right-winger, right-hand shot.
5′8″, 135 lb.
Last amateur team: the Valleyfield Braves.

SEASON	TEAM	GP	G	A	PTS	MIP
1953-54	Montreal Canadiens	3	0	1	1	0
	TOTALS	3	0	1	1	0

COUGHLIN, Jack

SEASON	TEAM	GP	G	A	PTS	MIP
*1919-20	Quebec Bulldogs/ Montreal Canadiens	11	0	0	0	—
	TOTALS	11	0	0	0	—

COURNOYER, Yvan Serge

Born in Drummondville, Quebec, November 22nd, 1943.
Right-winger, left-hand shot.
5′7″, 178 lb.
Last amateur team: the Montreal Canadiens jrs.

SEASON	TEAM	GP	G	A	PTS	MIP
1963-64	Montreal Canadiens	5	4	0	4	0
1964-65	Montreal Canadiens	55	7	10	17	10
1965-66	Montreal Canadiens	65	18	11	29	8
1966-67	Montreal Canadiens	69	25	15	40	14
1967-68	Montreal Canadiens	64	28	32	60	23
1968-69	Montreal Canadiens	76	43	44	87	31
1969-70	Montreal Canadiens	72	27	36	63	23
1970-71	Montreal Canadiens	65	37	36	73	21
1971-72	Montreal Canadiens	73	47	36	83	15
1972-73	Montreal Canadiens	67	40	39	79	18
1973-74	Montreal Canadiens	67	40	33	73	18
1974-75	Montreal Canadiens	76	29	45	74	32
1975-76	Montreal Canadiens	71	32	36	68	20
1976-77	Montreal Canadiens	60	25	28	53	8
1977-78	Montreal Canadiens	68	24	29	54	12
1978-79	Montreal Canadiens	15	2	5	7	2
	TOTALS	968	428	435	864	255

PLAYOFFS		GP	G	A	PTS	MIP
1964-65	Montreal Canadiens	12	3	1	4	0
1965-66	Montreal Canadiens	10	2	3	5	2
1966-67	Montreal Canadiens	10	2	3	5	6
1967-68	Montreal Canadiens	13	6	8	14	4
1968-69	Montreal Canadiens	14	4	7	11	5
1970-71	Montreal Canadiens	20	10	12	22	6
1971-72	Montreal Canadiens	6	2	1	3	2
1972-73	Montreal Canadiens	17	15	10	25	2
1973-74	Montreal Canadiens	6	5	2	7	2
1974-75	Montreal Canadiens	11	5	6	11	4
1975-76	Montreal Canadiens	13	3	6	9	4
1976-77	Montreal Canadiens	—	—	—	—	—
1977-78	Montreal Canadiens	15	7	4	11	10
	TOTALS	147	64	63	127	47

ALL-STAR GAMES		GP	G	A	PTS
1967	Montreal Canadiens	1	0	0	0
1971	All-Stars (Div. East)	1	1	0	1
1972	All-Stars (Div. East)	1	0	0	0
1973	All-Stars (Div. East)	1	0	0	0
1974	Prince of Wales	1	1	1	2
1978	Prince of Wales	1	0	0	0
	TOTALS	6	2	1	3

Played with the team that won the Prince of Wales Trophy in 1963-64, 1965-66, 1967-68, 1968-69, 1972-73, 1975-76, 1976-77, 1977-78.
Played with the team that won the Stanley Cup in 1964-65, 1965-66, 1967-68, 1968-69, 1970-71, 1972-73, 1975-76, 1976-77, 1977-78, 1978-79.
Won the Conn Smythe Trophy in 1972-73.
Member of the second All-Star team in 1968-69, 1970-71, 1971-72, 1972-73.
Appointed assistant captain of the Canadiens in 1972.
Appointed captain of the Canadiens in 1975, succeeding Henri Richard.
Retired in October, 1979.

COUTURE, Gerald Joseph Wilfred Arthur (Gerry)

Born in Saskatoon, Saskatchewan, August 6th, 1925.
Center, right-hand shot.
6′2″, 185 lb.
Last amateur team: the Saskatoon Quackers jrs.

SEASON	TEAM	GP	G	A	PTS	MIP
1951-52	Montreal Canadiens	10	0	1	1	4
	TOTALS	10	0	1	1	4

COUTURE, Rosario (Lolo)

Born in St. Boniface, Manitoba, July 24th, 1905.
Defenseman, right-winger, right-hand shot.
5′11″, 164 lb.
Last amateur team: the Winnipeg Rangers.

SEASON	TEAM	GP	G	A	PTS	MIP
1935-36	Montreal Canadiens	10	0	1	1	0
	TOTALS	10	0	1	1	0

Obtained from the Chicago Black Hawks for Wildor Larochelle (1935-36).

COUTURE, William Wilfred (Bill, Coutu)

Born Sault Ste-Marie, Ontario.
Defenseman.

SEASON	TEAM	GP	G	A	PTS	MIP
1916-17	Montreal Canadiens	15	0	—	0	—
1917-18	Montreal Canadiens	19	2	—	2	—
1918-19	Montreal Canadiens	15	1	1	2	18
1919-20	Montreal Canadiens	17	4	0	4	30
1921-22	Montreal Canadiens	23	4	3	7	4
1922-23	Montreal Canadiens	24	5	2	7	4
1923-24	Montreal Canadiens	16	3	1	4	8
1924-25	Montreal Canadiens	28	3	2	5	49
1925-26	Montreal Canadiens	33	2	4	6	95
	TOTALS	190	24	13	37	208

PLAYOFFS		GP	G	A	PTS	MIP
1916-17	Montreal Canadiens	5	0	—	0	—
1917-18	Montreal Canadiens	2	0	—	0	—
1918-19	Montreal Canadiens	10	0	—	0	—
1922-23	Montreal Canadiens	1	0	0	0	22
1923-24	Montreal Canadiens	6	0	0	0	2
1924-25	Montreal Canadiens	6	1	0	1	14
	TOTALS	30	1	0	1	38

Played with the team that won the Prince of Wales Trophy in 1924-25.
Played with the team that won the Stanley Cup in 1923-24.
Traded to the Hamilton Tigers in 1920.
Traded with Sprague Cleghorn for Harry Mummery, Carol Wilson and Amos Arbour in 1921.
Succeeded Sprague Cleghorn as captain of the Canadiens in 1925-26.

COX, Ab (Abbie)

Goaltender.

SEASON	TEAM	GP	GA	SO	AVE
1935-36	Montreal Canadiens	1	1	0	1.00
	TOTALS	1	1	0	1.00

OFFENSIVE RECORD		GP	G	A	PTS	MIP
1935-36	Montreal Canadiens	1	0	0	0	0
	TOTALS	1	0	0	0	0

CREIGHTON, William (Bill)

SEASON	TEAM	GP	G	A	PTS	MIP
*1916-17	Montreal Canadiens/ Toronto	2	0	—	0	—
	TOTALS	2	0	—	0	—

CRESSMAN, Glen

Born in Petersburg, Ontario, August 29th, 1934.
Center, right-hand shot.
5′9″, 155 lb.
Last amateur team: the Kitchener-Waterloo Canucks jrs.

SEASON	TEAM	GP	G	A	PTS	MIP
1956-57	Montreal Canadiens	4	0	0	0	2
	TOTALS	4	0	0	0	2

CRUTCHFIELD, Nelson (Nels)

Born in Knowlton, Quebec, July 12th, 1911.
Defenseman, center, left-hand shot.
6′1″, 175 lb.
Last amateur team: McGill University

SEASON	TEAM	GP	G	A	PTS	MIP
1934-35	Montreal Canadiens	41	5	5	10	20
	TOTALS	41	5	5	10	20

PLAYOFFS		GP	G	A	PTS	MIP
1934-35	Montreal Canadiens	2	0	1	1	22
	TOTALS	2	0	1	1	22

Obtained from the Montreal Maroons for Lionel Conacher and Herb Cain (1934-35).

CUDE, Wilfred (Wilf, Petch)

Born in Barry, Wales, August 4th, 1910.
Goaltender, left-hand shot.
5′9″, 146 lb.
Last amateur team: the Melville Millionnaires.

SEASON	TEAM	GP	GA	SO	AVE
*1933-34	Detroit Red Wings/ Montreal Canadiens	30	47	5	1.57
1934-35	Montreal Canadiens	48	145	1	3.02
1935-36	Montreal Canadiens	47	122	6	2.60
1936-37	Montreal Canadiens	44	99	5	2.25
1937-38	Montreal Canadiens	47	126	3	2.68
1938-39	Montreal Canadiens	23	77	2	3.35
1939-40	Montreal Canadiens	7	24	0	3.43
1940-41	Montreal Canadiens	3	13	0	4.33
	TOTALS	249	653	22	2.90

PLAYOFFS		GP	GA	SO	AVE
1934-35	Montreal Canadiens	2	6	0	3.00
1936-37	Montreal Canadiens	5	13	0	2.60
1937-38	Montreal Canadiens	3	11	0	3.67
	TOTALS	10	30	0	3.09

OFFENSIVE RECORD		GP	G	A	PTS	MIP
*1933-34	Detroit Red Wings/ Montreal Canadiens	30	0	0	0	0
1934-35	Montreal Canadiens	48	0	0	0	0
1935-36	Montreal Canadiens	47	0	0	0	0
1936-37	Montreal Canadiens	44	0	0	0	0
1937-38	Montreal Canadiens	47	0	0	0	0
1938-39	Montreal Canadiens	23	0	0	0	0
1939-40	Montreal Canadiens	7	0	0	0	0
1940-41	Montreal Canadiens	3	0	0	0	0
	TOTALS	249	0	0	0	0

PLAYOFFS		GP	G	A	PTS	MIP
1934-35	Montreal Canadiens	2	0	0	0	0
1936-37	Montreal Canadiens	5	0	0	0	0
1937-38	Montreal Canadiens	3	0	0	0	0
	TOTALS	10	0	0	0	0

Obtained from the Detroit Red Wings in 1934.
Member of the second All-Star team in 1935-36, 1936-37.
Died May 5, 1968.

CURRIE, Hugh Roy

Born in Saskatoon, Saskatchewan, October 22nd, 1925.
Defenseman. Right-hand shot.
6', 190 lb.
Last amateur team: the Baltimore Blades srs.

SEASON	TEAM	GP	G	A	PTS	MIP
1950-51	Montreal Canadiens	1	0	0	0	0
	TOTALS	1	0	0	0	0

CURRY, Floyd James (Busher)

Born in Chapleau, Ontario. August 11th, 1925.
Right-winger, right-hand shot.
5'11", 175 lb.
Last amateur team: the Montreal Royal srs.

SEASON	TEAM	GP	G	A	PTS	MIP
1947-48	Montreal Canadiens	31	1	5	6	0
1949-50	Montreal Canadiens	49	8	8	16	8
1950-51	Montreal Canadiens	69	13	14	27	23
1951-52	Montreal Canadiens	64	20	18	38	10
1952-53	Montreal Canadiens	68	16	6	22	10
1953-54	Montreal Canadiens	70	13	8	21	22
1954-55	Montreal Canadiens	68	11	10	21	36
1955-56	Montreal Canadiens	70	14	18	32	10
1956-57	Montreal Canadiens	70	7	9	16	20
1957-58	Montreal Canadiens	42	2	3	5	8
	TOTALS	601	105	99	204	147

PLAYOFFS		GP	G	A	PTS	MIP
1948-49	Montreal Canadiens	2	0	0	0	2
1949-50	Montreal Canadiens	5	1	0	1	2
1950-51	Montreal Canadiens	11	0	2	2	2
1951-52	Montreal Canadiens	11	4	3	7	6
1952-53	Montreal Canadiens	12	2	1	3	2
1953-54	Montreal Canadiens	11	4	0	4	4
1954-55	Montreal Canadiens	12	8	4	12	4
1955-56	Montreal Canadiens	10	1	5	6	12
1956-57	Montreal Canadiens	10	3	2	5	2
1957-58	Montreal Canadiens	7	0	0	0	2
	TOTALS	91	23	17	40	38

ALL-STAR GAMES		GP	G	A	PTS	MIP
1951	NHL All-Stars	1	0	0	0	0
1952	NHL All-Stars	1	0	0	0	0
1953	Montreal Canadiens	1	0	0	0	0
1956	Montreal Canadiens	1	0	0	0	0
1957	Montreal Canadiens	1	0	0	0	0
	TOTALS	5	0	0	0	0

Played with the team that won the Prince of Wales Trophy in 1955-56, 1957-58.
Played with the team that won the Stanley Cup in 1952-53, 1955-56, 1956-57, 1957-58.
Appointed assistant captain of the Canadiens in 1956.

CURTIS, Paul Edwin

Born in Peterborough, Ontario, September 29th, 1947.
Defenseman, left-hand shot.
6', 185 lb.
Last amateur team: the Peterborough Petes jrs.

SEASON	TEAM	GP	G	A	PTS	MIP
1969-70	Montreal Canadiens	1	0	0	0	0
	TOTALS	1	0	0	0	0

Drafted by the Los Angeles Kings, June 9th, 1970.

CUSHENAN, Ian Robertson

Born in Hamilton, Ontario, November 29th, 1933.
Defenseman, left-hand shot.
6'1", 195 lb.
Last amateur team: the St. Catharines Tee Pees jrs.

SEASON	TEAM	GP	G	A	PTS	MIP
1958-59	Montreal Canadiens	35	1	2	3	28
	TOTALS	35	1	2	3	28

ALL-STAR GAMES		GP	G	A	PTS
1958	Montreal Canadiens	1	0	0	0
	TOTALS	1	0	0	0

Played with the team that won the Prince of Wales Trophy in 1958-59.

CYR, Claude

Born in Montreal, Quebec, March 27th, 1939.
Goaltender.

SEASON	TEAM	GP	GA	SO	AVE
1958-59	Montreal Canadiens	1	1	0	1.00
	TOTALS	1	1	0	1.00

OFFENSIVE RECORD		GP	G	A	PTS	MIP
1958-59	Montreal Canadiens	1	0	0	0	0
	TOTALS	1	0	0	0	0

Played with the team that won the Prince of Wales Trophy in 1958-59.

DALLAIRE, Henri J.

SEASON	TEAM	GP	G	A	PTS	MIP
1910-11	Montreal Canadiens	11	11	—	11	—
1911-12	Montreal Canadiens	10	5	—	5	—
1913-14	Montreal Canadiens	5	2	—	2	—
	TOTALS	26	18	—	18	—

DAME, Aurella N. (Bunny)

Born in Edmonton, Alberta.

SEASON	TEAM	GP	G	A	PTS	MIP
1941-42	Montreal Canadiens	34	2	5	7	4
	TOTALS	34	2	5	7	4

DAVIS, Lorne Austin

Born in Regina, Saskatchewan, July 20th, 1930.
Right-winger, right-hand shot.
5'11", 190 lb.
Last amateur team: the Montreal Royal srs.

SEASON	TEAM	GP	G	A	PTS	MIP
1951-52	Montreal Canadiens	3	1	1	2	2
1953-54	Montreal Canadiens	37	6	4	10	2
	TOTALS	40	7	5	12	4

PLAYOFFS		GP	G	A	PTS	MIP
1952-53	Montreal Canadiens	7	1	1	2	2
1953-54	Montreal Canadiens	11	2	0	2	8
	TOTALS	18	3	1	4	10

ALL-STAR GAMES		GP	G	A	PTS
1953	Montreal Canadiens	1	0	0	0
	TOTALS	1	0	0	0

Played with the team that won the Stanley Cup in 1952-53.

DAWES, Robert James (Bob)

Born in Saskatoon, Saskatchewan, November 29th, 1924.
Defenseman, left-hand shot.
6'1", 170 lb.
Last amateur team: the Oshawa Generals jrs.

SEASON	TEAM	GP	G	A	PTS	MIP
1950-51	Montreal Canadiens	15	0	5	5	4
	TOTALS	15	0	5	5	4

PLAYOFFS		GP	G	A	PTS	MIP
1950-51	Montreal Canadiens	1	0	0	0	0
	TOTALS	1	0	0	0	0

DECARIE, Ed

SEASON	TEAM	GP	G	A	PTS	MIP
1909-10	Montreal Canadiens	1	0	—	0	—
	TOTALS	1	0	—	0	—

PLAYOFFS		GP	G	A	PTS	MIP
1909-10	Montreal Canadiens	12	7	—	7	—
	TOTALS	12	7	—	7	—

DEJORDY, Denis Emile

Born in St. Hyacinthe, Quebec, November 12th, 1938.
Goaltender, left-hand shot.
5'9", 185 lb.
Last amateur team: the St. Catharines Teepees jrs.

SEASON	TEAM	GP	GA	SO	AVE
1971-72	Montreal Canadiens	7	25	0	4.51
	TOTALS	7	25	0	4.51

OFFENSIVE RECORD		GP	G	A	PTS	MIP
1971-72	Montreal Canadiens	7	0	1	1	0
	TOTALS	7	0	1	1	0

Obtained from the Los Angeles Kings with Dale Hoganson, Noel Price and Doug Robinson for Rogatien Vachon, November 4, 1971.
Sold to the New York Islanders, June 12, 1972.

DEMERS, Antonio (Tony)

Born in Chambly Bassin, Quebec, July 22nd, 1917.
Right-winger, right-hand shot.
5'9", 180 lb.
Last amateur team: The Valleyfield Braves srs.

SEASON	TEAM	GP	G	A	PTS	MIP
1937-38	Montreal Canadiens	6	0	0	0	0
1939-40	Montreal Canadiens	14	2	3	5	2
1940-41	Montreal Canadiens	46	13	10	23	17
1941-42	Montreal Canadiens	7	3	4	7	4
1942-43	Montreal Canadiens	9	2	5	7	0
	TOTALS	82	20	22	42	23

PLAYOFFS		GP	G	A	PTS	MIP
1940-41	Montreal Canadiens	2	0	0	0	0
	TOTALS	2	0	0	0	0

DENIS, Louis Gilbert (Lulu)

Born in Vonda, Saskatchewan, June 7th, 1928.
Right-winger, right-hand shot.
5'8", 140 lb.
Last amateur team: the Montreal Royal srs.

SEASON	TEAM	GP	G	A	PTS	MIP
1949-50	Montreal Canadiens	2	0	1	1	0
1950-51	Montreal Canadiens	1	0	0	0	0
	TOTALS	3	0	1	1	0

DESAULNIERS, Gérard (Gerry)

Born in Shawinigan Falls, Quebec, December 31st, 1928.
Center, left-hand shot.
5'11", 152 lb.
Last amateur team: the Montreal Royal srs.

SEASON	TEAM	GP	G	A	PTS	MIP
1950-51	Montreal Canadiens	3	0	1	1	2
1952-53	Montreal Canadiens	2	0	1	1	2
1953-54	Montreal Canadiens	3	0	0	0	0
	TOTALS	8	0	2	2	4

DESILETS, Joffre Wilfred

Born in Capreol, Ontario, April 10th, 1915.
Right-winger, right-hand shot.
5'10", 175 lb.
Last amateur team: the St. John Beavers (N.B.).

SEASON	TEAM	GP	G	A	PTS	MIP
1935-36	Montreal Canadiens	38	7	6	13	0
1936-37	Montreal Canadiens	48	7	12	19	17
1937-38	Montreal Canadiens	32	6	7	13	6
	TOTALS	118	20	25	45	23

PLAYOFFS		GP	G	A	PTS	MIP
1936-37	Montreal Canadiens	5	1	0	1	0
1937-38	Montreal Canadiens	2	0	0	0	7
	TOTALS	7	1	0	1	7

Traded to the Chicago Black Hawks for Louis Trudel in 1938.

DESLAURIERS, Jacques

Born in Montreal, Quebec, September 3rd, 1928.
Defenseman, left-hand shot.
6', 170 lb.
Last amateur team: the Valleyfield Braves srs.

SEASON	TEAM	GP	G	A	PTS	MIP
1955-56	Montreal Canadiens	2	0	0	0	0
	TOTALS	2	0	0	0	0

Played with the team that won the Prince of Wales Trophy in 1955-56.

DESRIVIÈRES, ?

Incomplete record. Existence confirmed by Official Report of Match, Season 1929-30, NHL Office.

DHEERE, Marcel Albert (Ching)

Born in St. Boniface, Manitoba, December 19th, 1920.
Left-winger, left-hand shot.
5'7", 175 lb.
Last amateur team: Treherne (Man.) intermediate.

SEASON	TEAM	GP	G	A	PTS	MIP
1942-43	Montreal Canadiens	11	1	2	3	2
	TOTALS	11	1	2	3	2

PLAYOFFS		GP	G	A	PTS	MIP
1942-43	Montreal Canadiens	5	0	0	0	6
	TOTALS	5	0	0	0	6

DOHERTY, Fred H.

Forward.

SEASON	TEAM	GP	G	A	PTS	MIP
1918-19	Montreal Canadiens	3	0	0	0	—
	TOTALS	3	0	0	0	—

DORAN, John Michael (Red)

Born in Belleville, Ontario, May 24th, 1911.
Defenseman, left-hand shot.
6', 195 lb.
Last amateur team: the Toronto Marlboros srs.

SEASON	TEAM	GP	G	A	PTS	MIP
1939-40	Montreal Canadiens	6	0	3	3	6
	TOTALS	6	0	3	3	6

Died February 11th, 1975.

DOROHOY, Edward (Ed, The Pistol)

Born in Medicine Hat, Alberta, March 13th, 1929.
Center, left-hand shot.
5'9", 150 lb.
Last amateur team: the Lethbridge Native Sons jrs.

SEASON	TEAM	GP	G	A	PTS	MIP
1948-49	Montreal Canadiens	16	0	0	0	6
	TOTALS	16	0	0	0	6

DRILLON, Gordon Arthur (Gord)

Born in Moncton, New Brunswick, October 23rd, 1914.
Right-winger, right-hand shot.
6'2", 178 lb.
Last amateur team: the Pittsburgh Yellow Jackets.

SEASON	TEAM	GP	G	A	PTS	MIP
1942-43	Montreal Canadiens	49	28	22	50	14
	TOTALS	49	28	22	50	14

PLAYOFFS		GP	G	A	PTS	MIP
1942-43	Montreal Canadiens	5	4	2	6	0
	TOTALS	5	4	2	6	0

Bought from the Toronto Maple Leafs in 1942.
Member of the Hockey Hall of Fame in June, 1975.

DROUIN, Jude

Born in Mont-Louis, Quebec, October 28th, 1948.
Center, right-hand shot.
5'9", 160 lb.
Last amateur team: the Montreal Canadiens jrs.

SEASON	TEAM	GP	G	A	PTS	MIP
1968-69	Montreal Canadiens	9	0	1	1	0
1969-70	Montreal Canadiens	3	0	0	0	2
	TOTALS	12	0	1	1	2

Played with the team that won the Prince of Wales Trophy in 1968-69.
Traded to the Minnesota North Stars for Bill Collins, June 10, 1970.

DROUIN, Paul-Émile (Polly)

Born in Verdun, Quebec, January 16th, 1916.
Left-winger, left-hand shot.
5'7", 160 lb.
Last amateur team: The Ottawa Senators srs.

SEASON	TEAM	GP	G	A	PTS	MIP
1935-36	Montreal Canadiens	30	1	8	9	19
1936-37	Montreal Canadiens	4	0	0	0	0
1937-38	Montreal Canadiens	31	7	13	20	8
1938-39	Montreal Canadiens	28	7	11	18	2
1939-40	Montreal Canadiens	42	4	11	15	51
1940-41	Montreal Canadiens	21	4	7	11	0
	TOTALS	156	23	50	73	80

PLAYOFFS		GP	G	A	PTS	MIP
1937-38	Montreal Canadiens	1	0	0	0	0
1938-39	Montreal Canadiens	3	0	1	1	5
1940-41	Montreal Canadiens	1	0	0	0	0
	TOTALS	5	0	1	1	5

Drafted by the St. Louis Eagles in 1935.
Died January 2, 1967.

DRYDEN, Kenneth Wayne (Ken)

Born in Hamilton, Ontario, August 8th, 1947.
Goaltender, left-hand shot.
6'4", 210 lb.
Last amateur team: Canada's National Team.

SEASON	TEAM	GP	GA	SO	AVE
1970-71	Montreal Canadiens	6	9	0	1.65
1971-72	Montreal Canadiens	64	142	8	2.24
1972-73	Montreal Canadiens	54	119	6	2.26
1974-75	Montreal Canadiens	56	149	4	2.69
1975-76	Montreal Canadiens	62	121	8	2.03
1976-77	Montreal Canadiens	56	117	10	2.14
1977-78	Montreal Canadiens	52	105	5	2.05
1978-79	Montreal Canadiens	47	108	5	2.30
	TOTALS	397	870	46	2.34

PLAYOFFS		GP	GA	SO	AVE
1970-71	Montreal Canadiens	20	61	0	3.00
1971-72	Montreal Canadiens	6	17	0	2.83
1972-73	Montreal Canadiens	17	50	1	2.89
1974-75	Montreal Canadiens	11	29	2	2.53
1975-76	Montreal Canadiens	13	25	1	1.92
1976-77	Montreal Canadiens	14	22	4	1.55
1977-78	Montreal Canadiens	15	29	2	1.89
1978-79	Montreal Canadiens	16	41	0	2.48
	TOTALS	112	274	10	2.40

OFFENSIVE RECORD		GP	G	A	PTS	MIP
1970-71	Montreal Canadiens	6	0	0	0	0
1971-72	Montreal Canadiens	64	0	3	3	4
1972-73	Montreal Canadiens	54	0	4	4	2
1974-75	Montreal Canadiens	56	0	3	3	2
1975-76	Montreal Canadiens	62	0	2	2	0
1976-77	Montreal Canadiens	56	0	2	2	0
1977-78	Montreal Canadiens	52	0	2	2	0
1978-79	Montreal Canadiens	47	0	3	3	0
	TOTALS	397	0	19	19	8

PLAYOFFS		GP	G	A	PTS	MIP
1970-71	Montreal Canadiens	20	0	1	1	0
1971-72	Montreal Canadiens	6	0	0	0	0
1972-73	Montreal Canadiens	17	0	0	0	2
1974-75	Montreal Canadiens	11	0	0	0	0
1975-76	Montreal Canadiens	13	0	0	0	0
1976-77	Montreal Canadiens	14	0	0	0	0
1977-78	Montreal Canadiens	15	0	0	0	0
1978-79	Montreal Canadiens	16	0	4	4	4
	TOTALS	112	0	5	5	6

ALL-STAR GAMES		GP	GA	SO	AVE
1972	All-Stars (Div. East)	1	2	0	4.00
1975	Prince of Wales	1	0	0	0.00
1976	Prince of Wales	1	1	0	2.00
1977	Prince of Wales	1	1	0	2.00
1978	Prince of Wales	1	2	0	4.00
1979	Challenge Cup	2	7	0	3.50
	TOTALS	7	13	0	2.17

Played with the team that won the Prince of Wales Trophy in 1972-73, 1975-76, 1976-77, 1977-78.
Played with the team that won the Stanley Cup in 1970-71, 1972-73, 1975-76, 1976-77, 1977-78, 1978-79.
Won the Conn Smythe Trophy in 1970-71.
Won the Vezina Trophy in 1972-73, 1975-76, 1976-77, 1977-78, 1978-79 (last three shared with Bunny Larocque).
Won the Calder Trophy in 1971-72.
Member of the first All-Star team in 1972-73, 1975-76, 1976-77, 1977-78, 1978-79.
Member of the second All-Star team in 1971-72.
Brother of Dave Dryden.
Retired in June, 1979.

DUBÉ, Joseph Gilles

Born in Sherbrooke, Quebec, June 2nd, 1927.
Left-winger, left-hand shot.
5'11", 165 lb.
Last amateur team: the Sherbrooke Saints srs.

SEASON	TEAM	GP	G	A	PTS	MIP
1949-50	Montreal Canadiens	12	1	2	3	2
	TOTALS	12	1	2	3	2

DUBEAU, Ernest (Ernie)

SEASON	TEAM	GP	G	A	PTS	MIP
1911-12	Montreal Canadiens	18	3	—	3	—
1912-13	Montreal Canadiens	19	0	—	0	—
1913-14	Montreal Canadiens	20	7	—	7	—
1914-15	Montreal Canadiens	19	6	—	6	—
	TOTALS	76	16	—	16	—

PLAYOFFS		GP	G	A	PTS	MIP
1913-14	Montreal Canadiens	2	0	—	0	—
	TOTALS	2	0	—	0	—

Obtained from the Vancouver team for Edouard Lalonde in 1911.

DUCKETT, Richard

SEASON	TEAM	GP	G	A	PTS	MIP
1909-10	Montreal Canadiens					

Incomplete record: See *The Flying Frenchmen, Hockey's Greatest Dynasty*, by Stan Fischler and Maurice Richard, p. 17.

DUFF, Terrance Richard (Dick)

Born in Kirkland Lake, Ontario, February 18th, 1936.
Left-winger, left-hand shot.
5'9", 163 lb.
Last amateur team: The St. Michaels College jrs.

SEASON	TEAM	GP	G	A	PTS	MIP
1964-65	Montreal Canadiens	40	9	7	16	16
1965-66	Montreal Canadiens	63	21	24	45	78
1966-67	Montreal Canadiens	51	12	11	23	23
1967-68	Montreal Canadiens	66	25	21	46	21
1968-69	Montreal Canadiens	68	19	21	40	24
1969-70	Montreal Canadiens	17	1	1	2	4
	TOTALS	305	87	85	172	166

PLAYOFFS		GP	G	A	PTS	MIP
1964-65	Montreal Canadiens	13	3	6	9	17
1965-66	Montreal Canadiens	10	2	5	7	2
1966-67	Montreal Canadiens	10	2	5	7	4
1967-68	Montreal Canadiens	13	2	4	7	4
1968-69	Montreal Canadiens	14	6	8	14	11
	TOTALS	60	15	28	43	38

ALL-STAR GAMES		GP	G	A	PTS
1965	Montreal Canadiens	1	0	1	1
1967	Montreal Canadiens	1	0	0	0
	TOTALS	2	0	1	1

Obtained from the New York Rangers for Bill Hicke, December 22, 1964.
Played with the team that won the Prince of Wales Trophy in 1965-66, 1967-68, 1968-69.
Played with the team that won the Stanley Cup in 1964-65, 1965-66, 1967-68, 1968-69.
Sold to the Los Angeles Kings, January 23, 1970.

DUPONT, Normand

Born in Montreal, Quebec, February 5th, 1957.
Left-winger, left-hand shot.
5'10", 180 lb.
Last amateur team: Nova Scotia AHL.

SEASON	TEAM	GP	G	A	PTS	MIP
1979-80	Montreal Canadiens	35	1	3	4	4
	TOTALS	35	1	3	4	4

PLAYOFFS		GP	G	A	PTS	MIP
1979-80	Montreal Canadiens	8	1	1	2	0
	TOTALS	8	1	1	2	0

DURNAN, William Ronald (Bill)

Born in Toronto, Ontario, January 22nd, 1915.
Goaltender, ambidextrous.
6', 185 lb.
Last amateur team: the Montreal Royal srs.

SEASON	TEAM	GP	GA	SO	AVE
1943-44	Montreal Canadiens	50	109	2	2.18
1944-45	Montreal Canadiens	50	121	1	2.42
1945-46	Montreal Canadiens	40	104	4	2.60
1946-47	Montreal Canadiens	60	138	4	2.30
1947-48	Montreal Canadiens	59	162	5	2.74
1948-49	Montreal Canadiens	60	126	10	2.10
1949-50	Montreal Canadiens	64	141	8	2.20
	TOTALS	383	901	34	2.36

PLAYOFFS		GP	GA	SO	AVE
1943-44	Montreal Canadiens	9	14	1	1.55
1944-45	Montreal Canadiens	6	15	0	2.50
1945-46	Montreal Canadiens	9	20	0	2.22
1946-47	Montreal Canadiens	11	23	1	2.09
1948-49	Montreal Canadiens	7	17	0	2.43
1949-50	Montreal Canadiens	3	10	0	3.33
	TOTALS	45	99	2	2.35

ALL-STAR GAMES		GP	GA	SO	AVE
1947	NHL All-Stars	1	3	0	1.50
1948	NHL All-Stars	1	0	0	0.00
1949	NHL All-Stars	1	1	0	0.50
	TOTALS	3	4	0	0.66

OFFENSIVE RECORD		GP	G	A	PTS	MIP
1943-44	Montreal Canadiens	50	0	0	0	0
1944-45	Montreal Canadiens	50	0	0	0	0
1945-46	Montreal Canadiens	40	0	0	0	0
1946-47	Montreal Canadiens	60	0	0	0	0
1947-48	Montreal Canadiens	59	0	0	0	5
1948-49	Montreal Canadiens	60	0	0	0	0
1949-50	Montreal Canadiens	64	0	1	1	2
	TOTALS	383	0	1	1	7

PLAYOFFS		GP	G	A	PTS	MIP
1943-44	Montreal Canadiens	9	0	0	0	0
1944-45	Montreal Canadiens	6	0	0	0	0
1945-46	Montreal Canadiens	9	0	0	0	0
1946-47	Montreal Canadiens	11	0	0	0	0
1948-49	Montreal Canadiens	7	0	0	0	0
1949-50	Montreal Canadiens	3	0	0	0	0
	TOTALS	45	0	0	0	0

Played with the team that won the Prince of Wales Trophy in 1943-44, 1944-45, 1945-46, 1946-47.
Played with the team that won the Stanley Cup in 1943-44, 1945-46.
Won the Vezina Trophy in 1943-44, 1944-45, 1945-46, 1946-47, 1948-49, 1949-50.
Member of the first All-Star team in 1943-44, 1944-45, 1945-46, 1946-47, 1948-49, 1949-50.
Member of the Hockey Hall of Fame in June, 1964.
Appointed assistant captain in 1946.
Appointed captain of the Canadiens in 1948.

DUSSAULT, Joseph Normand (Norm, Ti-Nomme)

Born in Springfield, Massachusetts, September 26th, 1925.
Left-winger, left-hand shot.
5'6", 150 lb.
Last amateur team: the Victoriaville Tigers.

SEASON	TEAM	GP	G	A	PTS	MIP
1947-48	Montreal Canadiens	28	5	10	15	4
1948-49	Montreal Canadiens	47	9	8	17	6
1949-50	Montreal Canadiens	67	13	24	37	22
1950-51	Montreal Canadiens	64	4	20	24	15
	TOTALS	206	31	62	93	47

PLAYOFFS		GP	G	A	PTS	MIP
1948-49	Montreal Canadiens	2	0	0	0	0
1949-50	Montreal Canadiens	5	3	1	4	0
	TOTALS	7	3	1	4	0

DUTTON, Mervyn (Red)

Born in Russell, Manitoba, January 3, 1898.
Defenseman.

SEASON	TEAM	GP	G	A	PTS	MIP
1926-27	Montreal Maroons	—	4	4	8	—
1927-28	Montreal Maroons	—	7	6	13	—
1928-29	Montreal Maroons	—	1	3	4	—
1929-30	Montreal Maroons	—	3	13	16	—
	TOTALS	—	15	26	41	—

PLAYOFFS		GP	G	A	PTS	MIP
1926-27	Montreal Maroons	—	0	0	0	—
1927-28	Montreal Maroons	—	1	0	1	—
1929-30	Montreal Maroons	—	0	0	0	—
	TOTALS	—	1	0	1	—

EDDOLLS, Frank Herbert

Born in Lachine, Quebec, July 5th, 1921.
Defenseman, left-hand shot.
5'8", 180 lb.
Last amateur team: the Oshawa Generals jrs.

SEASON	TEAM	GP	G	A	PTS	MIP
1944-45	Montreal Canadiens	43	5	8	13	20
1945-46	Montreal Canadiens	8	0	1	1	6
1946-47	Montreal Canadiens	6	0	0	0	0
	TOTALS	57	5	9	14	26

PLAYOFFS		GP	G	A	PTS	MIP
1944-45	Montreal Canadiens	3	0	0	0	0
1945-46	Montreal Canadiens	8	0	1	1	2
1946-47	Montreal Canadiens	6	0	0	0	4
	TOTALS	17	0	1	1	6

Played with the team that won the Prince of Wales Trophy in 1944-45, 1945-46, 1946-47.
Played with the team that won the Stanley Cup in 1945-46.
Traded to the New York Rangers with "Buddy" O'Connor for Hal Laycoe, Joe Bell and George Robertson in 1948.

EDMUNDSON, Garry Frank

Born in Sexsmith, Alberta, May 6th, 1932.
Left-winger, left-hand shot.
6', 173 lb.
Last amateur team: the Cincinnati Mohawks srs.

SEASON	TEAM	GP	G	A	PTS	MIP
1951-52	Montreal Canadiens	1	0	0	0	0
	TOTALS	1	0	0	0	0

PLAYOFFS		GP	G	A	PTS	MIP
1951-52	Montreal Canadiens	2	0	0	0	4
	TOTALS	2	0	0	0	4

EMBERG, Edwin (Ed, Eddie)

Born in Verdun, Quebec, November 18th, 1921.
Left-winger, left-hand shot.
5'10", 160 lb.
Last amateur team: the Ottawa Senators srs.

PLAYOFFS		GP	G	A	PTS	MIP
1944-45	Montreal Canadiens	2	1	0	1	0
	TOTALS	2	1	0	1	0

ENGBLOM, Brian

Born in Winnipeg, Manitoba, January 27th, 1955.
Defenseman, left-hand shot.
6'2", 200 lb.
Last amateur team: Wisconsin University.

SEASON	TEAM	GP	G	A	PTS	MIP
1976-77	Montreal Canadiens	—	—	—	—	—
1977-78	Montreal Canadiens	28	1	2	3	23
1978-79	Montreal Canadiens	62	3	11	14	60
1979-80	Montreal Canadiens	70	3	20	23	43
	TOTALS	160	7	33	40	126

PLAYOFFS		GP	G	A	PTS	MIP
1976-77	Montreal Canadiens	2	0	0	0	2
1977-78	Montreal Canadiens	5	0	0	0	2
1978-79	Montreal Canadiens	16	0	0	1	11
1979-80	Montreal Canadiens	10	2	4	6	6
	TOTALS	33	2	4	7	21

Played with the team that won the Prince of Wales Trophy in 1977-78.
Played with the team that won the Stanley Cup in 1976-77, 1977-78, 1978-79.

ESPOSITO, Anthony James (Tony)

Born in Sault Ste-Marie, Ontario, April 23rd, 1943.
Goaltender, right-hand shot.
5'11", 185 lb.
Last amateur team: Michigan Tech.

SEASON	TEAM	GP	GA	SO	AVE
1968-69	Montreal Canadiens	13	34	2	2.73
	TOTALS	13	34	2	2.73

OFFENSIVE RECORD		GP	G	A	PTS	MIP
1968-69	Montreal Canadiens	13	0	0	0	0
	TOTALS	13	0	0	0	0

Played with the team that won the Prince of Wales Trophy in 1968-69.
Drafted by the Chicago Black Hawks, June 11, 1969.
Brother of Phil Esposito of the New York Rangers.

EVANS, Claude

Born in Longueuil, Quebec, April 28th, 1933.
Goaltender, left-hand shot.
Last amateur team: The Cincinnati Mohawks srs.

SEASON	TEAM	GP	GA	SO	AVE
1954-55	Montreal Canadiens	4	12	0	3.60
	TOTALS	4	12	0	3.60

OFFENSIVE RECORD		GP	G	A	PTS	MIP
1954-55	Montreal Canadiens	4	0	0	0	0
	TOTALS	4	0	0	0	0

EVANS, Stewart (Stew)

Born in Ottawa, Ontario, June 19th, 1908.
Defenseman, left-hand shot.
5' 10", 170 lb.
Last amateur team: The Portland Buckaroos.

SEASON	TEAM	GP	G	A	PTS	MIP
1938-39	Montreal Canadiens	43	2	7	9	58
	TOTALS	43	2	7	9	58

PLAYOFFS		GP	G	A	PTS	MIP
1938-39	Montreal Canadiens	3	0	0	0	2
	TOTALS	3	0	0	0	2

FERGUSON, John Bowie (Fergie)

Born in Vancouver, British Columbia, September 5th, 1938.
Left-winger, left-hand shot.
5' 11", 190 lb.
Last amateur team: The Fort Wayne Komets srs.

SEASON	TEAM	GP	G	A	PTS	MIP
1963-64	Montreal Canadiens	59	18	27	45	125
1964-65	Montreal Canadiens	69	17	27	44	156
1965-66	Montreal Canadiens	65	11	14	25	153
1966-67	Montreal Canadiens	67	20	22	42	177
1967-68	Montreal Canadiens	61	15	18	33	117
1968-69	Montreal Canadiens	71	29	23	52	185
1969-70	Montreal Canadiens	48	19	13	32	139
1970-71	Montreal Canadiens	60	16	14	30	162
	TOTALS	500	145	158	303	1214

PLAYOFFS		GP	G	A	PTS	MIP
1963-64	Montreal Canadiens	7	0	1	1	25
1964-65	Montreal Canadiens	13	3	1	4	28
1965-66	Montreal Canadiens	10	2	0	2	44
1966-67	Montreal Canadiens	10	4	2	6	22
1967-68	Montreal Canadiens	13	3	5	8	25
1968-69	Montreal Canadiens	14	4	3	7	80
1970-71	Montreal Canadiens	18	4	6	10	36
	TOTALS	85	20	18	38	260

ALL-STAR GAMES		GP	G	A	PTS
1965	Montreal Canadiens	1	0	0	0
1967	Montreal Canadiens	1	2	0	2
	TOTALS	2	2	0	2

Played with the team that won the Prince of Wales Trophy in 1963-64, 1964-65, 1965-66, 1967-68, 1968-69.
Played with the team that won the Stanley Cup in 1964-65, 1965-66, 1967-68, 1968-69, 1970-71.
Appointed assistant captain of the Canadiens in 1969.

FIELD, Wilfred Spence (Wilf)

Born in Winnipeg, Manitoba, April 29th, 1915.
Defenseman, right-hand shot.
5'11", 185 lb.
Last amateur team: the Winnipeg Monarchs jrs.

SEASON	TEAM	GP	G	A	PTS	MIP
*1944-45	Montreal Canadiens/ Chicago Black Hawks	48	4	4	8	32
	TOTALS	48	4	4	8	32

Drafted from the New York Americans in 1944.
Played with the team that won the Prince of Wales Trophy in 1944-45.

FILLION, Robert Louis (Bob)

Born in Thetford Mines, Quebec, July 12th, 1921.
Left-winger, left-hand shot.
5'10", 170 lb.
Last amateur team: the Montreal Army team.

SEASON	TEAM	GP	G	A	PTS	MIP
1943-44	Montreal Canadiens	41	7	23	30	14
1944-45	Montreal Canadiens	31	6	8	14	12
1945-46	Montreal Canadiens	50	10	6	16	12
1946-47	Montreal Canadiens	57	6	3	9	16
1947-48	Montreal Canadiens	32	9	9	18	8
1948-49	Montreal Canadiens	59	3	9	12	14
1949-50	Montreal Canadiens	57	1	3	4	8
	TOTALS	327	42	61	103	84

PLAYOFFS		GP	G	A	PTS	MIP
1943-44	Montreal Canadiens	3	0	0	0	2
1944-45	Montreal Canadiens	1	3	0	3	0
1945-46	Montreal Canadiens	9	4	3	7	6
1946-47	Montreal Canadiens	8	0	0	0	0
1948-49	Montreal Canadiens	7	0	1	1	4
1949-50	Montreal Canadiens	5	0	0	0	0
	TOTALS	33	7	4	11	12

Played with the team that won the Prince of Wales Trophy in 1943-44, 1944-45, 1945-46, 1946-47.
Played with the team that won the Stanley Cup in 1943-44, 1945-46.
Appointed assistant captain of the Canadiens in 1947.

FLEMING, Reginald Stephen (Reg)

Born in Montreal, Quebec, April 21st, 1936.
Defenseman, left-hand shot.
5'10", 185 lb.
Last amateur team: the Montreal Canadiens jrs.

SEASON	TEAM	GP	G	A	PTS	MIP
1959-60	Montreal Canadiens	3	0	0	0	2
	TOTALS	3	0	0	0	2

Played with the team that won the Prince of Wales Trophy in 1959-60.
Sold to the Chicago Black Hawks, June, 1960.

FONTINATO, Louis (Lou)

Born in Guelph, Ontario, January 20th, 1932.
Defenseman, left-hand shot.
6'1", 195 lb.
Last amateur team: the Guelph Biltmores jrs.

SEASON	TEAM	GP	G	A	PTS	MIP
1961-62	Montreal Canadiens	54	2	13	15	167
1962-63	Montreal Canadiens	63	2	8	10	141
	TOTALS	117	4	21	25	308

PLAYOFFS		GP	G	A	PTS	MIP
1961-62	Montreal Canadiens	6	0	1	1	23
	TOTALS	6	0	1	1	23

Bought from the New York Rangers in June, 1961.
Played with the team that won the Prince of Wales Trophy in 1961-62.

FORTIER, Charles

SEASON	TEAM	GP	G	A	PTS	MIP
1923-24	Montreal Canadiens	1	0	0	0	0
	TOTALS	1	0	0	0	0

FOURNIER, Jacques (Jack)

Forward.

SEASON	TEAM	GP	G	A	PTS	MIP
1914-15	Montreal Canadiens	9	0	—	0	—
1915-16	Montreal Canadiens	9	0	—	0	—
	TOTALS	18	0	—	0	—

FRAMPTON, Robert Percy James (Bob)

Born in Toronto, Ontario, January 20th, 1929.
Left-winger, left-hand shot.
5'10", 175 lb.
Last amateur team: the Montreal Royals srs.

SEASON	TEAM	GP	G	A	PTS	MIP
1949-50	Montreal Canadiens	2	0	0	0	0
	TOTALS	2	0	0	0	0

PLAYOFFS		GP	G	A	PTS	MIP
1949-50	Montreal Canadiens	3	0	0	0	0
	TOTALS	3	0	0	0	0

FRASER, Gordon (Gord)

Born in Pembroke, Ontario.
Defenseman.

SEASON	TEAM	GP	G	A	PTS	MIP
*1929-30	Montreal Canadiens/ Pittsburgh Pirates	40	6	4	10	41
	TOTALS	40	6	4	10	41

FRÉCHETTE, F.

SEASON	TEAM	GP	G	A	PTS	MIP
1912-13	Montreal Canadiens	1	0	—	0	—
1913-14	Montreal Canadiens	1	0	—	0	—
	TOTALS	2	0	—	0	—

FREW, Irvine

Born in Kilsyth, Scotland, August 16th, 1907.
Defenseman, right-hand shot.
5'10", 180 lb.
Last amateur team: the Calgary Canadiens jrs.

SEASON	TEAM	GP	G	A	PTS	MIP
1935	Montreal Canadiens	18	0	2	2	16
	TOTALS	18	0	2	2	16

Drafted from the St. Louis Eagles in 1935.

FRYDAY, Robert George (Bob)

Born in Toronto, Ontario, December 5th, 1928.
Right-winger, right-hand shot.
5'10", 155 lb.
Last amateur team: the Montreal Royals srs.

SEASON	TEAM	GP	G	A	PTS	MIP
1949-50	Montreal Canadiens	2	1	0	1	0
1951-52	Montreal Canadiens	3	0	0	0	0
	TOTALS	5	1	0	1	0

GAGNÉ, Arthur E. (Art)

Right-winger, right-hand shot.

SEASON	TEAM	GP	G	A	PTS	MIP
1926-27	Montreal Canadiens	44	14	3	17	42
1927-28	Montreal Canadiens	44	20	10	30	75
1928-29	Montreal Canadiens	44	7	3	10	52
	TOTALS	132	41	16	57	169

PLAYOFFS		GP	G	A	PTS	MIP
1926-27	Montreal Canadiens	4	0	0	0	0
1927-28	Montreal Canadiens	2	1	1	2	4
1928-29	Montreal Canadiens	3	0	0	0	12
	TOTALS	9	1	1	2	16

Traded to the Boston Bruins in 1929.

GAGNON, Germain

Born in Chicoutimi, Quebec, December 9th, 1942.
Left-winger, left-hand shot.
6', 172 lb.
Last amateur team: The Montreal Canadiens jrs.

SEASON	TEAM	GP	G	A	PTS	MIP
1971-72	Montreal Canadiens	4	0	0	0	0
	TOTALS	4	0	0	0	0

Traded to the New York Islanders on June 26th to complete the transaction of June 6, 1972, when the Islanders got Denis Dejordy, Tony Featherstone, Murray Anderson, Glen Resch and Alec Campbell for a certain amount of money and future considerations.

GAGNON, John (Black Cat, Johnny)

Born in Chicoutimi, Quebec, June 8th, 1905.
Right-winger, right-hand shot.
5'5", 140 lb.
Last amateur team: Sons of Ireland (Quebec).

SEASON	TEAM	GP	G	A	PTS	MIP
1930-31	Montreal Canadiens	41	18	7	25	43
1931-32	Montreal Canadiens	48	19	18	37	40
1932-33	Montreal Canadiens	48	12	23	35	64
1933-34	Montreal Canadiens	48	9	15	24	25
*1934-35	Boston Bruins/ Montreal Canadiens	47	2	6	8	11
1935-36	Montreal Canadiens	48	7	9	16	42
1936-37	Montreal Canadiens	48	20	16	36	38
1937-38	Montreal Canadiens	47	13	17	30	9
1938-39	Montreal Canadiens	45	12	22	34	23
*1939-40	Montreal Canadiens/ New York Americans	34	8	8	16	0
	TOTALS	444	120	141	261	295

PLAYOFFS		GP	G	A	PTS	MIP
1930-31	Montreal Canadiens	10	6	2	8	8
1931-32	Montreal Canadiens	4	1	1	2	4
1932-33	Montreal Canadiens	2	0	2	2	0
1933-34	Montreal Canadiens	2	1	0	1	2
1934-35	Montreal Canadiens	2	0	1	1	2
1936-37	Montreal Canadiens	5	2	1	3	9
1937-38	Montreal Canadiens	3	1	3	4	2
1938-39	Montreal Canadiens	3	0	2	2	10
	TOTALS	31	11	12	23	37

Played with the team that won the Stanley Cup in 1930-31.
Traded to the Boston Bruins for Tony Savage in 1934-35.
Bought back from Boston in 1934-35.
Sold to the New York Americans in 1939-40.

GAINEY, Robert Michael (Bob)

Born in Peterborough, Ontario, December 13th, 1953.
Left-winger, left-hand shot.
6'2", 190 lb.
Last amateur team: the Peterborough Petes jrs.

SEASON	TEAM	GP	G	A	PTS	MIP
1973-74	Montreal Canadiens	66	3	7	10	34
1974-75	Montreal Canadiens	80	17	20	37	49
1975-76	Montreal Canadiens	78	15	13	28	57
1976-77	Montreal Canadiens	80	14	19	33	41
1977-78	Montreal Canadiens	66	15	16	31	57
1978-79	Montreal Canadiens	79	20	18	38	44
1979-80	Montreal Canadiens	64	14	19	33	32
	TOTALS	513	98	113	200	312

PLAYOFFS		GP	G	A	PTS	MIP
1973-74	Montreal Canadiens	6	0	0	0	6
1974-75	Montreal Canadiens	11	2	4	6	4
1975-76	Montreal Canadiens	13	1	3	4	20
1976-77	Montreal Canadiens	14	4	1	5	25
1977-78	Montreal Canadiens	15	2	7	9	14
1978-79	Montreal Canadiens	16	6	10	16	10
1979-80	Montreal Canadiens	10	1	1	2	4
	TOTALS	85	16	26	42	83

ALL-STAR GAMES		GP	G	A	PTS
1977	Montreal Canadiens	1	0	1	0
1978	Montreal Canadiens	1	0	0	0
	TOTALS	2	0	1	1

First Amateur Draft choice of the Canadiens in 1973.
Played with the team that won the Prince of Wales Trophy in 1975-76, 1976-77, 1977-78.
Played with the team that won the Stanley Cup in 1975-76, 1976-77, 1977-78, 1978-79.
Won the Frank J. Selke Trophy in 1977-78 and 1978-79.
Won the Conn Smythe Trophy in 1978-79.
Won the Frank Selke Trophy in 1979-80.

GALLAGHER, John James Patrick (Johnny)

Born in Kenora, Ontario, January 19th, 1909.
Defenseman, left-hand shot.
5'11", 188 lb.
Last amateur team: M.A.A.A. srs.

SEASON	TEAM	GP	G	A	PTS	MIP
*1936-37	New York Americans/ Montreal Canadiens	20	1	0	1	12
	TOTALS	20	1	0	1	12

Drafted by the New York Americans (1936-37).

GAMBLE, Richard Frank (Dick)

Born in Moncton, New Brunswick, November 16th, 1928.
Left-winger, left-hand shot.
6', 177 lb.
Last amateur team: the Quebec Aces srs.

SEASON	TEAM	GP	G	A	PTS	MIP
1950-51	Montreal Canadiens	1	0	0	0	0
1951-52	Montreal Canadiens	64	23	17	40	8
1952-53	Montreal Canadiens	69	11	13	24	26
1953-54	Montreal Canadiens	32	4	8	12	18
1955-56	Montreal Canadiens	12	0	3	3	8
	TOTALS	178	38	41	79	60

PLAYOFFS		GP	G	A	PTS	MIP
1951-52	Montreal Canadiens	7	0	2	2	0
1952-53	Montreal Canadiens	5	1	0	1	2
1954-55	Montreal Canadiens	2	0	0	0	2
	TOTALS	14	1	2	3	4

Played with the team that won the Prince of Wales Trophy in 1955-56.
Played with the team that won the Stanley Cup in 1952-53.

GARDINER, Herbert Martin (Herb)

Born in Winnipeg, Manitoba, May 8th, 1891.
Defenseman.

SEASON	TEAM	GP	G	A	PTS	MIP
1926-27	Montreal Canadiens	44	6	6	12	26
1927-28	Montreal Canadiens	4	4	3	7	26
*1928-29	Montreal Canadiens/ Chicago Black Hawks	13	0	0	0	0
	TOTALS	61	10	9	19	52

PLAYOFFS		GP	G	A	PTS	MIP
1926-27	Montreal Canadiens	4	0	0	0	6
1927-28	Montreal Canadiens	2	0	1	1	4
	TOTALS	6	0	1	1	10

Traded to the Chicago Black Hawks for Arthur Lesieur in 1929.
Member of the Hockey Hall of Fame in April 1958.
Died January 11, 1972.

GARDINER, Wilbert Homer (Bert)

Born in Saskatoon, Saskatchewan, March 25th, 1913.
Goaltender, left-hand shot.
5'11", 160 lb.
Last amateur team: the Philadelphia Ramblers.

SEASON	TEAM	GP	GA	SO	AVE
1940-41	Montreal Canadiens	42	119	2	2.83
1941-42	Montreal Canadiens	10	42	0	4.20
	TOTALS	52	161	2	3.10

PLAYOFFS		GP	GA	SO	AVE
1940-41	Montreal Canadiens	3	8	0	2.67
	TOTALS	3	8	0	2.67

OFFENSIVE RECORD		GP	G	A	PTS	MIP
1940-41	Montreal Canadiens	42	0	0	0	0
1941-42	Montreal Canadiens	10	0	0	0	0
	TOTALS	52	0	0	0	0

PLAYOFFS		GP	G	A	PTS	MIP
1940-41	Montreal Canadiens	3	0	0	0	0
	TOTALS	3	0	0	0	0

Obtained from the New York Rangers in 1940.

GARDNER, David Calvin (Dave)

Born in Toronto, Ontario, August 23rd, 1952.
Center, right-hand shot.
6', 183 lb.
Last amateur team: The Toronto Marlboros jrs.

SEASON	TEAM	GP	G	A	PTS	MIP
1972-73	Montreal Canadiens	5	1	1	2	2
1973-74	Montreal Canadiens	31	1	10	11	2
	TOTALS	36	2	11	13	4

Played with the team that won the Prince of Wales Trophy in 1972-73.
Traded to the St. Louis Blues for the first Amateur Draft choice of 1974 (Doug Risebrough) March 9, 1974.
Son of Cal Gardner. Brother of Paul Gardner.

GARDNER, James Henry (Jim, Jimmy)

Born in Montreal, Quebec, May 21st, 1881.

SEASON	TEAM	GP	G	A	PTS	MIP
1913-14	Montreal Canadiens	13	10	—	10	—
1914-15	Montreal Canadiens	3	0	—	0	—
	TOTALS	16	10	—	10	—

Drafted from New Westminster in 1913.
Member of the Hockey Hall of Fame in August, 1962.
Died November, 1940.

GAUDREAULT, Léonard (Léo)

Born in Chicoutimi, Quebec.
Left-winger.
5'10", 152 lb.
Last amateur team: St-François-Xavier srs.

SEASON	TEAM	GP	G	A	PTS	MIP
1927-28	Montreal Canadiens	32	6	2	8	24
1928-29	Montreal Canadiens	11	0	0	0	4
1932-33	Montreal Canadiens	24	2	2	4	2
	TOTALS	67	8	4	12	30

GAUTHIER, Arthur (Art)

SEASON	TEAM	GP	G	A	PTS	MIP
1926-27	Montreal Canadiens	13	0	0	0	0
	TOTALS	13	0	0	0	0

PLAYOFFS		GP	G	A	PTS	MIP
1926-27	Montreal Canadiens	1	0	0	0	0
	TOTALS	1	0	0	0	0

GAUTHIER, Jean Philippe

Born in Montreal, Quebec, April 29th, 1937.
Defenseman, right-hand shot.
6'1", 196 lb.
Last amateur team: the Hull-Ottawa Canadiens srs.

SEASON	TEAM	GP	G	A	PTS	MIP
1960-61	Montreal Canadiens	4	0	1	1	8
1961-62	Montreal Canadiens	12	0	1	1	10
1962-63	Montreal Canadiens	65	1	17	18	46
1963-64	Montreal Canadiens	1	0	0	0	2
1965-66	Montreal Canadiens	2	0	0	0	0
1966-67	Montreal Canadiens	2	0	0	0	2
1969-70	Montreal Canadiens	4	0	1	1	0
	TOTALS	90	1	20	21	68

PLAYOFFS		GP	G	A	PTS	MIP
1962-63	Montreal Canadiens	5	0	0	0	12
1964-65	Montreal Canadiens	2	0	0	0	4
	TOTALS	7	0	0	0	16

Played with the team that won the Prince of Wales Trophy in 1960-61, 1961-62, 1963-64, 1965-66.
Played with the team that won the Stanley Cup in 1964-65.
Drafted by the Philadelphia Flyers during the 1967 expansion, June 6, 1967.
Recalled by the Cleveland Barons, farm team of the Canadiens, from the Oklahoma City Blazers, farm team of the Boston Bruins, June 12, 1969.

GAUTHIER, Joseph Alphonse Paul

Born in Winnipeg, Manitoba, March 6th, 1915.
Goaltender.
5'5", 125 lb.
Last amateur team: the Winnipeg Monarchs.

SEASON	TEAM	GP	GA	SO	AVE
1937-38	Montreal Canadiens	1	2	0	2.00
	TOTALS	1	2	0	2.00

OFFENSIVE RECORD		GP	G	A	PTS	MIP
1937-38	Montreal Canadiens	1	0	0	0	0
	TOTALS	1	0	0	0	0

Traded to the Boston Bruins for Terry Reardon in 1941.

GAUTHIER, René Fernand (Fern)

Born in Chicoutimi, Quebec, August 31st, 1919.
Right-winger, right-hand shot.
5'11", 175 lb.
Last amateur team: Shawinigan Falls srs.

SEASON	TEAM	GP	G	A	PTS	MIP
1944-45	Montreal Canadiens	50	18	13	31	23
	TOTALS	50	18	13	31	23

PLAYOFFS		GP	G	A	PTS	MIP
1944-45	Montreal Canadiens	4	0	0	0	0
	TOTALS	4	0	0	0	0

Played with the team that won the Prince of Wales Trophy in 1944-45.
Traded to the New York Rangers in 1943.
Traded from the New York Rangers with "Dutch" Hiller for Phil Watson in 1944.

GENDRON, Jean-Guy (Smitty)

Born in Montreal, Quebec, August 30th, 1934.
Left-winger, left-hand shot.
5'9", 157 lb.
Last amateur team: the Trois-Rivières Reds jrs.

SEASON	TEAM	GP	G	A	PTS	MIP
1960-61	Montreal Canadiens	43	9	12	21	51
	TOTALS	43	9	12	21	51

PLAYOFFS		GP	G	A	PTS	MIP
1960-61	Montreal Canadiens	5	0	0	0	2
	TOTALS	5	0	0	0	2

Obtained from the Boston Bruins for André Pronovost in November, 1960.
Played with the team that won the Prince of Wales Trophy in 1960-61.
Drafted by the New York Rangers in June, 1961.

GEOFFRION, Danny

Born in Montreal, Quebec, January 24th, 1958.
Right-winger, right-hand shot.
5'10", 182 lb.
Last amateur team: Cornwall QJHL.

SEASON	TEAM	GP	G	A	PTS	MIP
1979-80	Montreal Canadiens	32	0	6	6	12
	TOTALS	32	0	6	6	12

PLAYOFFS		GP	G	A	PTS	MIP
1979-80	Montreal Canadiens	2	0	0	0	7
	TOTALS	2	0	0	0	7

GEOFFRION, Joseph André Bernard (Boom Boom)

Born in Montreal, Quebec, February 14th, 1931.
Right-winger, right-hand shot.
5'9", 180 lb.
Last amateur team: the Montreal National jrs.

SEASON	TEAM	GP	G	A	PTS	MIP
1950-51	Montreal Canadiens	18	8	6	14	9
1951-52	Montreal Canadiens	67	30	24	54	66
1952-53	Montreal Canadiens	65	22	17	39	37
1953-54	Montreal Canadiens	54	29	25	54	87
1954-55	Montreal Canadiens	70	38	37	75	57
1955-56	Montreal Canadiens	59	29	33	62	66
1956-57	Montreal Canadiens	41	19	21	40	18
1957-58	Montreal Canadiens	42	27	23	50	51
1958-59	Montreal Canadiens	59	22	44	66	30
1959-60	Montreal Canadiens	59	30	41	71	36
1960-61	Montreal Canadiens	64	50	45	95	29
1961-62	Montreal Canadiens	62	23	36	59	36
1962-63	Montreal Canadiens	51	23	18	41	73
1963-64	Montreal Canadiens	55	21	18	39	41
	TOTALS	766	371	388	759	636

PLAYOFFS		GP	G	A	PTS	MIP
1950-51	Montreal Canadiens	11	1	1	2	6
1951-52	Montreal Canadiens	11	3	1	4	6
1952-53	Montreal Canadiens	12	6	4	10	12
1953-54	Montreal Canadiens	11	6	5	11	18
1954-55	Montreal Canadiens	12	8	5	13	8
1955-56	Montreal Canadiens	10	5	9	14	6
1956-57	Montreal Canadiens	10	11	7	18	2
1957-58	Montreal Canadiens	10	6	5	11	2
1958-59	Montreal Canadiens	11	5	8	13	10
1959-60	Montreal Canadiens	8	2	10	12	4
1960-61	Montreal Canadiens	4	2	1	3	0
1961-62	Montreal Canadiens	5	0	1	1	6
1962-63	Montreal Canadiens	5	0	1	1	4
1963-64	Montreal Canadiens	7	1	1	2	4
	TOTALS	127	56	59	115	88

ALL-STAR GAMES		GP	G	A	PTS
1952	NHL All-Stars (2nd team)	1	0	0	0
1953	Montreal Canadiens	1	0	0	0
1954	NHL All-Stars	1	0	0	0
1955	NHL All-Stars	1	0	0	0
1956	Montreal Canadiens	1	0	0	0
1958	Montreal Canadiens	1	1	0	1
1959	Montreal Canadiens	1	0	1	1
1960	Montreal Canadiens	1	0	0	0
1961	NHL All-Stars	1	0	0	0
1962	NHL All-Stars	1	0	0	0
1963	NHL All-Stars	1	0	1	1
	TOTALS	11	1	2	3

Played with the team that won the Prince of Wales Trophy in 1955-56, 1957-58, 1958-59, 1959-60, 1960-61, 1961-62, 1963-64.
Played with the team that won the Stanley Cup in 1952-53, 1956-57, 1957-58, 1958-59, 1959-60.
Won the Calder Trophy in 1951-52.
Won the Art Ross Trophy in 1954-55, 1960-61.
Won the Hart Trophy in 1960-61.
Member of the second All-Star team in 1954-55, 1959-60.
Member of the first All-Star team in 1960-61.
Appointed assistant captain of the Canadiens in 1958.
Recalled by the New York Rangers in June, 1966.
Son-in-law of Howie Morenz.
Father-in-law of Hartland Monahan of the Washington Capitals.
Member of the Hockey Hall of Fame in June, 1972.
Coach of the Canadiens 1979-80 season (until December 12, 1979).
Father of Danny Geoffrion of the Canadiens.

GETLIFFE, Raymond (Ray)

Born in Galt, Ontario, April, 1914.
Center, left-winger, left-hand shot.
5'11", 175 lb.
Last amateur team: St. John srs.

SEASON	TEAM	GP	G	A	PTS	MIP
1939-40	Montreal Canadiens	46	11	12	23	29
1940-41	Montreal Canadiens	39	15	10	25	25
1941-42	Montreal Canadiens	45	11	15	26	35
1942-43	Montreal Canadiens	50	18	28	46	26
1943-44	Montreal Canadiens	44	28	25	53	44
1944-45	Montreal Canadiens	41	16	7	23	34
	TOTALS	265	99	97	196	193

PLAYOFFS		GP	G	A	PTS	MIP
1940-41	Montreal Canadiens	3	1	1	2	0
1941-42	Montreal Canadiens	3	0	1	1	0
1942-43	Montreal Canadiens	5	0	1	1	8
1943-44	Montreal Canadiens	9	5	4	9	16
	TOTALS	26	6	7	13	26

Played with the team that won the Prince of Wales Trophy in 1943-44, 1944-45.
Played with the team that won the Stanley Cup in 1943-44.
Traded from the Boston Bruins with Charlie Sands for Herb Cain and Desse Smith in 1939.

GINGRAS, Gaston

Born in Temiscaming, Quebec, February 13th, 1959.
Defenseman, left-hand shot.
6'1", 195 lb.
Last amateur team: Kitchener OHA.

SEASON	TEAM	GP	G	A	PTS	MIP
1979-80	Montreal Canadiens	34	3	7	10	18
	TOTALS	34	3	7	10	18

PLAYOFFS		GP	G	A	PTS	MIP
1979-80	Montreal Canadiens	10	3	3	5	2
	TOTALS	10	3	3	5	2

GIROUX, Arthur (Art) Joseph

Born in Strathmore, Alberta, June 6th, 1907.
Right-winger, right-hand shot.
5'10", 165 lb.

SEASON	TEAM	GP	G	A	PTS	MIP
1932-33	Montreal Canadiens	40	5	2	7	14
	TOTALS	40	5	2	7	14

PLAYOFFS		GP	G	A	PTS	MIP
1932-33	Montreal Canadiens	2	0	0	0	0
	TOTALS	2	0	0	0	0

GLASS, Frank (Pud)

Born in 1884.

SEASON	TEAM	GP	G	A	PTS	MIP
1911-12	Montreal Canadiens	16	7	—	7	—
	TOTALS	16	7	—	7	—

Returned to the Montreal Red Bands Wanderers in 1910.
Died March 2, 1965.

GLOVER, Howard Edward (Howie)

Born in Toronto, Ontario, February 14th, 1935.
Right-winger, right-hand shot.
5'11", 175 lb.

Last amateur team: the North Bay Trappers srs.

SEASON	TEAM	GP	G	A	PTS	MIP
1968-69	Montreal Canadiens	1	0	0	0	0
	TOTALS	1	0	0	0	0

Played with the team that won the Prince of Wales Trophy in 1968-69.

GODIN, Samuel (Sam)

Born in Rockland, Ontario, September 20th, 1909.
Right-winger, right-hand shot.
5'10", 156 lb.
Last amateur team: the Hull Frontenacs.

SEASON	TEAM	GP	G	A	PTS	MIP
1933-34	Montreal Canadiens	36	2	2	4	15
	TOTALS	36	2	2	4	15

GOLDSWORTHY, Leroy D.

Born in Two Harbors, Minnesota, October 18th, 1908.
Defenseman, right-winger, right-hand shot.
6', 165 lb.
Last amateur team: the Edmonton Eskimos jrs.

SEASON	TEAM	GP	G	A	PTS	MIP
*1934-35	Chicago Black Hawks/ Montreal Canadiens	40	20	9	29	15
1935-36	Montreal Canadiens	47	15	11	26	8
	TOTALS	87	35	20	55	23

PLAYOFFS		GP	G	A	PTS	MIP
1934-35	Montreal Canadiens	2	1	0	1	0
	TOTALS	2	1	0	1	0

Obtained from the Chicago Black Hawks with Roger Jenkins and Lionel Conacher for Howie Morenz, Martin Burke and Lorne Chabot (1934-35).
Traded to the Chicago Black Hawks and brought back from the same team (1934-35).
Traded to the Boston Bruins for Albert "Babe" Siebert in 1936.

GOLDUP, Glenn Michael

Born in St. Catharines, Ontario, April 26th, 1953.
Left-winger, right-winger, left-hand shot.
6', 187 lb.
Last amateur team: the Toronto Marlboros jrs.

SEASON	TEAM	GP	G	A	PTS	MIP
1973-74	Montreal Canadiens	6	0	0	0	0
1974-75	Montreal Canadiens	9	0	1	1	2
1975-76	Montreal Canadiens	3	0	0	0	2
	TOTALS	18	0	1	1	4

Played with the team that won the Prince of Wales Trophy in 1975-76.
Sold to the Los Angeles June 11, 1976 for the first Round Draft choice.
Son of Henry "Hank" Goldup.

GOUPILLE, Clifford (Cliff, Red)

Born in Trois-Rivières, Quebec, September 2nd, 1915.
Defenseman, left-hand shot.
6', 190 lb.
Last amateur team: Plessisville, Quebec.

SEASON	TEAM	GP	G	A	PTS	MIP
1935-36	Montreal Canadiens	4	0	0	0	0
1936-37	Montreal Canadiens	4	0	0	0	0
1937-38	Montreal Canadiens	47	4	5	9	44
1938-39	Montreal Canadiens	18	0	2	2	24
1939-40	Montreal Canadiens	48	2	10	12	48
1940-41	Montreal Canadiens	48	3	6	9	81
1941-42	Montreal Canadiens	47	1	5	6	51
1942-43	Montreal Canadiens	6	2	0	2	8
	TOTALS	222	12	28	40	256

PLAYOFFS		GP	G	A	PTS	MIP
1937-38	Montreal Canadiens	3	2	0	2	4
1940-41	Montreal Canadiens	2	0	0	0	0
1941-42	Montreal Canadiens	3	0	0	0	2
	TOTALS	8	2	0	2	6

GOYETTE, Philippe (Phil)

Born in Lachine, Quebec, October 31st, 1933.
Center, left-hand shot.
5'11", 165 lb.
Last amateur team: the Cincinnati Mohawks srs.

SEASON	TEAM	GP	G	A	PTS	MIP
1956-57	Montreal Canadiens	14	3	4	7	0
1957-58	Montreal Canadiens	70	9	37	46	8
1958-59	Montreal Canadiens	63	10	18	28	8
1959-60	Montreal Canadiens	65	21	22	43	4
1960-61	Montreal Canadiens	62	7	4	11	4
1961-62	Montreal Canadiens	69	7	27	34	18
1962-63	Montreal Canadiens	32	5	8	13	2
	TOTALS	375	62	120	182	44

PLAYOFFS		GP	G	A	PTS	MIP
1956-57	Montreal Canadiens	10	2	1	3	4
1957-58	Montreal Canadiens	10	4	1	5	4
1958-59	Montreal Canadiens	10	0	4	4	0
1959-60	Montreal Canadiens	8	2	1	3	4
1960-61	Montreal Canadiens	6	3	3	6	0
1961-62	Montreal Canadiens	6	1	4	5	2
1962-63	Montreal Canadiens	2	0	0	0	0
	TOTALS	52	12	14	26	14

ALL-STAR GAMES		GP	G	A	PTS
1957	Montreal Canadiens	1	0	0	0
1958	Montreal Canadiens	1	0	0	0
1959	Montreal Canadiens	1	0	0	0
	TOTALS	3	0	0	0

Played with the team that won the Prince of Wales Trophy in 1957-58, 1958-59, 1959-60, 1960-61, 1961-62.
Played with the team that won the Stanley Cup in 1956-57, 1957-58, 1958-59, 1959-60.
Traded to the New York Rangers with Don Marshall and Jacques Plante for Lorne Worsley, Dave Balon, Léon Rochefort and Len Ronson, June 4, 1963.
Member of the famous Kid Line with Claude Provost at the right wing and André Pronovost at the left wing.

GRABOSKI, Anthony Rudel (Tony)

Born in Timmins, Ontario, May 9th, 1916.
Defenseman, forward, left-hand shot.
5'10", 170 lb.
Last amateur team: the Sudbury Millionnaires.

SEASON	TEAM	GP	G	A	PTS	MIP
1940-41	Montreal Canadiens	34	4	3	7	12
1941-42	Montreal Canadiens	23	2	5	7	8
1942-43	Montreal Canadiens	9	0	2	2	4
	TOTALS	66	6	10	16	24

PLAYOFFS		GP	G	A	PTS	MIP
1940-41	Montreal Canadiens	3	0	0	0	6
	TOTALS	3	0	0	0	6

GRACIE, Robert J. (Bob)

Born in North Bay, Ontario, November 8th, 1910.
Center, left-winger, left-hand shot.
5'9", 155 lb.
Last amateur team: the Toronto Marlboros.

SEASON	TEAM	GP	G	A	PTS	MIP
*1938-39	Montreal Canadiens/ Chicago Black Hawks	38	4	7	11	31
	TOTALS	38	4	7	11	31

Drafted from the Montreal Maroons in 1938.
Traded to the Chicago Black Hawks in 1938-39.
Died August 10, 1963.

GRANT, Daniel Frederick (Danny)

Born in Fredericton, New Brunswick, February 21st, 1946.
Left-winger, left-hand shot.
5'10", 192 lb.
Last amateur team: the Peterborough Petes jrs.

SEASON	TEAM	GP	G	A	PTS	MIP
1965-66	Montreal Canadiens	1	0	0	0	0
1967-68	Montreal Canadiens	22	3	4	7	10
	TOTALS	23	3	4	7	10

PLAYOFFS		GP	G	A	PTS	MIP
1967-68	Montreal Canadiens	10	0	3	3	5
	TOTALS	10	0	3	3	5

Played with the team that won the Prince of Wales Trophy in 1965-66, 1967-68.
Played with the team that won the Stanley Cup in 1967-68.
Traded to the Minnesota North Stars with Claude Larose for the first Amateur Draft choice of 1972 (Dave Gardner), a player chosen at a later date (Marshall Johnston) and a certain amount of money, June 10, 1968.

GRAVELLE, Joseph Gérard Léo (La Gazelle)

Born in Aylmer, Quebec, June 10th, 1925.
Right-winger, right-hand shot.
5'9", 158 lb.
Last amateur team: the Montreal Royals srs.

SEASON	TEAM	GP	G	A	PTS	MIP
1946-47	Montreal Canadiens	53	16	14	30	12
1947-48	Montreal Canadiens	15	0	0	0	0
1948-49	Montreal Canadiens	36	4	6	10	6
1949-50	Montreal Canadiens	70	19	10	29	18
*1950-51	Montreal Canadiens/ Detroit Red Wings	49	5	4	9	6
	TOTALS	223	44	34	78	42

PLAYOFFS		GP	G	A	PTS	MIP
1946-47	Montreal Canadiens	6	2	0	2	2
1948-49	Montreal Canadiens	7	2	1	3	0
1949-50	Montreal Canadiens	4	0	0	0	0
	TOTALS	17	4	1	5	2

Played with the team that won the Prince of Wales Trophy in 1946-47.
Traded to the Detroit Red Wings for Bert Olmstead in 1951.

GRAY, Terrence Stanley (Terry)

Born in Montreal, Quebec, March 21st, 1938.
Right-winger, right-hand shot.
6', 175 lb.
Last amateur team: the Hull-Ottawa Canadiens jrs.

SEASON	TEAM	GP	G	A	PTS	MIP
1963-64	Montreal Canadiens	4	0	0	0	6
	TOTALS	4	0	0	0	6

Played with the team that won the Prince of Wales Trophy in 1963-64.

GRENIER, Lucien S. J.

Born in Malartic, Quebec, November 3rd, 1946.
Left-winger, right-winger, left-hand shot.
5'10", 163 lb.
Last amateur team: the Montreal Canadiens jrs.

SEASON	TEAM	GP	G	A	PTS	MIP
1969-70	Montreal Canadiens	23	2	3	5	2
	TOTALS	23	2	3	5	2

PLAYOFFS		GP	G	A	PTS	MIP
1968-69	Montreal Canadiens	2	0	0	0	0
	TOTALS	2	0	0	0	0

Played with the team that won the Stanley Cup in 1968-69.
Traded to the Los Angeles Kings with Larry Mickey and Jack Norris for Léon Rochefort, Greg Boddy and Wayne Thomas, May 22, 1970.

GROULX, Ted (Teddy)

Goaltender.

PLAYOFFS		GP	GA	SO	AVE
1909-10	Montreal Canadiens	9	77	0	8.55
	TOTALS	9	77	0	8.55

OFFENSIVE RECORD		GP	G	A	PTS	MIP
1909-10	Montreal Canadiens	9	0	—	0	—
	TOTALS	9	0	—	0	—

GROSVENOR, Leonard (Len)

Born in Ottawa, Ontario.

SEASON	TEAM	GP	G	A	PTS	MIP
1932-33	Montreal Canadiens	4	0	0	0	0
	TOTALS	4	0	0	0	0

PLAYOFFS		GP	G	A	PTS	MIP
1932-33	Montreal Canadiens	2	0	0	0	0
	TOTALS	2	0	0	0	0

GUEVREMONT, ?

SEASON	TEAM	GP	G	A	PTS	MIP
1912-13	Montreal Canadiens	2	0	—	0	—
	TOTALS	2	0	—	0	—

HAGGERTY, James (Jim)

Born in Port Arthur, Ontario, April 14th, 1914.
Left-winger.
5′11″, 167 lb.

SEASON	TEAM	GP	G	A	PTS	MIP
1941-42	Montreal Canadiens	5	1	1	2	0
	TOTALS	5	1	1	2	0

PLAYOFFS		GP	G	A	PTS	MIP
1941-42	Montreal Canadiens	3	2	1	3	2
	TOTALS	3	2	1	3	2

HAINSWORTH, George

Born in Toronto, Ontario, June 26th, 1898.
Goaltender, left-hand shot.
5′6″, 150 lb.
Last amateur team: Kitchener.

SEASON	TEAM	GP	GA	SO	AVE
1926-27	Montreal Canadiens	44	67	14	1.52
1927-28	Montreal Canadiens	44	48	13	1.09
1928-29	Montreal Canadiens	44	43	22	0.98
1929-30	Montreal Canadiens	42	108	4	2.57
1930-31	Montreal Canadiens	44	89	8	2.02
1931-32	Montreal Canadiens	48	111	6	2.31
1932-33	Montreal Canadiens	48	115	7	2.40
*1936-37	Montreal Canadiens/ Toronto Maple Leafs	7	23	0	3.28
	TOTALS	321	604	74	1.88

PLAYOFFS		GP	GA	SO	AVE
1926-27	Montreal Canadiens	4	6	1	1.50
1927-28	Montreal Canadiens	2	3	0	1.50
1928-29	Montreal Canadiens	3	5	0	1.67
1929-30	Montreal Canadiens	6	6	3	1.00
1930-31	Montreal Canadiens	10	21	2	2.10
1931-32	Montreal Canadiens	4	13	0	3.25
1932-33	Montreal Canadiens	2	8	0	4.00
	TOTALS	31	62	6	2.00

OFFENSIVE RECORD		GP	G	A	PTS	MIP
1926-27	Montreal Canadiens	44	0	0	0	0
1927-28	Montreal Canadiens	44	0	0	0	0
1928-29	Montreal Canadiens	44	0	0	0	0
1929-30	Montreal Canadiens	42	0	0	0	0
1930-31	Montreal Canadiens	44	0	0	0	0
1931-32	Montreal Canadiens	48	0	0	0	0
1932-33	Montreal Canadiens	48	0	0	0	0
*1936-37	Montreal Canadiens/ Toronto Maple Leafs	7	0	0	0	0
	TOTALS	321	0	0	0	0

PLAYOFFS		GP	G	A	PTS	MIP
1926-27	Montreal Canadiens	4	0	0	0	0
1927-28	Montreal Canadiens	2	0	0	0	0
1928-29	Montreal Canadiens	3	0	0	0	0
1929-30	Montreal Canadiens	6	0	0	0	0
1930-31	Montreal Canadiens	10	0	0	0	0
1931-32	Montreal Canadiens	4	0	0	0	0
1933-32	Montreal Canadiens	2	0	0	0	0
	TOTALS	31	0	0	0	0

Bought from the Saskatoon Sheiks in 1926.
Played with the team that won the Stanley Cup in 1929-30, 1930-31.
Won the Vezina Trophy in 1926-27, 1927-28, 1928-29.
Appointed captain of the Canadiens in 1932-33.
Traded to the Toronto Maple Leafs for Lorne Chabot in 1933.
Drafted from the Toronto Maple Leafs in 1936-37.
Member of the Hockey Hall of Fame in June, 1961.
Died October 9, 1950.

HALL, Joseph Henry (Joe)

Born in Stratfordshire, England, in 1882.
Defenseman, point.

SEASON	TEAM	GP	G	A	PTS	MIP
1917-18	Montreal Canadiens	20	8	—	8	—
1918-19	Montreal Canadiens	17	7	1	8	85
	TOTALS	37	15	1	16	85

PLAYOFFS		GP	G	A	PTS	MIP
1917-18	Montreal Canadiens	2	0	2	2	—
1918-19	Montreal Canadiens	10	0	0	0	—
	TOTALS	12	0	2	2	—

Drafted from the Quebec Bulldogs in 1917.
Died following the Stanley Cup Series, April 5, 1919.
Member of the Hockey Hall of Fame in 1961.

HAMILTON, Charles (Chuck)

Born in Kirkland Lake, Ontario, January 18th, 1939.
Left-winger, left-hand shot.
5′11″, 175 lb.
Last amateur team: the Peterborough Petes jrs.

SEASON	TEAM	GP	G	A	PTS	MIP
1961-62	Montreal Canadiens	1	0	0	0	0
	TOTALS	1	0	0	0	0

Played with the team that won the Prince of Wales Trophy in 1961-62.

HANNA, John

Born in Sydney, Nova Scotia, April 5th, 1935.
Defenseman, right-hand shot.
5′10″, 175 lb.
Last amateur team: the Trois-Rivières Flambeaux jrs.

SEASON	TEAM	GP	G	A	PTS	MIP
1963-64	Montreal Canadiens	6	0	0	0	2
	TOTALS	6	0	0	0	2

Played with the team that won the Prince of Wales Trophy in 1963-64.

HARMON, David Glen

Born in Holland, Manitoba, January 2nd, 1921.
Defenseman, left-hand shot.
5′9″, 160 lb.
Last amateur team: the Montreal Canadiens srs.

SEASON	TEAM	GP	G	A	PTS	MIP
1942-43	Montreal Canadiens	27	5	9	14	25
1943-44	Montreal Canadiens	43	5	16	21	36
1944-45	Montreal Canadiens	42	5	8	13	41
1945-46	Montreal Canadiens	49	7	10	17	28
1946-47	Montreal Canadiens	57	5	9	14	53
1947-48	Montreal Canadiens	56	10	4	14	52
1948-49	Montreal Canadiens	59	8	12	20	44
1949-50	Montreal Canadiens	62	3	16	19	28
1950-51	Montreal Canadiens	57	2	12	14	27
	TOTALS	452	50	96	146	334

PLAYOFFS		GP	G	A	PTS	MIP
1942-43	Montreal Canadiens	5	0	1	1	2
1943-44	Montreal Canadiens	9	1	2	3	4
1944-45	Montreal Canadiens	6	1	0	1	2
1945-46	Montreal Canadiens	9	1	4	5	0
1946-47	Montreal Canadiens	11	1	1	2	4
1948-49	Montreal Canadiens	7	1	1	2	4
1949-50	Montreal Canadiens	5	0	1	1	21
1950-51	Montreal Canadiens	1	0	0	0	0
	TOTALS	53	5	10	15	37

ALL-STAR GAMES		GP	G	A	PTS
1949	NHL All-Stars	1	0	0	0
1950	NHL All-Stars	1	0	0	0
	TOTALS	2	0	0	0

Played with the team that won the Prince of Wales Trophy in 1943-44, 1944-45, 1945-46, 1946-47.
Played with the team that won the Stanley Cup in 1943-44, 1945-46.
Member of the second All-Star team in 1944-45, 1948-49.
Appointed assistant captain of the Canadiens in 1948.

HARPER, Terrance Victor (Terry)

Born in Regina, Saskatchewan, January 27th, 1940.
Defenseman, right-hand shot.
6′1″, 197 lb.
Last amateur team: the Regina Pats jrs.

SEASON	TEAM	GP	G	A	PTS	MIP
1962-63	Montreal Canadiens	14	1	1	2	10
1963-64	Montreal Canadiens	70	2	15	17	149
1964-65	Montreal Canadiens	62	0	7	7	93
1965-66	Montreal Canadiens	69	1	11	12	91
1966-67	Montreal Canadiens	56	0	16	16	99
1967-68	Montreal Canadiens	57	3	8	11	66
1968-69	Montreal Canadiens	21	0	3	3	37
1969-70	Montreal Canadiens	75	4	18	22	109
1970-71	Montreal Canadiens	78	1	21	22	116
1971-72	Montreal Canadiens	52	2	12	14	35
	TOTALS	554	14	112	126	805

PLAYOFFS		GP	G	A	PTS	MIP
1962-63	Montreal Canadiens	5	1	0	1	8
1963-64	Montreal Canadiens	7	0	0	0	6
1964-65	Montreal Canadiens	13	0	0	0	19
1965-66	Montreal Canadiens	10	2	3	5	18
1966-67	Montreal Canadiens	10	0	1	1	15
1967-68	Montreal Canadiens	13	0	1	1	8
1968-69	Montreal Canadiens	11	0	0	0	8
1970-71	Montreal Canadiens	20	0	6	6	28
1971-72	Montreal Canadiens	5	1	1	2	6
	TOTALS	94	4	12	16	116

ALL-STAR GAMES		GP	G	A	PTS
1965	Montreal Canadiens	1	0	0	0
1967	Montreal Canadiens	1	0	1	1
	TOTALS	2	0	1	1

Played with the team that won the Prince of Wales Trophy in 1963-64, 1965-66, 1967-68, 1968-69.
Played with the team that won the Stanley Cup in 1964-65, 1965-66, 1967-68, 1968-69, 1970-71.
Appointed assistant captain of the Canadiens in 1970.
Traded to the Los Angeles Kings for the 1974 second Amateur Draft choice (Gary MacGregor), the 1975 first Amateur Draft choice (Pierre Mondou), the 1975 third Amateur Draft choice (Paul Woods) and the 1976 first amateur Draft choice (Peter Lee), August 22, 1972.

HARRINGTON, Leland (Hago) K.

Born in Melrose, Massachusetts.
Left-winger.
5′8″, 163 lb.
Last amateur team: the Boston A.A.A.

SEASON	TEAM	GP	G	A	PTS	MIP
1932-33	Montreal Canadiens	24	1	1	2	2
	TOTALS	24	1	1	2	2

PLAYOFFS		GP	G	A	PTS	MIP
1932-33	Montreal Canadiens	2	1	0	1	2
	TOTALS	2	1	0	1	2

HARRIS, Edward Alexander (Ted)

Born in Winnipeg, Manitoba, July 18th, 1936.
Defenseman, left-hand shot.
6'2", 183 lb.
Last amateur team: the Philadelphia Ramblers (EHL).

SEASON	TEAM	GP	G	A	PTS	MIP
1963-64	Montreal Canadiens	4	0	1	1	0
1964-65	Montreal Canadiens	68	1	14	15	107
1965-66	Montreal Canadiens	53	0	13	13	87
1966-67	Montreal Canadiens	65	2	16	18	86
1967-68	Montreal Canadiens	67	5	16	21	78
1968-69	Montreal Canadiens	76	7	18	25	102
1969-70	Montreal Canadiens	74	3	17	20	116
	TOTALS	407	18	95	113	576

PLAYOFFS		GP	G	A	PTS	MIP
1964-65	Montreal Canadiens	13	0	5	5	45
1965-66	Montreal Canadiens	10	0	0	0	38
1966-67	Montreal Canadiens	10	0	1	1	19
1967-68	Montreal Canadiens	13	0	4	4	22
1968-69	Montreal Canadiens	14	1	2	3	34
	TOTALS	60	1	12	13	158

ALL-STAR GAMES		GP	G	A	PTS
1965	Montreal Canadiens	1	0	0	0
1967	Montreal Canadiens	1	0	0	0
1969	NHL All-Stars (Div. East)	1	0	1	1
	TOTALS	3	0	1	1

Played with the team that won the Prince of Wales Trophy in 1963-64, 1965-66, 1967-68, 1968-69.
Played with the team that won the Stanley Cup in 1964-65, 1965-66, 1967-68, 1968-69.
Member of the second All-Star team in 1968-69.
Drafted by the Minnesota North Stars, June 9, 1970.

HART, Wilfred (Wilf, Gizzy) Harold

Born in Weyburn, Saskatchewan, June 1st, 1902.
Left-winger.
5'9", 171 lb.
Last amateur team: Weyburn.

SEASON	TEAM	GP	G	A	PTS	MIP
1926-27	Montreal Canadiens	38	3	3	6	8
1927-28	Montreal Canadiens	44	3	2	5	4
1932-33	Montreal Canadiens	18	0	3	3	0
	TOTALS	100	6	8	14	12

PLAYOFFS		GP	G	A	PTS	MIP
1926-27	Montreal Canadiens	4	0	0	0	0
1927-28	Montreal Canadiens	2	0	0	0	0
1932-33	Montreal Canadiens	2	0	1	1	0
	TOTALS	8	0	1	1	0

HARVEY, Douglas Norman (Doug)

Born in Montreal, Quebec, December 19th, 1924.
Defenseman, left-hand shot.
5'11", 180 lb.
Last amateur team: the Montreal Royals srs.

SEASON	TEAM	GP	G	A	PTS	MIP
1947-48	Montreal Canadiens	35	4	4	8	32
1948-49	Montreal Canadiens	55	3	13	16	87
1949-50	Montreal Canadiens	70	4	20	24	76
1950-51	Montreal Canadiens	70	5	24	29	93
1951-52	Montreal Canadiens	68	6	23	29	82
1952-53	Montreal Canadiens	69	4	30	34	67
1953-54	Montreal Canadiens	68	8	29	37	110
1954-55	Montreal Canadiens	70	6	43	49	58
1955-56	Montreal Canadiens	62	5	39	44	60
1956-57	Montreal Canadiens	70	6	44	50	92
1957-58	Montreal Canadiens	68	9	32	41	131
1958-59	Montreal Canadiens	61	4	16	20	61
1959-60	Montreal Canadiens	66	6	21	27	45
1960-61	Montreal Canadiens	58	6	33	39	48
	TOTALS	890	76	371	447	1042

PLAYOFFS		GP	G	A	PTS	MIP
1948-49	Montreal Canadiens	7	0	1	1	10
1949-50	Montreal Canadiens	5	0	2	2	10
1950-51	Montreal Canadiens	11	0	5	5	12
1951-52	Montreal Canadiens	11	0	3	3	8
1952-53	Montreal Canadiens	12	0	5	5	8
1953-54	Montreal Canadiens	10	0	2	2	12
1954-55	Montreal Canadiens	12	0	8	8	6
1955-56	Montreal Canadiens	10	2	5	7	10
1956-57	Montreal Canadiens	10	0	7	7	10
1957-58	Montreal Canadiens	10	2	9	11	16
1958-59	Montreal Canadiens	11	1	11	12	22
1959-60	Montreal Canadiens	8	3	0	3	6
1960-61	Montreal Canadiens	6	0	1	1	8
	TOTALS	123	8	59	67	138

ALL-STAR GAMES		GP	G	A	PTS
1951	NHL All-Stars	1	0	0	0
1952	NHL All-Stars	1	0	0	0
1953	Montreal Canadiens	1	0	1	1
1954	NHL All-Stars	1	0	0	0
1955	NHL All-Stars	1	1	0	1
1956	Montreal Canadiens	1	0	1	1
1957	Montreal Canadiens	1	0	0	0
1958	Montreal Canadiens	1	0	1	1
1959	Montreal Canadiens	1	0	3	3
1960	Montreal Canadiens	1	0	0	0
	TOTALS	10	1	6	7

Played with the team that won the Prince of Wales Trophy in 1955-56, 1957-58, 1958-59, 1959-60, 1960-61.
Played with the team that won the Stanley Cup in 1952-53, 1955-56, 1956-57, 1957-58, 1958-59, 1959-60.
Won the James Norris Trophy in 1954-55, 1955-56, 1956-57, 1957-58, 1959-60, 1960-61.
Member of the first All-Star team in 1951-52, 1952-53, 1953-54, 1954-55, 1955-56, 1956-57, 1957-58, 1959-60, 1960-61.
Appointed assistant captain of the Canadiens in 1951-52.
Appointed captain of the Canadiens in 1960 (1960-61).
Member of the second All-Star team in 1958-59.
Sold to the New York Rangers in June, 1961.
Member of the Hockey Hall of Fame in June, 1973.

HAYNES, Paul

Born in Montreal, Quebec, March 1st, 1909.
Center, left-hand shot.
5'9", 160 lb.
Last amateur team: Windsor (IHL).

SEASON	TEAM	GP	G	A	PTS	MIP
1935-36	Montreal Canadiens	48	5	19	24	24
1936-37	Montreal Canadiens	47	8	18	26	24
1937-38	Montreal Canadiens	48	13	22	35	25
1938-39	Montreal Canadiens	47	5	33	38	27
1939-40	Montreal Canadiens	23	2	8	10	8
1940-41	Montreal Canadiens	7	0	0	0	12
	TOTALS	220	33	100	133	120

PLAYOFFS		GP	G	A	PTS	MIP
1936-37	Montreal Canadiens	5	2	3	5	0
1937-38	Montreal Canadiens	3	0	4	4	5
1938-39	Montreal Canadiens	3	0	0	0	4
	TOTALS	11	2	7	9	9

HEADLEY, Fern James (Curley)

Born in Chrystle, North Dakota, March 2nd, 1901.
Defenseman.
5'11", 175 lb.

SEASON	TEAM	GP	G	A	PTS	MIP
*1924-25	Montreal Canadiens/ Boston Bruins	27	1	1	2	6
	TOTALS	27	1	1	2	6

PLAYOFFS		GP	G	A	PTS	MIP
1924-25	Montreal Canadiens	5	0	—	0	—
	TOTALS	5	0	—	0	—

Obtained from the Saskatoon Sheiks with Jean Matz in 1924.
Played with the team that won the Prince of Wales Trophy in 1924-25.
Traded to the Boston Bruins in 1925.

HEFFERNAN, Gerald (Gerry, Jerry)

Born in Montreal, Quebec, July 24th, 1916.
Right-winger, right-hand shot.
5'9", 160 lb.
Last amateur team: the Montreal Royals srs.

SEASON	TEAM	GP	G	A	PTS	MIP
1941-42	Montreal Canadiens	40	5	15	20	15
1943-44	Montreal Canadiens	43	28	20	48	12
	TOTALS	83	33	35	68	27

PLAYOFFS		GP	G	A	PTS	MIP
1941-42	Montreal Canadiens	2	2	1	3	0
1942-43	Montreal Canadiens	2	0	0	0	0
1943-44	Montreal Canadiens	7	1	2	3	8
	TOTALS	11	3	3	6	8

Played with the team that won the Prince of Wales Trophy in 1943-44.
Played with the team that won the Stanley Cup in 1943-44.
Member of the famous "Razzle Dazzle" line with "Buddy" O'Connor at center and Pierre Morin at left wing.

HÉRON, Robert (Red)

Born in Toronto, Ontario, December 31st, 1917.
Left-winger, left-hand shot.
5'10", 170 lb.
Last amateur team: the Toronto Goodyears jrs.

SEASON	TEAM	GP	G	A	PTS	MIP
*1941-42	New York Americans/ Montreal Canadiens	23	1	2	3	14
	TOTALS	23	1	2	3	14

PLAYOFFS		GP	G	A	PTS	MIP
1941-42	Montreal Canadiens	3	0	0	0	0
	TOTALS	3	0	0	0	0

HERRON, Denis

Born in Chambly, Quebec, June 18th, 1952.
Goaltender, left-hand shot.
5'11", 165 lbs.
Last amateur team: Trois-Rivières jrs.

SEASON	TEAM	GP	GA	SO	AVE
1979-80	Montreal Canadiens	34	80	0	2.51
	TOTALS	34	80	0	2.51

PLAYOFFS		GP	GA	SO	AVE
1979-80	Montreal Canadiens	5	15	0	3.00
	TOTALS	5	15	0	3.00

Traded to the Canadiens for a second Draft choice from the Pittsburgh Penguins for Pat Hughes and goaltender Robert Holland in 1979.

HICKE, William Lawrence (Bill)

Born in Regina, Saskatchewan, March 31st, 1938.
Right-winger, left-hand shot.
5'8", 165 lb.
Last amateur team: the Regina Pats jrs.

SEASON	TEAM	GP	G	A	PTS	MIP
1959-60	Montreal Canadiens	43	3	10	13	17
1960-61	Montreal Canadiens	70	18	27	45	31
1961-62	Montreal Canadiens	70	20	31	51	42
1962-63	Montreal Canadiens	70	17	22	39	39
1963-64	Montreal Canadiens	48	11	9	20	41
1964-65	Montreal Canadiens	17	0	1	1	6
	TOTALS	318	69	100	169	176

PLAYOFFS		GP	G	A	PTS	MIP
1958-59	Montreal Canadiens	1	0	0	0	0
1959-60	Montreal Canadiens	7	1	2	3	0
1960-61	Montreal Canadiens	5	2	0	2	19
1961-62	Montreal Canadiens	6	0	2	2	14
1962-63	Montreal Canadiens	5	0	0	0	0
1963-64	Montreal Canadiens	7	0	2	2	2
	TOTALS	31	3	6	9	35

ALL-STAR GAMES		GP	G	A	PTS
1959	Montreal Canadiens	1	0	2	2
1960	Montreal Canadiens	1	0	0	0
	TOTALS	2	0	2	2

Played with the team that won the Prince of Wales Trophy in 1959-60, 1960-61, 1961-62, 1963-64.
Played with the team that won the Stanley Cup in 1958-59, 1959-60.
Traded to the New York Rangers for Dick Duff, December 22, 1964.

HICKS, Wayne Wilson

Born in Aberdeen, Washington, April 9th, 1937.
Right-winger, right-hand shot.
5′10″, 185 lb.
Last amateur team: the Melville Millionnaires jrs.

SEASON	TEAM	GP	G	A	PTS	MIP
1963-64	Montreal Canadiens	2	0	0	0	0
	TOTALS	2	0	0	0	0

Played with the team that won the Prince of Wales Trophy in 1963-64.

HILLER, Wilbert Carl (Dutch)

Born in Kitchener, Ontario, May 11th, 1915.
Left-winger, left-hand shot.
5′8″, 160 lb.
Last amateur team: the New York Rovers.

SEASON	TEAM	GP	G	A	PTS	MIP
*1942-43	Boston Bruins/ Montreal Canadiens	42	8	6	14	4
1944-45	Montreal Canadiens	48	20	16	36	20
1945-46	Montreal Canadiens	45	7	11	18	4
	TOTALS	135	35	33	68	28

PLAYOFFS		GP	G	A	PTS	MIP
1942-43	Montreal Canadiens	5	1	0	1	4
1944-45	Montreal Canadiens	6	1	1	2	4
1945-46	Montreal Canadiens	9	4	2	6	2
	TOTALS	20	6	3	9	10

Bought from the Boston Bruins in 1943.
Traded to the New York Rangers with Charlie Sands for Phil Watson.
Obtained from the New York Rangers with Fernand Gauthier for Phil Watson in 1944.
Played with the team that won the Prince of Wales Trophy in 1944-45, 1945-46.
Played with the team that won the Stanley Cup in 1945-46.
Loaned to the New York Rangers with John Mahaffey, Fernand Gauthier and Antonio Demers for Phil Watson.

HILLMAN, Larry Morley

Born in Kirkland Lake, Ontario, February 5th, 1937.
Defenseman, left-hand shot.
6′, 185 lb.
Last amateur team: the Hamilton Tiger Cubs.

SEASON	TEAM	GP	G	A	PTS	MIP
1968-69	Montreal Canadiens	25	0	5	5	17
	TOTALS	25	0	5	5	17

PLAYOFFS		GP	G	A	PTS	MIP
1968-69	Montreal Canadiens	1	0	0	0	0
	TOTALS	1	0	0	0	0

Obtained from the Pittsburgh Penguins for Jean-Guy Lagace and a certain amount of money, November 22, 1968.
Played with the team that won the Prince of Wales Trophy in 1968-69.
Played with the team that won the Stanley Cup in 1968-69.
Drafted by the Philadelphia Flyers June 11, 1969.

HIRSCHFELD, John Albert (Bert)

Born in Halifax, Nova Scotia, March 1st, 1929.
Left-winger, left-hand shot.
5′10″, 165 lb.
Last amateur team: the Montreal Royals srs.

SEASON	TEAM	GP	G	A	PTS	MIP
1949-50	Montreal Canadiens	13	1	2	3	2
1950-51	Montreal Canadiens	20	0	2	2	0
	TOTALS	33	1	4	5	2

Traded to the Detroit Red Wings for Gerald Couture in June, 1951.

HODGE, Charles Edward (Charlie)

Born in Lachine, Quebec, July 28th, 1933.
Goaltender, left-hand shot.
5′6″, 150 lb.
Last amateur team: the Cincinnati Mohawks srs.

SEASON	TEAM	GP	GA	SO	AVE
1954-55	Montreal Canadiens	14	31	1	2.27
1957-58	Montreal Canadiens	12	31	1	2.58
1958-59	Montreal Canadiens	2	6	0	3.00
1959-60	Montreal Canadiens	1	3	0	3.00
1960-61	Montreal Canadiens	30	76	4	2.53
1963-64	Montreal Canadiens	62	140	8	2.26
1964-65	Montreal Canadiens	52	135	3	2.60
1965-66	Montreal Canadiens	26	56	1	2.58
1966-67	Montreal Canadiens	37	88	3	2.60
	TOTALS	236	566	21	2.40

PLAYOFFS		GP	GA	SO	AVE
1954-55	Montreal Canadiens	4	6	0	1.50
1963-64	Montreal Canadiens	7	16	1	2.29
1964-65	Montreal Canadiens	5	10	1	2.00
	TOTALS	16	32	2	2.00

OFFENSIVE RECORD		GP	G	A	PTS	MIP
1954-55	Montreal Canadiens	14	0	0	0	0
1957-58	Montreal Canadiens	12	0	0	0	0
1958-59	Montreal Canadiens	2	0	0	0	0
1959-60	Montreal Canadiens	1	0	0	0	0
1960-61	Montreal Canadiens	30	0	0	0	0
1963-64	Montreal Canadiens	62	0	0	0	2
1964-65	Montreal Canadiens	52	0	0	0	2
1965-66	Montreal Canadiens	26	0	0	0	0
1966-67	Montreal Canadiens	37	0	0	0	2
	TOTALS	236	0	0	0	6

PLAYOFFS		GP	G	A	PTS	MIP
1954-55	Montreal Canadiens	4	0	0	0	0
1963-64	Montreal Canadiens	7	0	0	0	0
1964-65	Montreal Canadiens	5	0	0	0	0
	TOTALS	16	0	0	0	0

Played with the team that won the Prince of Wales Trophy in 1957-58, 1958-59, 1959-60, 1960-61, 1963-64, 1965-66.
Played with the team that won the Stanley Cup in 1958-59, 1959-60, 1964-65, 1965-66.
Won the Vezina Trophy in 1963-64, 1965-66 (with Lorne Worsley).
Member of the second All-Star team in 1963-64, 1964-65.
Drafted by the Oakland Seals at the 1967 Expansion, June 6, 1967.

HOEKSTRA, Cecil Thomas

Born in Winnipeg, Manitoba, April 2nd, 1935.
Left-winger, left-hand shot.
6′, 175 lb.
Last amateur team: the St. Catharines Tee Pees jrs.

SEASON	TEAM	GP	G	A	PTS	MIP
1959-60	Montreal Canadiens	4	0	0	0	0
	TOTALS	4	0	0	0	0

Played with the team that won the Prince of Wales Trophy in 1959-60.
Brother of Ed Hoekstra.

HOGANSON, Dale Gordon (Red)

Born in North Battleford, Saskatchewan, July 8th, 1949.
Defenseman, left-hand shot.
5′10″, 195 lb.
Last amateur team: the Estevan Bruins jrs.

SEASON	TEAM	GP	G	A	PTS	MIP
1971-72	Montreal Canadiens	21	0	0	0	2
1972-73	Montreal Canadiens	25	0	2	2	2
	TOTALS	46	0	2	2	4

Obtained from the Los Angeles Kings with Denis Dejordy, Noel Price and Doug Robinson for Rogatien Vachon, November 4, 1971.
Played with the team that won the Prince of Wales Trophy in 1972-73.
Traded to the Atlanta Flames with Charles Arnason and Bob Murray for a player chosen at a later date and a future Amateur Draft choice, May 29, 1973.
Signed with the Quebec Nordiques in May, 1973.

HOLMES, William (Bill)

Born in Weyburn, Saskatchewan, 1899.

SEASON	TEAM	GP	G	A	PTS	MIP
1925-26	Montreal Canadiens	9	1	0	1	2
	TOTALS	9	1	0	1	2

Died on March 14, 1961.

HORVATH, Bronco Joseph

Born in Port Colborne, Ontario, March 12th, 1930.
Center, left-hand shot.
5′11″, 185 lb.
Last amateur team: the Galt Black Hawks jrs.

SEASON	TEAM	GP	G	A	PTS	MIP
1956-57	Montreal Canadiens	1	0	0	0	0
	TOTALS	1	0	0	0	0

Obtained from the New York Rangers in November, 1956.
Drafted by the Boston Bruins in June, 1957.

HOULE, Réjean

Born in Rouyn, Quebec, October 25th, 1949.
Center, right-winger, left-winger, left-hand shot.
5′11″, 168 lb.
Last amateur team: the Montreal Canadiens jrs.

SEASON	TEAM	GP	G	A	PTS	MIP
1969-70	Montreal Canadiens	9	0	1	1	0
1970-71	Montreal Canadiens	66	10	9	19	28
1971-72	Montreal Canadiens	77	11	17	28	21
1972-73	Montreal Canadiens	72	13	35	48	36
1976-77	Montreal Canadiens	65	22	30	52	24
1977-78	Montreal Canadiens	76	30	28	58	50
1978-79	Montreal Canadiens	66	17	34	51	48
1979-80	Montreal Canadiens	60	18	27	45	68
	TOTALS	491	121	181	302	275

PLAYOFFS		GP	G	A	PTS	MIP
1970-71	Montreal Canadiens	20	2	5	7	20
1971-72	Montreal Canadiens	6	0	0	0	2
1972-73	Montreal Canadiens	17	3	6	9	0
1976-77	Montreal Canadiens	6	0	1	1	4
1977-78	Montreal Canadiens	15	3	8	11	14
1978-79	Montreal Canadiens	7	1	5	6	2
1979-80	Montreal Canadiens	10	4	5	9	12
	TOTALS	81	13	30	43	54

First Amateur Draft choice of the Canadiens in 1969.
Played with the team that won the Prince of Wales Trophy in 1972-73, 1976-77, 1977-78.
Played with the team that won the Stanley Cup in 1970-71, 1972-73, 1976-77, 1977-78, 1978-79.
With the Quebec Nordiques from 1973-74 to 1975-76.

HUCK, Anthony Francis (Fran)

Born in Regina, Saskatchewan, December 4th, 1945.
Center, left-hand shot.
5'7", 165 lb.
Last amateur team: the Canada's National team.

SEASON	TEAM	GP	G	A	PTS	MIP
1969-70	Montreal Canadiens	2	0	0	0	0
1970-71	Montreal Canadiens	5	1	2	3	0
	TOTALS	7	1	2	3	0

Traded to the St. Louis Blues for the second Amateur Draft choice of 1971 (Michel Deguise), January 28, 1971.

HUGHES, Pat

Born in Toronto, Ontario, March 25th, 1955.
Right-winger, right-hand shot.
6'1", 180 lb.
Last amateur team: Michigan University.

SEASON	TEAM	GP	G	A	PTS	MIP
1977-78	Montreal Canadiens	3	0	0	0	2
1978-79	Montreal Canadiens	41	9	8	17	22
	TOTALS	44	9	8	17	24

PLAYOFFS		GP	G	A	PTS	MIP
1978-79	Montreal Canadiens	8	1	2	3	4
	TOTALS	8	1	2	3	4

Played with the team that won the Stanley Cup in 1978-79.
Traded to the Pittsburgh Penguins with Robert Holland for goaltender Denis Herron and a future Draft choice.

HUNT, Bert

SEASON	TEAM	GP	G	A	PTS	MIP
*1914-15	Shamrocks/ Ontarios/ Montreal Canadiens	10	0	—	0	—
	TOTALS	10	0	—	0	—

Obtained from the Ontarios in 1914-15.

IRWIN, Ivan Duane (The Terrible)

Born in Chicago, Illinois, March 13th, 1927.
Defenseman, left-hand shot.
6'2", 185 lb.
Last amateur team: the Sherbrooke Saints srs.

SEASON	TEAM	GP	G	A	PTS	MIP
1952-53	Montreal Canadiens	4	0	1	1	0
	TOTALS	4	0	1	1	0

JARVIS, Douglas (Doug)

Born in Brantford, Ontario, March 24th, 1955.
Center, left-hand shot.
5'9", 165 lb.
Last amateur team: the Peterborough Petes jrs.

SEASON	TEAM	GP	G	A	PTS	MIP
1975-76	Montreal Canadiens	80	5	30	35	16
1976-77	Montreal Canadiens	80	16	22	38	14
1977-78	Montreal Canadiens	80	11	28	39	23
1978-79	Montreal Canadiens	80	10	13	23	16
1979-80	Montreal Canadiens	80	13	11	24	28
	TOTALS	400	55	104	159	97

PLAYOFFS		GP	G	A	PTS	MIP
1975-76	Montreal Canadiens	13	2	1	3	2
1976-77	Montreal Canadiens	14	0	7	7	2
1977-78	Montreal Canadiens	15	3	5	8	12
1978-79	Montreal Canadiens	12	1	3	4	4
1979-80	Montreal Canadiens	10	4	4	8	2
	TOTALS	64	10	20	30	22

Obtained from the Toronto Maple Leafs for Greg Hubick, June 26, 1975.
Played with the team that won the Prince of Wales Trophy in 1975-76, 1976-77, 1977-78.
Played with the team that won the Stanley Cup in 1975-76, 1976-77, 1977-78, 1978-79.

JENKINS, Roger Joseph

Born in Appleton, Wisconsin, November 18th, 1911.
Defenseman, right-hand shot.
5'11", 173 lb.
Last amateur team: the Edmonton Imperials.

SEASON	TEAM	GP	G	A	PTS	MIP
1934-35	Montreal Canadiens	45	4	6	10	63
*1936-37	Montreal Canadiens/ New York Americans/ Montreal Maroons	37	1	4	5	14
	TOTALS	82	5	10	15	77

PLAYOFFS		GP	G	A	PTS	MIP
1934-35	Montreal Canadiens	2	1	0	1	2
	TOTALS	2	1	0	1	2

Obtained from the Chicago Black Hawks with Lionel Conacher and Leroy Goldsworthy for Lorne Chabot, Howie Morenz and Martin Burke in 1934.
Sold to the Boston Bruins in 1935.

JETTE, Alphonse

Forward.

SEASON	TEAM	GP	G	A	PTS	MIP
1911-12	Montreal Canadiens	2	0	—	0	—
1912-13	Montreal Canadiens	3	0	—	0	—
1913-14	Montreal Canadiens	6	1	—	1	—
1914-15	Montreal Canadiens	3	0	—	0	—
	TOTALS	14	1	—	1	—

JOANETTE, Rosario (Kit) (Kitoute)

Born in Valleyfield, Quebec, August 27th, 1915.
Center, right-hand shot.
5'10", 160 lb.
Last amateur team: the Valleyfield Braves srs.

SEASON	TEAM	GP	G	A	PTS	MIP
1944-45	Montreal Canadiens	2	0	1	1	4
	TOTALS	2	0	1	1	4

Played with the team that won the Prince of Wales Trophy in 1944-45.

JOHNS, Donald Ernest (Don)

Born in St. George, Ontario, December 13th, 1937.
Defenseman, left-hand shot.
5'11", 178 lb.
Last amateur team: the Fort William Columbus Canadiens jrs.

SEASON	TEAM	GP	G	A	PTS	MIP
1965-66	Montreal Canadiens	1	0	0	0	0
	TOTALS	1	0	0	0	0

Played with the team that won the Prince of Wales Trophy in 1965-66.
Sold to the Minnesota North Stars in October, 1967.

JOHNSON, Allan Edmund (Al)

Born in Winnipeg, Manitoba, March 30th, 1935.
Right-winger, right-hand shot.
5'11", 185 lb.
Last amateur team: the Cincinnati Mohawks srs.

SEASON	TEAM	GP	G	A	PTS	MIP
1956-57	Montreal Canadiens	2	0	1	1	2
	TOTALS	2	0	1	1	2

JOHNSON, Thomas Christian (Tom)

Born in Baldur, Manitoba, February 18th, 1928.
Defenseman, left-hand shot.
6', 180 lb.
Last amateur team: the Montreal Royals srs.

SEASON	TEAM	GP	G	A	PTS	MIP
1947-48	Montreal Canadiens	1	0	0	0	0
1950-51	Montreal Canadiens	70	2	8	10	128
1951-52	Montreal Canadiens	67	0	7	7	76
1952-53	Montreal Canadiens	70	3	8	11	63
1953-54	Montreal Canadiens	70	7	11	18	85
1954-55	Montreal Canadiens	70	6	19	25	74
1955-56	Montreal Canadiens	64	3	10	13	75
1956-57	Montreal Canadiens	70	4	11	15	59
1957-58	Montreal Canadiens	66	3	18	21	75
1958-59	Montreal Canadiens	70	10	29	39	76
1959-60	Montreal Canadiens	64	4	25	29	59
1960-61	Montreal Canadiens	70	1	15	16	54
1961-62	Montreal Canadiens	62	1	17	18	45
1962-63	Montreal Canadiens	43	3	5	8	28
	TOTALS	857	47	183	230	897

PLAYOFFS		GP	G	A	PTS	MIP
1949-50	Montreal Canadiens	1	0	0	0	0
1950-51	Montreal Canadiens	11	0	0	0	6
1951-52	Montreal Canadiens	11	1	0	1	2
1952-53	Montreal Canadiens	12	2	3	5	8
1953-54	Montreal Canadiens	11	1	2	3	30
1954-55	Montreal Canadiens	12	2	0	2	22
1955-56	Montreal Canadiens	10	0	2	2	8
1956-57	Montreal Canadiens	10	0	2	2	13
1957-58	Montreal Canadiens	2	0	0	0	0
1958-59	Montreal Canadiens	11	2	3	5	8
1959-60	Montreal Canadiens	8	0	1	1	4
1960-61	Montreal Canadiens	6	0	1	1	8
1961-62	Montreal Canadiens	6	0	1	1	0
	TOTALS	111	8	15	23	109

ALL-STAR GAMES		GP	G	A	PTS
1952	NHL All-Stars	1	0	0	0
1953	Montreal Canadiens	1	0	0	0
1956	Montreal Canadiens	1	0	0	0
1957	Montreal Canadiens	1	0	1	1
1958	Montreal Canadiens	1	0	0	0
1959	Montreal Canadiens	1	0	1	1
1960	Montreal Canadiens	1	0	0	0
	TOTALS	7	0	2	2

Played with the team that won the Prince of Wales Trophy in 1955-56, 1957-58, 1958-59, 1959-60, 1960-61, 1961-62.
Played with the team that won the Stanley Cup in 1952-53, 1955-56, 1956-57, 1957-58, 1958-59, 1959-60.
Appointed assistant captain of the Canadiens in 1956.
Won the James-Norris Trophy in 1958-59.
Member of the first All-Star team in 1958-59.
Member of the second All-Star team in 1955-56.
Member of the Hockey Hall of Fame in June, 1970.
Drafted by the Boston Bruins June 4, 1963.

JOLIAT, Aurèle

Born in Ottawa, Ontario, August 29th, 1901.
Left-winger, left-hand shot.
5'7", 136 lb.
Last amateur team: Iroquois Falls.

SEASON	TEAM	GP	G	A	PTS	MIP
1922-23	Montreal Canadiens	24	13	9	22	31
1923-24	Montreal Canadiens	24	15	5	20	19
1924-25	Montreal Canadiens	24	29	11	40	85
1925-26	Montreal Canadiens	25	17	9	26	52
1926-27	Montreal Canadiens	43	14	4	18	79
1927-28	Montreal Canadiens	44	28	11	39	105
1928-29	Montreal Canadiens	44	12	5	17	59
1929-30	Montreal Canadiens	42	19	12	31	40
1930-31	Montreal Canadiens	43	13	22	35	73
1931-32	Montreal Canadiens	48	15	24	39	46
1932-33	Montreal Canadiens	48	18	21	39	53
1933-34	Montreal Canadiens	48	22	15	37	27
1934-35	Montreal Canadiens	48	17	12	29	18
1935-36	Montreal Canadiens	48	15	8	23	16
1936-37	Montreal Canadiens	47	17	15	32	30
1937-38	Montreal Canadiens	44	6	7	13	24
	TOTALS	644	270	190	460	757

PLAYOFFS		GP	G	A	PTS	MIP
1922-23	Montreal Canadiens	2	1	1	2	8
1923-24	Montreal Canadiens	6	4	4	8	10
1924-25	Montreal Canadiens	5	2	2	4	21
1926-27	Montreal Canadiens	4	1	0	1	10
1927-28	Montreal Canadiens	2	0	0	0	4
1928-29	Montreal Canadiens	3	1	1	2	10
1929-30	Montreal Canadiens	6	0	2	2	6
1930-31	Montreal Canadiens	10	0	4	4	12
1931-32	Montreal Canadiens	4	2	0	2	4
1932-33	Montreal Canadiens	2	2	1	3	2
1933-34	Montreal Canadiens	2	0	1	1	0
1934-35	Montreal Canadiens	2	1	0	1	0
1936-37	Montreal Canadiens	5	0	3	3	2
	TOTALS	53	14	19	33	89

Played with the team that won the Prince of Wales Trophy in 1924-25.
Played with the team that won the Stanley Cup in 1923-24, 1929-30, 1930-31.
Member of the first All-Star team in 1930-31.
Member of the second All-Star team in 1931-32, 1933-34, 1934-35.
Member of the Hockey Hall of Fame in April, 1945.
Brother of René "Bobby" Joliat.

JOLIAT, René (Bobby, Bobbie)

SEASON	TEAM	GP	G	A	PTS	MIP
1924-25	Montreal Canadiens	1	0	0	0	0
	TOTALS	1	0	0	0	0

Played with the team that won the Prince of Wales Trophy in 1924-25.

JOLY, Yvan

Born in Hawksbury, Ontario, February 6th, 1960.
Right-winger, right-hand shot.
5′8″, 169 lb.
Last amateur team: Ottawa OHA.

SEASON	TEAM	GP	G	A	PTS	MIP
1979-80	Montreal Canadiens (Playoffs)	1	0	0	0	0
	TOTALS	1	0	0	0	0

KAISER, Vernon Charles (Vern)

Born in Preston, Ontario, September 28th, 1925.
Left-winger, left-hand shot.
6′, 180 lb.
Last amateur team: the Preston Riversides jrs.

SEASON	TEAM	GP	G	A	PTS	MIP
1950-51	Montreal Canadiens	50	7	5	12	33
	TOTALS	50	7	5	12	33

KARAKAS, Michael (Mike)

Born in Aurora, Minnesota, December 12th, 1911.
Goaltender, left-hand shot.
5′10″, 161 lb.
Last amateur team: the Eveleth Rangers (Minn.).

SEASON	TEAM	GP	GA	SO	AVE
*1939-40	Chicago Black Hawks/ Montreal Canadiens	22	76	0	3.46
	TOTALS	22	76	0	3.46

OFFENSIVE RECORD		GP	G	A	PTS	MIP
*1939-40	Chicago Black Hawks/ Montreal Canadiens	22	0	0	0	0
	TOTALS	22	0	0	0	0

KING, Frank Edward

Born in Toronto, Ontario, March 7th, 1929.
Center, left-hand shot.
5′11″, 185 lb.
Last amateur team: the Brandon Wheat Kings jrs.

SEASON	TEAM	GP	G	A	PTS	MIP
1950-51	Montreal Canadiens	10	1	0	1	2
	TOTALS	10	1	0	1	2

LACH, Elmer James

Born in Nokomis, Saskatchewan, January 22nd, 1918.
Center, left-hand shot.
5′10″, 170 lb.
Last amateur team: The Moose Jaw Millers jrs.

SEASON	TEAM	GP	G	A	PTS	MIP
1940-41	Montreal Canadiens	43	7	14	21	16
1941-42	Montreal Canadiens	1	0	1	1	0
1942-43	Montreal Canadiens	45	18	40	58	14
1943-44	Montreal Canadiens	48	24	48	72	23
1944-45	Montreal Canadiens	50	26	54	80	37
1945-46	Montreal Canadiens	50	13	34	47	34
1946-47	Montreal Canadiens	31	14	16	30	22
1947-48	Montreal Canadiens	60	30	31	61	72
1948-49	Montreal Canadiens	36	11	18	29	59
1949-50	Montreal Canadiens	64	15	33	48	33
1950-51	Montreal Canadiens	65	21	24	45	48
1951-52	Montreal Canadiens	70	15	50	65	36
1952-53	Montreal Canadiens	53	16	25	41	56
1953-54	Montreal Canadiens	48	5	20	25	28
	TOTALS	664	215	408	623	478

PLAYOFFS		GP	G	A	PTS	MIP
1940-41	Montreal Canadiens	3	1	0	1	0
1942-43	Montreal Canadiens	5	2	4	6	6
1943-44	Montreal Canadiens	9	2	11	13	4
1944-45	Montreal Canadiens	6	4	4	8	2
1945-46	Montreal Canadiens	9	5	12	17	4
1948-49	Montreal Canadiens	1	0	0	0	4
1949-50	Montreal Canadiens	5	1	2	3	4
1950-51	Montreal Canadiens	11	2	2	4	2
1951-52	Montreal Canadiens	11	1	2	3	4
1952-53	Montreal Canadiens	12	1	6	7	6
1953-54	Montreal Canadiens	4	0	2	2	0
	TOTALS	76	19	45	64	36

ALL-STAR GAMES		GP	G	A	PTS
1948	NHL All-Stars	1	0	1	1
1952	NHL All-Stars (1st team)	1	0	0	0
1953	Montreal Canadiens	1	0	0	0
	TOTALS	3	0	1	1

Played with the team that won the Prince of Wales Trophy in 1943-44, 1944-45, 1945-46, 1946-47.
Played with the team that won the Stanley Cup in 1943-44, 1945-46, 1952-53.
Won the Hart Trophy in 1944-45.
Won the Art-Ross Trophy in 1947-48, 1944-45.
Member of the first All-Star Team in 1944-45, 1947-48, 1951-52.
Member of the second All-Star team in 1943-44, 1945-46.
Member of the famous Punch Line with Maurice Richard at right wing and Toe Blake at left wing.
Appointed assistant captain of the Canadiens in 1948.
Member of the Hockey Hall of Fame in June, 1966.

LACHANCE, ?

Incomplete record: Existence confirmed by, Official Report of Match, Season 1926-27, NHL Office.

LACROIX, Alphonse (Frenchy)

Goaltender.

SEASON	TEAM	GP	GA	SO	AVE
1925-26	Montreal Canadiens	5	15	0	3.00
	TOTALS	5	15	0	3.00

OFFENSIVE RECORD		GP	G	A	PTS	MIP
1925-26	Montreal Canadiens	5	0	0	0	0
	TOTALS	5	0	0	0	0

LAFLEUR, Guy Damien

Born in Thurso, Québec, September 20th, 1951.
Right-winger, center, right-hand shot.
6′, 178 lb.
Last amateur team: the Quebec Remparts jrs.

SEASON	TEAM	GP	G	A	PTS	MIP
1971-72	Montreal Canadiens	73	29	35	64	48
1972-73	Montreal Canadiens	69	28	27	55	51
1973-74	Montreal Canadiens	73	21	35	56	29
1074-75	Montreal Canadiens	70	53	66	119	37
1975-76	Montreal Canadiens	80	56	69	125	36
1976-77	Montreal Canadiens	80	56	80	136	20
1977-78	Montreal Canadiens	78	60	72	132	26
1978-79	Montreal Canadiens	80	52	77	129	28
1979-80	Montreal Canadiens	74	50	75	125	12
	TOTALS	677	405	536	941	287

PLAYOFFS		GP	G	A	PTS	MIP
1971-72	Montreal Canadiens	6	1	4	5	2
1972-73	Montreal Canadiens	17	3	5	8	9
1973-74	Montreal Canadiens	6	0	1	1	4
1974-75	Montreal Canadiens	11	12	7	19	15
1975-76	Montreal Canadiens	13	7	10	17	2
1976-77	Montreal Canadiens	14	9	17	26	6
1977-78	Montreal Canadiens	15	10	11	21	16
1978-79	Montreal Canadiens	16	10	13	23	0
1979-80	Montreal Canadiens	3	3	1	4	0
	TOTALS	101	55	69	124	54

ALL-STAR GAMES		GP	G	A	PTS
1975	Montreal Canadiens	1	0	3	3
1976	Montreal Canadiens	1	1	2	3
1977	Montreal Canadiens	1	0	1	1
1978	Montreal Canadiens	1	0	0	0
1980	Montreal Canadiens	1	0	1	1
	TOTALS	5	1	7	8

First Amateur Draft choice of the Canadiens in 1971.
Played with the team that won the Prince of Wales Trophy in 1972-73, 1975-76, 1976-77, 1977-78.
Played with the team that won the Stanley Cup in 1972-73, 1975-76, 1976-77, 1977-78, 1978-79.
Won the Art-Ross Trophy in 1975-76, 1976-77, 1977-78.
Member of the First All-Star team in 1974-75, 1975-76, 1976-77, 1977-78, 1978-79.
Won the Lester B. Pearson Trophy in 1975-76.
Won the "Seagram's Seven Crowns Sports Award" in 1976.
Won the Hart Trophy in 1976-77.
Won the Molson Cup 1974-75, 1975-76, 1976-77, 1977-78, 1978-79, 1979-80.

LAFLEUR, Rene

SEASON	TEAM	GP	G	A	PTS	MIP
1924-25	Montreal Canadiens	1	0	0	0	0
	TOTALS	1	0	0	0	0

Played with the team that won the Prince of Wales Trophy in 1924-25.

LAFORCE, Ernest (Ernie)

Born in Montreal, Quebec, June 23rd, 1916.
Defenseman.
Last amateur team: the Montreal Royals srs.

SEASON	TEAM	GP	G	A	PTS	MIP
1942-43	Montreal Canadiens	1	0	0	0	0
	TOTALS	1	0	0	0	0

LAFORGE, Claude Roger

Born in Sorel, Quebec, July 1st, 1936.
Left-winger, left-hand shot.
5'9", 160 lb.
Last amateur team: the Cincinnati Mohawks srs.

SEASON	TEAM	GP	G	A	PTS	MIP
1957-58	Montreal Canadiens	5	0	0	0	0
	TOTALS	5	0	0	0	0

Played with the team that won the Prince of Wales Trophy in 1957-58.
Sold to the Detroit Red Wings in June, 1958.

LAFRANCE, Adelard

Born in Chapleau, Ontario, January 13th, 1912.

SEASON	TEAM	GP	G	A	PTS	MIP
1933-34	Montreal Canadiens	3	0	0	0	2
	TOTALS	3	0	0	0	2

PLAYOFFS		GP	G	A	PTS	MIP
1933-34	Montreal Canadiens	2	0	0	0	0
	TOTALS	2	0	0	0	0

LAFRANCE, Leo

SEASON	TEAM	GP	G	A	PTS	MIP
*1926-27	Montreal Canadiens	4	0	0	0	0
1927-28	Montreal Canadiens/ Chicago Black Hawks	29	0	2	2	6
	TOTALS	33	0	2	2	6

LALONDE, Edouard Charles (Newsy)

Born in Cornwall, Ontario, October 31st, 1887.
Defenseman, right-winger, center, rover.

SEASON	TEAM	GP	G	A	PTS	MIP
1909-10	Montreal Canadiens	1	2	—	2	—
1910-11	Montreal Canadiens	16	19	—	19	—
1912-13	Montreal Canadiens	18	25	—	25	—
1913-14	Montreal Canadiens	14	22	—	22	—
1914-15	Montreal Canadiens	6	4	—	4	—
1915-16	Montreal Canadiens	24	31	—	31	—
1916-17	Montreal Canadiens	18	27	—	27	—
1917-18	Montreal Canadiens	14	23	—	23	—
1918-19	Montreal Canadiens	17	23	9	32	40
1919-20	Montreal Canadiens	23	36	6	42	33
1920-21	Montreal Canadiens	24	33	8	41	36
1921-22	Montreal Canadiens	20	9	4	13	11
	TOTALS	195	254	27	281	120

PLAYOFFS		GP	G	A	PTS	MIP
*1909-10	Montreal Canadiens/ Renfrew Creamery Kings	11	38	—	38	—
1913-14	Montreal Canadiens	2	0	—	0	—
1915-16	Montreal Canadiens	4	3	—	3	—
1916-17	Montreal Canadiens	6	2	—	2	—
1917-18	Montreal Canadiens	2	4	—	4	—
1918-19	Montreal Canadiens	10	17	—	18	—
	TOTALS	35	64	—	65	—

Signed up with the Canadiens in 1909.
Loaned to the Renfrew Creamery Kings for the playoffs in 1910.
Traded to the Vancouver team for Ernest Dubeau in 1911. Came back to the Canadiens afterward; the Canadiens yielded Didier Pitre's contract to complete the transaction in 1913.
Played with the team that won the Stanley Cup in 1915-16.
Traded to the Saskatoon Sheiks for Aurèle Joliat in 1922.
Member of the Hockey Hall of Fame in June, 1950.
Appointed captain of the Canadiens from 1917-18 to 1920-21.
Died at Montreal November 21, 1970.
Succeeded Cecil Hart as coach of the Canadiens in 1932 (1932-33 to 1933-34, 1934-35 with Leo Dandurand).

LAMB, Joseph Gordon (Joe)

Born in Sussex, New Brunswick, June 18th, 1906.
Right-winger, right-hand shot.
5'10", 170 lb.
Last amateur team: the Montreal Victorias srs.

SEASON	TEAM	GP	G	A	PTS	MIP
*1934-35	Montreal Canadiens/ St. Louis Eagles	38	14	14	28	23
	TOTALS	38	14	14	28	23

LAMBERT, Yvon Pierre

Born in St. Germain-de-Grantham, Drummondville, Quebec, May 20th, 1950.
Left-winger, left-hand shot.
6', 195 lb.
Last amateur team: Drummondville jrs.

SEASON	TEAM	GP	G	A	PTS	MIP
1972-73	Montreal Canadiens	1	0	0	0	0
1973-74	Montreal Canadiens	60	6	10	16	42
1974-75	Montreal Canadiens	80	32	35	67	74
1975-76	Montreal Canadiens	80	32	35	67	28
1976-77	Montreal Canadiens	79	24	28	52	50
1977-78	Montreal Canadiens	77	18	22	40	20
1978-79	Montreal Canadiens	79	26	40	66	26
1979-80	Montreal Canadiens	77	21	32	53	23
	TOTALS	533	159	202	361	263

PLAYOFFS		GP	G	A	PTS	MIP
1973-74	Montreal Canadiens	5	0	0	0	7
1974-75	Montreal Canadiens	11	4	2	6	0
1975-76	Montreal Canadiens	12	2	3	5	18
1976-77	Montreal Canadiens	14	3	3	6	12
1977-78	Montreal Canadiens	15	2	4	6	6
1978-79	Montreal Canadiens	16	5	6	11	16
1979-80	Montreal Canadiens	10	8	4	12	4
	TOTALS	83	24	22	46	63

Played with the team that won the Prince of Wales Trophy in 1972-73, 1975-76, 1976-77, 1977-78.
Played with the team that won the Stanley Cup in 1975-76, 1976-77, 1977-78, 1978-79.

LAMIRANDE, Jean-Paul (J.P.)

Born in Shawinigan Falls, Quebec, August 21st, 1923.
Defenseman, right-hand shot.
5'8", 170 lb.
Last amateur team: the Montreal Royals srs.

SEASON	TEAM	GP	G	A	PTS	MIP
1954-55	Montreal Canadiens	1	0	0	0	0
	TOTALS	1	0	0	0	0

Died January 30, 1976.

LAMOUREUX, Leo Peter

Born in Espanola, Ontario, October 1st, 1916.
Defenseman, left-hand shot.
5'11", 197 lb.
Last amateur team: the Hamilton Tigers srs.

SEASON	TEAM	GP	G	A	PTS	MIP
1942-43	Montreal Canadiens	46	2	16	18	43
1943-44	Montreal Canadiens	44	8	23	31	32
1944-45	Montreal Canadiens	49	2	22	24	38
1945-46	Montreal Canadiens	45	5	7	12	18
1946-47	Montreal Canadiens	50	2	11	13	14
	TOTALS	234	19	79	98	145

PLAYOFFS		GP	G	A	PTS	MIP
1943-44	Montreal Canadiens	9	0	3	3	8
1944-45	Montreal Canadiens	6	1	1	2	2
1945-46	Montreal Canadiens	9	0	2	2	2
1946-47	Montreal Canadiens	4	0	0	0	4
	TOTALS	28	1	6	7	16

Played with the team that won the Prince of Wales Trophy in 1943-44, 1944-45, 1945-46, 1946-47.
Played with the team that won the Stanley Cup in 1943-44, 1945-46.
Died January 11, 1961.

LANGLOIS, Albert (Junior, Al)

Born in Magog, Quebec, November 6th, 1934.
Defenseman, left-hand shot.
6', 205 lb.
Last amateur team: the Quebec Frontenacs srs.

SEASON	TEAM	GP	G	A	PTS	MIP
1957-58	Montreal Canadiens	1	0	0	0	0
1958-59	Montreal Canadiens	48	0	3	3	26
1959-60	Montreal Canadiens	67	1	14	15	43
1960-61	Montreal Canadiens	61	1	12	13	56
	TOTALS	177	2	29	31	130

PLAYOFFS		GP	G	A	PTS	MIP
1957-58	Montreal Canadiens	7	0	1	1	4
1958-59	Montreal Canadiens	7	0	0	0	4
1959-60	Montreal Canadiens	8	0	3	3	18
1960-61	Montreal Canadiens	5	0	0	0	6
	TOTALS	27	0	4	4	32

Played with the team that won the Prince of Wales Trophy in 1957-58, 1958-59, 1959-60, 1960-61.
Played with the team that won the Stanley Cup in 1957-58, 1958-59, 1959-60.
Traded to the New York Rangers for John Hanna in June, 1961.

LANGLOIS, Charles (Charlie)

Born in Lotbiniere, Quebec, August 25th, 1894.
Defenseman.

SEASON	TEAM	GP	G	A	PTS	MIP
*1927-28	Pittsburgh Pirates/ Montreal Canadiens	40	0	0	0	22
	TOTALS	40	0	0	0	22

PLAYOFFS		GP	G	A	PTS	MIP
1927-28	Montreal Canadiens	2	0	0	0	0
	TOTALS	2	0	0	0	0

Obtained from the Pittsburgh Pirates for Martin Burke in 1927.

LANGWAY, Rod

Born in Formosa, Taiwan, May 3rd, 1957.
Defenseman, left-hand shot.
6'3", 215 lb.
Last amateur team: New Hampshire University.

SEASON	TEAM	GP	G	A	PTS	MIP
1978-79	Montreal Canadiens	45	3	4	7	30
1979-80	Montreal Canadiens	77	7	29	36	81
	TOTALS	122	10	33	43	111

PLAYOFFS		GP	G	A	PTS	MIP
1978-79	Montreal Canadiens	8	0	0	0	16
1979-80	Montreal Canadiens	10	3	3	6	2
	TOTALS	18	3	3	6	18

Played with the team that won the Stanley Cup in 1978-79.

LAPERRIERE, Joseph Jacques Hugues (Lappy)

Born in Rouyn, Quebec, November 22nd, 1941.
Defenseman, left-hand shot.
6'2", 190 lb.
Last amateur team: the Montreal Canadiens jrs.

SEASON	TEAM	GP	G	A	PTS	MIP
1962-63	Montreal Canadiens	6	0	2	2	2
1963-64	Montreal Canadiens	65	2	28	30	102
1964-65	Montreal Canadiens	67	5	22	27	92
1965-66	Montreal Canadiens	57	6	25	31	85
1966-67	Montreal Canadiens	61	0	20	20	48
1967-68	Montreal Canadiens	72	4	21	25	84
1968-69	Montreal Canadiens	69	5	26	31	45
1969-70	Montreal Canadiens	73	6	31	37	98
1970-71	Montreal Canadiens	49	0	16	16	20
1971-72	Montreal Canadiens	73	3	25	28	50
1972-73	Montreal Canadiens	57	7	16	23	34
1973-74	Montreal Canadiens	42	2	10	12	14
	TOTALS	691	40	242	282	674

PLAYOFFS		GP	G	A	PTS	MIP
1962-63	Montreal Canadiens	5	0	1	1	4
1963-64	Montreal Canadiens	7	1	1	2	8
1964-65	Montreal Canadiens	6	1	1	2	16
1966-67	Montreal Canadiens	9	0	1	1	9
1967-68	Montreal Canadiens	13	1	3	4	20
1968-69	Montreal Canadiens	14	1	3	4	28
1970-71	Montreal Canadiens	20	4	9	13	12
1971-72	Montreal Canadiens	4	0	0	0	2
1972-73	Montreal Canadiens	10	1	3	4	2
	TOTALS	88	9	22	31	101

ALL-STAR GAMES		GP	G	A	PTS
1964	NHL All-Stars	1	0	1	1
1965	Montreal Canadiens	1	1	0	1
1967	Montreal Canadiens	1	0	0	0
1968	NHL All-Stars	1	0	0	0
1970	NHL All-Stars	1	1	0	1
	TOTALS	5	2	1	3

Played with the team that won the Prince of Wales Trophy in 1963-64, 1965-66, 1967-68, 1968-69, 1972-73.
Played with the team that won the Stanley Cup in 1964-65, 1967-68, 1968-69, 1970-71, 1972-73.
Won the Calder Trophy in 1963-64.
Won the James Norris Trophy in 1965-66.
Member of the first All-Star team in 1964-65, 1965-66.
Member of the second All-Star team in 1963-64, 1969-70.
Appointed assistant captain of the Canadiens in 1972.

LAPOINTE, Guy Gerard

Born in Montreal, Quebec, March 18th, 1948.
Defenseman, left-hand shot.
6', 204 lb.
Last amateur team: the Montreal Canadiens jrs.

SEASON	TEAM	GP	G	A	PTS	MIP
1968-69	Montreal Canadiens	1	0	0	0	2
1969-70	Montreal Canadiens	5	0	0	0	4
1970-71	Montreal Canadiens	78	15	29	44	107
1971-72	Montreal Canadiens	69	11	38	49	58
1972-73	Montreal Canadiens	76	19	35	54	117
1973-74	Montreal Canadiens	71	13	40	53	63
1974-75	Montreal Canadiens	80	28	47	75	88
1975-76	Montreal Canadiens	77	21	47	68	78
1976-77	Montreal Canadiens	77	25	51	76	53
1977-78	Montreal Canadiens	49	13	29	42	19
1978-79	Montreal Canadiens	69	13	42	55	48
1979-80	Montreal Canadiens	45	6	20	26	29
	TOTALS	697	164	378	542	666

PLAYOFFS		GP	G	A	PTS	MIP
1970-71	Montreal Canadiens	20	4	5	9	34
1971-72	Montreal Canadiens	6	0	1	1	0
1972-73	Montreal Canadiens	17	6	7	13	20
1973-74	Montreal Canadiens	6	0	2	2	4
1974-75	Montreal Canadiens	11	6	4	10	4
1975-76	Montreal Canadiens	13	3	3	6	12
1976-77	Montreal Canadiens	12	3	9	12	4
1977-78	Montreal Canadiens	14	1	6	7	16
1978-79	Montreal Canadiens	10	2	6	8	10
1979-80	Montreal Canadiens	2	0	0	0	0
	TOTALS	111	25	43	68	104

ALL-STAR GAMES		GP	G	A	PTS
1973	All-Stars (Div. East)	1	0	0	0
1975	All-Stars (Div. East)	1	0	0	0
1976	All-Stars (Div. East)	1	0	1	1
1977	All-Stars (Div. East)	1	0	0	0
	TOTALS	4	0	1	1

Played with the team that won the Prince of Wales Trophy in 1968-69, 1972-73, 1975-76, 1976-77, 1977-78.
Played with the team that won the Stanley Cup in 1970-71, 1972-73, 1975-76, 1976-77, 1977-78, 1978-79.
Member of the first All-Star team in 1972-73.
Member of the second All-Star team in 1974-75, 1975-76, 1976-77.
Appointed assistant captain of the Canadiens in 1974.

LAROCHELLE, Wildor

Born in Sorel, Quebec, September 23rd, 1906.
Right-winger, right-hand shot.
5'8", 158 lb.
Last amateur team: Sorel jrs.

SEASON	TEAM	GP	G	A	PTS	MIP
1925-26	Montreal Canadiens	33	2	1	3	10
1926-27	Montreal Canadiens	41	0	1	1	6
1927-28	Montreal Canadiens	40	3	1	4	30
1928-29	Montreal Canadiens	2	0	0	0	0
1929-30	Montreal Canadiens	44	14	11	25	28
1930-31	Montreal Canadiens	40	8	5	13	35
1931-32	Montreal Canadiens	48	18	8	26	16
1932-33	Montreal Canadiens	47	11	4	15	27
1933-34	Montreal Canadiens	48	16	11	27	27
1934-35	Montreal Canadiens	48	9	19	28	12
*1935-36	Montreal Canadiens/ Chicago Black Hawks	40	2	3	5	14
	TOTALS	431	83	64	147	205

PLAYOFFS		GP	G	A	PTS	MIP
1926-27	Montreal Canadiens	4	0	0	0	0
1927-28	Montreal Canadiens	2	0	0	0	0
1929-30	Montreal Canadiens	6	1	0	1	12
1930-31	Montreal Canadiens	10	1	2	3	8
1931-32	Montreal Canadiens	4	2	1	3	4
1932-33	Montreal Canadiens	2	1	0	1	0
1933-34	Montreal Canadiens	2	1	1	2	0
1934-35	Montreal Canadiens	2	0	0	0	0
	TOTALS	32	6	4	10	24

Played with the team that won the Stanley Cup in 1929-30, 1930-31.
Traded to the Chicago Black Hawks for Rosario Couture in 1935-36.
Died March 21, 1964.

LAROCQUE, Michel Raymond (Bunny)

Born in Hull, Quebec, April 6th, 1952.
Goaltender, left-hand shot.
5'10", 185 lb.
Last amateur team: the Ottawa 67 jrs.

SEASON	TEAM	GP	GA	SO	AVE
1973-74	Montreal Canadiens	27	69	0	2.89
1974-75	Montreal Canadiens	25	74	3	3.00
1975-76	Montreal Canadiens	22	50	2	2.46
1976-77	Montreal Canadiens	26	53	4	2.09
1977-78	Montreal Canadiens	30	77	1	2.67
1978-79	Montreal Canadiens	34	94	3	2.84
1979-80	Montreal Canadiens	39	125	3	3.32
	TOTALS	203	542	16	2.67

PLAYOFFS		GP	GA	SO	AVE
1973-74	Montreal Canadiens	6	18	0	2.97
1976-77	Montreal Canadiens	—	—	—	—
1978-79	Montreal Canadiens	1	0	0	0.00
1979-80	Montreal Canadiens	5	11	1	2.20
	TOTALS	12	29	1	2.42

OFFENSIVE RECORD		GP	G	A	PTS	MIP
1973-74	Montreal Canadiens	27	0	2	2	0
1974-75	Montreal Canadiens	25	0	1	1	2
1975-76	Montreal Canadiens	22	0	2	2	4
1976-77	Montreal Canadiens	26	0	0	0	0
1977-78	Montreal Canadiens	30	0	4	4	0
1978-79	Montreal Canadiens	34	0	3	3	2
	TOTALS	164	0	12	12	8

PLAYOFFS		GP	G	A	PTS	MIP
1973-74	Montreal Canadiens	6	0	2	2	0
1978-79	Montreal Canadiens	1	0	0	0	0
1979-80	Montreal Canadiens	5	0	0	0	0
	TOTALS	12	0	2	2	0

Second Amateur Draft Choice of the Canadiens in 1972.
Played with the team that won the Prince of Wales Trophy in 1975-76, 1976-77, 1977-78.
Played with the team that won the Stanley Cup in 1975-76, 1976-77, 1977-78, 1978-79.
Won the Vezina Trophy in 1976-77, 1977-78, 1978-79 (with Ken Dryden).

LAROSE, Claude David

Born in Hearst, Ontario, March 2nd, 1942.
Right-winger, right-hand shot.
6', 170 lb.
Last amateur team: the Peterborough Petes jrs.

SEASON	TEAM	GP	G	A	PTS	MIP
1962-63	Montreal Canadiens	4	0	0	0	0
1963-64	Montreal Canadiens	21	1	1	2	43
1964-65	Montreal Canadiens	68	21	16	37	82
1965-66	Montreal Canadiens	64	15	18	33	67
1966-67	Montreal Canadiens	69	19	16	35	82
1967-68	Montreal Canadiens	42	2	9	11	28
1970-71	Montreal Canadiens	64	10	13	23	90
1971-72	Montreal Canadiens	77	20	18	38	64
1972-73	Montreal Canadiens	73	11	23	34	30
1973-74	Montreal Canadiens	39	17	7	24	30
1974-75	Montreal Canadiens	8	1	2	3	6
	TOTALS	529	117	123	240	522

PLAYOFFS		GP	G	A	PTS	MIP
1963-64	Montreal Canadiens	2	1	0	1	0
1964-65	Montreal Canadiens	13	0	1	1	14
1965-66	Montreal Canadiens	6	0	1	1	31
1966-67	Montreal Canadiens	10	1	5	6	15
1967-68	Montreal Canadiens	12	3	2	5	8
1970-71	Montreal Canadiens	11	1	0	1	10
1971-72	Montreal Canadiens	6	2	1	3	23
1972-73	Montreal Canadiens	17	3	4	7	6
1973-74	Montreal Canadiens	5	0	2	2	11
	TOTALS	82	11	16	27	118

ALL-STAR GAMES		GP	G	A	PTS
1965	Montreal Canadiens	1	0	1	1
1967	Montreal Canadiens	1	0	1	1
	TOTALS	2	0	2	2

Played with the team that won the Prince of Wales Trophy in 1963-64, 1965-66, 1967-68, 1972-73.
Played with the team that won the Stanley Cup in 1964-65, 1965-66, 1967-68, 1970-71, 1972-73.
Traded to the Minnesota North Stars with Dan Grant for the first Amateur Draft choice of 1972 (Dave Gardner), Marshall Johnson and a certain amount of money, June 10, 1968.
Obtained from the Minnesota North Stars for Robert Rousseau, June 10, 1970.
Sold to the St. Louis Blues, December 5, 1974.
Appointed assistant captain for the 1974-75 season.

LAROUCHE, Pierre

Born in Tachereau, Quebec, November 16th, 1955.
Center, right-hand shot.
5'11", 175 lb.
Last amateur team: Sorel jrs.

SEASON	TEAM	GP	G	A	PTS	MIP
1977-78	Montreal Canadiens	44	17	32	49	11
1978-79	Montreal Canadiens	36	9	13	22	4
1979-80	Montreal Canadiens	73	50	41	91	16
	TOTALS	153	76	86	162	31

PLAYOFFS		GP	G	A	PTS	MIP
1977-78	Montreal Canadiens	5	2	1	3	4
1978-79	Montreal Canadiens	6	1	3	4	0
1979-80	Montreal Canadiens	9	1	7	8	2
	TOTALS	20	4	11	15	6

Obtained from the Pittsburgh Penguins with a player to be named later (Peter Marsh, December 15, 1977) for Peter Mahovlich and Peter Lee, November 29, 1977.
Played with the team that won the Prince of Wales Trophy in 1977-78.
Played with the team that won the Stanley Cup in 1977-78, 1978-79.

LAVIOLETTE, Jean-Baptiste (Jack)

Born in Belleville, Ontario, July 27th, 1879.
Defenseman, left-winger.

SEASON	TEAM	GP	G	A	PTS	MIP
1909-10	Montreal Canadiens	1	1	—	1	—
1910-11	Montreal Canadiens	16	0	—	0	—
1911-12	Montreal Canadiens	18	7	—	7	—
1912-13	Montreal Canadiens	20	8	0	8	—
1913-14	Montreal Canadiens	20	7	—	7	—
1914-15	Montreal Canadiens	18	6	—	6	—
1915-16	Montreal Canadiens	18	7	—	7	—
1916-17	Montreal Canadiens	18	7	—	7	—
1917-18	Montreal Canadiens	18	2	—	2	—
	TOTALS	147	45	—	45	—

PLAYOFFS		GP	G	A	PTS	MIP
1909-10	Montreal Canadiens	11	3	—	3	—
1913-14	Montreal Canadiens	2	0	—	0	—
1915-16	Montreal Canadiens	4	0	—	0	—
	TOTALS	17	3	—	3	—

Played with the team that won the Stanley Cup in 1915-16.
Member of the Hockey Hall of Fame in August, 1962.

LAYCOE, Harold Richardson (Hal)

Born in Sutherland, Saskatchewan, June 23rd, 1922.
Defenseman, left-hand shot.
6'1", 175 lb.
Last amateur team: the New York Rovers srs.

SEASON	TEAM	GP	G	A	PTS	MIP
1947-48	Montreal Canadiens	14	1	2	3	4
1948-49	Montreal Canadiens	51	3	5	8	31
1949-50	Montreal Canadiens	30	0	2	2	21
1950-51	Montreal Canadiens/ Boston Bruins	44	1	3	4	29
	TOTALS	139	5	12	17	85

PLAYOFFS		GP	G	A	PTS	MIP
1948-49	Montreal Canadiens	7	0	1	1	13
1949-50	Montreal Canadiens	2	0	0	0	0
	TOTALS	9	0	1	1	13

Obtained from the New York Rangers with Joe Bell and George Robertson for "Buddy" O'Connor and Frank Eddolls in 1947.
Traded to the Boston Bruins for Ross Lowe in 1949-50.

LECLAIR, Jean-Louis (Jackie)

Born in Quebec, Quebec, May 30th, 1929.
Center, left-hand shot.
5'11", 175 lb.
Last amateur team: the Ottawa Senators srs.

SEASON	TEAM	GP	G	A	PTS	MIP
1954-55	Montreal Canadiens	59	11	22	33	12
1955-56	Montreal Canadiens	54	6	8	14	30
1956-57	Montreal Canadiens	47	3	10	13	14
	TOTALS	160	20	40	60	56

PLAYOFFS		GP	G	A	PTS	MIP
1954-55	Montreal Canadiens	12	5	0	5	2
1955-56	Montreal Canadiens	8	1	1	2	4
	TOTALS	20	6	1	7	6

ALL-STAR GAMES		GP	G	A	PTS
1956	Montreal Canadiens	1	0	0	0
	TOTALS	1	0	0	0

Played with the team that won the Prince of Wales Trophy in 1955-56.
Played with the team that won the Stanley Cup in 1955-56.

LEDUC, Albert (Battleship)

Born in Valleyfield, Quebec, November 22nd, 1902.
Defenseman, right-hand shot.
5'9", 180 lb.

SEASON	TEAM	GP	G	A	PTS	MIP
1925-26	Montreal Canadiens	32	10	3	13	62
1926-27	Montreal Canadiens	43	5	2	7	62
1927-28	Montreal Canadiens	42	8	5	13	73
1928-29	Montreal Canadiens	43	9	2	11	79
1929-30	Montreal Canadiens	44	6	8	14	90
1930-31	Montreal Canadiens	44	8	6	14	82
1931-32	Montreal Canadiens	41	5	3	8	60
1932-33	Montreal Canadiens	48	5	3	8	62
1934-35	Montreal Canadiens	4	0	0	0	4
	TOTALS	341	56	32	88	574

PLAYOFFS		GP	G	A	PTS	MIP
1926-27	Montreal Canadiens	4	0	0	0	2
1927-28	Montreal Canadiens	2	1	0	1	5
1928-29	Montreal Canadiens	3	1	0	1	4
1929-30	Montreal Canadiens	6	1	3	4	8
1930-31	Montreal Canadiens	7	0	2	2	9
1931-32	Montreal Canadiens	4	1	1	2	2
1932-33	Montreal Canadiens	2	1	0	1	2
	TOTALS	28	5	6	11	32

Played with the team that won the Stanley Cup in 1929-30, 1930-31.
Traded to the Ottawa Senators for Martin Burke (1933-34).

LEDUC, R. Edgar

SEASON	TEAM	GP	G	A	PTS	MIP
	Montreal Canadiens	3	0	—	0	—
	TOTALS	3	0	—	0	—

PLAYOFFS		GP	G	A	PTS	MIP
	Montreal Canadiens	3	3	—	3	—
	TOTALS	3	3	—	3	—

LEE, R.

Incomplete record: Existence confirmed by, Official Report of Match, Season 1942-43, NHL Office.

LEFLEY, Charles Thomas (Chuck)

Born in Winnipeg, Manitoba, January 20th, 1950.
Left-winger, left-hand shot.
6'1", 185 lb.
Last amateur team: Canada's National Team.

SEASON	TEAM	GP	G	A	PTS	MIP
1971-72	Montreal Canadiens	16	0	2	2	0
1972-73	Montreal Canadiens	65	21	26	46	22
1973-74	Montreal Canadiens	74	23	31	54	34
1974-75	Montreal Canadiens	19	1	2	3	4
	TOTALS	174	45	60	105	60

PLAYOFFS		GP	G	A	PTS	MIP
1970-71	Montreal Canadiens	1	0	0	0	0
1972-73	Montreal Canadiens	17	3	5	8	6
1973-74	Montreal Canadiens	6	0	1	1	0
	TOTALS	24	3	6	9	6

Played with the team that won the Prince of Wales Trophy in 1972-73.
Played with the team that won the Stanley Cup in 1970-71, 1972-73.
Traded to the St. Louis Blues for Don Awrey November 28, 1974.
Brother of Bryan Lefley.

LEGER, Roger

Born in Annonciation, Quebec, March 26th, 1919.
Defenseman, right-hand shot.
5'11", 210 lb.
Last amateur team: the Valleyfield Braves.

SEASON	TEAM	GP	G	A	PTS	MIP
1946-47	Montreal Canadiens	49	4	18	22	12
1947-48	Montreal Canadiens	48	4	14	18	26
1948-59	Montreal Canadiens	28	6	7	13	10
1949-50	Montreal Canadiens	55	3	12	15	21
	TOTALS	180	17	51	68	69

PLAYOFFS		GP	G	A	PTS	MIP
1946-47	Montreal Canadiens	11	0	6	6	10
1948-49	Montreal Canadiens	5	0	1	1	2
1949-50	Montreal Canadiens	4	0	0	0	2
	TOTALS	20	0	7	7	14

Played with the team that won the Prince of Wales Trophy in 1946-47.

LEMAIRE, Jacques Gerard

Born in Ville Lasalle, Quebec, September 7th, 1945.
Center, left-winger, left-hand shot.
5'10", 180 lb.
Last amateur team: the Montreal Canadiens jrs.

SEASON	TEAM	GP	G	A	PTS	MIP
1967-68	Montreal Canadiens	69	22	20	42	16
1968-69	Montreal Canadiens	75	29	34	63	29
1969-70	Montreal Canadiens	69	32	28	60	16
1970-71	Montreal Canadiens	78	28	28	56	18
1971-72	Montreal Canadiens	77	32	49	81	26
1972-73	Montreal Canadiens	77	44	51	95	16
1973-74	Montreal Canadiens	66	29	38	67	10
1974-75	Montreal Canadiens	80	36	56	92	20
1975-76	Montreal Canadiens	61	20	32	52	20
1976-77	Montreal Canadiens	75	34	41	75	22
1977-78	Montreal Canadiens	76	36	61	97	14
1978-79	Montreal Canadiens	50	24	31	55	10
	TOTALS	853	366	469	835	217

PLAYOFFS		GP	G	A	PTS	MIP
1967-68	Montreal Canadiens	13	7	6	13	6
1968-69	Montreal Canadiens	14	4	2	6	6
1970-71	Montreal Canadiens	20	9	10	19	17
1971-72	Montreal Canadiens	6	2	1	3	2
1972-73	Montreal Canadiens	17	7	13	20	2
1973-74	Montreal Canadiens	6	0	4	4	2
1974-75	Montreal Canadiens	11	5	7	12	4
1975-76	Montreal Canadiens	13	3	3	6	2
1976-77	Montreal Canadiens	14	7	12	19	6
1977-78	Montreal Canadiens	15	6	8	14	10
1978-79	Montreal Canadiens	16	11	12	23	6
	TOTALS	145	61	78	139	63

ALL-STAR GAMES		GP	G	A	PTS
1970	All-Stars (Div. East)	1	0	1	1
1973	All-Stars (Div. East)	1	1	0	1
	TOTALS	2	1	1	2

Played with the team that won the Prince of Wales Trophy in 1967-68, 1968-69, 1972-73, 1975-76, 1976-77, 1977-78.
Played with the team that won the Stanley Cup in 1967-68, 1968-69, 1970-71, 1972-73, 1975-76, 1976-77, 1977-78, 1978-79.
Appointed assistant captain of the Canadiens in 1974.
Took a job as a coach in Switzerland in June, 1979.

LEPINE, Alfred (Pit)

Born in Ste-Anne-de-Bellevue, Quebec, July 30th, 1901.
Center, left-hand shot.
6', 168 lb.
Last amateur team: the Pittsburgh Yellow Jackets.

SEASON	TEAM	GP	G	A	PTS	MIP
1925-26	Montreal Canadiens	27	9	1	10	18
1926-27	Montreal Canadiens	44	16	1	17	20
1927-28	Montreal Canadiens	20	4	1	5	6
1928-29	Montreal Canadiens	44	6	1	7	48
1929-30	Montreal Canadiens	44	24	9	33	47

SEASON	TEAM	GP	G	A	PTS	MIP
1930-31	Montreal Canadiens	44	17	7	24	63
1931-32	Montreal Canadiens	48	19	11	30	42
1932-33	Montreal Canadiens	46	8	8	16	45
1933-34	Montreal Canadiens	48	10	8	18	44
1934-35	Montreal Canadiens	48	12	19	31	16
1935-36	Montreal Canadiens	32	6	10	16	4
1936-37	Montreal Canadiens	34	7	8	15	15
1937-38	Montreal Canadiens	47	5	14	19	24
	TOTALS	526	143	98	241	392

PLAYOFFS		GP	G	A	PTS	MIP
1926-27	Montreal Canadiens	4	0	0	0	2
1927-28	Montreal Canadiens	1	0	0	0	0
1928-29	Montreal Canadiens	3	0	0	0	2
1929-30	Montreal Canadiens	6	2	2	4	6
1930-31	Montreal Canadiens	10	4	2	6	6
1931-32	Montreal Canadiens	3	1	0	1	4
1932-33	Montreal Canadiens	2	0	0	0	0
1933-34	Montreal Canadiens	2	0	0	0	0
1934-35	Montreal Canadiens	2	0	0	0	2
1936-37	Montreal Canadiens	5	0	1	1	0
1937-38	Montreal Canadiens	3	0	0	0	0
	TOTALS	41	7	5	12	22

Played with the team that won the Stanley Cup in 1929-30, 1930-31.
Succeeded "Babe" Seibert as coach of the Canadiens in 1939.
Died August 2, 1955.

LEPINE, Hector

SEASON	TEAM	GP	G	A	PTS	MIP
1925-26	Montreal Canadiens	33	5	2	7	2
	TOTALS	33	5	2	7	2

LEROUX, G.

SEASON	TEAM	GP	G	A	PTS	MIP
1935-36	Montreal Canadiens	2	0	0	0	0
	TOTALS	2	0	0	0	0

LESIEUR, Arthur (Art)

Born in Fall River, Massachusetts, September 13th, 1907.
Defenseman, right-hand shot.
5'11", 190 lb.
Last amateur team: St. Cesaire jrs.

SEASON	TEAM	GP	G	A	PTS	MIP
*1928-29	Chicago Black Hawks/ Montreal Canadiens	17	0	0	0	0
1930-31	Montreal Canadiens	21	2	0	2	14
1931-32	Montreal Canadiens	24	1	2	3	12
1935-36	Montreal Canadiens	38	1	0	1	24
	TOTALS	100	4	2	6	50

PLAYOFFS		GP	G	A	PTS	MIP
1930-31	Montreal Canadiens	10	0	0	0	4
1931-32	Montreal Canadiens	4	0	0	0	0
	TOTALS	14	0	0	0	4

Played with the team that won the Stanley Cup in 1930-31.
Obtained from the Chicago Black Hawks for Herb Gardiner in 1928-29.

LEWIS, Douglas (Doug)

Born in Winnipeg, Manitoba, March 3rd, 1921.
Left-winger, left-hand shot.
5'8", 155 lb.
Last amateur team: the Edmonton A.C. jrs.

SEASON	TEAM	GP	G	A	PTS	MIP
1946-47	Montreal Canadiens	3	0	0	0	0
	TOTALS	3	0	0	0	0

Played with the team that won the Prince of Wales Trophy in 1946-47.

LITZENBERGER, Edward C. J. (Eddie, Litz)

Born in Neudorf, Saskatchewan, July 15th, 1932.
Right-winger, right-hand shot.
6'3", 194 lb.
Last amateur team: the Montreal Royals srs.

SEASON	TEAM	GP	G	A	PTS	MIP
1952-53	Montreal Canadiens	2	1	0	1	2
1953-54	Montreal Canadiens	3	0	0	0	0
1954-55	Montreal Canadiens	29	7	4	11	12
	TOTALS	34	8	4	12	14

Sold to Chicago, December, 1954.

LOCAS, Jacques

Born in Montreal, Quebec, February 12th, 1926.
Right-winger, right-hand shot.
5'11", 175 lb.
Last amateur team: the Sherbrooke Saints.

SEASON	TEAM	GP	G	A	PTS	MIP
1947-48	Montreal Canadiens	56	7	8	15	66
1948-49	Montreal Canadiens	3	0	0	0	0
	TOTALS	59	7	8	15	66

LONG, Stanley Gordon (Stan)

Born in Owen Sound, Ontario, November 6th, 1929.
Defenseman, left-hand shot.
5'11", 190 lb.
Last amateur team: the Montreal Royals srs.

PLAYOFFS		GP	G	A	PTS	MIP
1951-52	Montreal Canadiens	3	0	0	0	0
	TOTALS	3	0	0	0	0

LORRAIN, Rodrigue (Rod)

Born in Buckingham, Quebec, July, 1915.
Right-winger, right-hand shot.
5'5", 156 lb.
Last amateur team: the Ottawa Senators srs.

SEASON	TEAM	GP	G	A	PTS	MIP
1935-36	Montreal Canadiens	1	0	0	0	2
1936-37	Montreal Canadiens	47	3	6	9	8
1937-38	Montreal Canadiens	48	13	19	32	14
1938-39	Montreal Canadiens	38	10	9	19	0
1939-40	Montreal Canadiens	41	1	5	6	6
1941-42	Montreal Canadiens	4	1	0	1	0
	TOTALS	179	28	39	67	30

PLAYOFFS		GP	G	A	PTS	MIP
1936-37	Montreal Canadiens	5	0	0	0	0
1937-38	Montreal Canadiens	3	0	0	0	0
1938-39	Montreal Canadiens	3	0	3	3	0
	TOTALS	11	0	3	3	0

Died October 22, 1980.

LOWE, Ross Robert

Born in Oshawa, Ontario, September 21st, 1928.
Defenseman, right-hand shot.
6'1", 180 lb.
Last amateur team: the Oshawa Generals jrs.

SEASON	TEAM	GP	G	A	PTS	MIP
1951-52	Montreal Canadiens	31	1	5	6	42
	TOTALS	31	1	5	6	42

PLAYOFFS		GP	G	A	PTS	MIP
1950-51	Montreal Canadiens	2	0	0	0	0
	TOTALS	2	0	0	0	0

Obtained from the Boston Bruins for Hal Laycoe in 1951.

LOWREY, Ed (Eddie)

Born in 1894.
Forward.

SEASON	TEAM	GP	G	A	PTS	MIP
*1914-15	Montreal Canadiens/ Ottawa Senators	5	2	—	2	—
	TOTALS	2	2	—	2	—

LUMLEY, David

Born in Toronto, Ontario, September 1st, 1954.
Center, right-winger, right-hand shot.
6', 185 lb.
Last amateur team: New Hampshire University.

SEASON	TEAM	GP	G	A	PTS	MIP
1978-79	Montreal Canadiens	3	0	0	0	0
	TOTALS	3	0	0	0	0

Traded to the Edmonton Oilers with Dan Newman for future considerations.

LUPIEN, Gilles

Born in Lachute, Quebec, April 20th, 1954.
Defenseman, left-hand shot.
6'6", 210 lb.
Last amateur team: Montreal jrs.

SEASON	TEAM	GP	G	A	PTS	MIP
1977-78	Montreal Canadiens	46	1	3	4	108
1978-79	Montreal Canadiens	72	1	9	10	124
1979-80	Montreal Canadiens	56	1	7	8	109
	TOTALS	174	3	19	22	341

PLAYOFFS		GP	G	A	PTS	MIP
1977-78	Montreal Canadiens	8	0	0	0	17
1978-79	Montreal Canadiens	13	0	0	0	2
1979-80	Montreal Canadiens	4	0	0	0	2
	TOTALS	25	0	0	0	21

Played with the team that won the Prince of Wales Trophy in 1977-78.
Played with the team that won the Stanley Cup in 1977-78, 1978-79.

LYNN, Victor Ivan (Vic)

Born in Saskatoon, Saskatchewan, January 26th, 1925.
Defenseman, left-hand shot.
5'9", 185 lb.
Last amateur team: the New York Rovers.

SEASON	TEAM	GP	G	A	PTS	MIP
1945-46	Montreal Canadiens	2	0	0	0	0
	TOTALS	2	0	0	0	0

Played with the team that won the Prince of Wales Trophy in 1945-46.

McAVOY, George

Born in Edmonton, Alberta, June 21st, 1931.
Defenseman, left-hand shot.
5'11", 165 lb.
Last amateur team: the Penticton "V's" srs.

SEASON	TEAM	GP	G	A	PTS	MIP
1954-55	Montreal Canadiens	4	0	0	0	0
	TOTALS	4	0	0	0	0

McCAFFREY, Albert "Bert"

Born in Listowel, Ontario.
Defenseman.

SEASON	TEAM	GP	G	A	PTS	MIP
*1929-30	Montreal Canadiens/ Pittsburgh Pirates	43	4	7	11	38
1930-31	Montreal Canadiens	22	2	1	3	10
	TOTALS	65	6	8	14	48

PLAYOFFS		GP	G	A	PTS	MIP
1929-30	Montreal Canadiens	6	1	1	2	6
	TOTALS	6	1	1	2	6

Played with the team that won the Stanley Cup in 1929-30.

McCARTNEY, R. Walter Herbert

Born in Regina, Saskatchewan, April 26th, 1911.
Left-winger, left-hand shot.
5'10", 160 lb.

SEASON	TEAM	GP	G	A	PTS	MIP
1932-33	Montreal Canadiens	2	0	0	0	0
	TOTALS	2	0	0	0	0

McCORMACK, John Ronald (Goose)

Born in Edmonton, Alberta, August 2nd, 1925.
Center, left-hand shot.
6', 185 lb.
Last amateur team: the St. Michaels College jrs.

SEASON	TEAM	GP	G	A	PTS	MIP
1951-52	Montreal Canadiens	54	2	10	12	4
1952-53	Montreal Canadiens	59	1	9	10	9
1953-54	Montreal Canadiens	51	5	10	15	12
	TOTALS	164	8	29	37	25

PLAYOFFS		GP	G	A	PTS	MIP
1952-53	Montreal Canadiens	9	0	0	0	0
1953-54	Montreal Canadiens	7	0	1	1	0
	TOTALS	16	0	1	1	0

Played with the team that won the Stanley Cup in 1952-53.

McCREARY, Vernon Keith

Born in Sundridge, Ontario, June 19th, 1940.
Left-winger, left-hand shot.
5'10", 175 lb.
Last amateur team: the Hull-Ottawa Canadiens jrs.

SEASON	TEAM	GP	G	A	PTS	MIP
1964-65	Montreal Canadiens	9	0	3	3	4
	TOTALS	9	0	3	3	4

PLAYOFFS		GP	G	A	PTS	MIP
1961-62	Montreal Canadiens	1	0	0	0	0
	TOTALS	1	0	0	0	0

Drafted by the Pittsburgh Penguins during the 1967 Expansion, June 6, 1967.

McCREARY, William Edward (Bill)

Born in Sundridge, Ontario, December 2nd, 1934.
Left-winger, left-hand shot.
5'10", 172 lb.
Last amateur team: the Guelph Biltmores jrs.

SEASON	TEAM	GP	G	A	PTS	MIP
1962-63	Montreal Canadiens	14	2	3	5	0
	TOTALS	14	2	3	5	0

Traded to the St. Louis Blues for Claude Cardin and Phil Obendorf in June, 1967.

McCULLY, Bob

SEASON	TEAM	GP	G	A	PTS	MIP
1934-35	Montreal Canadiens	1	0	0	0	0
	TOTALS	1	0	0	0	0

McDONALD, Alvin Brian (Ab)

Born in Winnipeg, Manitoba, February 18th, 1936.
Left-winger, left-hand shot.
6'2", 194 lb.
Last amateur team: the St. Catharines Tee Pees jrs.

SEASON	TEAM	GP	G	A	PTS	MIP
1958-59	Montreal Canadiens	69	13	23	36	35
1959-60	Montreal Canadiens	68	9	13	22	26
	TOTALS	137	22	36	58	61

PLAYOFFS		GP	G	A	PTS	MIP
1957-58	Montreal Canadiens	2	0	0	0	2
1958-59	Montreal Canadiens	11	1	1	2	6
	TOTALS	13	1	1	2	8

ALL-STAR GAMES		GP	G	A	PTS
1958	Montreal Canadiens	1	1	0	1
1959	Montreal Canadiens	1	1	0	1
	TOTALS	2	2	0	2

Played with the team that won the Prince of Wales Trophy in 1958-59, 1959-60.
Played with the team that won the Stanley Cup in 1957-58, 1958-59.
Sold to the Chicago Black Hawks in June, 1960.

McDONALD, Jack

Left-winger, center, rover.

SEASON	TEAM	GP	G	A	PTS	MIP
*1917-18	Montreal Wanderers/ Montreal Canadiens	12	12	—	12	—
1918-19	Montreal Canadiens	18	8	4	12	9
1920-21	Montreal Canadiens/ Toronto St. Patricks	17	0	1	1	0
1921-22	Montreal Canadiens	2	0	0	0	0
	TOTALS	49	20	5	25	9

PLAYOFFS		GP	G	A	PTS	MIP
1917-18	Montreal Canadiens	2	1	0	1	—
1918-19	Montreal Canadiens	10	1	0	1	—
	TOTALS	12	2	0	2	—

Traded to the Quebec Bulldogs in 1919.
Died January 24, 1958.

McGIBBON, Irving John

SEASON	TEAM	GP	G	A	PTS	MIP
1942-43	Montreal Canadiens	1	0	0	0	2
	TOTALS	1	0	0	0	2

McGILL, John George (Jack)

Born in Ottawa, Ontario, November 3rd, 1910.
Left-hand shot.
5'10", 150 lb.
Last amateur team: McGill University.

SEASON	TEAM	GP	G	A	PTS	MIP
1934-35	Montreal Canadiens	44	9	1	10	34
1935-36	Montreal Canadiens	46	13	7	20	28
1936-37	Montreal Canadiens	44	5	2	7	9
	TOTALS	134	27	10	37	71

PLAYOFFS		GP	G	A	PTS	MIP
1934-35	Montreal Canadiens	2	2	0	2	0
1936-37	Montreal Canadiens	1	0	0	0	0
	TOTALS	3	2	0	2	0

MacKAY, Calum (Baldy)

Born in Toronto, Ontario, January 1st, 1927.
Left-winger, left-hand shot.
5'9", 185 lb.
Last amateur team: the Oshawa Generals jrs.

SEASON	TEAM	GP	G	A	PTS	MIP
1949-50	Montreal Canadiens	52	8	10	18	44
1950-51	Montreal Canadiens	70	18	10	28	69
1951-52	Montreal Canadiens	12	0	1	1	8
1953-54	Montreal Canadiens	47	10	13	23	54
1954-55	Montreal Canadiens	50	14	21	35	39
	TOTALS	231	50	55	105	214

PLAYOFFS		GP	G	A	PTS	MIP
1949-50	Montreal Canadiens	5	0	1	1	2
1950-51	Montreal Canadiens	11	1	0	1	0
1952-53	Montreal Canadiens	7	1	3	4	10
1953-54	Montreal Canadiens	3	0	1	1	0
1954-55	Montreal Canadiens	12	3	8	11	8
	TOTALS	38	5	13	18	20

ALL-STAR GAMES		GP	G	A	PTS
1949-50	Montreal Canadiens	1	0	0	0
	TOTALS	1	0	0	0

Obtained from the Detroit Red Wings for Joe Carveth.
Played with the team that won the Stanley Cup in 1952-53.

MacKAY, Murdo John

Born in Fort William, Ontario, August 8th, 1917.
Center, right-hand shot.
6', 175 lb.
Last amateur team: the New York Rovers srs.

SEASON	TEAM	GP	G	A	PTS	MIP
1945-46	Montreal Canadiens	5	0	1	1	0
1947-48	Montreal Canadiens	14	0	2	2	0
	TOTALS	19	0	3	3	0

PLAYOFFS		GP	G	A	PTS	MIP
1946-47	Montreal Canadiens	9	0	1	1	0
1948-49	Montreal Canadiens	6	1	1	2	0
	TOTALS	15	1	2	3	0

Played with the team that won the Prince of Wales Trophy in 1945-46.

MacKENZIE, William Kenneth (Bill)

Born in Winnipeg, Manitoba, December 12th, 1911.
Defenseman, right-hand shot.
5'11", 175 lb.
Last amateur team: the Montreal Royals srs.

SEASON	TEAM	GP	G	A	PTS	MIP
*1936-37	Montreal Maroons/ Montreal Canadiens	49	4	4	8	28
*1937-38	Montreal Canadiens/ Chicago Black Hawks	46	1	2	3	24
	TOTALS	95	5	6	11	52

PLAYOFFS		GP	G	A	PTS	MIP
1936-37	Montreal Canadiens	5	1	0	1	0
	TOTALS	5	1	0	1	0

Obtained from the Montreal Maroons for Paul Runge (1936-37).
Traded to the Chicago Black Hawks for Martin Burke (1937-38).

McKINNON, John Douglas

Born in Guysborough, Nova Scotia, July 15th, 1902.
Defenseman, right-winger, right-hand shot.
5'8", 170 lb.

SEASON	TEAM	GP	G	A	PTS	MIP
1925-26	Montreal Canadiens	2	0	0	0	0
	TOTALS	2	0	0	0	0

McMAHON, Michael Clarence (Mike)

Born in Brockville, Ontario, February 1st, 1917.
Defenseman, left-hand shot.
5'8", 215 lb.
Last amateur team: the Quebec Aces srs.

SEASON	TEAM	GP	G	A	PTS	MIP
1943-44	Montreal Canadiens	42	7	17	24	98
*1945-46	Montreal Canadiens/ Boston Bruins	15	0	1	1	4
	TOTALS	57	7	18	25	102

PLAYOFFS		GP	G	A	PTS	MIP
1942-43	Montreal Canadiens	5	0	0	0	14
1943-44	Montreal Canadiens	8	1	2	3	16
	TOTALS	13	1	2	3	30

Played with the team that won the Prince of Wales Trophy in 1943-44, 1945-46.
Played with the team that won the Stanley Cup in 1943-44.
Loaned to the Boston Bruins with an option to recall him in 1945-46.
Father of Mike McMahon, Jr.

McNABNEY, Sidney (Sid, Syd)

Born in Toronto, Ontario, January 15th, 1929.
Center, left-hand shot.
5'7", 158 lb.
Last amateur team: the Barrie Flyers jrs.

PLAYOFFS		GP	G	A	PTS	MIP
1950-51	Montreal Canadiens	5	0	1	1	2
	TOTALS	5	0	1	1	2

McNAMARA, Harold (Hal)

Defenseman.

SEASON	TEAM	GP	G	A	PTS	MIP
1916-17	Montreal Canadiens	1	0	—	0	—
	TOTALS	1	0	—	0	—

McNAMARA, Howard

Defenceman.
240 lb.

SEASON	TEAM	GP	G	A	PTS	MIP
1915-16	Montreal Canadiens	24	10	—	10	—
1919-20	Montreal Canadiens	11	1	0	1	2
	TOTALS	35	11	0	11	2

PLAYOFFS		GP	G	A	PTS	MIP
1915-16	Montreal Canadiens	5	0	—	0	—
	TOTALS	5	0	—	0	—

Played with the team that won the Stanley Cup in 1915-16.

MacNEIL, Allister Wences (Al)

Born in Sydney, Nova Scotia, September 27th, 1935.
Defenseman, left-hand shot.
5'10", 185 lb.
Last amateur team: the Toronto Marlboros jrs.

SEASON	TEAM	GP	G	A	PTS	MIP
	Montreal Canadiens	61	1	7	8	74
	TOTALS	61	1	7	8	74

PLAYOFFS		GP	G	A	PTS	MIP
	Montreal Canadiens	5	0	0	0	2
	TOTALS	5	0	0	0	2

Obtained from the Toronto Maple Leafs for Stan Smrke, in June, 1960.
Played with the team that won the Prince of Wales Trophy in 1961-62.
Traded to the Chicago Black Hawks for Wayne Hicks in May, 1962.
Obtained from the Chicago Black Hawks and drafted by the New York Rangers in June, 1966.
Succeeded Claude Ruel as coach of the Canadiens in 1970 (1970-71).

McNEIL, Gerard George (Gerry)

Born in Quebec, Quebec, April 17th, 1926.
Goaltender, left-hand shot.
5'7", 155 lb.
Last amateur team: the Montreal Royal srs.

SEASON	TEAM	GP	GA	SO	AVE
1947-48	Montreal Canadiens	2	7	0	3.50
1949-50	Montreal Canadiens	6	9	1	1.50
1950-51	Montreal Canadiens	70	184	6	2.63
1951-52	Montreal Canadiens	70	164	5	2.34
1952-53	Montreal Canadiens	66	140	10	2.12
1953-54	Montreal Canadiens	53	114	6	2.15
1956-57	Montreal Canadiens	9	32	0	3.55
	TOTALS	276	650	28	2.36

PLAYOFFS		GP	GA	SO	AVE
1949-50	Montreal Canadiens	2	5	0	2.50
1950-51	Montreal Canadiens	11	25	1	2.27
1951-52	Montreal Canadiens	11	23	1	2.09
1952-53	Montreal Canadiens	8	16	2	2.00
1953-54	Montreal Canadiens	3	3	1	1.00
	TOTALS	35	72	5	2.05

OFFENSIVE RECORD		GP	G	A	PTS	MIP
1947-48	Montreal Canadiens	2	0	0	0	0
1949-50	Montreal Canadiens	6	0	0	0	0
1950-51	Montreal Canadiens	70	0	0	0	0
1951-52	Montreal Canadiens	70	0	0	0	0
1952-53	Montreal Canadiens	66	0	0	0	0
1953-54	Montreal Canadiens	53	0	0	0	0
1956-57	Montreal Canadiens	9	0	0	0	2
	TOTALS	276	0	0	0	2

PLAYOFFS		GP	G	A	PTS	MIP
1949-50	Montreal Canadiens	2	0	0	0	0
1950-51	Montreal Canadiens	11	0	0	0	0
1951-52	Montreal Canadiens	11	0	0	0	0
1952-53	Montreal Canadiens	8	0	0	0	0
1953-54	Montreal Canadiens	3	0	0	0	0
	TOTALS	35	0	0	0	0

ALL-STAR GAMES		GP	GA	SO	AVE
1951	NHL All-Stars	1	1	0	0.67
1953	Montreal Canadiens	1	3	0	3.00
	TOTALS	3	5	0	0.83

Played with the team that won the Stanley Cup in 1952-53.
Member of the second All-Star team in 1952-53.

MacPHERSON, James Albert (Bud)

Born in Edmonton, Alberta, March 21st, 1927.
Defenseman, left-hand shot.
6'3", 205 lb.
Last amateur team: the Edmonton Flyers srs.

SEASON	TEAM	GP	G	A	PTS	MIP
1948-49	Montreal Canadiens	3	0	0	0	2
1950-51	Montreal Canadiens	62	0	16	16	40
1951-52	Montreal Canadiens	54	2	1	3	24
1952-53	Montreal Canadiens	59	2	3	5	67
1953-54	Montreal Canadiens	41	0	5	5	41
1954-55	Montreal Canadiens	30	1	8	9	55
1956-57	Montreal Canadiens	10	0	0	0	4
	TOTALS	259	5	33	38	233

		GP	G	A	PTS	MIP
1950-51	Montreal Canadiens	11	0	2	2	8
1951-52	Montreal Canadiens	11	0	0	0	0
1952-53	Montreal Canadiens	4	0	1	1	9
1953-54	Montreal Canadiens	3	0	0	0	4
	TOTALS	29	0	3	3	21

ALL-STAR GAMES		GP	G	A	PTS
1953	Montreal Canadiens	1	0	0	0
	TOTALS	1	0	0	0

Played with the team that won the Stanley Cup in 1952-53.

MACEY, Hubert (Hub)

Born in Big River, Saskatchewan, April 13th, 1921.
Center, left-hand shot, left-winger.
5'8", 178 lb.
Last amateur team: the New York Rovers.

SEASON	TEAM	GP	G	A	PTS	MIP
1946-47	Montreal Canadiens	12	0	1	1	0
	TOTALS	12	0	1	1	0

PLAYOFFS		GP	G	A	PTS	MIP
1946-47	Montreal Canadiens	7	0	0	0	0
	TOTALS	7	0	0	0	0

Played with the team that won the Prince of Wales Trophy in 1946-47.

MAHAFFEY, John

Born in Montreal, Quebec, July 18th, 1919.
Center, left-hand shot.
5'7", 165 lb.
Last amateur team: the Montreal Royals srs.

SEASON	TEAM	GP	G	A	PTS	MIP
1942-43	Montreal Canadiens	9	2	5	7	4
	TOTALS	9	2	5	7	4

PLAYOFFS		GP	G	A	PTS	MIP
1944-45	Montreal Canadiens	1	0	1	1	0
	TOTALS	1	0	1	1	0

Traded to the New York Rangers in 1943.

MAHOVLICH, Francis William (Frank, The Big M)

Born in Timmins, Ontario, January 10th, 1938.
Left-winger, left-hand shot.
6', 205 lb.
Last amateur team: the St. Michaels College jrs.

SEASON	TEAM	GP	G	A	PTS	MIP
1970-71	Montreal Canadiens	38	17	24	41	11
1971-72	Montreal Canadiens	76	43	53	96	36
1972-73	Montreal Canadiens	78	38	55	93	51
1973-74	Montreal Canadiens	71	31	49	80	47
	TOTALS	263	129	181	310	145

PLAYOFFS		GP	G	A	PTS	MIP
1970-71	Montreal Canadiens	20	14	13	27	18
1971-72	Montreal Canadiens	6	3	2	5	2
1972-73	Montreal Canadiens	17	9	14	23	6
1973-74	Montreal Canadiens	6	1	2	3	0
	TOTALS	49	27	31	58	26

ALL-STAR GAMES		GP	G	A	PTS
1970	NHL All-Stars (Div. East)	1	0	0	0
1971	NHL All-Stars (Div. East)	1	0	0	0
1972	NHL All-Stars (Div. East)	1	0	0	0
1973	NHL All-Stars (Div. East)	1	1	1	2
1974	NHL All-Stars (Div. East)	1	1	0	1
	TOTALS	5	2	1	3

Obtained from the Detroit Red Wings for Mickey Redmond, Bill Collins and Guy Charron, January 13, 1971.
Played with the team that won the Prince of Wales Trophy in 1972-73.
Played with the team that won the Stanley Cup in 1970-71, 1972-73.
Signed up with the Toronto Toros in June, 1974.
Member of the First All-Star team in 1972-73.
Appointed assistant captain of the Canadiens in 1971.
Brother of Peter Mahovlich.

MAHOVLICH, Peter Joseph (Pete)

Born in Timmins, Ontario, October 10th, 1946.
Center, left-winger, left-hand shot.
6'5", 215 lb.
Last amateur team: the Hamilton Red Wings jrs.

SEASON	TEAM	GP	G	A	PTS	MIP
1969-70	Montreal Canadiens	36	9	8	17	51
1970-71	Montreal Canadiens	78	35	26	61	181
1971-72	Montreal Canadiens	75	35	32	67	103

SEASON	TEAM	GP	G	A	PTS	MIP
1972-73	Montreal Canadiens	61	21	38	59	49
1973-74	Montreal Canadiens	78	36	37	73	122
1974-75	Montreal Canadiens	80	35	82	117	64
1975-76	Montreal Canadiens	80	34	71	105	76
1976-77	Montreal Canadiens	76	15	47	62	45
1977-78	Montreal Canadiens	17	3	5	8	4
	TOTALS	581	223	346	569	695

PLAYOFFS		GP	G	A	PTS	MIP
1970-71	Montreal Canadiens	20	10	6	16	43
1971-72	Montreal Canadiens	6	0	2	2	12
1972-73	Montreal Canadiens	17	4	9	13	22
1973-74	Montreal Canadiens	6	2	1	3	4
1974-75	Montreal Canadiens	11	6	10	16	10
1975-76	Montreal Canadiens	13	4	8	12	24
1976-77	Montreal Canadiens	13	4	5	9	19
	TOTALS	86	30	41	71	134

ALL-STAR GAMES		GP	GA	SO	AVE
1971	NHL All-Stars (Div. East)	1	0	0	0
1976	NHL All-Stars (Prince of Wales)	1	1	3	4
	TOTALS	2	1	3	4

Obtained from the Detroit Red Wings with Bart Crashley for Garry Monahan and Doug Piper, June 6, 1969.
Played with the team that won the Prince of Wales Trophy in 1972-73, 1975-76, 1976-77.
Played with the team that won the Stanley Cup in 1970-71, 1972-73, 1975-76, 1976-77.
Appointed assistant captain of the Canadiens in 1973.
Traded to the Penguins with Peter Lee for Pierre Larouche and the rights to Peter Marsh of Cincinnati of the WHA.
Brother of Frank Mahovlich.

MAILLEY, Frank

SEASON	TEAM	GP	G	A	PTS	MIP
1942-43	Montreal Canadiens	1	0	0	0	0
	TOTALS	1	0	0	0	0

MAJEAU, Fernand (Fern)

Born in Verdun, Quebec, May 3rd, 1916.
Center, left-winger, left-hand shot.
5′9″, 155 lb.
Last amateur team: Verdun.

SEASON	TEAM	GP	G	A	PTS	MIP
1943-44	Montreal Canadiens	44	20	18	38	39
1944-45	Montreal Canadiens	12	2	6	8	4
	TOTALS	56	22	24	46	43

PLAYOFFS		GP	G	A	PTS	MIP
1943-44	Montreal Canadiens	1	0	0	0	0
	TOTALS	1	0	0	0	0

Played with the team that won the Prince of Wales Trophy in 1943-44, 1944-45.
Played with the team that won the Stanley Cup in 1943-44.
Died June 21, 1966.

MAJOR ?

SEASON	TEAM	GP	G	A	PTS	MIP
1916-17	Montreal Canadiens	2	0	—	0	—
	TOTALS	2	0	—	0	—

MALONE, Clifford (Cliff)

Born in Quebec, Quebec, September 4th, 1925.
Right-winger, right-hand shot.
5′10″, 155 lb.
Last amateur team: the Montreal Royals srs.

SEASON	TEAM	GP	G	A	PTS	MIP
1951-52	Montreal Canadiens	3	0	0	0	0
	TOTALS	3	0	0	0	0

MALONE, Maurice Joseph (Joe)

Born in Sillery, Quebec, February 28th, 1890.
Center, left-winger.
Last amateur team: Quebec srs.

SEASON	TEAM	GP	G	A	PTS	MIP
1917-18	Montreal Canadiens	20	44	—	44	—
1918-19	Montreal Canadiens	8	7	1	8	3
1922-23	Montreal Canadiens	9	1	0	1	2
1923-24	Montreal Canadiens	9	0	0	0	0
	TOTALS	46	52	1	53	5

PLAYOFFS		GP	G	A	PTS	MIP
1917-18	Montreal Canadiens	2	1	—	1	—
1918-19	Montreal Canadiens	5	6	1	7	—
1922-23	Montreal Canadiens	2	0	0	0	0
	TOTALS	9	7	1	8	0

Drafted from the Quebec Bulldogs in 1917.
Returned to the Quebec Bulldogs in 1919.
Obtained from the Hamilton Tigers for Albert Corbeau and Edmond Bouchard in 1922.
Member of the Hockey Hall of Fame in June, 1950.
Died May 15, 1969.

MALONE, Sarsfield

SEASON	TEAM	GP	G	A	PTS	MIP
1913-14	Montreal Canadiens	1	0	—	0	—
1916-17	Montreal Canadiens	8	1	—	1	—
	TOTALS	9	1	—	1	—

PLAYOFFS		GP	G	A	PTS	MIP
1916-17	Montreal Canadiens	1	0	—	0	—
	TOTALS	1	0	—	0	—

MALTAIS, ?

SEASON	TEAM	GP	G	A	PTS	MIP
1916-17	Montreal Canadiens	1	0	—	0	—
	TOTALS	1	0	—	0	—

MANASTERSKY, Timothy (Tom, Tony)

Born in Montreal, Quebec, March 7th, 1929.
Defenseman, right-hand shot.
5′9″, 185 lb.
Last amateur team: the Montreal Royal srs.

SEASON	TEAM	GP	G	A	PTS	MIP
1950-51	Montreal Canadiens	6	0	0	0	11
	TOTALS	6	0	0	0	11

MANCUSO, Felix (Gus)

Born in Niagara Falls, Ontario, April 11th, 1914.
Right-winger.
5′7″, 160 lb.

SEASON	TEAM	GP	G	A	PTS	MIP
1937-38	Montreal Canadiens	17	1	1	2	4
1938-39	Montreal Canadiens	2	0	0	0	0
1939-40	Montreal Canadiens	2	0	0	0	0
	TOTALS	21	1	1	2	4

MANIAGO, Cesare

Born in Trail, British Columbia, January 13th, 1939.
Goaltender, left-hand shot.
6′3″, 195 lb.
Last amateur team: the Chatham Maroons srs.

SEASON	TEAM	GP	GA	SO	AVE
1962-63	Montreal Canadiens	14	42	0	3.00
	TOTALS	14	42	0	3.00

OFFENSIVE RECORD		GP	G	A	PTS	MIP
1962-63	Montreal Canadiens	14	0	0	0	2
	TOTALS	14	0	0	0	2

Drafted from the Toronto Maple Leafs, June 13, 1961.
Traded to the New York Rangers with Garry Peters for Earl Ingarfield, Noel Price, Gord Labossiere and Dave McComb, June 8, 1965.

MANTHA, Georges Leon

Born in Lachine, Quebec, November 29th, 1908.
Left-winger, left-hand shot.
5′8″, 162 lb.
Last amateur team: Bell Telephone srs.

SEASON	TEAM	GP	G	A	PTS	MIP
1928-29	Montreal Canadiens	21	0	0	0	8
1929-30	Montreal Canadiens	44	5	2	7	16
1930-31	Montreal Canadiens	44	11	6	17	25
1931-32	Montreal Canadiens	48	1	7	8	8
1932-33	Montreal Canadiens	43	3	6	9	10
1933-34	Montreal Canadiens	44	6	9	15	12
1934-35	Montreal Canadiens	42	12	10	22	14
1935-36	Montreal Canadiens	35	1	12	13	14
1936-37	Montreal Canadiens	47	13	14	27	17
1937-38	Montreal Canadiens	47	23	19	42	12
1938-39	Montreal Canadiens	25	5	5	10	6
1939-40	Montreal Canadiens	42	9	11	20	6
1940-41	Montreal Canadiens	6	0	1	1	0
	TOTALS	488	89	102	191	141

PLAYOFFS		GP	G	A	PTS	MIP
1928-29	Montreal Canadiens	3	0	0	0	0
1929-30	Montreal Canadiens	6	0	0	0	0
1930-31	Montreal Canadiens	10	5	1	6	4
1931-32	Montreal Canadiens	4	0	0	0	2
1934-35	Montreal Canadiens	2	0	0	0	4
1936-37	Montreal Canadiens	5	0	0	0	0
1937-38	Montreal Canadiens	3	1	0	1	0
1938-39	Montreal Canadiens	3	0	0	0	0
	TOTALS	36	6	1	7	18

Played with the team that won the Stanley Cup in 1929-30, 1930-31.
Brother of Sylvio Mantha.

MANTHA, Sylvio

Born in Montreal, Quebec, April 14th, 1902.
Defenseman, right-hand shot.
5′10″, 173 lb.
Last amateur team: the Montreal National srs.

SEASON	TEAM	GP	G	A	PTS	MIP
1923-24	Montreal Canadiens	24	1	0	1	9
1924-25	Montreal Canadiens	30	2	0	2	16
1925-26	Montreal Canadiens	34	2	1	3	66
1926-27	Montreal Canadiens	43	10	5	15	77
1927-28	Montreal Canadiens	43	4	11	15	61
1928-29	Montreal Canadiens	44	9	4	13	56
1929-30	Montreal Canadiens	44	13	11	24	108
1930-31	Montreal Canadiens	44	4	7	11	75
1931-32	Montreal Canadiens	47	5	5	10	62
1932-33	Montreal Canadiens	48	4	7	11	50
1933-34	Montreal Canadiens	48	4	6	10	24
1934-35	Montreal Canadiens	47	3	11	14	36
1935-36	Montreal Canadiens	42	2	4	6	25
	TOTALS	538	63	72	135	665

PLAYOFFS		GP	G	A	PTS	MIP
1923-24	Montreal Canadiens	5	0	—	0	—
1924-25	Montreal Canadiens	6	0	0	0	2
1926-27	Montreal Canadiens	4	1	0	1	0
1927-28	Montreal Canadiens	2	0	0	0	6
1928-29	Montreal Canadiens	3	0	0	0	0
1929-30	Montreal Canadiens	6	2	1	3	18
1930-31	Montreal Canadiens	10	2	1	3	26
1931-32	Montreal Canadiens	4	0	1	1	8
1932-33	Montreal Canadiens	2	0	1	1	2
1933-34	Montreal Canadiens	2	0	0	0	2
1934-35	Montreal Canadiens	2	0	0	0	2
	TOTALS	46	5	4	9	66

Played with the team that won the Prince of Wales Trophy in 1924-25.
Played with the team that won the Stanley Cup in 1923-24, 1929-30, 1930-31.
Member of the Hockey Hall of Fame in September, 1960.

Member of the second All-Star team in 1930-31, 1931-32.
Signed up with the Boston Bruins in 1936.
Appointed captain of the Canadiens from 1926-27 to 1935-36.
Succeeded Leo Dandurand as coach of the Canadiens (1935-36).
Brother of Georges Mantha.
Died August 7, 1974.

MARCHAND, ?

Incomplete record: Existence confirmed by the Official Report of Match, season 1922-23, NHL office.

MARSHALL, Donald Robert (Don)

Born in Verdun, Quebec, March 23rd, 1932.
Left-winger, left-hand shot.
5'10", 165 lb.
Last amateur team: the Cincinnati Mohawks srs.

SEASON	TEAM	GP	G	A	PTS	MIP
1951-52	Montreal Canadiens	1	0	0	0	0
1954-55	Montreal Canadiens	39	5	3	8	9
1955-56	Montreal Canadiens	66	4	1	5	10
1956-57	Montreal Canadiens	70	12	8	20	6
1957-58	Montreal Canadiens	68	22	19	41	14
1958-59	Montreal Canadiens	70	10	22	32	12
1959-60	Montreal Canadiens	70	16	22	38	4
1960-61	Montreal Canadiens	70	14	17	31	8
1961-62	Montreal Canadiens	66	18	28	46	12
1962-63	Montreal Canadiens	65	13	20	33	6
	TOTALS	585	114	140	254	81

PLAYOFFS		GP	G	A	PTS	MIP
1954-55	Montreal Canadiens	12	1	1	2	2
1955-56	Montreal Canadiens	10	1	0	1	0
1956-57	Montreal Canadiens	10	1	3	4	2
1957-58	Montreal Canadiens	10	0	2	2	4
1958-59	Montreal Canadiens	11	0	2	2	2
1959-60	Montreal Canadiens	8	2	2	4	0
1960-61	Montreal Canadiens	6	0	2	2	0
1961-62	Montreal Canadiens	6	0	1	1	2
1962-63	Montreal Canadiens	5	0	0	0	0
	TOTALS	78	5	13	18	12

ALL-STAR GAMES		GP	G	A	PTS
1956	Montreal Canadiens	1	0	0	0
1957	Montreal Canadiens	1	0	0	0
1958	Montreal Canadiens	1	1	1	2
1959	Montreal Canadiens	1	0	0	0
1960	Montreal Canadiens	1	0	0	0
1961	NHL All-Stars	1	0	0	0
	TOTALS	6	1	1	2

Played with the team that won the Prince of Wales Trophy in 1955-56, 1957-58, 1958-59, 1959-60, 1960-61, 1961-62.
Played with the team that won the Stanley Cup in 1955-56, 1956-57, 1957-58, 1958-59, 1959-60.
Traded to the New York Rangers with Philippe Goyette and Jacques Plante for Lorne Worsley, Dave Balon, Leon Rochefort and Len Ronson, June 4, 1963.

MASNICK, Paul Andrew

Born in Regina, Saskatchewan, April 14th, 1931.
Center, right-hand shot.
5'9", 165 lb.
Last amateur team: the Regina Pats jrs.

SEASON	TEAM	GP	G	A	PTS	MIP
1950-51	Montreal Canadiens	43	4	1	5	14
1951-52	Montreal Canadiens	15	1	2	3	2
1952-53	Montreal Canadiens	53	5	7	12	44
1953-54	Montreal Canadiens	50	5	21	26	57
*1954-55	Chicago Black Hawks/ Montreal Canadiens	30	1	1	2	8
	TOTALS	191	16	32	48	125

PLAYOFFS		GP	G	A	PTS	MIP
1950-51	Montreal Canadiens	11	2	1	3	4
1951-52	Montreal Canadiens	6	1	0	1	12
1952-53	Montreal Canadiens	6	1	0	1	7
1953-54	Montreal Canadiens	10	0	4	4	4
	TOTALS	33	4	5	9	27

Played with the team that won the Stanley Cup in 1952-53.

MATTE, Joseph (Joe)

Born in 1893.
Defenseman.

SEASON	TEAM	GP	G	A	PTS	MIP
*1925-26	Boston Bruins/ Montreal Canadiens	9	0	0	0	0
	TOTALS	9	0	0	0	0

Died June 13, 1961.

MATZ, Jean (John)

SEASON	TEAM	GP	G	A	PTS	MIP
1924-25	Montreal Canadiens	30	3	2	5	0
	TOTALS	30	3	2	5	0

PLAYOFFS		GP	G	A	PTS	MIP
1924-25	Montreal Canadiens	5	0	0	0	2
	TOTALS	5	0	0	0	2

Obtained from the Saskatoon Sheiks with Fern Headley in 1924.
Played with the team that won the Prince of Wales Trophy in 1924-25.

MAZUR, Edward Joseph (Spider)

Born in Winnipeg, Manitoba, July 25th, 1929.
Left-winger, left-hand shot.
6'2", 186 lb.
Last amateur team: the Winnipeg Monarchs jrs.

SEASON	TEAM	GP	G	A	PTS	MIP
1953-54	Montreal Canadiens	67	7	14	21	95
1954-55	Montreal Canadiens	25	1	5	6	21
	TOTALS	92	8	19	27	116

PLAYOFFS		GP	G	A	PTS	MIP
1950-51	Montreal Canadiens	2	0	0	0	0
1951-52	Montreal Canadiens	5	2	0	2	4
1952-53	Montreal Canadiens	7	2	2	4	11
1953-54	Montreal Canadiens	11	0	3	3	7
	TOTALS	25	4	5	9	22

ALL-STAR GAMES		GP	G	A	PTS
1953	Montreal Canadiens	1	0	0	0
	TOTALS	1	0	0	0

Played with the team that won the Stanley Cup in 1952-53.

MEAGHER, Rick

Born in Belleville, Ontario, November 4th, 1953.
Center, right-hand shot.
5'10", 175 lb.
Last amateur team: Nova Scotia (AHL).

SEASON	TEAM	GP	G	A	PTS	MIP
1979-80	Montreal Canadiens	2	0	0	0	0
	TOTALS	2	0	0	0	0

MEGER, Paul Carl

Born in Watrous, Saskatchewan, February 17th, 1929.
Left-winger, left-hand shot.
5'7", 160 lb.
Last amateur team: the Barrie Flyers jrs.

SEASON	TEAM	GP	G	A	PTS	MIP
1950-51	Montreal Canadiens	17	2	4	6	6
1951-52	Montreal Canadiens	69	24	18	42	44
1952-53	Montreal Canadiens	69	9	17	26	38
1953-54	Montreal Canadiens	44	4	9	13	24
1954-55	Montreal Canadiens	13	0	4	4	6
	TOTALS	212	39	52	91	118

PLAYOFFS		GP	G	A	PTS	MIP
1949-50	Montreal Canadiens	2	0	0	0	2
1950-51	Montreal Canadiens	11	1	3	4	4
1951-52	Montreal Canadiens	11	0	3	3	2
1952-53	Montreal Canadiens	5	1	2	3	4
1953-54	Montreal Canadiens	6	1	0	1	4
	TOTALS	35	3	8	11	16

Played with the team that won the Stanley Cup in 1952-53.

MERONEK, William (Will, Smiley)

Born in Stony Mountain, Manitoba, April 5th, 1917.
Last amateur team: the Montreal Canadiens srs.

SEASON	TEAM	GP	G	A	PTS	MIP
1939-40	Montreal Canadiens	7	2	2	4	0
1942-43	Montreal Canadiens	12	3	6	9	0
	TOTALS	19	5	8	13	0

PLAYOFFS		GP	G	A	PTS	MIP
1942-43	Montreal Canadiens	1	0	0	0	0
	TOTALS	1	0	0	0	0

MICKEY, Robert Larry

Born in Lacombe, Alberta, October 21st, 1943.
Right-winger, right-hand shot.
5'11", 180 lb.
Last amateur team: the St. Catharines Black Hawks jrs.

SEASON	TEAM	GP	G	A	PTS	MIP
1969-70	Montreal Canadiens	21	4	4	8	4
	TOTALS	21	4	4	8	4

Drafted from the Toronto Maple Leafs, June 11, 1969.
Traded to the Los Angeles Kings with Lucien Grenier and Jack Norris for Leon Rochefort, Wayne Thomas and Greg Boddy, May 22, 1970.

MILLAIRE, Edouard (Ed)

PLAYOFFS		GP	G	A	PTS	MIP
1909-10	Montreal Canadiens	1	0	—	0	—
	TOTALS	1	0	—	0	—

MILLER, William (Bill)

Born in Campbelltown, New Brunswick, August 1st, 1911.
Center, defenseman, right-hand shot.
6', 160 lb.
Last amateur team: the Moncton Hawks.

SEASON	TEAM	GP	G	A	PTS	MIP
*1935-36	Montreal Maroons/ Montreal Canadiens	25	1	2	3	2
1936-37	Montreal Canadiens	48	3	1	4	12
	TOTALS	73	4	3	7	14

PLAYOFFS		GP	G	A	PTS	MIP
1936-37	Montreal Canadiens	5	0	0	0	0
	TOTALS	5	0	0	0	0

MONAHAN, Garry Michael

Born in Barrie, Ontario, October 20th, 1946.
Center, left-hand shot.
6', 185 lb.
Last amateur team: the Peterborough Petes jrs.

SEASON	TEAM	GP	G	A	PTS	MIP
1967-68	Montreal Canadiens	11	0	0	0	8
1968-69	Montreal Canadiens	3	0	0	0	0
	TOTALS	14	0	0	0	8

Played with the team that won the Prince of Wales Trophy in 1967-68, 1968-69.
Traded to the Detroit Red Wings with Doug Piper for Peter Mahovlich and Bart Crashley, June 6, 1969.

MONDOU, Armand

Born in Yamaska, Quebec, June 27th, 1905.
Left-winger, left-hand shot.
5'10", 175 lb.
Last amateur team: St. François-Xavier.

SEASON	TEAM	GP	G	A	PTS	MIP
1928-29	Montreal Canadiens	32	3	4	7	6
1929-30	Montreal Canadiens	44	3	5	8	24
1930-31	Montreal Canadiens	40	5	4	9	10
1931-32	Montreal Canadiens	47	6	12	18	22
1932-33	Montreal Canadiens	24	1	3	4	15
1933-34	Montreal Canadiens	48	5	3	8	4
1934-35	Montreal Canadiens	46	9	15	24	6
1935-36	Montreal Canadiens	36	7	11	18	10
1936-37	Montreal Canadiens	7	1	1	2	0
1937-38	Montreal Canadiens	7	2	4	6	0
1938-39	Montreal Canadiens	34	3	7	10	2
1939-40	Montreal Canadiens	21	2	2	4	0
	TOTALS	386	47	71	118	99

PLAYOFFS		GP	G	A	PTS	MIP
1928-29	Montreal Canadiens	3	0	0	0	2
1929-30	Montreal Canadiens	6	1	1	2	6
1930-31	Montreal Canadiens	8	0	0	0	0
1931-32	Montreal Canadiens	4	1	2	3	2
1933-34	Montreal Canadiens	1	0	1	1	0
1934-35	Montreal Canadiens	2	0	1	1	0
1936-37	Montreal Canadiens	5	0	0	0	0
1938-39	Montreal Canadiens	3	1	0	1	2
	TOTALS	32	3	5	8	12

Played with the team that won the Stanley Cup in 1929-30, 1930-31.
Died September 13, 1976.

MONDOU, Pierre

Born in Sorel, Quebec, November 27th, 1955.
Center, right-hand shot.
5'11", 175 lb.
Last amateur team: the Montreal Canadiens jrs.

SEASON	TEAM	GP	G	A	PTS	MIP
1977-78	Montreal Canadiens	71	19	30	49	8
1978-79	Montreal Canadiens	77	31	41	72	26
1979-80	Montreal Canadiens	75	30	36	66	12
	TOTALS	223	80	107	187	46

PLAYOFFS		GP	G	A	PTS	MIP
1976-77	Montreal Canadiens	4	0	0	0	0
1977-78	Montreal Canadiens	15	3	7	10	4
1978-79	Montreal Canadiens	16	3	6	9	4
1979-80	Montreal Canadiens	4	1	4	5	4
	TOTALS	39	7	17	24	12

Played with the team that won the Prince of Wales Trophy in 1977-78.
Played with the team that won the Stanley Cup in 1976-77, 1977-78, 1978-79.

MOORE, Richard Winston (Dickie)

Born in Montreal, Quebec, January 6th, 1931.
Left-winger, left-hand shot.
5'11", 178 lb.
Last amateur team: the Montreal Canadiens jrs.

SEASON	TEAM	GP	G	A	PTS	MIP
1951-52	Montreal Canadiens	33	18	15	33	44
1952-53	Montreal Canadiens	18	2	6	8	19
1953-54	Montreal Canadiens	13	1	4	5	12
1954-55	Montreal Canadiens	67	16	20	36	32
1955-56	Montreal Canadiens	70	11	39	50	55
1956-57	Montreal Canadiens	70	29	29	58	56
1957-58	Montreal Canadiens	70	36	48	84	65
1958-59	Montreal Canadiens	70	41	55	96	61
1959-60	Montreal Canadiens	62	22	42	64	54
1960-61	Montreal Canadiens	57	35	34	69	62
1961-62	Montreal Canadiens	57	19	22	41	54
1962-63	Montreal Canadiens	67	24	26	50	61
	TOTALS	654	254	340	594	575

PLAYOFFS		GP	G	A	PTS	MIP
1951-52	Montreal Canadiens	11	1	1	2	12
1952-53	Montreal Canadiens	12	3	2	5	13
1953-54	Montreal Canadiens	11	5	8	13	8
1954-55	Montreal Canadiens	12	1	5	6	22
1955-56	Montreal Canadiens	10	3	6	9	12
1956-57	Montreal Canadiens	10	3	7	10	4
1957-58	Montreal Canadiens	10	4	7	11	4
1958-59	Montreal Canadiens	11	5	12	17	8
1959-60	Montreal Canadiens	8	6	4	10	4
1960-61	Montreal Canadiens	6	3	1	4	4
1961-62	Montreal Canadiens	6	4	2	6	8
1962-63	Montreal Canadiens	5	0	1	1	2
	TOTALS	112	38	56	94	101

ALL-STAR GAMES		GP	G	A	PTS
1953	Montreal Canadiens	1	0	0	0
1956	Montreal Canadiens	1	0	0	0
1957	Montreal Canadiens	1	0	1	1
1958	Montreal Canadiens	1	0	3	3
1959	Montreal Canadiens	1	1	1	2
1960	Montreal Canadiens	1	0	0	0
1961	NHL All-Stars	1	0	0	0
	TOTALS	7	1	5	6

Played with the team that won the Prince of Wales Trophy in 1955-56, 1957-58, 1958-59, 1959-60, 1960-61, 1961-62.
Played with the team that won the Stanley Cup in 1952-53, 1955-56, 1956-57, 1957-58, 1958-59, 1959-60.
Won the Art Ross Trophy in 1957-58, 1958-59.
Member of the first All-Star team in 1957-58, 1958-59.
Appointed assistant captain of the Canadiens in 1960.
Member of the second All-Star team in 1960-61.
Drafted by the Toronto Maple Leafs in June, 1964.
Member of the Hockey Hall of Fame in June, 1974.

MORAN, Ambrose Jason (Amby)

Defenseman.

SEASON	TEAM	GP	G	A	PTS	MIP
1926-27	Montreal Canadiens	12	0	0	0	10
	TOTALS	12	0	0	0	10

MORENZ, Howarth William Howard (Howie)

Born in Mitchell, Ontario, September 21st, 1902.
Center, left-hand shot.
5'9", 165 lb.
Last amateur team: Stratford jrs.

SEASON	TEAM	GP	G	A	PTS	MIP
1923-24	Montreal Canadiens	24	13	3	16	20
1924-25	Montreal Canadiens	30	27	7	34	31
1925-26	Montreal Canadiens	31	23	3	26	39
1926-27	Montreal Canadiens	44	25	7	32	49
1927-28	Montreal Canadiens	43	33	18	51	66
1928-29	Montreal Canadiens	42	17	10	27	47
1929-30	Montreal Canadiens	44	40	10	50	72
1930-31	Montreal Canadiens	39	28	23	51	49
1931-32	Montreal Canadiens	48	24	25	49	46
1932-33	Montreal Canadiens	46	14	21	35	32
1933-34	Montreal Canadiens	39	8	13	21	21
1936-37	Montreal Canadiens	30	4	16	20	12
	TOTALS	460	256	156	412	484

PLAYOFFS		GP	G	A	PTS	MIP
1923-24	Montreal Canadiens	6	7	2	9	10
1924-25	Montreal Canadiens	6	7	1	8	10
1926-27	Montreal Canadiens	4	1	0	1	4
1927-28	Montreal Canadiens	2	0	0	0	12
1928-29	Montreal Canadiens	3	0	0	0	6
1929-30	Montreal Canadiens	6	3	0	3	10
1930-31	Montreal Canadiens	10	1	4	5	10
1931-32	Montreal Canadiens	4	1	0	1	4
1932-33	Montreal Canadiens	2	0	3	3	2
1933-34	Montreal Canadiens	2	1	1	2	0
	TOTALS	45	21	11	32	68

Played with the team that won the Prince of Wales Trophy in 1924-25.
Played with the team that won the Stanley Cup in 1923-24, 1929-30, 1930-31.
Member of the first All-Star team in 1930-31, 1931-32.
Member of the second All-Star team in 1932-33.
Traded to the Chicago Black Hawks with Martin Burke and Lorne Chabot for Lionel Conacher, Roger Jenkins and Leroy Goldsworthy in 1934.
Obtained from the New York Rangers in 1936.
Father-in-law of Bernard Geoffrion.
Grandfather of Linda Geoffrion, wife of Hartland Monahan.
Member of the Hockey Hall of Fame in April, 1945.
Died March 8, 1937 (following an injury during the game against Chicago on January 28 at the Forum).

MORIN, Pierre (Pete, Pit)

Born in Lachine, Quebec, December 8th, 1915.
Left-winger, left-hand shot.
5'6", 150 lb.
Last amateur team: the Montreal Royals srs.

SEASON	TEAM	GP	G	A	PTS	MIP
1941-42	Montreal Canadiens	31	10	12	22	7
	TOTALS	31	10	12	22	7

PLAYOFFS		GP	G	A	PTS	MIP
1941-42	Montreal Canadiens	1	0	0	0	0
	TOTALS	1	0	0	0	0

Member of the famous "Razzle-Dazzle" line with "Buddy" O'Connor at center and Gerry Heffernan at right wing.

MORISSETTE, Jean-Guy

Born in Causapscal, Quebec, December 16th, 1937.
Goaltender, left-hand shot.
5'6", 140 lb.
Last amateur team: Moncton srs.

SEASON	TEAM	GP	GA	SO	AVE
1963-64	Montreal Canadiens	1	4	0	4.00
	TOTALS	1	4	0	4.00

OFFENSIVE RECORD		GP	G	A	PTS	MIP
1963-64	Montreal Canadiens	1	0	0	0	0
	TOTALS	1	0	0	0	0

Played with the team that won the Prince of Wales Trophy in 1963-64.

MOSDELL, Kenneth (Ken)

Born in Montreal, Quebec, July 13th, 1922.
Center, left-hand shot.
6'1", 170 lb.
Last amateur team: the Montreal Royals srs.

SEASON	TEAM	GP	G	A	PTS	MIP
1944-45	Montreal Canadiens	31	12	6	18	16
1945-46	Montreal Canadiens	13	2	1	3	8
1946-47	Montreal Canadiens	54	5	10	15	50
1947-48	Montreal Canadiens	23	1	0	1	19
1948-49	Montreal Canadiens	60	17	9	26	50
1949-50	Montreal Canadiens	67	15	12	27	42
1950-51	Montreal Canadiens	66	13	18	31	24
1951-52	Montreal Canadiens	44	5	11	16	19
1952-53	Montreal Canadiens	63	5	14	19	27
1953-54	Montreal Canadiens	67	22	24	46	64
1954-55	Montreal Canadiens	70	22	32	54	82
1955-56	Montreal Canadiens	67	13	17	30	48
1957-58	Montreal Canadiens	2	0	1	1	0
	TOTALS	627	132	155	287	449

PLAYOFFS		GP	G	A	PTS	MIP
1945-46	Montreal Canadiens	9	4	1	5	6
1946-47	Montreal Canadiens	4	2	0	2	4
1948-49	Montreal Canadiens	7	1	1	2	4
1949-50	Montreal Canadiens	5	0	0	0	12
1950-51	Montreal Canadiens	11	1	1	2	4
1951-52	Montreal Canadiens	2	1	0	1	0
1952-53	Montreal Canadiens	7	3	2	5	4
1953-54	Montreal Canadiens	11	1	0	1	4
1954-55	Montreal Canadiens	12	2	7	9	8
1955-56	Montreal Canadiens	9	1	1	2	2
1958-59	Montreal Canadiens	2	0	0	0	0
	TOTALS	79	16	13	29	48

ALL-STAR GAMES		GP	G	A	PTS
1951	NHL All-Stars	1	1	0	1
1952	NHL All-Stars	1	0	0	0
1953	Montreal Canadiens	1	0	0	0
1954	NHL All-Stars	1	0	0	0
1955	NHL All-Stars	1	0	0	0
	TOTALS	5	1	0	1

Bought from the New York Americans in 1944.
Played with the team that won the Prince of Wales Trophy in 1944-45, 1945-46, 1946-47, 1955-56, 1957-58.
Played with the team that won the Stanley Cup in 1945-46, 1952-53, 1955-56, 1958-59.
Appointed assistant captain of the Canadiens in 1951.
Member of the first All-Star team in 1953-54.
Member of the second All-Star team in 1954-55.

MUMMERY, Harry

Defenseman, point.
245 lb.

SEASON	TEAM	GP	G	A	PTS	MIP
1916-17	Montreal Canadiens	20	4	—	4	—
1920-21	Montreal Canadiens	24	15	5	20	68
	TOTALS	44	19	5	24	68

PLAYOFFS		GP	G	A	PTS	MIP
1916-17	Montreal Canadiens	6	0	—	0	—
	TOTALS	6	0	—	0	—

Drafted from the Quebec Bulldogs in 1916.

MUNRO, Duncan (Dunc) B.

Born in Toronto, Ontario.

SEASON	TEAM	GP	G	A	PTS	MIP
1931-32	Montreal Canadiens	48	1	1	2	14
	TOTALS	48	1	1	2	14

PLAYOFFS		GP	G	A	PTS	MIP
1931-32	Montreal Canadiens	2	0	0	0	2
	TOTALS	2	0	0	0	2

Drafted from the Maroons (1931-32).
Died in 1958.

MURDOCH, Robert John (Bob)

Born in Kirkland Lake, Ontario, November 20th, 1946.
Defenseman, right-hand shot.
6', 190 lb.
Last amateur team: Canada's National Team.

SEASON	TEAM	GP	G	A	PTS	MIP
1970-71	Montreal Canadiens	1	0	2	2	2
1971-72	Montreal Canadiens	11	1	1	2	8
1972-73	Montreal Canadiens	69	2	22	24	55
	TOTALS	81	3	25	28	65

PLAYOFFS		GP	G	A	PTS	MIP
1970-71	Montreal Canadiens	2	0	0	0	0
1971-72	Montreal Canadiens	1	0	0	0	0
1972-73	Montreal Canadiens	13	0	3	3	10
	TOTALS	16	0	3	3	10

Played with the team that won the Prince of Wales Trophy in 1972-73.
Played with the team that won the Stanley Cup in 1970-71, 1972-73.
Traded to the Los Angeles Kings with Randy Rota for the first Amateur Draft choice of 1974 (Mario Tremblay) and a certain amount of money, May 29, 1973.

MURPHY, Harold (Hal)

Born in Montreal, Quebec, July 6th, 1927.
Goaltender, right-hand shot.
Last amateur team: the Montreal Royals srs.

SEASON	TEAM	GP	GA	SO	AVE
1952-53	Montreal Canadiens	1	4	0	4.00
	TOTALS	1	4	0	4.00

OFFENSIVE RECORD		GP	G	A	PTS	MIP
1952-53	Montreal Canadiens	1	0	0	0	0
	TOTALS	1	0	0	0	0

MURRAY, Leo

Born in Portage-la-Prairie, Manitoba, February 15th, 1902.

SEASON	TEAM	GP	G	A	PTS	MIP
1932-33	Montreal Canadiens	6	0	0	0	2
	TOTALS	6	0	0	0	2

MURRAY, Thomas (Tom, Mickey)

Goaltender.

SEASON	TEAM	GP	GA	SO	AVE
1929-30	Montreal Canadiens	1	4	0	4.00
	TOTALS	1	4	0	4.00

OFFENSIVE RECORD		GP	G	A	PTS	MIP
1929-30	Montreal Canadiens	1	0	0	0	0
	TOTALS	1	0	0	0	0

MYRE, Louis Philippe (Phil)

Born in Ste-Anne-de-Bellevue, Quebec, November 1st, 1948.
Goaltender, left-hand shot.
6'1", 180 lb.
Last amateur team: the Niagara Falls Flyers jrs.

SEASON	TEAM	GP	GA	SO	AVE
1969-70	Montreal Canadiens	10	19	0	2.15
1970-71	Montreal Canadiens	30	87	1	3.11
1971-72	Montreal Canadiens	9	32	0	3.63
	TOTALS	49	138	1	2.81

OFFENSIVE RECORD		GP	G	A	PTS	MIP
1969-70	Montreal Canadiens	10	0	0	0	2
1970-71	Montreal Canadiens	30	0	1	1	17
1971-72	Montreal Canadiens	9	0	0	0	4
	TOTALS	49	0	1	1	23

Drafted by the Atlanta Flames, June 6, 1972.

NAPIER, Mark

Born in Toronto, Ontario, January 28th, 1957.
Right-winger, left-hand shot.
5'10", 185 lb.
Last amateur team: Toronto Marlboros jrs.

SEASON	TEAM	GP	G	A	PTS	MIP
1978-79	Montreal Canadiens	54	11	20	31	11
1979-80	Montreal Canadiens	76	16	33	49	7
	TOTALS	130	27	53	80	18

PLAYOFFS		GP	G	A	PTS	MIP
1978-79	Montreal Canadiens	12	3	2	5	2
1979-80	Montreal Canadiens	10	2	6	8	0
	TOTALS	22	5	8	13	2

Played with the team that won the Stanley Cup in 1978-79.

NEWMAN, Daniel Kenneth (Dan)

Born in Windsor, Ontario, January 26th, 1952.
Left-winger, left-hand shot.
6'1", 195 lb.
Last amateur team: St. Clair College.

SEASON	TEAM	GP	G	A	PTS	MIP
1978-79	Montreal Canadiens	16	0	0	2	4
	TOTALS	16	0	0	2	4

PLAYOFFS		GP	G	A	PTS	MIP
1978-79	Montreal Canadiens	0	0	0	0	0
	TOTALS	0	0	0	0	0

Traded to the Edmonton Oilers with Dave Lumley for future considerations.

NILAN, Chris

Born in Boston, Massachusetts, February 9th, 1958.
Forward, right-hand shot.
6', 200 lb.
Last amateur team: North Eastern University.

SEASON	TEAM	GP	G	A	PTS	MIP
1979-80	Montreal Canadiens	15	0	2	2	50
	TOTALS	15	0	2	2	50

PLAYOFFS		GP	G	A	PTS	MIP
1979-80	Montreal Canadiens	5	0	0	0	2
	TOTALS	5	0	0	0	2

NOBLE, Edward Reginald (Reg)

Born in Collingwood, Ontario, June 23rd, 1896.
Left-winger, center, defenseman, left-hand shot.
5'8", 180 lb.
Last amateur team: Riverside srs.

SEASON	TEAM	GP	G	A	PTS	MIP
*1916-17	Toronto Arenas/ Montreal Canadiens	19	13	—	13	—
	TOTALS	19	13	—	13	—

PLAYOFFS		GP	G	A	PTS	MIP
1916-17	Montreal Canadiens	2	0	—	0	—
	TOTALS	2	0	—	0	—

Obtained from the Toronto Arenas in 1916-17.
Member of the Hockey Hall of Fame in June, 1962.
Died June 20, 1962.

NYROP, William (Bill)

Born in Washington, D.C., July 23rd, 1952.
Defenseman, left-hand shot.
6'2", 209 lb.
Last amateur team: Notre-Dame University.

SEASON	TEAM	GP	G	A	PTS	MIP
1975-76	Montreal Canadiens	19	0	3	3	8
1976-77	Montreal Canadiens	74	3	19	22	21
1977-78	Montreal Canadiens	72	5	21	26	37
1978-79	Montreal Canadiens	—	—	—	—	—
	TOTALS	165	8	43	51	66

PLAYOFFS		GP	G	A	PTS	MIP
1975-76	Montreal Canadiens	13	0	3	3	12
1976-77	Montreal Canadiens	8	1	0	1	4
1977-78	Montreal Canadiens	12	0	4	4	6
1978-79	Montreal Canadiens	—	—	—	—	—
	TOTALS	33	1	7	8	22

Seventh Amateur Draft choice in 1972.
Played with the team that won the Prince of Wales Trophy in 1975-76, 1976-77, 1977-78.
Played with the team that won the Stanley Cup in 1975-76, 1976-77, 1977-78.
Took a leave of absence for one year (1978-79).
Traded to the Minnesota North Stars for a second Amateur Draft choice (Gaston Gingras) in 1979.

O'CONNOR, Herbert William (Buddy, Bud)

Born in Montreal, Quebec, June 21st, 1916.
Center, left-hand shot.
5'7", 145 lb.
Last amateur team: the Montreal Royals srs.

SEASON	TEAM	GP	G	A	PTS	MIP
1941-42	Montreal Canadiens	36	9	16	25	4
1942-43	Montreal Canadiens	50	15	43	58	2
1943-44	Montreal Canadiens	44	12	42	54	6
1944-45	Montreal Canadiens	50	21	23	44	2
1945-46	Montreal Canadiens	45	11	11	22	2
1946-47	Montreal Canadiens	46	10	20	30	6
	TOTALS	271	78	155	233	22

PLAYOFFS		GP	G	A	PTS	MIP
1941-42	Montreal Canadiens	3	0	1	1	0
1942-43	Montreal Canadiens	5	4	5	9	0
1943-44	Montreal Canadiens	8	1	2	3	2
1944-45	Montreal Canadiens	2	0	0	0	0
1945-46	Montreal Canadiens	9	2	3	5	0
1946-47	Montreal Canadiens	8	3	4	7	0
	TOTALS	35	10	15	25	2

Played with the team that won the Prince of Wales Trophy in 1943-44, 1944-45, 1945-46, 1946-47.
Played with the team that won the Stanley Cup in 1943-44, 1945-46.
Member of the famous "Razzle-Dazzle" line with Gerry Heffernan at right wing and Pierre Morin at left wing.

O'NEILL, James Beaton (Peggy)

Born in Semans, Saskatchewan, April 3rd, 1913.
Center, right-winger, right-hand shot.
5'8", 160 lb.
Last amateur team: Wesleys jrs. (Saskatoon).

SEASON	TEAM	GP	G	A	PTS	MIP
1940-41	Montreal Canadiens	12	0	3	3	0
1941-42	Montreal Canadiens	4	0	1	1	4
	TOTALS	16	0	4	4	4

PLAYOFFS		GP	G	A	PTS	MIP
1940-41	Montreal Canadiens	3	0	0	0	0
	TOTALS	3	0	0	0	0

OLMSTEAD, Murray Bert

Born in Scepter, Saskatchewan, September 4th, 1926.
Left-winger, left-hand shot.
6'2", 183 lb.
Last amateur team: the Moose Jaw Canucks jrs.

SEASON	TEAM	GP	G	A	PTS	MIP
*1950-51	Chicago Black Hawks/ Montreal Canadiens	38	18	23	41	50
1951-52	Montreal Canadiens	69	7	28	35	49
1952-53	Montreal Canadiens	69	17	28	45	83
1953-54	Montreal Canadiens	70	15	37	52	85
1954-55	Montreal Canadiens	70	10	48	58	103
1955-56	Montreal Canadiens	70	14	56	70	94
1956-57	Montreal Canadiens	64	15	33	48	74
1957-58	Montreal Canadiens	57	9	28	37	71
	TOTALS	507	105	281	386	609

PLAYOFFS		GP	G	A	PTS	MIP
1950-51	Montreal Canadiens	11	2	3	5	9
1951-52	Montreal Canadiens	11	0	1	1	4
1952-53	Montreal Canadiens	12	2	2	4	4
1953-54	Montreal Canadiens	11	0	1	1	19
1954-55	Montreal Canadiens	12	0	4	4	21
1955-56	Montreal Canadiens	10	4	10	14	8
1956-57	Montreal Canadiens	10	0	9	9	13
1957-58	Montreal Canadiens	9	0	3	3	0
	TOTALS	86	8	33	41	78

ALL-STAR GAMES		GP	G	A	PTS
1953	Montreal Canadiens	1	0	0	0
1956	Montreal Canadiens	1	0	1	1
1957	Montreal Canadiens	1	1	0	1
1959	Montreal Canadiens	1	0	0	0
	TOTALS	4	1	1	2

Obtained from the Chicago Black Hawks for Leo Gravelle in December, 1950.
Played with the team that won the Prince of Wales Trophy in 1955-56, 1957-58.
Played with the team that won the Stanley Cup in 1952-53, 1955-56, 1956-57, 1957-58.
Member of the second All-Star team in 1952-53, 1955-56.
Appointed assistant captain of the Canadiens in 1954.
Drafted by the Toronto Maple Leafs in June, 1958.

PALANGIO, Peter Albert (Pete)

Born in North Bay, Ontario, September 10th, 1908.
Left-winger, left-hand shot.
5'11", 175 lb.
Last amateur team: the North Bay Trappers srs.

SEASON	TEAM	GP	G	A	PTS	MIP
1926-27	Montreal Canadiens	6	0	0	0	0
1928-29	Montreal Canadiens	2	0	0	0	0
	TOTALS	8	0	0	0	0

PLAYOFFS		GP	G	A	PTS	MIP
1926-27	Montreal Canadiens	4	0	0	0	0
	TOTALS	4	0	0	0	0

PARGETER, George William

Born in Calgary, Alberta, February 24th, 1923.
Left-winger, left-hand shot.
5'7", 168 lb.
Last amateur team: the Red Deer Wheelers jrs.

SEASON	TEAM	GP	G	A	PTS	MIP
1946-47	Montreal Canadiens	4	0	0	0	0
	TOTALS	4	0	0	0	0

Played with the team that won the Prince of Wales Trophy in 1946-47.

PATTERSON, George (Pat)

Born in Kingston, Ontario, May 22nd, 1906.
Right-winger.
6'1", 176 lb.
Last amateur team: Kingston jrs.

SEASON	TEAM	GP	G	A	PTS	MIP
*1927-28	Montreal Canadiens/ Toronto Maple Leafs	28	4	2	6	17
1928-29	Montreal Canadiens	44	4	5	9	34
	TOTALS	72	8	7	15	51

PLAYOFFS		GP	G	A	PTS	MIP
1928-29	Montreal Canadiens	3	0	0	0	2
	TOTALS	3	0	0	0	2

Traded to the New York Americans in 1929.

PAULHUS, Roland

Defenseman.

SEASON	TEAM	GP	G	A	PTS	MIP
1925-26	Montreal Canadiens	33	0	0	0	0
	TOTALS	33	0	0	0	0

PAYAN, Eugene (Pete, Pit)

SEASON	TEAM	GP	G	A	PTS	MIP
1910-11	Montreal Canadiens	16	12	—	12	—
1911-12	Montreal Canadiens	17	9	—	9	—
1912-13	Montreal Canadiens	6	3	—	3	—
1913-14	Montreal Canadiens	17	5	—	5	—
	TOTALS	56	29	—	29	—

PLAYOFFS		GP	G	A	PTS	MIP
1913-14	Montreal Canadiens	2	0	—	0	—
	TOTALS	2	0	—	0	—

PAYER, Evariste P.

Forward.

SEASON	TEAM	GP	G	A	PTS	MIP
1910-11	Montreal Canadiens	5	0	—	0	—
1911-12	Montreal Canadiens	3	0	—	0	—
1917-18	Montreal Canadiens	1	0	—	0	—
	TOTALS	9	0	—	0	—

PENNINGTON, Clifford (Cliff)

Born in Winnipeg, Manitoba, April 18th, 1940.
Center, right-hand shot.
6', 170 lb.
Last amateur team: the St. Boniface Canadiens jrs.

SEASON	TEAM	GP	G	A	PTS	MIP
1960-61	Montreal Canadiens	4	1	0	1	0
	TOTALS	4	1	0	1	0

Played with the team that won the Prince of Wales Trophy in 1960-61.

PERREAULT, Robert (Bob, Miche)

Born in Trois-Rivières, Quebec, January 28th, 1931.
Goaltender, left-hand shot.
5'8", 170 lb.
Last amateur team: the Trois-Rivières Reds jrs.

SEASON	TEAM	GP	GA	SO	AVE
1955-56	Montreal Canadiens	6	12	1	2.00
	TOTALS	6	12	1	2.00

OFFENSIVE RECORD		GP	G	A	PTS	MIP
1955-56	Montreal Canadiens	6	0	0	0	0
	TOTALS	6	0	0	0	0

Played with the team that won the Prince of Wales Trophy in 1955-56.

PETERS, Garry Lorne

Born in Regina, Saskatchewan, October 9th, 1942.
Center, left-hand shot.
5'10", 170 lb.
Last amateur team: the Regina Pats jrs.

SEASON	TEAM	GP	G	A	PTS	MIP
1964-65	Montreal Canadiens	13	0	2	2	6
1966-67	Montreal Canadiens	4	0	1	1	2
	TOTALS	17	0	3	3	8

Traded to the New York Rangers with Cesare Maniago for Earl Ingarfield, Gord Labossière, Noel Price and Dave McComb, June 8, 1965.
Obtained from the New York Rangers with Ted Taylor for Gord Berenson, June 13, 1966.
Drafted by the Philadelphia Flyers during the 1967 Expansion, June 6, 1967.

PETERS, James Meldrum (Jim)

Born in Verdun, Quebec, October 2nd, 1922.
Right-winger, right-hand shot.
5′11″, 165 lb.
Last amateur team: Canadian Army Team (Kingston, Ont.).

SEASON	TEAM	GP	G	A	PTS	MIP
1945-46	Montreal Canadiens	47	11	19	30	10
1946-47	Montreal Canadiens	60	11	13	24	27
*1947-48	Montreal Canadiens/ Boston Bruins	59	13	18	31	44
	TOTALS	166	35	50	85	81

PLAYOFFS		GP	G	A	PTS	MIP
1945-46	Montreal Canadiens	9	3	1	4	6
1946-47	Montreal Canadiens	11	1	2	3	10
	TOTALS	20	4	3	7	16

Played with the team that won the Prince of Wales Trophy in 1945-46, 1946-47.
Played with the team that won the Stanley Cup in 1945-46.
Traded to the Boston Bruins with John Quilty for Joe Carveth.
Father of Jim Peters, Jr.

PHILLIPS, Charles (Charlie)

Born in Toronto, Ontario, May 19th, 1917.
Defenseman.

SEASON	TEAM	GP	G	A	PTS	MIP
1942-43	Montreal Canadiens	17	0	0	0	6
	TOTALS	17	0	0	0	6

PICARD, Jean-Noel (Noel)

Born in Montreal, Quebec, December 25th, 1938.
Defenseman, right-hand shot.
6′1″, 185 lb.
Last amateur team: the Montreal Olympics srs.

SEASON	TEAM	GP	G	A	PTS	MIP
1964-65	Montreal Canadiens	16	0	7	7	33
	TOTALS	16	0	7	7	33

PLAYOFFS		GP	G	A	PTS	MIP
1964-65	Montreal Canadiens	3	0	1	1	0
	TOTALS	3	0	1	1	0

Played with the team that won the Stanley Cup in 1964-65.
Drafted by the St. Louis Blues durings the 1967 Expansion in June, 1967.
Brother of Roger Picard.

PITRE, Didier (Pit, Cannonball)

Born in Sault Ste-Marie, Ontario, in 1884.
Right-winger, defenseman, rover.
200 lb.

SEASON	TEAM	GP	G	A	PTS	MIP
1909-10	Montreal Canadiens	1	0	—	—	—
1910-11	Montreal Canadiens	16	19	—	19	—
1911-12	Montreal Canadiens	18	28	—	28	—
1912-13	Montreal Canadiens	17	24	—	24	—
1914-15	Montreal Canadiens	20	30	—	30	—
1915-16	Montreal Canadiens	24	23	—	23	—
1916-17	Montreal Canadiens	20	22	—	22	—
1917-18	Montreal Canadiens	19	17	—	17	—
1918-19	Montreal Canadiens	17	14	4	18	9
1919-20	Montreal Canadiens	22	15	7	22	6
1920-21	Montreal Canadiens	23	15	1	16	23
1921-22	Montreal Canadiens	23	2	3	5	12
1922-23	Montreal Canadiens	23	1	2	3	0
	TOTALS	243	210	17	227	50

PLAYOFFS		GP	G	A	PTS	MIP
1909-10	Montreal Canadiens	12	11	—	11	—
1915-16	Montreal Canadiens	5	4	—	4	—
1916-17	Montreal Canadiens	6	7	—	7	—
1917-18	Montreal Canadiens	2	0	0	0	0
1918-19	Montreal Canadiens	10	2	2	4	—
1922-23	Montreal Canadiens	2	0	—	—	—
	TOTALS	37	24	2	26	—

Signed up with the Canadiens in 1909.
Traded to the Vancouver team to complete the exchange that sent Newsy Lalonde to the Canadiens in 1913.
Played with the team that won the Stanley Cup in 1915-16.
Member of the Hockey Hall of Fame in August, 1962.
Died July 29, 1934.

PLAMONDON, Gerard Roger (Gerry, Eagle Eye)

Born in Sherbrooke, Quebec, January 5th, 1925.
Left-winger, left-hand shot.
5′8″, 170 lb.
Last amateur team: the Montreal Royals srs.

SEASON	TEAM	GP	G	A	PTS	MIP
1945-46	Montreal Canadiens	6	0	2	2	2
1947-48	Montreal Canadiens	3	1	1	2	0
1948-49	Montreal Canadiens	27	5	5	10	8
1949-50	Montreal Canadiens	37	1	5	6	0
1950-51	Montreal Canadiens	1	0	0	0	0
	TOTALS	74	7	13	20	10

PLAYOFFS		GP	G	A	PTS	MIP
1945-46	Montreal Canadiens	1	0	0	0	0
1948-49	Montreal Canadiens	7	5	1	6	0
1949-50	Montreal Canadiens	3	0	1	1	2
	TOTALS	11	5	2	7	2

Played with the team that won the Prince of Wales Trophy in 1945-46.
Played with the team that won the Stanley Cup in 1945-46.

PLANTE, Joseph Jacques Omer (The Snake)

Born in Mont-Carmel, Quebec, January 17th, 1929.
Goaltender, left-hand shot.
6′, 175 lb.
Last amateur team: the Montreal Royals srs.

SEASON	TEAM	GP	GA	SO	AVE
1952-53	Montreal Canadiens	3	4	0	1.33
1953-54	Montreal Canadiens	17	27	5	1.59
1954-55	Montreal Canadiens	52	110	5	2.11
1955-56	Montreal Canadiens	64	119	7	1.86
1956-57	Montreal Canadiens	61	123	9	2.02
1957-58	Montreal Canadiens	57	119	9	2.09
1958-59	Montreal Canadiens	67	144	9	2.15
1959-60	Montreal Canadiens	69	175	3	2.54
1960-61	Montreal Canadiens	40	112	2	2.80
1961-62	Montreal Canadiens	70	166	4	2.37
1962-63	Montreal Canadiens	56	138	5	2.46
	TOTALS	556	1237	58	2.22

PLAYOFFS		GP	GA	SO	AVE
1952-53	Montreal Canadiens	4	7	1	1.75
1953-54	Montreal Canadiens	8	15	2	1.87
1954-55	Montreal Canadiens	12	30	0	2.50
1955-56	Montreal Canadiens	10	18	2	1.80
1956-57	Montreal Canadiens	10	18	1	1.80
1957-58	Montreal Canadiens	10	20	1	2.00
1958-59	Montreal Canadiens	11	28	0	2.54
1959-60	Montreal Canadiens	8	11	3	1.37
1960-61	Montreal Canadiens	6	16	0	2.67
1961-62	Montreal Canadiens	6	19	0	3.17
1962-63	Montreal Canadiens	5	14	0	2.80
	TOTALS	90	196	10	2.13

OFFENSIVE RECORD		GP	G	A	PTS	MIP
1952-53	Montreal Canadiens	3	0	0	0	0
1953-54	Montreal Canadiens	17	0	0	0	0
1954-55	Montreal Canadiens	52	0	0	0	2
1955-56	Montreal Canadiens	64	0	0	0	10
1956-57	Montreal Canadiens	61	0	0	0	16
1957-58	Montreal Canadiens	57	0	0	0	13
1958-59	Montreal Canadiens	67	0	1	1	11
1959-60	Montreal Canadiens	69	0	0	0	2
1960-61	Montreal Canadiens	40	0	0	0	2
1961-62	Montreal Canadiens	70	0	0	0	14
1962-63	Montreal Canadiens	56	0	1	1	2
	TOTALS	556	0	2	2	72

ALL-STAR GAMES		GP	GA	SO	AVE
1956	Montreal Canadiens	1	1	0	0.33
1957	Montreal Canadiens	1	5	0	1.67
1958	Montreal Canadiens	1	3	0	1.00
1959	Montreal Canadiens	1	1	0	0.33
1960	Montreal Canadiens	1	2	0	0.67
1962	NHL All-Stars	1	4	0	4.00
	TOTALS	6	16	0	2.66

Played with the team that won the Prince of Wales Trophy in 1955-56, 1957-58, 1958-59, 1959-60, 1960-61, 1961-62.
Played with the team that won the Stanley Cup in 1952-53, 1955-56, 1956-57, 1957-58, 1958-59, 1959-60.
Member of the first All-Star team in 1955-56, 1958-59, 1961-62.
Member of the second All-Star team in 1956-57, 1957-58, 1959-60.
Won the Vezina Trophy in 1955-56, 1956-57, 1957-58, 1958-59, 1959-60, 1961-62.
Won the Hart Trophy in 1961-62.

PLASSE, Michel Pierre

Born in Montreal, Quebec, June 1st, 1948.
Goaltender, left-hand shot.
5′11″, 161 lb.
Last amateur team: the Jacksonville Rockets srs.

SEASON	TEAM	GP	GA	SO	AVE
1972-73	Montreal Canadiens	17	40	0	2.58
1973-74	Montreal Canadiens	15	57	0	4.08
	TOTALS	32	97	0	3.03

OFFENSIVE RECORD		GP	G	A	PTS	MIP
1972-73	Montreal Canadiens	17	0	0	0	4
1973-74	Montreal Canadiens	15	0	0	0	0
	TOTALS	32	0	0	0	4

Played with the team that won the Prince of Wales Trophy in 1972-73.
Played with the team that won the Stanley Cup in 1972-73.
Drafted by the Kansas City Scouts, June 12, 1974.

PLEAU, Lawrence Winslow (Larry)

Born in Lynn, Massachusetts, January 29th, 1947.
Center, left-hand shot.
6′1″, 190 lb.
Last amateur team: the New Jersey Devils (IHL).

SEASON	TEAM	GP	G	A	PTS	MIP
1969-70	Montreal Canadiens	20	1	0	1	0
1970-71	Montreal Canadiens	19	1	5	6	8
1971-72	Montreal Canadiens	55	7	10	17	19
	TOTALS	94	9	15	24	27

PLAYOFFS		GP	G	A	PTS	MIP
1971-72	Montreal Canadiens	4	0	0	0	0
	TOTALS	4	0	0	0	0

Selected by the New England Whalers during the World Hockey Association Draft in February, 1972.
Drafted by the Toronto Maple Leafs in June, 1972.

POIRIER, Gordon C. (Gord)

Born in Maple Creek, Saskatchewan, October 27th, 1913.

SEASON	TEAM	GP	G	A	PTS	MIP
1939-40	Montreal Canadiens	10	0	0	0	0
	TOTALS	10	0	0	0	0

POLICH, Mike

Born in Hibbing, Minnesota, December 19th, 1952.
Center, left-winger, left-hand shot.
5′8″, 170 lb.
Last amateur team: Minnesota University.

SEASON	TEAM	GP	G	A	PTS	MIP
1976-77	Montreal Canadiens	0	0	0	0	0
1977-78	Montreal Canadiens	1	0	0	0	0
	TOTALS	1	0	0	0	0

PLAYOFFS		GP	G	A	PTS	MIP
1976-77	Montreal Canadiens	5	0	0	0	0
	TOTALS	5	0	0	0	0

Played with the team that won the Prince of Wales Trophy in 1977-78.
Played with the team that won the Stanley Cup in 1977-78.
Signed on by Minnesota as a free agent, September 6, 1978; in compensation Montreal got Jerry Engele.

PORTLAND, John Frederick (Jack)

Born in Waubaushene, Ontario, July 30th, 1912.
Defenseman, left-hand shot.
6′2″, 185 lb.
Last amateur team: Collingwood jrs.

SEASON	TEAM	GP	G	A	PTS	MIP
1933-34	Montreal Canadiens	31	0	2	2	10
*1934-35	Montreal Canadiens/ Boston Bruins	20	1	1	2	4
*1940-41	Chicago Black Hawks/ Montreal Canadiens	47	2	7	9	38
1941-42	Montreal Canadiens	46	2	9	11	53
1942-43	Montreal Canadiens	49	3	14	17	52
	TOTALS	193	8	33	41	157

PLAYOFFS		GP	G	A	PTS	MIP
1933-34	Montreal Canadiens	2	0	0	0	0
1940-41	Montreal Canadiens	3	0	1	1	2
1941-42	Montreal Canadiens	3	0	0	0	0
1942-43	Montreal Canadiens	5	1	2	3	2
	TOTALS	13	1	3	4	4

Obtained from the Chicago Black Hawks in 1940-41.

POULIN, George (Skinner)

Forward.

SEASON	TEAM	GP	G	A	PTS	MIP
1909-10	Montreal Canadiens	1	2	—	2	—
1910-11	Montreal Canadiens	13	3	—	3	—
1915-16	Montreal Canadiens	16	5	—	5	—
*1916-17	Montreal Canadiens/ Montreal Wanderers	10	3	—	3	—
	TOTALS	40	13	—	13	—

PLAYOFFS		GP	G	A	PTS	MIP
1909-10	Montreal Canadiens	12	7	—	7	—
1915-16	Montreal Canadiens	3	1	—	1	—
	TOTALS	15	8	—	8	—

Played with the team that won the Stanley Cup in 1915-16.
Traded to the Montreal Red Bands Wanderers in 1916-17.

POVEY, Fred

Born in Sherbrooke, Quebec, March 1st, 1884.
Forward.

SEASON	TEAM	GP	G	A	PTS	MIP
1912-13	Montreal Canadiens	4	0	—	0	—
	TOTALS	4	0	—	0	—

POWER, "Rocket"

Defenseman.

SEASON	TEAM	GP	G	A	PTS	MIP
*1910-11	Montreal Canadiens/ Quebec Bulldogs	14	3	—	3	—
	TOTALS	14	3	—	3	—

Brother of Charles and Joe Power.

PRICE, Garry Noel

Born in Brockville, Ontario, December 9th, 1935.
Defenseman, left-hand shot.
6′, 185 lb.
Last amateur team: St. Michaels College jrs.

SEASON	TEAM	GP	G	A	PTS	MIP
1965-66	Montreal Canadiens	15	0	6	6	8
1966-67	Montreal Canadiens	24	0	3	3	8
	TOTALS	39	0	9	9	16

PLAYOFFS		GP	G	A	PTS	MIP
1965-66	Montreal Canadiens	3	0	1	1	0
	TOTALS	3	0	1	1	0

Obtained from the New York Rangers with Earl Ingarfield, Gord Labossière, and Dave McComb for Garry Peters and Cesare Maniago, June 8, 1965.
Played with the team that won the Prince of Wales Trophy in 1965-66.
Played with the team that won the Stanley Cup in 1965-66.
Drafted by the Pittsburgh Penguins during the 1967 Expansion, June 6, 1967.
Obtained from the Los Angeles Kings with Denis Dejordy, Dale Hoganson and Doug Robinson for Rogatien Vachon, November 4, 1971.
Sold to the Atlanta Flames, August 14, 1972.

PRODGERS, George (Goldie)

Born in 1892.
Defenseman.

SEASON	TEAM	GP	G	A	PTS	MIP
1915-16	Montreal Canadiens	24	8	—	8	—
	TOTALS	24	8	—	8	—

PLAYOFFS		GP	G	A	PTS	MIP
1915-16	Montreal Canadiens	4	3	—	3	—
	TOTALS	4	3	—	3	—

Played with the team that won the Stanley Cup in 1915-16.

PRONOVOST, Andre Joseph Armand

Born in Shawinigan Falls, Quebec, July 9th, 1936.
Left-winger, left-hand shot.
5′9″, 165 lb.
Last amateur team: the Montreal Canadiens jrs.

SEASON	TEAM	GP	G	A	PTS	MIP
1956-57	Montreal Canadiens	64	10	11	21	58
1957-58	Montreal Canadiens	66	16	12	28	55
1958-59	Montreal Canadiens	70	9	14	23	48
1959-60	Montreal Canadiens	69	12	19	31	61
1960-61	Montreal Canadiens	21	1	5	6	4
	TOTALS	290	48	61	109	226

PLAYOFFS		GP	G	A	PTS	MIP
1956-57	Montreal Canadiens	8	1	0	1	4
1957-58	Montreal Canadiens	10	2	0	2	16
1958-59	Montreal Canadiens	11	2	1	3	6
1959-60	Montreal Canadiens	8	1	2	3	0
	TOTALS	37	6	3	9	26

ALL-STAR GAMES		GP	GA	SO	AVE
1957	Montreal Canadiens	1	0	0	0
1958	Montreal Canadiens	1	0	0	0
1959	Montreal Canadiens	1	1	0	1
1960	Montreal Canadiens	1	0	1	1
	TOTALS	4	1	1	2

Played with the team that won the Prince of Wales Trophy in 1957-58, 1958-59, 1959-60, 1960-61.
Played with the team that won the Stanley Cup in 1956-57, 1957-58, 1958-59, 1959-60.
Traded to the Boston Bruins for Jean-Guy Gendron in November, 1960.
Member of the famous Kid Line with Philippe Goyette at center and Claude Provost at right wing.

PRONOVOST, Claude (Suitcase)

Born in Shawinigan Falls, Quebec, July 22nd, 1935.
Goaltender, left-hand shot.
5′9″.
Last amateur team: the Montreal Canadiens jrs.

SEASON	TEAM	GP	GA	SO	AVE
1958-59	Montreal Canadiens	2	7	0	3.50
	TOTALS	2	7	0	3.50

OFFENSIVE RECORD		GP	G	A	PTS	MIP
1958-59	Montreal Canadiens	2	0	0	0	0
	TOTALS	2	0	0	0	0

Played with the team that won the Prince of Wales Trophy in 1958-59.

PROVOST, Joseph Antoine Claude (Jos)

Born in Montreal, Quebec, September 17th, 1933.
Right-winger, right-hand shot.
5′9″, 175 lb.
Last amateur team: the Montreal Canadiens jrs.

SEASON	TEAM	GP	G	A	PTS	MIP
1955-56	Montreal Canadiens	60	13	16	29	30
1956-57	Montreal Canadiens	67	16	14	30	24
1957-58	Montreal Canadiens	70	19	32	51	71
1958-59	Montreal Canadiens	69	16	22	38	37
1959-60	Montreal Canadiens	70	17	29	46	42
1960-61	Montreal Canadiens	49	11	4	15	32
1961-62	Montreal Canadiens	70	33	29	62	22
1962-63	Montreal Canadiens	67	20	30	50	26
1963-64	Montreal Canadiens	68	15	17	32	37
1964-65	Montreal Canadiens	70	27	37	64	28
1965-66	Montreal Canadiens	70	19	36	55	38
1966-67	Montreal Canadiens	64	11	13	24	16
1967-68	Montreal Canadiens	73	14	30	44	26
1968-69	Montreal Canadiens	73	13	15	28	18
1969-70	Montreal Canadiens	65	10	11	21	22
	TOTALS	1005	254	335	589	469

PLAYOFFS		GP	G	A	PTS	MIP
1955-56	Montreal Canadiens	10	3	3	6	12
1956-57	Montreal Canadiens	10	0	1	1	8
1957-58	Montreal Canadiens	10	1	3	4	8
1958-59	Montreal Canadiens	11	6	2	8	2
1959-60	Montreal Canadiens	8	1	1	2	0
1960-61	Montreal Canadiens	6	1	3	4	4
1961-62	Montreal Canadiens	6	2	2	4	2
1962-63	Montreal Canadiens	5	0	1	1	2
1963-64	Montreal Canadiens	7	2	2	4	22
1964-65	Montreal Canadiens	13	2	6	8	12
1965-66	Montreal Canadiens	10	2	3	5	2
1966-67	Montreal Canadiens	7	1	1	2	0
1967-68	Montreal Canadiens	13	2	8	10	10
1968-69	Montreal Canadiens	10	2	2	4	2
	TOTALS	126	25	38	63	86

ALL-STAR GAMES		GP	G	A	PTS
1956	Montreal Canadiens	1	0	0	0
1957	Montreal Canadiens	1	0	0	0
1958	Montreal Canadiens	1	0	2	2
1959	Montreal Canadiens	1	0	0	0
1960	Montreal Canadiens	1	1	0	1
1961	NHL All-Stars	1	0	0	0

ALL-STAR GAMES		GP	G	A	PTS
1963	NHL All-Stars	1	0	0	0
1964	NHL All-Stars	1	0	0	0
1965	Montreal Canadiens	1	0	0	0
1967	Montreal Canadiens	1	0	0	0
	TOTALS	10	1	2	3

Played with the team that won the Prince of Wales Trophy in 1955-56, 1957-58, 1958-59, 1959-60, 1960-61, 1961-62, 1963-64, 1965-66, 1967-68, 1968-69.
Played with the team that won the Stanley Cup in 1955-56, 1956-57, 1957-58, 1958-59, 1959-60, 1964-65, 1965-66, 1967-68, 1968-69.
Member of the first All-Star team in 1964-65.
Won the Bill Masterton Trophy in 1967-68.
Appointed assistant captain of the Canadiens in 1967.
Sold to the Los Angeles Kings in June, 1971.
Member of the famous Kid Line with Philippe Goyette at center and Andre Pronovost at left wing.

PUSIE, Jean-Baptiste (Jean)

Born in Montreal, Quebec, October 15th, 1910.
Defenseman, left-hand shot.
6', 205 lb.
Last amateur team: Verdun.

SEASON	TEAM	GP	G	A	PTS	MIP
1930-31	Montreal Canadiens	6	0	0	0	0
1931-32	Montreal Canadiens	1	0	0	0	0
1935-36	Montreal Canadiens	31	0	2	2	11
	TOTALS	38	0	2	2	11

PLAYOFFS		GP	G	A	PTS	MIP
1930-31	Montreal Canadiens	3	0	0	0	0
	TOTALS	3	0	0	0	0

Died April 21, 1956.

QUILTY, John Francis

Born in Ottawa, Ontario, January 21st, 1921.
Center, left-hand shot.
6', 180 lb.
Last amateur team: Glebe Collegiate jrs.

SEASON	TEAM	GP	G	A	PTS	MIP
1940-41	Montreal Canadiens	48	18	16	34	31
1941-42	Montreal Canadiens	48	12	12	24	44
1946-47	Montreal Canadiens	3	1	1	2	0
*1947-48	Montreal Canadiens/ Boston Bruins	26	5	5	10	6
	TOTALS	125	36	34	70	81

PLAYOFFS		GP	G	A	PTS	MIP
1940-41	Montreal Canadiens	3	0	2	2	0
1941-42	Montreal Canadiens	3	0	1	1	0
1946-47	Montreal Canadiens	7	3	2	5	9
	TOTALS	13	3	5	8	9

Won the Calder Trophy in 1940-41.
Won the Prince of Wales Trophy during the 1946-47 season.
Died September 12, 1969.

RAYMOND, Armand

Born in Mechanicsville, New York, January 12th, 1913.
Defenseman.

SEASON	TEAM	GP	G	A	PTS	MIP
1937-38	Montreal Canadiens	11	0	1	1	10
	TOTALS	11	0	1	1	10

RAYMOND, Paul-Marcel

Born in Montreal, Quebec, February 27th, 1913.
Right-winger, right-hand shot.
5'8", 138 lb.
Last amateur team: Canadian Pacific Railway srs.

SEASON	TEAM	GP	G	A	PTS	MIP
1932-33	Montreal Canadiens	16	0	0	0	0
1933-34	Montreal Canadiens	29	1	0	1	2
1934-35	Montreal Canadiens	20	1	1	2	0
1937-38	Montreal Canadiens	11	0	2	2	4
	TOTALS	76	2	3	5	6

PLAYOFFS		GP	G	A	PTS	MIP
1933-34	Montreal Canadiens	2	0	0	0	0
1937-38	Montreal Canadiens	3	0	0	0	2
	TOTALS	5	0	0	0	2

REARDON, Kenneth Joseph (Ken)

Born in Winnipeg, Manitoba, April 1st, 1921.
Defenseman, left-hand shot.
5'11", 180 lb.
Last amateur team: Ottawa Commandos srs.

SEASON	TEAM	GP	G	A	PTS	MIP
1940-41	Montreal Canadiens	46	2	8	10	41
1941-42	Montreal Canadiens	41	3	12	15	83
1945-46	Montreal Canadiens	43	5	4	9	45
1946-47	Montreal Canadiens	52	5	17	22	84
1947-48	Montreal Canadiens	58	7	15	22	129
1948-49	Montreal Canadiens	46	3	13	16	103
1949-50	Montreal Canadiens	67	1	27	28	109
	TOTALS	353	26	96	122	594

PLAYOFFS		GP	G	A	PTS	MIP
1940-41	Montreal Canadiens	2	0	0	0	4
1941-42	Montreal Canadiens	3	0	0	0	4
1945-46	Montreal Canadiens	9	1	1	2	4
1946-47	Montreal Canadiens	7	1	2	3	20
1948-49	Montreal Canadiens	7	0	0	0	18
1949-50	Montreal Canadiens	2	0	2	2	12
	TOTALS	30	2	5	7	62

Played with the team that won the Prince of Wales Trophy in 1945-46, 1946-47.
Played with the team that won the Stanley Cup in 1945-46.
Member of the first All-Star team in 1946-47, 1949-50.
Member of the second All-Star team in 1945-46, 1947-48, 1948-49.
Appointed assistant captain of the Canadiens in 1949.
Brother of Terry Reardon.
Member of the Hockey Hall of Fame in June, 1966.

REARDON, Terrance George (Terry)

Born in Winnipeg, Manitoba, April 6th, 1919.
Defenseman, right-winger.
5'10", 170 lb.
Last amateur team: the Brandon Wheat Kings jrs.

SEASON	TEAM	GP	G	A	PTS	MIP
1941-42	Montreal Canadiens	33	17	17	34	24
1942-43	Montreal Canadiens	13	6	6	12	2
	TOTALS	46	23	23	46	26

PLAYOFFS		GP	G	A	PTS	MIP
1941-42	Montreal Canadiens	3	2	2	4	2
	TOTALS	3	2	2	4	2

Obtained from the Boston Bruins for Paul Gauthier.
Brother of Ken Reardon.

REAUME, Marc Avellin

Born in Lasalle, Ontario, February 7th, 1934.
Defenseman, left-hand shot.
6'1", 185 lb.
Last amateur team: the St. Michaels College jrs.

SEASON	TEAM	GP	G	A	PTS	MIP
1963-64	Montreal Canadiens	3	0	0	0	2
	TOTALS	3	0	0	0	2

Played with the team that won the Prince of Wales Trophy in 1963-64.

REAY, William (Bill)

Born in Winnipeg, Manitoba, August 21st, 1918.
Center, left-hand shot.
5'7", 155 lb.
Last amateur team: the Quebec Aces srs.

SEASON	TEAM	GP	G	A	PTS	MIP
1945-46	Montreal Canadiens	44	17	12	29	10
1946-47	Montreal Canadiens	59	22	20	42	17
1947-48	Montreal Canadiens	60	6	14	20	24
1948-49	Montreal Canadiens	60	22	23	45	33
1949-50	Montreal Canadiens	68	19	26	45	48
1950-51	Montreal Canadiens	60	6	18	24	24
1951-52	Montreal Canadiens	68	7	34	41	20
1952-53	Montreal Canadiens	56	4	15	19	26
	TOTALS	475	103	162	265	202

PLAYOFFS		GP	G	A	PTS	MIP
1945-46	Montreal Canadiens	9	1	2	3	4
1946-47	Montreal Canadiens	11	6	1	7	14
1948-49	Montreal Canadiens	7	1	5	6	4
1949-50	Montreal Canadiens	4	0	1	1	0
1950-51	Montreal Canadiens	11	3	3	6	10
1951-52	Montreal Canadiens	10	2	2	4	7
1952-53	Montreal Canadiens	11	0	2	2	4
	TOTALS	63	13	16	29	43

ALL-STAR GAMES		GP	G	A	PTS
1952	NHL All-Stars	1	0	0	0
	TOTALS	1	0	0	0

Played with the team that won the Prince of Wales Trophy in 1945-46, 1946-47.
Played with the team that won the Stanley Cup in 1945-46, 1952-53.
Appointed assistant captain of the Canadiens in 1948.
Member of the second All-Star Team in 1952.

REDMOND, Michael Edward (Mickey)

Born in Kirkland Lake, Ontario, December 27th, 1947.
Right-winger, right-hand shot.
5'11", 185 lbs.
Last amateur team: the Peterborough Petes jrs.

SEASON	TEAM	GP	G	A	PTS	MIP
1967-68	Montreal Canadiens	41	6	5	11	4
1968-69	Montreal Canadiens	65	9	15	24	12
1969-70	Montreal Canadiens	75	27	27	54	61
1970-71	Montreal Canadiens	40	14	16	30	35
	TOTALS	221	56	63	119	112

PLAYOFFS		GP	G	A	PTS	MIP
1967-68	Montreal Canadiens	2	0	0	0	0
1968-69	Montreal Canadiens	14	2	3	5	2
	TOTALS	16	2	3	5	2

Played with the team that won the Prince of Wales Trophy in 1967-68, 1968-69.
Played with the team that won the Stanley Cup in 1967-68, 1968-69.
Traded to the Detroit Red Wings with Guy Charron and Bill Collins for Frank Mahovlich, January 13, 1971.
Brother of Dick Redmond of the Chicago Black Hawks.

RHEAUME, Herbert (Herb)

Goaltender.

SEASON	TEAM	GP	GA	SO	AVE
1925-26	Montreal Canadiens	30	92	0	3.07
	TOTALS	30	92	0	3.07

OFFENSIVE RECORD		GP	G	A	PTS	MIP
1925-26	Montreal Canadiens	30	0	0	0	0
	TOTALS	30	0	0	0	0

RICHARD, Joseph Henri (Pocket Rocket)

Born in Montreal, Quebec, February 29th, 1936.
Center, right-hand shot.
5'7", 160 lb.
Last amateur team: the Montreal Canadiens jrs.

SEASON	TEAM	GP	G	A	PTS	MIP
1955-56	Montreal Canadiens	64	19	21	40	46
1956-57	Montreal Canadiens	63	18	36	54	71
1957-58	Montreal Canadiens	67	28	52	80	56
1958-59	Montreal Canadiens	63	21	30	51	33
1959-60	Montreal Canadiens	70	30	43	73	66
1960-61	Montreal Canadiens	70	24	44	68	91
1961-62	Montreal Canadiens	54	21	29	50	48
1962-63	Montreal Canadiens	67	23	50	73	57
1963-64	Montreal Canadiens	66	14	39	53	73
1964-65	Montreal Canadiens	53	23	29	52	43
1965-66	Montreal Canadiens	62	22	39	61	47
1966-67	Montreal Canadiens	65	21	34	55	28
1967-68	Montreal Canadiens	54	9	19	28	16
1968-69	Montreal Canadiens	64	15	37	52	45
1969-70	Montreal Canadiens	62	16	36	52	61
1970-71	Montreal Canadiens	75	12	37	49	46
1971-72	Montreal Canadiens	75	12	32	44	48
1972-73	Montreal Canadiens	71	8	35	43	21
1973-74	Montreal Canadiens	75	19	36	55	28
1974-75	Montreal Canadiens	16	3	10	13	4
	TOTALS	1256	358	688	1046	928

PLAYOFFS		GP	G	A	PTS	MIP
1955-56	Montreal Canadiens	10	4	4	8	21
1956-57	Montreal Canadiens	10	2	6	8	10
1957-58	Montreal Canadiens	10	1	7	8	11
1958-59	Montreal Canadiens	11	3	8	11	13
1959-60	Montreal Canadiens	8	3	9	12	9
1960-61	Montreal Canadiens	6	2	4	6	22
1962-63	Montreal Canadiens	5	1	1	2	2
1963-64	Montreal Canadiens	7	1	1	2	9
1964-65	Montreal Canadiens	13	7	4	11	24
1965-66	Montreal Canadiens	8	1	4	5	2
1966-67	Montreal Canadiens	10	4	6	10	2
1967-68	Montreal Canadiens	13	4	4	8	4
1968-69	Montreal Canadiens	14	2	4	6	8
1970-71	Montreal Canadiens	20	5	7	12	20
1971-72	Montreal Canadiens	6	0	3	3	4
1972-73	Montreal Canadiens	17	6	4	10	14
1973-74	Montreal Canadiens	6	2	2	4	2
1974-75	Montreal Canadiens	6	1	2	3	4
	TOTALS	180	49	80	129	181

ALL-STAR GAMES		GP	G	A	PTS
1956	Montreal Canadiens	1	0	0	0
1957	Montreal Canadiens	1	0	1	1
1958	Montreal Canadiens	1	1	2	3
1959	Montreal Canadiens	1	1	1	2
1960	Montreal Canadiens	1	0	0	0
1961	NHL All-Stars	1	0	0	0
1963	NHL All-Stars	1	1	0	1
1965	Montreal Canadiens	1	0	0	0
1967	Montreal Canadiens	1	1	1	2
	TOTALS	9	4	5	9

Played with the team that won the Prince of Wales Trophy in 1955-56, 1957-58, 1958-59, 1959-60, 1960-61, 1961-62, 1963-64, 1965-66, 1967-68, 1968-69, 1972-73.
Played with the team that won the Stanley Cup in 1955-56, 1956-57, 1957-58, 1958-59, 1959-60, 1964-65, 1965-66, 1967-68, 1968-69, 1970-71, 1972-73.
Appointed assistant captain in 1963 and captain in 1971 (1971-75).
Won the Bill Masterton Trophy in 1973-74.
Member of the first All-Star team in 1957-58.
Member of the second All-Star team in 1958-59, 1960-61, 1962-63.
Brother of Maurice Richard.

RICHARD, Joseph Henri Maurice (Rocket)

Born in Montreal, Quebec, August 4th, 1921.
Right-winger, left-hand shot.
5'10", 195 lb.
Last amateur team: the Montreal Canadiens srs.

SEASON	TEAM	GP	G	A	PTS	MIP
1942-43	Montreal Canadiens	16	5	6	11	4
1943-44	Montreal Canadiens	46	32	22	54	45
1944-45	Montreal Canadiens	50	50	23	73	46
1945-46	Montreal Canadiens	50	27	21	48	50
1946-47	Montreal Canadiens	60	45	26	71	69
1947-48	Montreal Canadiens	53	28	25	53	89
1948-49	Montreal Canadiens	59	20	18	38	110
1949-50	Montreal Canadiens	70	43	22	65	114
1950-51	Montreal Canadiens	65	42	24	66	97
1951-52	Montreal Canadiens	48	27	17	44	44
1952-53	Montreal Canadiens	70	28	33	61	112
1953-54	Montreal Canadiens	70	37	30	67	112
1954-55	Montreal Canadiens	67	38	36	74	125
1955-56	Montreal Canadiens	70	38	33	71	89
1956-57	Montreal Canadiens	63	33	29	62	74
1957-58	Montreal Canadiens	28	15	19	34	28
1958-59	Montreal Canadiens	42	17	21	38	27
1959-60	Montreal Canadiens	51	19	16	35	50
	TOTALS	978	544	421	965	1285

PLAYOFFS		GP	G	A	PTS	MIP
1943-44	Montreal Canadiens	9	12	5	17	10
1944-45	Montreal Canadiens	6	6	2	8	10
1945-46	Montreal Canadiens	9	7	4	11	15
1946-47	Montreal Canadiens	10	6	5	11	44
1948-49	Montreal Canadiens	7	2	1	3	14
1949-50	Montreal Canadiens	5	1	1	2	6
1950-51	Montreal Canadiens	11	9	4	13	13
1951-52	Montreal Canadiens	11	4	2	6	6
1952-53	Montreal Canadiens	12	7	1	8	2
1953-54	Montreal Canadiens	11	3	0	3	22
1955-56	Montreal Canadiens	10	5	9	14	24
1956-57	Montreal Canadiens	10	8	3	11	8
1957-58	Montreal Canadiens	10	11	4	15	10
1958-59	Montreal Canadiens	4	0	0	0	2
1959-60	Montreal Canadiens	8	1	3	4	2
	TOTALS	133	82	44	126	188

ALL-STAR GAMES		GP	G	A	PTS
1947	NHL All-Stars	1	1	1	2
1948	NHL All-Stars	1	0	1	1
1949	NHL All-Stars	1	0	0	0
1950	NHL All-Stars	1	0	0	0
1951	NHL All-Stars	1	0	0	0
1952	NHL All-Stars	1	1	0	1
1953	Montreal Canadiens	1	1	0	1
1954	NHL All-Stars	1	0	0	0
1955	NHL All-Stars	1	0	0	0
1956	Montreal Canadiens	1	1	0	1
1957	Montreal Canadiens	1	1	0	1
1958	Montreal Canadiens	1	2	0	2
1959	Montreal Canadiens	1	0	0	0
	TOTALS	13	7	2	9

Played with the team that won the Prince of Wales Trophy in 1943-44, 1944-45, 1945-46, 1946-47, 1955-56, 1957-58, 1958-59, 1959-60.
Played with the team that won the Stanley Cup in 1943-44, 1945-46, 1952-53, 1955-56, 1956-57, 1957-58, 1958-59, 1959-60.
Member of the first All-Star team in 1944-45, 1945-46, 1946-47, 1947-48, 1948-49, 1949-50, 1954-55, 1955-56.
Member of the second All-Star team in 1943-44, 1950-51, 1951-52, 1952-53, 1953-54, 1956-57.
Won the Hart Trophy in 1946-47.
Appointed assistant captain in 1952 and captain in 1956 (1956-60).
Member of the famous Punch Line with Elmer Lach at center and Toe Blake at left wing.
Brother of Henri Richard.
Member of the Hockey Hall of Fame in June, 1961.

RILEY John (Jack)

Born in Berckenia, Ireland, December 29th, 1910.
Center, left-hand shot.
5'11", 160 lb.
Last amateur team: the Vancouver King George jrs.

SEASON	TEAM	GP	G	A	PTS	MIP
1933-34	Montreal Canadiens	48	6	11	17	4
1934-35	Montreal Canadiens	47	4	11	15	4
	TOTALS	95	10	22	32	8

PLAYOFFS		GP	G	A	PTS	MIP
1933-34	Montreal Canadiens	2	0	1	1	0
1934-35	Montreal Canadiens	2	0	2	2	0
	TOTALS	4	0	3	3	0

RIOPELLE, Howard Joseph (Howie, Rip)

Born in Ottawa, Ontario, January 30th, 1922.
Left-winger, left-hand shot.
5'11", 165 lb.
Last amateur team: the Montreal Royal srs.

SEASON	TEAM	GP	G	A	PTS	MIP
1947-48	Montreal Canadiens	55	5	2	7	12
1948-49	Montreal Canadiens	48	10	6	16	34
1949-50	Montreal Canadiens	66	12	8	20	27
	TOTALS	169	27	16	43	73

PLAYOFFS		GP	G	A	PTS	MIP
1948-49	Montreal Canadiens	7	1	1	2	2
1949-50	Montreal Canadiens	1	0	0	0	0
	TOTALS	8	1	1	2	2

RISEBROUGH, Douglas (Doug)

Born in Guelph, Ontario, January 29th, 1954.
Center, left-hand shot.
5'11", 180 lb.
Last amateur team: the Kitchener Rangers jrs.

SEASON	TEAM	GP	G	A	PTS	MIP
1974-75	Montreal Canadiens	64	15	32	47	198
1975-76	Montreal Canadiens	80	16	28	44	180
1976-77	Montreal Canadiens	78	22	38	60	132
1977-78	Montreal Canadiens	72	18	23	41	97
1978-79	Montreal Canadiens	48	10	15	25	62
1979-80	Montreal Canadiens	44	8	10	18	81
	TOTALS	386	89	146	235	750

PLAYOFFS		GP	G	A	PTS	MIP
1974-75	Montreal Canadiens	11	3	5	8	37
1975-76	Montreal Canadiens	13	0	3	3	30
1976-77	Montreal Canadiens	12	2	3	5	16
1977-78	Montreal Canadiens	15	2	2	4	17
1978-79	Montreal Canadiens	15	1	6	7	32
	TOTALS	66	8	19	27	132

Second Amateur Draft choice of the Canadiens in 1974.
Played with the team that won the Prince of Wales Trophy in 1975-76, 1976-77, 1977-78.
Played with the team that won the Stanley Cup in 1975-76, 1976-77, 1977-78, 1978-79.

RITCHIE, David (Dave)

Defenseman.

SEASON	TEAM	GP	G	A	PTS	MIP
1920-21	Montreal Canadiens	5	0	0	0	—
1924-25	Montreal Canadiens	5	0	0	0	0
1925-26	Montreal Canadiens	2	0	0	0	0
	TOTALS	12	0	0	0	0

PLAYOFFS		GP	G	A	PTS	MIP
1924-25	Montreal Canadiens	1	0	—	0	—
	TOTALS	1	0	—	0	—

Played with the team that won the Prince of Wales Trophy in 1924-25.

RIVERS, George (Gus)

Born in Winnipeg, Manitoba, November 19th, 1909.
5'11", 160 lb.
Last amateur team: the Winnipeg jrs.

SEASON	TEAM	GP	G	A	PTS	MIP
1929-30	Montreal Canadiens	19	1	0	1	2
1930-31	Montreal Canadiens	44	2	5	7	6
1931-32	Montreal Canadiens	25	1	0	1	4
	TOTALS	88	4	5	9	12

PLAYOFFS		GP	G	A	PTS	MIP
1929-30	Montreal Canadiens	6	1	0	1	2
1930-31	Montreal Canadiens	10	1	0	1	0
	TOTALS	16	2	0	2	2

Played with the team that won the Stanley Cup in 1930-31.

ROBERT, Claude

Born in Montreal, Quebec, August 10th, 1928.
Left-winger, center, left-hand shot.
5'11", 175 lb.
Last amateur team: the Chicoutimi Sagueneens srs.

SEASON	TEAM	GP	G	A	PTS	MIP
1950-51	Montreal Canadiens	23	1	0	1	9
	TOTALS	23	1	0	1	9

ROBERTO, Phillip Joseph (Phil)

Born in Niagara Falls, Ontario, January 1st, 1949.
Right-winger, right-hand shot.
6'1", 190 lb.
Last amateur team: the Niagara Falls Flyers jrs.

SEASON	TEAM	GP	G	A	PTS	MIP
1969-70	Montreal Canadiens	8	0	1	1	8
1970-71	Montreal Canadiens	39	14	7	21	21
1971-72	Montreal Canadiens	27	3	2	5	22
	TOTALS	74	17	10	27	51

PLAYOFFS		GP	G	A	PTS	MIP
1970-71	Montreal Canadiens	15	0	1	1	36
	TOTALS	15	0	1	1	36

Played with the team that won the Stanley Cup in 1970-71.
Traded to the St. Louis Blues for Jim Roberts, December 13, 1971.

ROBERTS, James Wilfred (Jim)

Born in Toronto, Ontario, April 9th, 1940.
Defenseman, right-winger, right-hand shot.
5'10", 185 lb.
Last amateur team: Peterborough Petes jrs.

SEASON	TEAM	GP	G	A	PTS	MIP
1963-64	Montreal Canadiens	15	0	1	1	2
1964-65	Montreal Canadiens	70	3	10	13	40
1965-66	Montreal Canadiens	70	5	5	10	20
1966-67	Montreal Canadiens	63	3	0	3	16
1971-72	Montreal Canadiens	51	7	15	22	49
1972-73	Montreal Canadiens	77	14	18	32	28
1973-74	Montreal Canadiens	67	8	16	24	39
1974-75	Montreal Canadiens	79	5	13	18	52
1975-76	Montreal Canadiens	74	13	8	21	35
1976-77	Montreal Canadiens	45	5	14	19	18
	TOTALS	611	63	100	163	299

PLAYOFFS		GP	G	A	PTS	MIP
1963-64	Montreal Canadiens	7	0	1	1	14
1964-65	Montreal Canadiens	13	0	0	0	30
1965-66	Montreal Canadiens	10	1	1	2	10
1966-67	Montreal Canadiens	4	1	0	1	0
1971-72	Montreal Canadiens	6	1	0	1	0
1972-73	Montreal Canadiens	17	0	2	2	22
1973-74	Montreal Canadiens	6	0	0	0	4
1974-75	Montreal Canadiens	11	2	2	4	2
1975-76	Montreal Canadiens	13	3	1	4	2
1976-77	Montreal Canadiens	14	3	0	3	6
	TOTALS	101	11	7	18	90

Played on team that won the Prince of Wales Trophy in 1964-65, 1965-66, 1972-73, 1975-76 and 1976-77.
Played on team that won the Stanley Cup in 1964-65, 1965-66, 1972-73, 1975-76 and 1976-77.
Drafted by St. Louis from Montreal in the Expansion Draft, June 6, 1967. Traded to Montreal by St. Louis for Phil Roberto, December 13, 1971. Traded to St. Louis by Montreal for St. Louis' 3rd round 1979 Amateur Draft choice, August 18, 1977.

ROBERTSON, George Thomas

Born in Winnipeg, Manitoba, May 11th, 1928.
Center, left-hand shot.
6'1", 172 lb.
Last amateur team: the Montreal Royals srs.

SEASON	TEAM	GP	G	A	PTS	MIP
1947-48	Montreal Canadiens	1	0	0	0	0
1948-49	Montreal Canadiens	30	2	5	7	6
	TOTALS	31	2	5	7	6

ROBINSON, Earl Henry (Earle)

Born in Montreal, Quebec, March 11th, 1907.
Right-winger, right-hand shot.
5'10", 160 lb.
Last amateur team: the Montreal Victorias srs.

SEASON	TEAM	GP	G	A	PTS	MIP
1939-40	Montreal Canadiens	11	1	4	5	4
	TOTALS	11	1	4	5	4

ROBINSON, Larry Clark

Born in Winchester, Ontario, June 2nd, 1951.
Defenseman, left-hand shot.
6'3", 210 lb.
Last amateur team: the Kitchener Rangers jrs.

SEASON	TEAM	GP	G	A	PTS	MIP
1972-73	Montreal Canadiens	36	2	4	6	20
1973-74	Montreal Canadiens	78	6	20	26	66
1974-75	Montreal Canadiens	80	14	47	61	76
1975-76	Montreal Canadiens	80	10	30	40	59
1976-77	Montreal Canadiens	77	19	66	85	45
1977-78	Montreal Canadiens	80	13	52	65	39
1978-79	Montreal Canadiens	67	16	45	61	33
1979-80	Montreal Canadiens	72	14	61	75	39
	TOTALS	570	94	325	419	377

PLAYOFFS		GP	G	A	PTS	MIP
1972-73	Montreal Canadiens	11	1	4	5	9
1973-74	Montreal Canadiens	6	0	1	1	26
1974-75	Montreal Canadiens	11	0	4	4	27
1975-76	Montreal Canadiens	13	3	3	6	10
1976-77	Montreal Canadiens	14	2	10	12	12
1977-78	Montreal Canadiens	15	4	17	21	6
1978-79	Montreal Canadiens	16	6	9	15	8
1979-80	Montreal Canadiens	10	0	4	4	2
	TOTALS	96	16	52	68	100

Fourth Amateur Draft choice of the Canadiens in 1971.
Played with the team that won the Prince of Wales Trophy in 1972-73, 1975-76, 1976-77, 1977-78.
Played with the team that won the Stanley Cup in 1972-73, 1975-76, 1976-77, 1977-78, 1978-79.
Won the James Norris Trophy in 1976-77, 1979-80.
Member of the second All-Star team in 1977-78.
Won the Conn Smythe Trophy in 1977-78.
Member of the first All-Star team in 1976-77, 1978-79, 1979-80.

ROBINSON, Morris (Moe)

Born in Winchester, Ontario, May 29th, 1957.
Defenseman, right-hand shot.
6'3", 190 lb.
Last amateur team: Nova Scotia (AHL).

SEASON	TEAM	GP	G	A	PTS	MIP
1979-80	Montreal Canadiens	1	0	0	0	0
	TOTALS	1	0	0	0	0

ROCHE, Ernest Charles (Ernie)

Born in Montreal, Quebec, February 4th, 1930.
Defenseman, left-hand shot.
6'1", 170 lb.
Last amateur team: the Montreal Canadiens jrs.

SEASON	TEAM	GP	G	A	PTS	MIP
1950-51	Montreal Canadiens	4	0	0	0	2
	TOTALS	4	0	0	0	2

ROCHE, Michael Patrick Desmond (Des)

Born in Kemptville, Ontario, February 1st, 1909.
Right-winger, right-hand shot.
5'7", 188 lb.
Last amateur team: MAAA srs.

SEASON	TEAM	GP	G	A	PTS	MIP
*1934-35	Detroit Red Wings/ St. Louis Eagles/ Montreal Canadiens	27	3	1	4	10
	TOTALS	27	3	1	4	10

ROCHEFORT, Leon Joseph Fernand

Born in Cap-de-la-Madeleine, Quebec, May 4th, 1939.
Right-winger, right-hand shot.
6', 185 lb.
Last amateur team: the Guelph Biltmores jrs.

SEASON	TEAM	GP	G	A	PTS	MIP
1963-64	Montreal Canadiens	3	0	0	0	0
1964-65	Montreal Canadiens	9	2	0	2	0
1965-66	Montreal Canadiens	1	0	1	1	0
1966-67	Montreal Canadiens	27	9	7	16	6
1970-71	Montreal Canadiens	57	5	10	15	4
	TOTALS	97	16	18	34	10

PLAYOFFS		GP	G	A	PTS	MIP
1965-66	Montreal Canadiens	4	1	1	2	4
1966-67	Montreal Canadiens	10	1	1	2	4
1970-71	Montreal Canadiens	10	0	0	0	6
	TOTALS	24	2	2	4	14

Obtained from the New York Rangers with Dave Balon, Len Ronson and Lorne Worsley for Philippe Goyette, Jacques Plante and Don Marshall, June 4, 1963.
Played with the team that won the Prince of Wales Trophy in 1963-64, 1965-66.
Played with the team that won the Stanley Cup in 1965-66, 1970-71.
Drafted by the Philadelphia Flyers during the 1967 Expansion, June 6, 1967.
Obtained from the Los Angeles Kings with Wayne Thomas and Greg Boddy for Larry Mickey, Lucien Grenier and Jack Norris, May 22, 1970.
Traded to the Detroit Red Wings for Kerry Ketter and a certain amount of money, May 25, 1971.

ROCHON, J.

SEASON	TEAM	GP	G	A	PTS	MIP
1916-17	Montreal Canadiens	1	0	—	0	—
	TOTALS	1	0	—	0	—

RONAN, Erskine (Skene, Skein)

Forward.

SEASON	TEAM	GP	G	A	PTS	MIP
*1915-16	Montreal Canadiens/ Toronto	17	6	—	6	—
	TOTALS	17	6	—	6	—

PLAYOFFS		GP	G	A	PTS	MIP
1915-16	Montreal Canadiens	2	1	—	1	—
	TOTALS	2	1	—	1	—

Played with the team that won the Stanley Cup in 1915-16.

RONTY, Paul

Born in Toronto, Ontario, June 12th, 1928.
Center, left-hand shot.
6', 160 lb.
Last amateur team: the Boston Olympics srs.

SEASON	TEAM	GP	G	A	PTS	MIP
*1954-55	New York Rangers/ Montreal Canadiens	59	4	11	15	10
	TOTALS	59	4	11	15	10

PLAYOFFS		GP	G	A	PTS	MIP
1954-55	Montreal Canadiens	5	0	0	0	2
	TOTALS	5	0	0	0	2

ALL-STAR GAMES		GP	G	A	PTS
1954	NHL All-Stars	1	0	0	0
	TOTALS	1	0	0	0

ROSSIGNOL, Roland

Born in Edmundston, New Brunswick, October 18th, 1921.
Right-winger, right-hand shot.
5'9", 165 lb.
Last amateur team: the Quebec Aces srs.

SEASON	TEAM	GP	G	A	PTS	MIP
1944-45	Montreal Canadiens	5	2	2	4	2
	TOTALS	5	2	2	4	2
PLAYOFFS		GP	G	A	PTS	MIP
1944-45	Montreal Canadiens	1	0	0	0	2
	TOTALS	1	0	0	0	2

Played with the team that won the Prince of Wales Trophy in 1944-45.

ROTA, Randy Frank

Born in Creston, British Columbia, August 16th, 1950.
Left-winger, left-hand shot.
5'8", 170 lb.
Last amateur team: the Calgary Centennials jrs.

SEASON	TEAM	GP	G	A	PTS	MIP
1972-73	Montreal Canadiens	2	1	1	2	0
	TOTALS	2	1	1	2	0

Played with the team that won the Prince of Wales Trophy in 1972-73.
Traded to the Los Angeles Kings with Bob Murdoch for the first Amateur Draft choice of 1974 (Mario Tremblay) and a certain amount of money, May 29, 1973.
Cousin of Darcy Rota of the Chicago Black Hawks.

ROUSSEAU, Guy

Born in Montreal, Quebec, December 21st, 1934.
Left-winger, left-hand shot.
5'6", 140 lb.
Last amateur team: the Quebec Frontenacs jrs.

SEASON	TEAM	GP	G	A	PTS	MIP
1954-55	Montreal Canadiens	2	0	1	1	0
1956-57	Montreal Canadiens	2	0	0	0	2
	TOTALS	4	0	1	1	2

ROUSSEAU, Joseph Jean-Paul Robert (Bobby)

Born in Montreal, Quebec, July 26th, 1940.
Right-winger, right-hand shot.
5'10", 178 lb.
Last amateur team: the Montreal Canadiens jrs.

SEASON	TEAM	GP	G	A	PTS	MIP
1960-61	Montreal Canadiens	15	1	2	3	4
1961-62	Montreal Canadiens	70	21	24	45	26
1962-63	Montreal Canadiens	62	19	18	37	15
1963-64	Montreal Canadiens	70	25	31	56	32
1964-65	Montreal Canadiens	66	12	35	47	26
1965-66	Montreal Canadiens	70	30	48	78	20
1966-67	Montreal Canadiens	68	19	44	63	58
1967-68	Montreal Canadiens	74	19	46	65	47
1968-69	Montreal Canadiens	76	30	40	70	59
1969-70	Montreal Canadiens	72	24	34	58	30
	TOTALS	643	200	322	522	317
PLAYOFFS		GP	G	A	PTS	MIP
1961-62	Montreal Canadiens	6	0	2	2	0
1962-63	Montreal Canadiens	5	0	1	1	2
1963-64	Montreal Canadiens	7	1	1	2	2
1964-65	Montreal Canadiens	13	5	8	13	24
1965-66	Montreal Canadiens	10	4	4	8	6
1966-67	Montreal Canadiens	10	1	7	8	4
1967-68	Montreal Canadiens	13	2	4	6	8
1968-69	Montreal Canadiens	14	3	2	5	8
	TOTALS	78	16	29	45	54

ALL-STAR GAMES		GP	G	A	PTS
1965	Montreal Canadiens	1	0	1	1
1967	Montreal Canadiens	1	0	2	2
1969	NHL All-Stars (Div. East)	1	0	1	1
	TOTALS	3	0	4	4

Played with the team that won the Prince of Wales Trophy in 1960-61, 1961-62, 1963-64, 1965-66, 1967-68, 1968-69.
Played with the team that won the Stanley Cup in 1964-65, 1965-66, 1967-68, 1968-69.
Won the Calder Trophy in 1961-62.
Member of the second All-Star team in 1965-66.
Traded to the Minnesota North Stars for Claude Larose, June 10, 1970.

ROUSSEAU, Roland

Born in Montreal, Quebec, December 1st, 1929.
Defenseman, left-hand shot.
5'8", 160 lb.
Last amateur team: the Montreal Royals srs.

SEASON	TEAM	GP	G	A	PTS	MIP
1952-53	Montreal Canadiens	2	0	0	0	0
	TOTALS	2	0	0	0	0

ROY, ?

PLAYOFFS		GP	G	A	PTS	MIP
1916-17	Montreal Canadiens	1	0	—	0	—
	TOTALS	1	0	—	0	—

RUNGE, Paul

Born in Edmonton, Alberta, September 10th, 1908.
Left-winger, left-hand shot.
5'11", 167 lb.

SEASON	TEAM	GP	G	A	PTS	MIP
1934-35	Montreal Canadiens	3	0	0	0	2
*1935-36	Montreal Canadiens/ Boston Bruins	45	8	4	12	18
*1936-37	Montreal Canadiens/ Montreal Maroons	34	5	10	15	8
	TOTALS	82	13	14	27	28

Traded to the Montreal Maroons for Bill MacKenzie (1936-37).

ST. LAURENT, Dollard Herve

Born in Verdun, Quebec, May 12, 1929.
Defenseman, left-hand shot.
5'11", 180 lb.
Last amateur team: the Montreal Royals srs.

SEASON	TEAM	GP	G	A	PTS	MIP
1950-51	Montreal Canadiens	3	0	0	0	0
1951-52	Montreal Canadiens	40	3	10	13	30
1952-53	Montreal Canadiens	54	2	6	8	34
1953-54	Montreal Canadiens	53	3	12	15	43
1954-55	Montreal Canadiens	58	3	14	17	24
1955-56	Montreal Canadiens	46	4	9	13	58
1956-57	Montreal Canadiens	64	1	11	12	49
1957-58	Montreal Canadiens	65	3	20	23	68
	TOTALS	383	19	82	101	306
PLAYOFFS		GP	G	A	PTS	MIP
1951-52	Montreal Canadiens	9	0	3	3	6
1952-53	Montreal Canadiens	12	0	3	3	4
1953-54	Montreal Canadiens	10	1	2	3	8
1954-55	Montreal Canadiens	12	0	5	5	12
1955-56	Montreal Canadiens	4	0	0	0	2
1956-57	Montreal Canadiens	7	0	1	1	13
1957-58	Montreal Canadiens	5	0	0	0	10
	TOTALS	59	1	14	15	55

ALL-STAR GAMES		GP	G	A	PTS
1953	Montreal Canadiens	1	0	0	0
1956	Montreal Canadiens	1	0	0	0
1957	Montreal Canadiens	1	0	0	0
1958	Montreal Canadiens	1	0	0	0
	TOTALS	4	0	0	0

Played with the team that won the Prince of Wales Trophy in 1955-56, 1957-58.
Played with the team that won the Stanley Cup in 1952-53, 1955-56, 1956-57, 1957-58.
Sold to the Chicago Black Hawks in June, 1958.

SANDS, Charles Henry (Charlie)

Born in Fort William, Ontario, March 23rd, 1911.
Center, right-winger, right-hand shot.
5'9", 160 lb.

SEASON	TEAM	GP	G	A	PTS	MIP
1939-40	Montreal Canadiens	47	9	20	29	10
1940-41	Montreal Canadiens	43	5	13	18	4
1941-42	Montreal Canadiens	39	11	16	27	6
1942-43	Montreal Canadiens	31	3	9	12	0
	TOTALS	160	28	58	86	20
PLAYOFFS		GP	G	A	PTS	MIP
1940-41	Montreal Canadiens	2	1	0	1	0
1941-42	Montreal Canadiens	3	0	1	1	2
1942-43	Montreal Canadiens	2	0	0	0	0
	TOTALS	7	1	1	2	2

GOALTENDER RECORD		GP	GA	SO	AVE
1939-40	Montreal Canadiens	1	5	0	60.00
	TOTALS	1	5	0	60.00

Obtained from the Boston Bruins with Ray Getliffe for Herb Cain and Desse Smith in 1939.
Replaced Wilf Cude with only 5 minutes left in the February 22, 1940 game against the Chicago Black Hawks.
Traded to the New York Rangers for Phil Watson and "Dutch" Hiller in 1943.

SATHER, Glen Cameron (Slats)

Born in High River, Alberta, September 2nd, 1943.
Left-winger, left-hand shot.
5'11", 180 lb.
Last amateur team: the Edmonton Oil Kings jrs.

SEASON	TEAM	GP	G	A	PTS	MIP
1974-75	Montreal Canadiens	63	6	10	16	44
	TOTALS	63	6	10	16	44
PLAYOFFS		GP	G	A	PTS	MIP
1974-75	Montreal Canadiens	11	1	1	2	4
	TOTALS	11	1	1	2	4

Obtained from the St. Louis Blues to complete the transaction which sent Rick Wilson and the fifth Amateur Draft choice of 1974 (Don Wheldon) for Glen and the fourth Amateur Draft choice of 1974 (Barry Legge), May 27, 1974.
Traded to the Minnesota North Stars for a certain amount of money and the third Amateur Draft choice of 1977, July 9, 1975.

SAVAGE, Gordon (Tony)

Born in Calgary, Alberta, July 18th, 1906.
Defenseman, left-hand shot.
5'11", 170 lb.
Last amateur team: the Calgary Canadiens jrs.

SEASON	TEAM	GP	G	A	PTS	MIP
*1934-35	Montreal Canadiens/ Boston Bruins	49	1	5	6	6
	TOTALS	49	1	5	6	6
PLAYOFFS		GP	G	A	PTS	MIP
1934-35	Montreal Canadiens	2	0	0	0	0
	TOTALS	2	0	0	0	0

Obtained from the Boston Bruins for Arthur Gagne in 1934.

SAVARD, Serge A.

Born in Montreal, Quebec, January 22nd, 1946.
Defenseman, left-hand shot.
6'2", 210 lb.
Last amateur team: the Montreal Canadiens jrs. (OHA).

SEASON	TEAM	GP	G	A	PTS	MIP
1966-67	Montreal Canadiens	2	0	0	0	0
1967-68	Montreal Canadiens	67	2	13	15	34
1968-69	Montreal Canadiens	74	8	23	31	73
1969-70	Montreal Canadiens	64	12	19	31	38

SEASON	TEAM	GP	G	A	PTS	MIP
1970-71	Montreal Canadiens	37	5	10	15	30
1971-72	Montreal Canadiens	23	1	8	9	16
1972-73	Montreal Canadiens	74	7	32	39	58
1973-74	Montreal Canadiens	67	4	14	18	49
1974-75	Montreal Canadiens	80	20	40	60	64
1975-76	Montreal Canadiens	71	8	39	47	38
1976-77	Montreal Canadiens	78	9	33	42	35
1977-78	Montreal Canadiens	77	8	34	42	24
1978-79	Montreal Canadiens	80	7	26	33	30
1979-80	Montreal Canadiens	46	5	8	13	18
	TOTALS	840	96	299	395	507

PLAYOFFS		GP	G	A	PTS	MIP
1967-68	Montreal Canadiens	6	2	0	2	0
1968-69	Montreal Canadiens	14	4	6	10	24
1971-72	Montreal Canadiens	6	0	0	0	10
1972-73	Montreal Canadiens	17	3	8	11	22
1973-74	Montreal Canadiens	6	1	1	2	4
1974-75	Montreal Canadiens	11	1	7	8	2
1975-76	Montreal Canadiens	13	3	6	9	6
1976-77	Montreal Canadiens	14	2	7	9	2
1977-78	Montreal Canadiens	15	1	7	8	8
1978-79	Montreal Canadiens	16	2	7	9	6
1979-80	Montreal Canadiens	2	0	0	0	0
	TOTALS	120	19	49	68	84

ALL-STAR GAMES		GP	G	A	PTS
1970	NHL All-Stars (Div. East)	1	0	0	0
1973	NHL All-Stars (Div. East)	1	0	1	1
	TOTALS	2	0	1	1

Played with the team that won the Prince of Wales Trophy in 1967-68, 1968-69, 1972-73, 1975-76, 1976-77, 1977-78.
Played with the team that won the Stanley Cup in 1967-68, 1968-69, 1972-73, 1975-76, 1976-77, 1977-78, 1978-79.
Won the Conn Smythe Trophy in 1968-69.
Appointed assistant captain of the Canadiens in 1973.
Appointed captain in the interim in 1976-77.
Won the Bill Masterton Trophy in 1978-79.
Member of the second All-Star team in 1978-79.
Appointed captain in October, 1979, following Yvan Cournoyer's retirement.

SCHUTT, Rodney (Rod)

Born in Bancroft, Ontario, October 13th, 1956.
Left-winger, left-hand shot.
5'9", 185 lb.
Last amateur team: Sudbury jrs. (OHA).

SEASON	TEAM	GP	G	A	PTS	MIP
1977-78	Montreal Canadiens	2	0	0	0	0
	TOTALS	2	0	0	0	0

Played with the team that won the Prince of Wales Trophy in 1977-78.
Traded to the Pittsburgh Penguins for the first Amateur Draft choice of 1981.

SCOTT, Harry

Left-winger.

SEASON	TEAM	GP	G	A	PTS	MIP
*1913-14	Ontarios/ Montreal Canadiens	15	13	—	13	—
1914-15	Montreal Canadiens	15	8	—	8	—
	TOTALS	30	21	—	21	—

PLAYOFFS		GP	G	A	PTS	MIP
1913-14	Montreal Canadiens	2	1	—	1	—
	TOTALS	2	1	—	1	—

SEGUIN, Pat

PLAYOFFS		GP	G	A	PTS	MIP
1909-10	Montreal Canadiens	2	1	—	1	—
	TOTALS	2	1	—	1	—

SEIBERT, Albert Charles (Babe)

Born in Plattsville, Ontario, January 14th, 1904.
Defenseman, left-winger, left-hand shot.
5'10", 182 lb.
Last amateur team: Niagara Falls srs.

SEASON	TEAM	GP	G	A	PTS	MIP
1936-37	Montreal Canadiens	44	8	20	28	38
1937-38	Montreal Canadiens	37	8	11	19	56
1938-39	Montreal Canadiens	44	9	7	16	26
	TOTALS	125	25	38	63	120

PLAYOFFS		GP	G	A	PTS	MIP
1936-37	Montreal Canadiens	5	1	2	3	2
1937-38	Montreal Canadiens	3	1	1	2	0
1938-39	Montreal Canadiens	3	0	0	0	0
	TOTALS	11	2	3	5	2

Obtained from the Boston Bruins for Leroy Goldsworthy (1936-37).
Member of the first All-Star team in 1936-37, 1937-38.
Succeeded Jules Dugal as coach of the Canadiens (1939). Babe was appointed coach during the summer, but he passed away before the beginning of the 1939-40 season.
Appointed captain of the Canadiens from 1937-38 to 1938-39.
Died August 25, 1939.
Member of the Hockey Hall of Fame in 1964.

SEVIGNY, Richard

Born in Montreal, Quebec, November 4th, 1957.
Goaltender, left-hand shot.
5'8", 178 lb.
Last amateur team: Nova Scotia (AHL).

SEASON	TEAM	GP	GA	SO	AVE
1979-80	Montreal Canadiens	11	31	0	2.94
	TOTALS	11	31	0	2.94

OFFENSIVE RECORD		GP	G	A	PTS	MIP
1979-80	Montreal Canadiens	11	0	0	0	4
	TOTALS	11	0	0	0	4

SHANAHAN, Sean Bryan

Born in Toronto, Ontario, February 8th, 1951.
Left-winger, left-hand shot.
6'3", 205 lb.
Last amateur team: Providence College.

SEASON	TEAM	GP	G	A	PTS	MIP
1975-76	Montreal Canadiens	4	0	0	0	0
	TOTALS	4	0	0	0	0

Played with the team that won the Prince of Wales Trophy in 1975-76.

SHEEHAN, Robert Richard (Bob)

Born in Weymouth, Massachusetts, January 11th, 1949.
Center, left-hand shot.
5'7", 155 lb.
Last amateur team: the St. Catharines Black Hawks jrs.

SEASON	TEAM	GP	G	A	PTS	MIP
1969-70	Montreal Canadiens	16	2	1	3	2
1970-71	Montreal Canadiens	29	6	5	11	2
	TOTALS	45	8	6	14	4

PLAYOFFS		GP	G	A	PTS	MIP
1970-71	Montreal Canadiens	6	0	0	0	0
	TOTALS	6	0	0	0	0

Played with the team that won the Stanley Cup in 1970-71.
Sold to the California Golden Seals, May 25, 1971.

SHUTT, Stephen John (Steve)

Born in Toronto, Ontario, July 1st, 1952.
Left-winger, left-hand shot.
5'11", 180 lb.
Last amateur team: the Toronto Marlboros jrs.

SEASON	TEAM	GP	G	A	PTS	MIP
1972-73	Montreal Canadiens	50	8	8	16	24
1973-74	Montreal Canadiens	70	15	20	35	17
1974-75	Montreal Canadiens	77	30	35	65	40
1975-76	Montreal Canadiens	80	45	34	79	47
1976-77	Montreal Canadiens	80	60	45	105	28
1977-78	Montreal Canadiens	80	49	37	86	24
1978-79	Montreal Canadiens	72	37	40	77	31
1979-80	Montreal Canadiens	77	47	42	89	34
	TOTALS	586	291	261	552	245

PLAYOFFS		GP	G	A	PTS	MIP
1972-73	Montreal Canadiens	1	0	0	0	0
1973-74	Montreal Canadiens	6	5	3	8	9
1974-75	Montreal Canadiens	9	1	6	7	4
1975-76	Montreal Canadiens	13	7	8	15	2
1976-77	Montreal Canadiens	14	8	10	18	2
1977-78	Montreal Canadiens	15	9	8	17	20
1978-79	Montreal Canadiens	11	4	7	11	6
1979-80	Montreal Canadiens	10	6	3	9	6
	TOTALS	79	40	45	85	49

First Amateur Draft choice of the Canadiens in 1972.
Played with the team that won the Prince of Wales Trophy in 1972-73, 1975-76, 1976-77, 1977-78.
Played with the team that won the Stanley Cup in 1972-73, 1975-76, 1976-77, 1977-78, 1978-79.
New record for the most goals scored by a left-winger (60) 1976-77.
Member of the first All-Star team in 1976-77.
Member of the second All-Star team in 1977-78.

SINGBUSH, Alexander (Alex) E.

Born in Winnipeg, Manitoba, 1915.
Defenseman.

SEASON	TEAM	GP	G	A	PTS	MIP
1940-41	Montreal Canadiens	32	0	5	5	15
	TOTALS	32	0	5	5	15

PLAYOFFS		GP	G	A	PTS	MIP
1940-41	Montreal Canadiens	3	0	0	0	4
	TOTALS	3	0	0	0	4

SKOV, Glen Frederick

Born in Wheatley, Ontario, January 26th, 1931.
Center, left-hand shot.
6'1", 185 lb.
Last amateur team: the Windsor Spitfires jrs.

SEASON	TEAM	GP	G	A	PTS	MIP
1960-61	Montreal Canadiens	3	0	0	0	0
	TOTALS	3	0	0	0	0

Played with the team that won the Prince of Wales Trophy in 1960-61.

SMART, Alexander (Alex)

Born in Brandon, Manitoba, May 29th, 1918.

SEASON	TEAM	GP	G	A	PTS	MIP
1942-43	Montreal Canadiens	8	5	2	7	0
	TOTALS	8	5	2	7	0

SMITH, Desmond Patrick (Dessie)

Born in Ottawa, Ontario, February 22nd, 1914.
Defenseman, left-hand shot.
6', 185 lb.
Last amateur team: the Wembley Lions (England).

SEASON	TEAM	GP	G	A	PTS	MIP
1938-39	Montreal Canadiens	16	3	3	6	8
	TOTALS	16	3	3	6	8

PLAYOFFS		GP	G	A	PTS	MIP
1938-39	Montreal Canadiens	3	0	0	0	4
	TOTALS	3	0	0	0	4

Drafted from the Montreal Maroons in 1938.
Traded to the Boston Bruins with Herb Cain for Ray Getliffe and Charlie Sands in 1939.
Father of Gary and Brian Smith.

SMITH, Donald (Don)

Born in 1889.
Center, left-winger.

SEASON	TEAM	GP	G	A	PTS	MIP
1912-13	Montreal Canadiens	20	19	—	19	—
1913-14	Montreal Canadiens	20	18	—	18	—
*1914-15	Montreal Canadiens/ Montreal Wanderers	18	6	—	6	—
1919-20	Montreal Canadiens	10	1	0	1	4
	TOTALS	68	44	0	44	4

PLAYOFFS		GP	G	A	PTS	MIP
1913-14	Montreal Canadiens	2	1	—	1	—
	TOTALS	2	1	—	1	—

Obtained from the Victoria team in 1912.

SMITH, Stuart Ernest (Stu)

SEASON	TEAM	GP	G	A	PTS	MIP
1940-41	Montreal Canadiens	3	2	1	3	0
1941-42	Montreal Canadiens	1	0	1	1	0
	TOTALS	4	2	2	4	0

PLAYOFFS		GP	G	A	PTS	MIP
1940-41	Montreal Canadiens	1	0	0	0	0
	TOTALS	1	0	0	0	0

SMITH, Thomas James

Born in 1888.
Center, left-winger, rover.

SEASON	TEAM	GP	G	A	PTS	MIP
1916-17	Montreal Canadiens	15	9	—	9	—
	TOTALS	15	9	—	9	—

PLAYOFFS		GP	G	A	PTS	MIP
1916-17	Montreal Canadiens	6	4	—	4	—
	TOTALS	6	4	—	4	—

Drafted from the Quebec Bulldogs in 1916.
Member of the Hockey Hall of Fame in June, 1973.
Died in August, 1966.

SMRKE, Stanley (Stan)

Born in Belgrade, Yugoslavia, September 2nd, 1928.
Left-winger, left-hand shot.
5'11", 180 lb.
Last amateur team: the Chicoutimi Sagueneens srs.

SEASON	TEAM	GP	G	A	PTS	MIP
1956-57	Montreal Canadiens	4	0	0	0	0
1957-58	Montreal Canadiens	5	0	3	3	0
	TOTALS	9	0	3	3	0

ALL-STAR GAMES		GP	G	A	PTS
1957	Montreal Canadiens	1	1	0	1
	TOTALS	1	1	0	1

Played with the team that won the Prince of Wales Trophy in 1957-58.

STAHAN, Frank Ralph (Butch)

Born in Minnesdosa, Manitoba, October 29th, 1915.
Defenseman, left-hand shot.
6'1", 195 lb.
Last amateur team: the Ottawa Senators srs.

PLAYOFFS		GP	G	A	PTS	MIP
1944-45	Montreal Canadiens	3	0	1	1	2
	TOTALS	3	0	1	1	2

STARR, Harold

Born in Ottawa, Ontario, July 6th, 1906.
Defenseman, left-hand shot.
5'11", 176 lb.

SEASON	TEAM	GP	G	A	PTS	MIP
*1932-33	Ottawa Senators/ Montreal Canadiens	46	0	0	0	36
	TOTALS	46	0	0	0	36

PLAYOFFS		GP	G	A	PTS	MIP
1932-33	Montreal Canadiens	2	0	0	0	2
	TOTALS	2	0	0	0	2

Obtained from the Ottawa Senators in 1932-33.

STEPHENS, Philip (Phil)

Defenseman, center.

SEASON	TEAM	GP	G	A	PTS	MIP
1921-22	Montreal Canadiens	4	0	0	0	0
	TOTALS	4	0	0	0	0

STEWART, James Gaye

Born in Fort William, Ontario, June 28th, 1923.
Left-winger, left-hand shot.
5'11", 174 lb.
Last amateur team: the Toronto Marlboros jrs.

SEASON	TEAM	GP	G	A	PTS	MIP
*1952-53	New York Rangers/ Montreal Canadiens	23	1	3	4	8
	TOTALS	23	1	3	4	8

PLAYOFFS		GP	G	A	PTS	MIP
1953-54	Montreal Canadiens	3	0	0	0	0
	TOTALS	3	0	0	0	0

SUMMERHILL, William Arthur (Bill)

Born in Toronto, Ontario, July 9th, 1915.
Right-winger, right-hand shot.
5'9", 170 lb.
Last amateur team: the Verdun Maple Leafs srs.

SEASON	TEAM	GP	G	A	PTS	MIP
1938-39	Montreal Canadiens	43	6	10	16	28
1939-40	Montreal Canadiens	13	3	2	5	24
	TOTALS	56	9	12	21	52

PLAYOFFS		GP	G	A	PTS	MIP
1938-39	Montreal Canadiens	2	0	0	0	2
	TOTALS	2	0	0	0	2

SUTHERLAND, William Fraser (Bill)

Born in Regina, Saskatchewan, November 10th, 1934.
Center, left-hand shot.
5'10", 160 lb.
Last amateur team: the Cincinnati Mohawks srs.

PLAYOFFS		GP	G	A	PTS	MIP
1962-63	Montreal Canadiens	2	0	0	0	0
	TOTALS	2	0	0	0	0

TALBOT, Jean-Guy

Born in Cap-de-la-Madeleine, Quebec, July 11th, 1932.
Defenseman, left-hand shot.
5'11", 170 lb.
Last amateur team: the Quebec Aces jrs.

SEASON	TEAM	GP	G	A	PTS	MIP
1954-55	Montreal Canadiens	3	0	1	1	0
1955-56	Montreal Canadiens	66	1	13	14	80
1956-57	Montreal Canadiens	59	0	13	13	70
1957-58	Montreal Canadiens	55	4	15	19	65
1958-59	Montreal Canadiens	69	4	17	21	77
1959-60	Montreal Canadiens	69	1	14	15	60
1960-61	Montreal Canadiens	70	5	26	31	143
1961-62	Montreal Canadiens	70	5	42	47	90
1962-63	Montreal Canadiens	70	3	22	25	51
1963-64	Montreal Canadiens	66	1	13	14	83
1964-65	Montreal Canadiens	67	8	14	22	64
1965-66	Montreal Canadiens	59	1	14	15	50
1966-67	Montreal Canadiens	68	3	5	8	51
	TOTALS	791	36	209	245	884

PLAYOFFS		GP	G	A	PTS	MIP
1955-56	Montreal Canadiens	9	0	2	2	4
1956-57	Montreal Canadiens	10	0	2	2	10
1957-58	Montreal Canadiens	10	0	3	3	12
1958-59	Montreal Canadiens	11	0	1	1	10
1959-60	Montreal Canadiens	8	1	1	2	8
1960-61	Montreal Canadiens	6	1	1	2	10
1961-62	Montreal Canadiens	6	1	1	2	10
1962-63	Montreal Canadiens	5	0	0	0	8
1963-64	Montreal Canadiens	7	0	2	2	10
1964-65	Montreal Canadiens	13	0	1	1	22
1965-66	Montreal Canadiens	10	0	2	2	8
1966-67	Montreal Canadiens	10	0	0	0	0
	TOTALS	105	3	16	19	112

ALL-STAR GAMES		GP	G	A	PTS
1956	Montreal Canadiens	1	0	0	0
1957	Montreal Canadiens	1	0	0	0
1958	Montreal Canadiens	1	0	1	1
1960	Montreal Canadiens	1	0	0	0
1962	NHL All-Stars	1	0	0	0
1965	Montreal Canadiens	1	0	0	0
1967	Montreal Canadiens	1	0	0	0
	TOTALS	7	0	1	1

Played with the team that won the Prince of Wales Trophy in 1955-56, 1957-58, 1958-59, 1959-60, 1960-61, 1961-62, 1963-64, 1965-66.
Played with the team that won the Stanley Cup in 1955-56, 1956-57, 1957-58, 1958-59, 1959-60, 1964-65, 1965-66.
Member of the first All-Star team in 1961-62.
Appointed assistant captain of the Canadiens in 1963.
Drafted by the Minnesota North Stars during the 1967 Expansion, June 6, 1967.

TARDIF, Marc

Born in Granby, Quebec, June 12th, 1949.
Left-winger, left-hand shot.
6', 180 lb.
Last amateur team: the Montreal Canadiens jrs.

SEASON	TEAM	GP	G	A	PTS	MIP
1969-70	Montreal Canadiens	18	3	2	5	27
1970-71	Montreal Canadiens	76	19	30	49	133
1971-72	Montreal Canadiens	75	31	22	53	81
1972-73	Montreal Canadiens	76	25	25	50	48
	TOTALS	245	78	79	157	289

PLAYOFFS		GP	G	A	PTS	MIP
1970-71	Montreal Canadiens	20	3	1	4	40
1971-72	Montreal Canadiens	6	2	3	5	9
1972-73	Montreal Canadiens	14	6	6	12	6
	TOTALS	40	11	10	21	55

Played with the team that won the Prince of Wales Trophy in 1972-73.
Played with the team that won the Stanley Cup in 1970-71, 1972-73.
Signed up with the Los Angeles Sharks of the WHA in June, 1973.
Rights sold to the Nordiques for future considerations in 1979.

TAUGHER, William (Bill)

Goaltender.

SEASON	TEAM	GP	GA	SO	AVE
1925-26	Montreal Canadiens	1	3	0	3.00
	TOTALS	1	3	0	3.00

OFFENSIVE RECORD		GP	G	A	PTS	MIP
1925-26	Montreal Canadiens	1	0	0	0	0
	TOTALS	1	0	0	0	0

TESSIER, Orval Ray

Born in Cornwall, Ontario, June 30th, 1933.
Right-winger, center, right-hand shot.
5'8", 160 lb.
Last amateur team: the Barrie Flyers jrs.

SEASON	TEAM	GP	G	A	PTS	MIP
1954-55	Montreal Canadiens	4	0	0	0	0
	TOTALS	4	0	0	0	0

THIBEAULT, Lawrence Lorrain (Larry)

Born in Charletone, Ontario, October 2nd, 1918.
Left-winger, left-hand shot.
5'7", 180 lb.
Last amateur team: the Hull Volants srs.

SEASON	TEAM	GP	G	A	PTS	MIP
1945-46	Montreal Canadiens	1	0	0	0	0
	TOTALS	1	0	0	0	0

Played with the team that won the Prince of Wales Trophy in 1945-46.

THOMAS, Robert Wayne

Born in Ottawa, Ontario, October 9th, 1947.
Goaltender, left-hand shot.
6'2", 195 lb.
Last amateur team: Wisconsin University.

SEASON	TEAM	GP	GA	SO	AVE
1972-73	Montreal Canadiens	10	23	1	2.37
1973-74	Montreal Canadiens	42	111	1	2.76
	TOTALS	52	134	2	2.69

OFFENSIVE RECORD		GP	G	A	PTS	MIP
1972-73	Montreal Canadiens	10	0	1	1	2
1973-74	Montreal Canadiens	42	0	2	2	6
	TOTALS	52	0	3	3	8

Obtained from the Los Angeles Kings with Leon Rochefort and Greg Boddy for Larry Mickey, Lucien Grenier and Jack Norris in May, 1970.
Played with the team that won the Prince of Wales Trophy in 1972-73.
Traded to the Toronto Maple Leafs for the first Amateur Draft choice of 1976 (Peter Lee), June 17, 1975.

THOMSON, Rhys

Born in Toronto, Ontario, August 9th, 1918.
Defenseman.

SEASON	TEAM	GP	G	A	PTS	MIP
1939-40	Montreal Canadiens	7	0	0	0	16
	TOTALS	7	0	0	0	16

TREMBLAY, Gilles

Born in Montmorency, Quebec, December 17th, 1938.
Left-winger, left-hand shot.
5'10", 170 lb.
Last amateur team: the Hull-Ottawa Canadiens jrs.

SEASON	TEAM	GP	G	A	PTS	MIP
1960-61	Montreal Canadiens	45	7	11	18	4
1961-62	Montreal Canadiens	70	32	22	54	28
1962-63	Montreal Canadiens	60	25	24	49	42
1963-64	Montreal Canadiens	61	22	15	37	21
1964-65	Montreal Canadiens	26	9	7	16	16
1965-66	Montreal Canadiens	70	27	21	48	24
1966-67	Montreal Canadiens	62	13	19	32	16
1967-68	Montreal Canadiens	71	23	28	51	8
1968-69	Montreal Canadiens	44	10	15	25	2
	TOTALS	509	168	162	330	161

PLAYOFFS		GP	G	A	PTS	MIP
1960-61	Montreal Canadiens	6	1	3	4	0
1961-62	Montreal Canadiens	6	1	0	1	2
1962-63	Montreal Canadiens	5	2	0	2	0
1963-64	Montreal Canadiens	2	0	0	0	0
1965-66	Montreal Canadiens	10	4	5	9	0
1966-67	Montreal Canadiens	10	0	1	1	0
1967-68	Montreal Canadiens	9	1	5	6	2
	TOTALS	48	9	14	23	4

ALL-STAR GAMES		GP	G	A	PTS
1965	Montreal Canadiens	1	0	0	0
1967	Montreal Canadiens	1	0	0	0
	TOTALS	2	0	0	0

Played with the team that won the Prince of Wales Trophy in 1960-61, 1961-62, 1963-64, 1965-66, 1967-68, 1968-69.
Played with the team that won the Stanley Cup in 1965-66, 1967-68.

TREMBLAY, Jean-Claude (J.C.)

Born in Bagotville, Quebec, January 22, 1939.
Defenseman, left-hand shot.
5'11", 178 lb.
Last amateur team: the Hull-Ottawa Canadiens jrs.

SEASON	TEAM	GP	G	A	PTS	MIP
1959-60	Montreal Canadiens	11	0	1	1	0
1960-61	Montreal Canadiens	29	1	3	4	18
1961-62	Montreal Canadiens	70	3	17	20	18
1962-63	Montreal Canadiens	69	1	17	18	10
1963-64	Montreal Canadiens	70	5	16	21	24
1964-65	Montreal Canadiens	68	3	17	20	22
1965-66	Montreal Canadiens	59	6	29	35	8
1966-67	Montreal Canadiens	60	8	26	34	14
1967-68	Montreal Canadiens	73	4	26	30	18
1968-69	Montreal Canadiens	75	7	32	39	18
1969-70	Montreal Canadiens	58	2	19	21	7
1970-71	Montreal Canadiens	76	11	52	63	23
1971-72	Montreal Canadiens	76	6	51	57	24
	TOTALS	794	57	306	363	204

PLAYOFFS		GP	G	A	PTS	MIP
1960-61	Montreal Canadiens	5	0	0	0	0
1961-62	Montreal Canadiens	6	0	2	2	2
1962-63	Montreal Canadiens	5	0	0	0	0
1963-64	Montreal Canadiens	7	2	1	3	9
1964-65	Montreal Canadiens	13	1	9	10	18
1965-66	Montreal Canadiens	10	2	9	11	2
1966-67	Montreal Canadiens	10	2	4	6	2
1967-68	Montreal Canadiens	13	3	6	9	2
1968-69	Montreal Canadiens	13	1	4	5	6
1970-71	Montreal Canadiens	20	3	14	17	15
1971-72	Montreal Canadiens	6	0	2	2	0
	TOTALS	108	14	51	65	58

ALL-STAR GAMES		GP	G	A	PTS
1959	Montreal Canadiens	1	0	0	0
1965	Montreal Canadiens	1	0	0	0
1967	Montreal Canadiens	1	0	0	0
1968	NHL All-Stars	1	0	1	1
1969	NHL All-Stars (Div. East)	1	0	0	0
1971	NHL All-Stars (Div. East)	1	0	0	0
1972	NHL All-Stars (Div. East)	1	0	1	1
	TOTALS	7	0	2	2

Played with the team that won the Prince of Wales Trophy in 1959-60, 1960-61, 1961-62, 1963-64, 1965-66, 1967-68, 1968-69.
Played with the team that won the Stanley Cup in 1964-65, 1965-66, 1967-68, 1968-69, 1970-71.
Appointed assistant captain of the Canadiens in 1971.
Selected by the Los Angeles Sharks of the WHA in February, 1972, his rights were later obtained by the Quebec Nordiques.

TREMBLAY, Louis Nils

Born in Malbaie, Quebec, July 26th, 1923.
Center, left-hand shot.
5'8", 158 lb.
Last amateur team: the Sherbrooke Saints srs.

SEASON	TEAM	GP	G	A	PTS	MIP
1944-45	Montreal Canadiens	1	0	1	1	0
1945-46	Montreal Canadiens	2	0	0	0	0
	TOTALS	3	0	1	1	0

PLAYOFFS		GP	G	A	PTS	MIP
1944-45	Montreal Canadiens	2	0	0	0	0
	TOTALS	2	0	0	0	0

Played with the team that won the Prince of Wales Trophy in 1944-45, 1945-46.

TREMBLAY, Marcel

Born in Winnipeg, Manitoba, July 4th, 1915.

SEASON	TEAM	GP	G	A	PTS	MIP
1938-39	Montreal Canadiens	10	0	2	2	0
	TOTALS	10	0	2	2	0

TREMBLAY, Mario

Born in Alma, Quebec, September 2nd, 1956.
Right-winger, right-hand shot.
6', 185 lb.
Last amateur team: the Montreal "Bleu, Blanc, Rouge" jrs.

SEASON	TEAM	GP	G	A	PTS	MIP
1974-75	Montreal Canadiens	63	21	18	39	108
1975-76	Montreal Canadiens	71	11	16	27	88
1976-77	Montreal Canadiens	74	18	28	46	61
1977-78	Montreal Canadiens	56	10	14	24	44
1978-79	Montreal Canadiens	76	30	29	59	74
1979-80	Montreal Canadiens	77	16	26	42	105
	TOTALS	417	106	131	237	480

PLAYOFFS		GP	G	A	PTS	MIP
1974-75	Montreal Canadiens	11	0	1	1	7
1975-76	Montreal Canadiens	10	0	1	1	27
1976-77	Montreal Canadiens	14	3	0	3	9
1977-78	Montreal Canadiens	5	2	1	3	16
1978-79	Montreal Canadiens	13	3	4	7	13
1979-80	Montreal Canadiens	10	0	11	11	14
	TOTALS	63	8	18	26	86

Fourth Amateur Draft choice of the Canadiens in 1974.
Played with the team that won the Prince of Wales Trophy in 1975-76, 1976-77, 1977-78.
Played with the team that won the Stanley Cup in 1975-76, 1976-77, 1977-78, 1978-79.

TRUDEL, Louis Napoleon

Born in Salem, Massachusetts, July 21st, 1912.
Left-winger, left-hand shot.
5'11", 165 lb.
Last amateur team: the Edmonton Poslers.

SEASON	TEAM	GP	G	A	PTS	MIP
1938-39	Montreal Canadiens	31	8	13	21	2
1939-40	Montreal Canadiens	47	12	7	19	24
1940-41	Montreal Canadiens	16	2	3	5	2
	TOTALS	94	22	23	45	28

PLAYOFFS		GP	G	A	PTS	MIP
1938-39	Montreal Canadiens	3	1	0	1	0
	TOTALS	3	1	0	1	0

Obtained from the Chicago Black Hawks for Joffre Desilets in 1938.

TUDIN, Cornell (Connie, Conny)

SEASON	TEAM	GP	G	A	PTS	MIP
1941-42	Montreal Canadiens	4	0	1	1	4
	TOTALS	4	0	1	1	4

TURNER, Robert George (Bob)

Born in Regina, Saskatchewan, January 31st, 1934.
Defenseman, left-hand shot.
6', 178 lb.
Last amateur team: the Regina Pats jrs.

SEASON	TEAM	GP	G	A	PTS	MIP
1955-56	Montreal Canadiens	33	1	4	5	35
1956-57	Montreal Canadiens	58	1	4	5	48
1957-58	Montreal Canadiens	66	0	3	3	30
1958-59	Montreal Canadiens	68	4	24	28	66

SEASON	TEAM	GP	G	A	PTS	MIP
1959-60	Montreal Canadiens	54	0	9	9	40
1960-61	Montreal Canadiens	60	2	2	4	16
	TOTALS	339	8	46	54	235

PLAYOFFS		GP	G	A	PTS	MIP
1955-56	Montreal Canadiens	10	0	1	1	10
1956-57	Montreal Canadiens	6	0	1	1	0
1957-58	Montreal Canadiens	10	0	0	0	2
1958-59	Montreal Canadiens	11	0	2	2	20
1959-60	Montreal Canadiens	8	0	0	0	0
1960-61	Montreal Canadiens	5	0	0	0	0
	TOTALS	50	0	4	4	32

ALL-STAR GAMES		GP	G	A	PTS
1956	Montreal Canadiens	1	0	0	0
1957	Montreal Canadiens	1	0	0	0
1958	Montreal Canadiens	1	0	0	0
1959	Montreal Canadiens	1	0	0	0
1960	Montreal Canadiens	1	0	0	0
	TOTALS	5	0	0	0

Played with the team that won the Prince of Wales Trophy in 1955-56, 1957-58, 1958-59, 1959-60, 1960-61.
Played with the team that won the Stanley Cup in 1955-56, 1956-57, 1957-58, 1958-59, 1959-60.
Traded to the Chicago Black Hawks for Fred Hilts in June, 1961.

VACHON, Rogatien Rosaire (Roggy)

Born in Palmarolle, Quebec, September 8th, 1945.
Goaltender, left-hand shot.
5'7", 165 lb.
Last amateur team: the Thedford Mines Canadiens jrs.

SEASON	TEAM	GP	GA	SO	AVE
1966-67	Montreal Canadiens	19	47	1	2.48
1967-68	Montreal Canadiens	39	92	4	2.48
1968-69	Montreal Canadiens	36	98	2	2.87
1969-70	Montreal Canadiens	64	162	4	2.63
1970-71	Montreal Canadiens	47	118	2	2.64
1971-72	Montreal Canadiens	1	4	0	12.00
	TOTALS	206	521	13	2.53

PLAYOFFS		GP	GA	SO	AVE
1966-67	Montreal Canadiens	9	22	0	2.54
1967-68	Montreal Canadiens	2	4	0	2.13
1968-69	Montreal Canadiens	8	12	1	1.42
	TOTALS	19	38	1	2.00

OFFENSIVE RECORD		GP	G	A	PTS	MIP
1966-67	Montreal Canadiens	19	0	1	1	0
1967-68	Montreal Canadiens	39	0	0	0	2
1968-69	Montreal Canadiens	36	0	0	0	2
1969-70	Montreal Canadiens	64	0	0	0	0
1970-71	Montreal Canadiens	47	0	0	0	0
1971-72	Montreal Canadiens	1	0	0	0	0
	TOTALS	206	0	1	1	4

PLAYOFFS		GP	G	A	PTS	MIP
1966-67	Montreal Canadiens	9	0	0	0	0
1967-68	Montreal Canadiens	2	0	0	0	0
1968-69	Montreal Canadiens	8	0	0	0	2
	TOTALS	19	0	0	0	2

Won the Vezina Trophy (with Lorne Worsley) in 1967-68.
Traded to the Los Angeles Kings for Denis Dejordy, Noel Price, Dale Hoganson and Doug Robinson, November 4, 1971.

VADNAIS, Carol Marcel

Born in Montreal, Quebec, September 25th, 1945.
Defenseman, left-hand shot.
6'1", 212 lb.
Last amateur team: the Montreal Canadiens jrs.

SEASON	TEAM	GP	G	A	PTS	MIP
1966-67	Montreal Canadiens	11	0	3	3	35
1967-68	Montreal Canadiens	31	1	1	2	31
	TOTALS	42	1	4	5	66

PLAYOFFS		GP	G	A	PTS	MIP
1966-67	Montreal Canadiens	1	0	0	0	2
1967-68	Montreal Canadiens	1	0	0	0	0
	TOTALS	2	0	0	0	2

Played with the team that won the Prince of Wales Trophy in 1967-68.
Played with the team that won the Stanley Cup in 1967-68.
Drafted by the Oakland Seals, June 12, 1968.

VAN BOXMEER, John Martin

Born in Petrolia, Ontario, September 9th, 1952.
Defenseman, right-winger, right-hand shot.
6', 185 lb.
Last amateur team: the Guelph Royals jrs.

SEASON	TEAM	GP	G	A	PTS	MIP
1973-74	Montreal Canadiens	20	1	4	5	18
1974-75	Montreal Canadiens	9	0	2	2	0
1975-76	Montreal Canadiens	46	6	11	17	31
1976-77	Montreal Canadiens	4	0	1	1	0
	TOTALS	79	7	18	25	49

PLAYOFFS		GP	G	A	PTS	MIP
1973-74	Montreal Canadiens	1	0	0	0	0
	TOTALS	1	0	0	0	0

Fourth Amateur Draft choice of the Canadiens in 1972.
Played with the team that won the Prince of Wales Trophy in 1975-76.
Played with the team that won the Stanley Cup in 1975-76.
Traded to the Colorado Rockies, November 24, 1976 for a choice at the 1980 Amateur Draft.

VEZINA, Georges (The Chicoutimi Cucumber)

Born in Chicoutimi, Quebec, January, 1887.
Goaltender.
Last amateur team: Chicoutimi srs.

SEASON	TEAM	GP	GA	SO	AVE
1910-11	Montreal Canadiens	16	62	0	3.26
1911-12	Montreal Canadiens	18	66	0	3.66
1912-13	Montreal Canadiens	20	81	1	4.50
1913-14	Montreal Canadiens	20	65	1	3.25
1914-15	Montreal Canadiens	20	81	0	4.50
1915-16	Montreal Canadiens	24	76	0	3.15
1916-17	Montreal Canadiens	20	80	0	4.00
1917-18	Montreal Canadiens	21	84	1	4.00
1918-19	Montreal Canadiens	18	78	1	4.33
1919-20	Montreal Canadiens	24	113	0	4.71
1920-21	Montreal Canadiens	24	99	1	4.13
1921-22	Montreal Canadiens	24	94	0	3.91
1922-23	Montreal Canadiens	24	61	2	2.58
1923-24	Montreal Canadiens	24	48	3	2.00
1924-25	Montreal Canadiens	30	56	5	1.87
1925-26	Montreal Canadiens	1	1	0	1.00
	TOTALS	328	1145	15	3.49

PLAYOFFS		GP	GA	SO	AVE
1913-14	Montreal Canadiens	2	6	1	3.00
1915-16	Montreal Canadiens	5	13	0	2.60
1916-17	Montreal Canadiens	6	29	0	4.83
1917-18	Montreal Canadiens	2	10	0	5.00
1918-19	Montreal Canadiens	9	37	1	3.70
1922-23	Montreal Canadiens	2	3	0	1.50
1923-24	Montreal Canadiens	6	6	2	1.00
1924-25	Montreal Canadiens	6	18	1	3.00
	TOTALS	38	122	5	3.21

OFFENSIVE RECORD		GP	G	A	PTS	MIP
1910-11	Montreal Canadiens	16	0	—	0	—
1911-12	Montreal Canadiens	18	0	—	0	—
1912-13	Montreal Canadiens	20	0	—	0	—
1913-14	Montreal Canadiens	20	0	—	0	—
1914-15	Montreal Canadiens	20	0	—	0	—
1915-16	Montreal Canadiens	24	0	—	0	—
1916-17	Montreal Canadiens	20	0	—	0	—
1917-18	Montreal Canadiens	21	0	—	0	—
1918-19	Montreal Canadiens	18	0	0	0	0
1919-20	Montreal Canadiens	24	0	0	0	0
1920-21	Montreal Canadiens	24	0	0	0	0
1921-22	Montreal Canadiens	24	0	0	0	2
1922-23	Montreal Canadiens	24	0	0	0	0
1923-24	Montreal Canadiens	24	0	0	0	0
1924-25	Montreal Canadiens	30	0	0	0	0
1925-26	Montreal Canadiens	1	0	0	0	0
	TOTALS	328	0	0	0	2

OFFENSIVE RECORD (PLAYOFFS)		GP	G	A	PTS	MIP
1913-14	Montreal Canadiens	2	0	—	0	—
1915-16	Montreal Canadiens	5	0	—	0	—
1916-17	Montreal Canadiens	6	0	—	0	—
1917-18	Montreal Canadiens	2	0	—	0	—
1918-19	Montreal Canadiens	9	0	0	0	0
1922-23	Montreal Canadiens	2	0	0	0	0
1923-24	Montreal Canadiens	6	0	0	0	0
1924-25	Montreal Canadiens	6	0	0	0	0
	TOTALS	38	0	0	0	0

Played with the team that won the Prince of Wales Trophy in 1924-25.
Played with the team that won the Stanley Cup in 1915-16, 1923-24.
The NHL gave his name to the trophy for the best goaltender in the league.
Member of the Hockey Hall of Fame in April, 1945.
Died March 24, 1926.

WAKELY, Ernest Alfred Linton (Ernie)

Born in Flin Flon, Manitoba, November 27th, 1940.
Goaltender, left-hand shot.
5'11", 160 lb.
Last amateur team: the Winnipeg Braves jrs.

SEASON	TEAM	GP	G	GA	SO	AVE
1962-63	Montreal Canadiens	1	60	3	0	3.00
1968-69	Montreal Canadiens	1	60	4	0	4.00
	TOTALS	2	120	7	0	3.50

OFFENSIVE RECORD		GP	G	A	PTS	MIP
1962-63	Montreal Canadiens	1	0	0	0	0
1968-69	Montreal Canadiens	1	0	0	0	0
	TOTALS	2	0	0	0	0

Played with the Team that won the Prince of Wales Trophy in 1968-69.
Traded to the St. Louis Blues for Norman Beaudin and Bob Schmautz, June 27, 1969.

WALTON, Robert Charles (Bob)

Born in Ottawa, Ontario, August 5th, 1917.
Right-winger, right-hand shot.
5'9", 165 lb.
Last amateur team: the Sydney (N.S.) Millionnaires.

SEASON	TEAM	GP	G	A	PTS	MIP
1943-44	Montreal Canadiens	4	0	0	0	0
	TOTALS	4	0	0	0	0

Played with the team that won the Prince of Wales Trophy in 1943-44.

WARD, James William (Jim, Jimmy)

Born in Fort William, Ontario, September 1st, 1906.
Right-winger, right-hand shot.
5'11", 167 lb.
Last amateur team: Fort William srs.

SEASON	TEAM	GP	G	A	PTS	MIP
1938-39	Montreal Canadiens	36	4	3	7	0
	TOTALS	36	4	3	7	0

PLAYOFFS		GP	G	A	PTS	MIP
1938-39	Montreal Canadiens	1	0	0	0	0
	TOTALS	1	0	0	0	0

Drafted from the Montreal Maroons in 1938.
Father of Peter Ward, baseball player.

WARWICK, Grant David (Knobby)

Born in Regina, Saskatchewan, October 11th, 1921.
Right-winger, right-hand shot.

5'6", 165 lb.
Last amateur team: the Regina Rangers srs.

SEASON	TEAM	GP	G	A	PTS	MIP
1949-50	Montreal Canadiens	30	2	6	8	19
	TOTALS	30	2	6	8	19

Bought from the Boston Bruins, October 10, 1949.

WASNIE, Nicholas (Nick)

Born in Winnipeg, Manitoba, January 1st, 1904.
5'10", 174 lb.
Right-winger, right-hand shot.
Last amateur team: the Coleman Tigers srs.

SEASON	TEAM	GP	G	A	PTS	MIP
1929-30	Montreal Canadiens	44	12	11	23	64
1930-31	Montreal Canadiens	44	9	2	11	26
1931-32	Montreal Canadiens	48	10	2	12	16
	TOTALS	136	31	15	46	106

PLAYOFFS		GP	G	A	PTS	MIP
1929-30	Montreal Canadiens	6	2	2	4	12
1930-31	Montreal Canadiens	10	4	1	5	8
1931-32	Montreal Canadiens	4	0	0	0	0
	TOTALS	20	6	3	9	20

Obtained from Chicago (1929-30).
Played with the team that won the Stanley Cup in 1929-30, 1930-31.
Traded to the New York Americans (1932-33).

WATSON, Bryan Joseph (Bugsy)

Born in Bancroft, Ontario, November 14th, 1942.
Defenseman, right-hand shot.
5'10", 175 lb.
Last amateur team: the Peterborough Petes jrs.

SEASON	TEAM	GP	G	A	PTS	MIP
1963-64	Montreal Canadiens	39	0	2	2	18
1964-65	Montreal Canadiens	5	0	1	1	7
1967-68	Montreal Canadiens	12	0	1	1	9
	TOTALS	56	0	4	4	34

PLAYOFFS		GP	G	A	PTS	MIP
1963-64	Montreal Canadiens	6	0	0	0	2
	TOTALS	6	0	0	0	2

Traded to the Chicago Black Hawks for Don Johns, June 8, 1965.
Obtained from the Minnesota North Stars for Bill Plager, Leo Thiffault and Barrie Meissner, June 6, 1967.
Played with the team that won the Prince of Wales Trophy in 1963-64, 1967-68.
Traded to the Oakland Seals with a certain amount of money for the first Amateur Draft choice of 1972 (Steve Shutt), June 10, 1968.

WATSON, Phillip Henry (Phil)

Born in Montreal, Quebec, April 24th, 1914.
Center, right-hand shot.
5'11", 170 lb.
Last amateur team: the Montreal Royals srs.

SEASON	TEAM	GP	G	A	PTS	MIP
1943-44	Montreal Canadiens	44	17	32	49	61
	TOTALS	44	17	32	49	61

PLAYOFFS		GP	G	A	PTS	MIP
1943-44	Montreal Canadiens	9	3	5	8	16
	TOTALS	9	3	5	8	16

Obtained from the New York Rangers for Charlie Sands and "Dutch" Hiller in 1943.
Played with the team that won the Prince of Wales Trophy in 1943-44.
Played with the team that won the Stanley Cup in 1943-44.
Traded to the New York Rangers for Fernand Gauthier and "Dutch" Hiller in 1944.

WENTWORTH, Marvin (Cy)

Born in Grimsby, Ontario, January 24th, 1905.
Defenseman, right-hand shot.
5'10", 170 lb.
Last amateur team: Windsor.

SEASON	TEAM	GP	G	A	PTS	MIP
1938-39	Montreal Canadiens	45	0	3	3	12
1939-40	Montreal Canadiens	32	1	3	4	6
	TOTALS	77	1	6	7	18

PLAYOFFS		GP	G	A	PTS	MIP
1938-39	Montreal Canadiens	3	0	0	0	4
	TOTALS	3	0	0	0	4

WHITE, Leonard Arthur (Moe)

Born in Verdun, Quebec, July 28th, 1919.
Center, left-hand shot.
5'11", 180 lb.
Last amateur team: the Canadian Army team.

SEASON	TEAM	GP	G	A	PTS	MIP
1945-46	Montreal Canadiens	4	0	1	1	2
	TOTALS	4	0	1	1	2

Played with the team that won the Prince of Wales Trophy in 1945-46.

WILLSON, Donald Arthur (Don)

Born in Chatham, Ontario, January 1st, 1914.

SEASON	TEAM	GP	G	A	PTS	MIP
1937-38	Montreal Canadiens	18	2	7	9	0
1938-39	Montreal Canadiens	4	0	0	0	0
	TOTALS	22	2	7	9	0

PLAYOFFS		GP	G	A	PTS	MIP
1937-38	Montreal Canadiens	3	0	0	0	0
	TOTALS	3	0	0	0	0

WILSON, Carol (Cully)

Born in 1893.
Right-winger.

SEASON	TEAM	GP	G	A	PTS	MIP
*1920-21	Toronto St. Patricks/ Montreal Canadiens	17	8	2	10	16
	TOTALS	17	8	2	10	16

Obtained from the Toronto St. Patricks in 1920-21.
Traded with Harry Mummery and Amos Arbour for Sprague Cleghorn and Bill Couture in 1921.

WILSON, Gerald (Gerry)

Born in Edmonton, Alberta, April 10th, 1937.
Center, left-hand shot.
6'2", 200 lb.

SEASON	TEAM	GP	G	A	PTS	MIP
1956-57	Montreal Canadiens	3	0	0	0	2
	TOTALS	3	0	0	0	2

WILSON, Murray Charles

Born in Ottawa, Ontario, November 7th, 1951.
Left-winger, right-winger, left-hand shot.
6'1", 180 lb.
Last amateur team: the Ottawa '67s jrs.

SEASON	TEAM	GP	G	A	PTS	MIP
1972-73	Montreal Canadiens	52	18	9	27	16
1973-74	Montreal Canadiens	72	17	14	31	26
1974-75	Montreal Canadiens	73	24	18	42	44
1975-76	Montreal Canadiens	59	11	24	35	36
1976-77	Montreal Canadiens	60	13	14	27	26
1977-78	Montreal Canadiens	12	0	1	1	0
	TOTALS	328	83	80	163	148

PLAYOFFS		GP	G	A	PTS	MIP
1972-73	Montreal Canadiens	16	2	4	6	6
1973-74	Montreal Canadiens	5	1	0	1	2
1974-75	Montreal Canadiens	5	0	3	3	4
1975-76	Montreal Canadiens	12	1	1	2	6
1976-77	Montreal Canadiens	14	1	6	7	14
	TOTALS	52	5	14	19	32

Third Amateur Draft choice of the Canadiens in 1971.
Played with the team that won the Prince of Wales Trophy in 1972-73, 1975-76, 1976-77, 1977-78.
Played with the team that won the Stanley Cup in 1972-73, 1975-76, 1976-77, 1977-78.
Traded to the Los Angeles Kings with the first Amateur Draft choice of the Canadiens in 1979 for the first 1981 choice of the Kings.

WILSON, Richard Gordon (Rick)

Born in Prince Albert, Saskatchewan, August 10th, 1950.
Defenseman, left-hand shot.
6'1", 195 lb.
Last amateur team: North Dakota University.

SEASON	TEAM	GP	G	A	PTS	MIP
1973-74	Montreal Canadiens	21	0	2	2	6
	TOTALS	21	0	2	2	6

Traded to the St. Louis Blues with the fifth Amateur Draft choice of 1974 (Don Wheldon) for the fourth Amateur Draft choice of 1974 (Barry Legge) and Glen Sather, May 27, 1974.

WORSLEY, Lorne John (Gump, Gumper)

Born in Montreal, Quebec, May 14th, 1929.
Goaltender, left-hand shot.
5'7", 180 lb.
Last amateur team: the New York Rovers srs.

SEASON	TEAM	GP	GA	SO	AVE
1963-64	Montreal Canadiens	8	22	1	2.97
1964-65	Montreal Canadiens	18	50	1	2.94
1965-66	Montreal Canadiens	51	114	2	2.36
1966-67	Montreal Canadiens	18	47	1	3.18
1967-68	Montreal Canadiens	40	73	6	1.98
1968-69	Montreal Canadiens	30	64	5	2.26
1969-70	Montreal Canadiens	6	14	0	2.33
	TOTALS	171	384	16	2.25

PLAYOFFS		GP	GA	SO	AVE
1964-65	Montreal Canadiens	8	14	2	1.68
1965-66	Montreal Canadiens	10	20	1	1.99
1966-67	Montreal Canadiens	2	2	0	1.50
1967-68	Montreal Canadiens	12	21	1	1.88
1968-69	Montreal Canadiens	7	14	0	2.27
	TOTALS	39	71	4	1.82

ALL-STAR GAMES		GP	GA	SO	AVE
1965	Montreal Canadiens	1	1	0	0.67
	TOTALS	1	1	0	0.67

OFFENSIVE RECORD		GP	G	A	PTS	MIP
1963-64	Montreal Canadiens	8	0	0	0	0
1964-65	Montreal Canadiens	18	0	0	0	0
1965-66	Montreal Canadiens	51	0	1	1	4
1966-67	Montreal Canadiens	18	0	0	0	4
1967-68	Montreal Canadiens	40	0	0	0	10
1968-69	Montreal Canadiens	30	0	0	0	0
1969-70	Montreal Canadiens	6	0	0	0	0
	TOTALS	171	0	1	1	18

PLAYOFFS		GP	G	A	PTS	MIP
1964-65	Montreal Canadiens	8	0	0	0	0
1965-66	Montreal Canadiens	10	0	0	0	0
1966-67	Montreal Canadiens	2	0	0	0	0
1967-68	Montreal Canadiens	12	0	0	0	10
1968-69	Montreal Canadiens	7	0	0	0	5
	TOTALS	39	0	0	0	15

Obtained from the New York Rangers with Dave Balon, Leon Rochefort and Len Ronson for Jacques Plante, Philippe Goyette and Don Marshall, June 4, 1963.
Played with the team that won the Prince of Wales Trophy in 1963-64, 1965-66, 1967-68, 1968-69.
Played with the team that won the Stanley Cup in

1964-65, 1965-66, 1967-68, 1968-69.
Won the Vezina Trophy in 1965-66 (with Charlie Hodge) and in 1967-68 (with Rogatien Vachon).
Member of the first All-Star team in 1967-68.
Member of the second All-Star team in 1965-66.
Sold to the Minnesota North Stars, February 26, 1970.
Member of the Hall of Fame June, 1980.

WORTERS, Roy (Schrimp)

Born in Toronto, Ontario, October 19th, 1900.
Goaltender, left-hand shot.
5'3", 135 lb.
Last amateur team: the Pittsburgh Yellow Jackets.

SEASON	TEAM	GP	GA	SO	AVE
*1929-30	New York Americans/ Montreal Canadiens	37	137	2	3.70
	TOTALS	37	137	2	3.70

OFFENSIVE RECORD		GP	G	A	PTS	MIP
	New York Americans/ Montreal Canadiens	37	0	0	0	0
	TOTALS	37	0	0	0	0

Lent to the New York Americans in 1930.
Member of the Hockey Hall of Fame in June, 1969.
Died November 7, 1957.

YOUNG, Douglas G. (Doug)

Born in Medicine Hat, Alberta, October 1st, 1908.
Defenseman, right-hand shot.
5'10", 190 lb.
Last amateur team: Kitchener.

SEASON	TEAM	GP	G	A	PTS	MIP
1939-40	Montreal Canadiens	47	3	9	12	22
1940-41	Montreal Canadiens	3	0	0	0	4
	TOTALS	50	3	9	12	26

Bought from the Detroit Red Wings in 1939.

Index of Names in Text

CCM